# Violence against Women in Politics

# Violence against Women in Politics

Mona Lena Krook

# OXFORD
UNIVERSITY PRESS

Oxford University Press is a department of the University of Oxford. It furthers
the University's objective of excellence in research, scholarship, and education
by publishing worldwide. Oxford is a registered trade mark of Oxford University
Press in the UK and certain other countries.

Published in the United States of America by Oxford University Press
198 Madison Avenue, New York, NY 10016, United States of America.

© Oxford University Press 2020

Library of Congress Cataloging-in-Publication Data
Names: Krook, Mona Lena, author.
Title: Violence against women in politics / Mona Lena Krook.
Description: New York : Oxford University Press, 2020. |
Includes bibliographical references and index.
Identifiers: LCCN 2020008346 (print) | LCCN 2020008347 (ebook) |
ISBN 9780190088460 (hardback) | ISBN 9780190088477 (paperback) |
ISBN 9780190088491 (epub) | ISBN 9780190088507 (online)
Subjects: LCSH: Women—Political activity—Cross-cultural studies. |
Women—Violence against—Cross-cultural studies. |
Sexism in political culture—Cross-cultural studies.
Classification: LCC HQ1236 .K77 2020 (print) | LCC HQ1236 (ebook) |
DDC 320.082—dc23
LC record available at https://lccn.loc.gov/2020008346
LC ebook record available at https://lccn.loc.gov/2020008347

9 8 7 6 5 4 3 2 1

Paperback printed by LSC Communications, United States of America
Hardback printed by Bridgeport National Bindery, Inc., United States of America

For Lars and Soren

# CONTENTS

## Part IV: **A Call to Action**

# ACKNOWLEDGMENTS

This book is about feminist collaborations contributing to the global emergence, development, and diffusion of the concept of violence against women in politics. My own process of writing it was similarly made possible by numerous collaborations along the way. I began exploring this topic in 2014 with Juliana Restrepo Sanín, my graduate student at the time, with an eye to perhaps producing a short research note. As we delved into the emerging debates, however, it became clear it was a much bigger task than we had initially imagined. We spent the next few years collecting news items, exploring different literatures, talking to colleagues, and presenting our work to diverse audiences, all of which pushed us to refine how we thought about violence against women in the political realm—and ultimately leading to several co-authored papers. Although we eventually began to pursue our own research agendas—Juliana went on to write her doctoral dissertation on developments in Latin America, while I decided to research and write this book from a more global perspective—I will always be grateful to her for sharing my enthusiasm in the early days, which powered us both to keep going in spite of many challenges. I am very proud of the scholar she has become, and it goes without saying that the imprints of her work are everywhere in this book.

The Rutgers Women & Politics Program, more generally, has been the ideal place to work on a project of this nature and scope. My colleagues Sue Carroll, Mary Hawkesworth, Kira Sanbonmatsu, and Kelly Dittmar provided key thoughts and literature suggestions, while Cyndi Daniels is the best cheerleader anyone could ever have. I am deeply indebted to Nikol Alexander-Floyd for suggesting a writing retreat at Easton's Nook, which enabled me to write the extremely complex chapter on sexual violence over two weekends, sustained by Nadine's amazing cooking and hospitality. Several cohorts of graduate students also read and commented on papers and chapters. In particular, I would like to thank Mary Nugent, Rebecca Kuperberg, Haley Norris, Anja Vojvodic, Elizabeth Corredor, Isabel Köhler, Meriem Aissa, and Brit Anlar, who not only participated in local seminars but also attended many conference panels in the United States and abroad and helped inform my thinking. At Rutgers University more broadly, I appreciate the support of my department chair, Richard Lau, and the School of Arts and Sciences for finding new ways to fund the research that went into this book, including nominating me for an Andrew Carnegie Fellowship. Wendy Silverman and Daniel Portalatin also went above and beyond in helping me administer my various grants.

My practitioner colleagues inspire me every time we meet, and I feel privileged to have been able to get to know them and their work more closely over the last few years. Zeina Hilal and Kareen Jabre at the Inter-Parliamentary Union were the first to invite me to participate in an event on this topic back in 2014, and generously shared their thoughts with me on Skype and in person in Geneva and New York on many occasions. They also introduced me to Brigitte Filion, a veritable fountain of knowledge who inspired numerous new directions in my research. In 2015, I began an amazing collaboration with Caroline Hubbard and Sandra Pepera at the National Democratic Institute which was born at a café near the United Nations and resulted, one year later, in the launch of the #NotTheCost campaign to stop violence against women in politics. In the years since, our conversations have given me invaluable first-hand insights into the important work being done on the ground to tackle violence against women in politics—as well as provided much needed critical feedback on how to conceptualize this phenomenon from an academic perspective. As attention to this issue has accelerated around the world, I also consider myself extremely lucky to have spent so much time in seminars, workshops, and one-on-one meetings with Julie Ballington at UN Women; Marta Martínez, Betilde Muñoz-Pogossian, and Sara Mía Noguera at the Organization of American States; and María del Carmen Alanís Figueroa from the Mexican Federal Electoral Tribunal.

The opportunity to participate in numerous academic as well as scholar-practitioner events on violence against women in politics, further, has informed this project at every step. On the scholarly side, I appreciate the sustained critical engagement of Elin Bjarnegård, Jennifer Piscopo, and Gabrielle Bardall with my single-authored papers as well as my co-authored work with Juliana. Conversations and workshops with Cheryl Collier, Tracey Raney, Sandra Håkansson, Rebekah Herrick, Paige Schneider, Suzanne Dovi, Eleonora Esposito, Erica Rayment, Pippa Norris, Sofia Collignon, and Pär Zetterberg have also been extremely valuable and stimulating. Additionally, numerous faculty and students – both graduate and undergraduate – offered very helpful feedback on the project as a whole in the course of presentations at Columbia University, Rutgers University, Brigham Young University, Uppsala University, Johns Hopkins University, The College of New Jersey, Emory University, Sewanee: The University of the South, Oklahoma State University, the University of Bucharest, the Universidad Nacional Autónoma de México, the University of New South Wales, Monash University, the Australian National University, Harvard University, Princeton University, Indiana University, and Vrije Universiteit Brussel.

In the world of politics, I had the chance to meet many incredible women around the globe who generously spoke to me about their experiences. This travel and fieldwork was supported, at various stages, by a National Science Foundation CAREER Award (2010–2017), a Chancellor's Scholarship at

Rutgers University (2015–2020), and an Andrew Carnegie Fellowship (2017–2019). I also deeply appreciate having been included in meetings organized by UN Women, the National Democratic Institute, the Inter-Parliamentary Union, the Organization of American States, the Westminster Foundation for Democracy, and the Party of European Socialists. These events brought together political women from around the world to share their testimonies on this topic, many for the very first time. Inspired by these diverse collaborations, in early 2020 I created a companion website to this book at vawpolitics.org to catalogue scholarly and practitioner contributions to these debates, and—in the spirit of ongoing collective theorizing—to incorporate and reflect new directions in the field as it develops.

Finishing this book would not have been conceivable in any shape or form, however, without the collaboration of my husband, Ewan Harrison. Only with his help has it been possible to undertake the extensive traveling required to research this book, as well as to find the time and space to write it. He has been a devoted, talented, and loving lead parent for our two boys. As an academic himself, he has also been a useful theoretical sounding board and has helpfully pointed me to numerous relevant news articles over the years. I feel fortunate to have found a partner in life who is willing and able to provide so much moral, practical, and intellectual support. I am also grateful to Fiona, Frances, and John Harrison; Louise Anderson; and my parents, Leena and Christer Krook, for lending a helping hand.

This book is dedicated, nonetheless, to our sons, Lars and Soren. Fascinated by the concept of writing a book, Lars replaced my father as the person most interested in knowing when I would finally finish writing it. Soren took a more relaxed approach, asking me just once, very politely, what my "story" was about. Along with their unconditional support for all my endeavors, they remind me why this book is important and motivated me to push through to the end. While this book consumed a great deal of my attention for a sustained period of time, these two are and will always be the most important focus of my life. This book is for you, my darlings.

# ABBREVIATIONS

Armed Conflict Location and Event Data Project   (ACLED)
Asia Pacific Forum on Women, Law, and Development   (APWLD)
Association for Women's Rights in Development   (AWID)
Association of Locally Elected Women of Bolivia   (ACOBOL)
Center for Women's Global Leadership   (CWGL)
Chief Human Resources Officer   (CHRO)
Commission on the Status of Women   (CSW)
Committee on Standards in Public Life   (CSPL)
Committee to Protect Journalists   (CPJ)
Convention on the Elimination of All Forms of Discrimination against
   Women   (CEDAW)
Declaration of Principles   (DoP)
Economic Commission for Latin America and the Caribbean   (ECLAC)
European Parliament   (EP)
European Union   (EU)
Federal Bureau of Investigation   (FBI)
Federal Electoral Institute   (IFE)
Federation of Women Lawyers   (FIDA)
Fixated Threat Assessment Centre   (FTAC)
Global Journalist Security   (GJS)
Human Rights Council   (HRC)
Human Rights Watch   (HRW)
Illinois Anti-Harassment, Equality, and Access   (AHEA)
Inter-American Commission of Women   (CIM)
Inter-American Convention on the Prevention, Punishment, and Eradication
   of Violence against Women   (Belém do Pará Convention)
Inter-Parliamentary Union   (IPU)
International Federation of Journalists   (IFJ)
International Foundation for Electoral Systems   (IFES)
International Gay and Lesbian Human Rights Commission   (IGLHRC)
International Institute for Democracy and Electoral Assistance   (IDEA)
International Labour Conference   (ILC)
International Labour Organization   (ILO)
International News Safety Institute   (INSI)
International Press Institute   (IPI)
International Women's Media Foundation   (IWMF)

Lesbian, Gay, Bisexual, and Transgender   (LGBT)
Member of Parliament   (MP)
Member of the European Parliament   (MEP)
Mesoamerican Women Human Rights Defenders Initiative   (IM-Defensoras)
Movement for Democratic Change   (MDC)
National Democratic Institute   (NDI)
Non-Governmental Organization   (NGO)
Office of Compliance   (OOC)
Operation Anti Sexual Harassment   (OpAntiSH)
Organization for Security and Cooperation in Europe   (OSCE)
Organization of American States   (OAS)
Parliamentary Liaison and Investigation Team   (PLaIT)
Real Academia Española   (RAE)
South Asia Partnership   (SAP)
Tanzania Media Women's Association   (TAMWA)
Tanzania Women Cross-Party Platform   (TWCP)
UK Independence Party   (UKIP)
UN Development Fund for Women   (UNIFEM)
UN Development Program   (UNDP)
United Nations   (UN)
United Nations Educational, Scientific and Cultural
    Organization   (UNESCO)
United Nations Entity for Gender Equality and the Empowerment of
    Women   (UN Women)
United Nations Population Fund   (UNFPA)
Urgent Action Fund   (UAF)
Women Human Rights Defenders International Coalition   (WHRDIC)
Women Influencing Nations   (WIN)
Women Living Under Muslim Laws   (WLUML)
Women's Media Center   (WMC)
Women's Social and Political Union   (WSPU)
Young Women's Leadership Network   (YWLN)
Zimbabwe African National Union—Patriotic Front   (ZANU–PF)

# Introduction

# 1

# A "Problem with No Name"

In October 2016, former Australian prime minister Julia Gillard spoke at an event held in memory of Jo Cox, a female member of parliament (MP) in the United Kingdom who had been murdered four months earlier. A supporter of the campaign to remain in the European Union, Cox was fatally shot and stabbed while arriving at a routine walk-in session for constituents one week before the contested Brexit referendum. Gillard stated that she had been asked to give "an honest account of the reality of being in politics," in the context of the meeting's broader focus on promoting women's participation in public life.

Gillard began with a frank catalogue of sexist insults and gendered critiques she had faced as prime minister, content familiar to many scholars and political observers. But she soon pivoted into darker territory, noting that "threats of violence have become more prevalent for women in public life." These ranged from "detailed death threats, or threats against family, friends, and staff" to rape threats, which a "woman in public view may expect to receive . . . almost daily." Such acts sought to "challenge the resolve of the women who cop the abuse," as well as to "deter other women from raising their hand to serve in public life" (Gillard 2016).

While born of her personal experiences, Gillard's remarks echo concerns voiced by a growing number of politically active women around the world, despite very different political systems and local cultures. These women explicitly reject the idea that such acts are simply the "cost of doing politics." A striking proportion, moreover, perceive these acts to be gender-based, aimed specifically at deterring women's political participation as women. Brought together and theorized by local activists and international practitioners, these testimonies have led to the recognition of a new global problem: violence against women in politics.

*Violence against Women in Politics.* Mona Lena Krook, Oxford University Press (2020). © Oxford University Press.
DOI: 10.1093/oso/9780190088460.001.0001.

The organic and inductive origins of this concept, however, have resulted in lingering ambiguities regarding its contours. This book seeks to bring clarity to these debates. Written for both scholars and practitioners, it draws on academic research in multiple disciplines, as well as empirical examples from around the world. It argues, in short, that this phenomenon is not simply a gendered extension of existing definitions of political violence privileging physical aggressions against political rivals (Collier 2009; Della Porta 1995). Rather, the book proposes that violence against women in politics is a distinct phenomenon involving a broad range of harms to attack and undermine women as political actors. Its central motivation is thus not to gain the upper hand in a game of partisan competition, but rather to exclude women as a group from public life.

This analytical distinction, in turn, means that violence against women in politics does *not* include *all forms* of violence faced by politically active women. It is not the *only* or even the *most common* form of violence they may experience. Rather, it is a *specific form* of violence that can, and often does, *coexist* with other forms of violence in the political sphere. Not recognizing it as a separate phenomenon, however, overlooks a crucial source of bias and discrimination against women in politics—and, in turn, its acute and underappreciated costs for democracy, human rights, and gender equality.

## A Hidden Problem

Understanding how and why violence against women in politics emerged as a concept requires first considering why it remained hidden for so long— and, indeed, why many women still hesitate to speak out. Testimonies by politically active women reveal at least four reasons. Some women normalize violence as part of the political game and thus simply do not perceive it as a "problem" (a cognitive gap). Others recognize that violence is not an acceptable cost of political engagement, but nonetheless remain quiet to protect their political careers and/or their political parties (a political gap), or to avoid scorn or blame from others for purportedly bringing the abuse upon themselves (a receptivity gap). A final group would speak out but feels there is no one to tell or no adequate language to describe their experiences (a resources gap).

### A COGNITIVE GAP

The cognitive gap is perhaps the most common. The comments of Norwegian prime minister Erna Solberg illustrate this approach: appearing on a television program to discuss online hate speech directed at her, she commented: "this kind of abuse isn't a big deal . . . As a female politician you get used to being judged . . . so you become thick-skinned" ("Norway PM" 2015). The reasons for this cognitive gap are complex, but a driving factor is post-feminism, or the widespread belief in many countries that gender equality has been already achieved. With equality for women taken for granted, explanations of collective failures to achieve gender parity devolve to listing the shortcomings of individual women (Johnson 2007).

These developments have given rise to what scholars term neo- or modern sexism. "Old-fashioned" sexism is relatively unambiguous: presuming the inferiority of women as a group, it leads to prejudicial attitudes and discriminatory behaviors against women. In contrast, newer versions of sexism are less overt, creating obstacles to them being recognized as a form of sexism at all. Neosexism emerges from a conflict between new egalitarian values and residual negative feelings toward women, arguing that discrimination is a relic of the past—but the gains women are making are unfair or moving too fast (Tougas et al. 1995). Modern sexism adopts a slightly subtler approach, proposing that—because discrimination no longer exists—unequal outcomes are not the product of systematic disadvantage (Ellemers and Barreto 2009).

Post-feminist discourses have at least three implications for recognizing the phenomenon of violence against women in politics. First, women facing sexist violence confront an apparent contradiction between their supposedly equal status as political actors and their experiences of blatant discrimination. To resolve their cognitive dissonance, abused women may cope with hurt by rationalizing it, defining it as tolerable or normal, "forgetting" it, or refusing to acknowledge it (Ferraro and Johnson 1983; Kelly 1988). Second, beliefs that discrimination against women is rare can lead to the discounting of individual instances of prejudice. This is especially true when targets share a close relationship with their perpetrators. Nonetheless, these women are likely to suffer the same negative psychological, work, and health consequences as those who are more willing to label their experiences as a form of "violence" (Magley et al. 1999). Third, women who lack—or are discouraged from developing—awareness of group-based discrimination are unlikely to perceive sexist acts against them as a form of injustice, deterring collective action to change the status quo (Ellemers and Barreto 2009).

A POLITICAL GAP

Political reasons provide a different set of motivations for women to remain silent. In these cases, women recognize violence as both sexist and deeply problematic. They decide, however, to keep these experiences private for strategic reasons. Some remain quiet to avoid reinforcing stereotypes of women as "weak" and "unsuited" to the rough world of politics. In her post-election memoir, Hillary Clinton (2017) reflected on an October 2016 U.S. presidential debate in which Donald Trump hovered menacingly behind her on the stage.

Weighing whether or not she should call out his obvious attempts to intimidate her, she explained: "I chose option A. I kept my cool, aided by a lifetime of dealing with difficult men trying to throw me off . . . I wonder, though, whether I should have chosen option B" (136). She then went on to say that, had she "told Trump off, he surely would have capitalized on it gleefully," pointing to other female politicians who had been called "angry" or "hysterical" as a means to undermine their credibility as political actors (137).

Calling out sexism is a fraught enterprise: no matter how justified the claim, it can invite a wide range of negative responses. At the most immediate level, verbally confronting sexist acts can affect personal relationships between the accuser and the accused. Feeling attacked, the latter may retaliate by disliking or denigrating the accuser (Shelton and Stewart 2004). The accuser, in turn, may lose prestige within the broader community, who may view them as "complainers" who merit less respect. For this reason, Swim and Hyers (1999) find that most women—when faced with the decision to react or not to a sexist incident—prefer the least risky option of not responding at all. This is not due, they emphasize, to personal failings on the part of women. Rather, it stems from traditional gender roles socializing women to defer to others and maintain relationships at all costs. Consequently, while "self-silencing may appear to be a choice, it is done within a social context that can impose negative consequences for speaking one's voice" (Swim et al 2010, 494).

A second set of political considerations revolves around preventing scandals that might be weaponized by rival political parties. Data from the National Democratic Institute (NDI 2018) and the Centre for Social Research and UN Women (2014) find that most perpetrators are members of a woman's own party. This is consistent with findings in the broader violence against women literature showing that women tend to know their offenders, whether they are family members, friends, or colleagues (Watts and Zimmerman 2002). Pressures to remain loyal to this "trusted circle" make it difficult to break the silence by divulging these incidents publicly. However, this does not mean that these acts remain a complete secret. As a female party member in Tunisia explained: "This topic . . . has stayed a taboo. A woman can't go up to a man and confront him for sexual harassment. [But] as women in the political party, we talk amongst ourselves."[1] Even if a woman has not personally experienced violence, therefore, she often knows of other politically active women who have (Cerva Cerna 2014).

A RECEPTIVITY GAP

A third reason women do not speak out stems from the lack of a receptive audience. In 2017, Democrat Kim Weaver stood down as a candidate in an Iowa congressional race against Republican incumbent Steve King. In a Facebook post to her supporters, she explained that she had grown increasingly concerned about "very alarming acts of intimidation, including death threats."[2] Responding via Twitter, King claimed that Democrats drove her out of the race, not Republicans, and "Death threats likely didn't happen but a fabrication."[3] Although women have long been dismissed as reliable witnesses of their own lives (Gilmore 2017), recent work in philosophy theorizes this trend as a form of "gaslighting," which occurs when a hearer tells a speaker that their claims are not serious, they are overreacting, they are being too sensitive, or they are not interpreting events properly (McKinnon 2017). Gaslighting is a tactic commonly employed against women to raise doubts not only about their "ability to discern harm but [also] their standing as one who is owed better treatment" (Stark 2019, 231).

A variation on this theme is to accuse women who speak up of "playing the gender card." According to Falk (2008), female politicians are "'accused,' 'called out,' and 'criticized' for playing the gender card," which involves "referencing the barriers women have faced in the political sphere" or suggesting that a woman in politics gets "different treatment because of her sex" (174). This phrase dogged Gillard (2014) following her famous misogyny speech in parliament in 2012: "That speech brought me the reputation of being the one who was brave enough to name sexism and misogyny. And it brought with it all the baggage that stops women naming sexism and misogyny when they see it: I was accused of playing the gender card, of playing the victim" (112).

"Playing the gender card" undercuts the possibility of serious discussions of sexism in politics by suggesting that women who call it out do so for reasons other than genuine grievance (Donaghue 2015). Gillard's case, however, also points to the existence of multiple audiences. While her speech received a negative and often scornful response from political opponents, as well as many Australian media outlets, her words and delivery resonated strongly with women at home and around the world (Sawer 2013). In her autobiography, Gillard (2014) thus argues for redefining the term: "Someone who acts in a sexist manner, who imposes gender stereotypes, is playing the gender card. It is that person who is misusing gender to dismiss, to confine, to humiliate: not the woman who calls it out for what it is. Calling the sexism out is not playing the victim. I have done it and I know how it made me feel. Strong. I am nobody's victim. It is the only strategy that will enable change" (112).

## A RESOURCES GAP

A final barrier to naming this problem stems from a deficit of resources. In recent years, a number of veteran female politicians have come forward to disclose incidents experienced decades earlier. In 2016, former minister Monique Pelletier responded to campaigns against sexual harassment in French politics by tweeting: "Minister of women in 1979, I was harassed by a senator . . . shame on me for my silence!"[4] She explained in a subsequent interview that she had not spoken out previously because "it was a climate that very few people talked about at the time" ("Agression Sexuelle" 2016). Former deputy prime minister of Canada, Sheila Copps, made similar remarks in an editorial in 2014 in which she disclosed that she had been sexually assaulted by a political colleague in the 1980s: "I never reported it . . . I was the only woman in my caucus. There wasn't a safe place to go talk about it" (Copps 2014). Widespread silence on these issues leads politically active women to adopt a wide range of individualized coping strategies to deal with threats and acts of violence (Barry 2011).

A related challenge is the dearth of adequate language for women to describe their experiences. When female candidates in the United States were approached by a reporter about intimidation on the campaign trail, some "said initially that they had not been harassed—but then, when given examples like menacing social media messages, said yes, they had experienced those things . . . a certain level of misogyny is so expected as to feel unremarkable" (Astor 2018, 14). Similarly, a local councilor in Colombia observed: "At first, it was hard to recognize that I was a victim of political violence . . . I saw things that made me think, 'why are they doing this to me?' But I did not identify those things as political violence" (Restrepo Sanín 2016, 44).

## Aims of this Book

This book explains how, despite these challenges, women came to name the problem of violence against women in politics. It then develops a more robust version of this concept to support ongoing activism and inform future scholarly work. From a feminist perspective, these aims are deeply interconnected. Stretching at least as far back as Betty Friedan's (1963) discussion of the "problem with no name" (15), feminists have noted the lack of adequate language to describe women's experiences. This is because, as Robin L. West (2000) observes, "an injury uniquely sustained by a disempowered group will lack a name, a history, and in general a linguistic reality" (153).

Putting a name to such harms, however, can help de-normalize these injustices, "making visible what was invisible, defining as unacceptable what was acceptable, and insisting that what was naturalized is problematic" (Kelly 1988, 139). By such means, naming highlights the structural nature of these harms, stressing their shared and systematic character as opposed to dismissing them as "matters of intense, private shame" and "idiosyncratic, individual, and rare occurrences" (Mantilla 2015, 153). Discovering a language by which to interpret women's experiences, in turn, can help link individual recognition of inequality or mistreatment to a collective resolve to take action (Klatch 2001).

The book tackles this project in four parts. The first traces how the concept of violence against women in politics emerged on the global stage through the collective theorizing of many different actors. Chapter 2 maps its multiple, parallel origins across the global South and subsequent efforts by international actors to connect these debates into one overarching concept. Chapter 3 identifies incidents of political sexism and misogyny in other regions—including the global North—that, together with the #MeToo movement, helped propel recognition of violence against women in politics as a truly global problem. Chapter 4 argues for a further expansion of the concept to incorporate all categories of politically active women, pointing to equivalent and contemporaneous campaigns to address violence against women human rights defenders and female journalists. Chapter 5 traces how these discussions have become embedded, in turn, in a growing number of international normative frameworks.

In light of these developments, Chapter 6 explores whether violence against women in politics is in fact a "new" phenomenon. Existing evidence points to at least three scenarios: it is a new expression of an old problem; it stems from technological advances and rising levels of incivility in world politics; and it constitutes a backlash against women's increased political presence. While the lack of prior research complicates the task of testing these various explanations, the chapter ultimately argues that the search for a definitive answer may be misplaced: rather than constituting competing hypotheses, these accounts more likely collectively capture distinct elements driving this phenomenon.

Chapter 7 applies a more critical, comparative lens to these developments. It outlines a series of debates and controversies emerging from practitioner work, which have been subject at times to tense academic engagement. These disagreements include disputes over terminology; violence against women or gender-based violence as the defining feature of this phenomenon; differing typologies and classifications of specific forms of violence; views on targets and perpetrators of violence; the presence of intersecting forms of violence based on race, class, age, and other identities; and contextual factors and their role in shaping incidents of violence. The discussion stakes out the position of this book in relation to each of these debates, providing a short summary of the ideas subsequently elaborated at length in the next part of the volume.

The second section of the book develops a theoretical framework for understanding what violence against women in politics is—and, in particular, how it is distinct from other forms of violence experienced in the political sphere. Chapter 8 considers arguments suggesting politics is simply a hostile space and catalogues analogous campaigns focused on mapping and addressing violence against politicians, human rights defenders, and journalists. Chapter 9 rejects the view that violence against women in politics is simply a gendered version of already-recognized forms of political violence. It argues that this phenomenon is distinct because it specifically aims to exclude women *as women* from the political sphere via dynamics of structural, cultural, and symbolic violence. Theorizing the phenomenon in relation to these forms of violence also explains why, until recently, it has remained largely "normalized" and hidden from view.

Chapter 10 discusses how to identify empirical cases. Addressing methodological challenges related to under-reporting, comparisons, and intersectionality, the chapter draws from the literature on hate crimes to propose a bias event approach, presenting six criteria to ascertain whether an incident was potentially motivated by bias. Chapter 11 outlines competing views on defining "violence" and argues in favor of adopting a comprehensive approach, limited not to the use of force but attending to violations of personal integrity more broadly. Feminist work theorizing a continuum of violence against women highlights why identifying a more complete spectrum of violent acts is vital, as manifestations of violence not only overlap but also inform and reinforce one another (Kelly 1988).

The third part of the book identifies five forms of violence against women in politics. Four of these—physical, psychological, sexual, and economic—are widely recognized among both activist and research communities. The book also theorizes a fifth type, semiotic violence, which emerged inductively in the course of the research. These five forms are taken up in chapters 12 through 16, respectively, which elaborate manifestations and emerging solutions, drawing on a global dataset of news items, practitioner reports, autobiographies, and original interviews. The discussion in each chapter is not intended to be exhaustive, but illustrative, providing an initial architecture for future theorizing and elaboration of this phenomenon.

The fourth and final section of the book issues a call to action, outlining what activists and scholars might do to tackle and raise awareness of violence against women in politics. Chapter 17 focuses on practitioner solutions cutting across different kinds of violence, cataloguing legal reforms and other initiatives to call out perpetrators and provide redress and care for targets. Chapter 18 outlines and assesses current data collection efforts. Highlighting the need for quantitative and qualitative data, it enumerates practical strategies and methodological challenges in documenting this phenomenon. Chapter 19 considers the political and social implications of allowing violence against women in politics to continue unabated. Utilizing data from around the world, it delineates the threats this problem poses to democracy, human rights, and gender equality. Chapter 20 concludes the volume by looking to the future, arguing that tackling violence against women in politics requires ongoing dialogue and collaboration to ensure women's equal rights to participate—freely and safely—in political life around the world.

PART I

# An Emerging Concept

2

# A Global Genealogy

Global debates on violence against women in politics cannot be traced back to a single source. As Kingdon (1984) argues in his influential book on agenda-setting, public policy never originates with a single actor; rather, a community of people working in a particular domain help an idea grow and take hold. Interacting extensively with one another, these specialists exchange visions, proposals, and research, and work together to gain the support of prominent actors to move a subject onto the political agenda. Such networks may be national and/or transnational, with the latter helping to circulate new ideas and strategies across countries and world regions (Keck and Sikkink 1998). A central focus of these efforts involves developing language that "names, interprets, and dramatizes" problems in ways that inspire and mobilize campaigns for change (Finnemore and Sikkink 1998, 897).

## Inductive Origins across the Global South

The first moves to name the problem of violence against women in politics emerged in parallel across different parts of the global South. Working inductively, locally elected women in Bolivia theorized their experiences as "political harassment and violence against women" in the late 1990s; networks of elected women across South Asia, with support from global organizations, mapped and condemned manifestations of "violence against women in politics" in the mid-2000s; and state and non-state actors in Kenya recognized and sought to tackle "electoral gender-based violence" in the late 2000s. Taking women's lived experiences as a shared starting point, these campaigns named the problem in different ways, but overlapped in their concerns to condemn the use of violence as a method to deter women's political participation.

*Violence against Women in Politics*. Mona Lena Krook, Oxford University Press (2020). © Oxford University Press. DOI: 10.1093/oso/9780190088460.001.0001.

BOLIVIA: POLITICAL HARASSMENT AND VIOLENCE AGAINST WOMEN

Women in Bolivia first began to talk about "political harassment and violence against women" within meetings of the Association of Locally Elected Women of Bolivia (ACOBOL). Soon after its creation in 1999, ACOBOL started receiving reports of violent incidents against female councilors and mayors. After realizing the attacks were not isolated events, they began distributing surveys at their meetings to gain a better sense of the manifestations and frequency of these acts (Restrepo Sanín 2018b). In 2000, ACOBOL organized a seminar with the Vice Minister of Gender Affairs and the Family, followed a few months later by a public hearing hosted by the Commission of Decentralization and Popular Participation. In 2001, they started working with state and civil society institutions on drafting a bill on political harassment and violence for reasons of gender, taking the first steps toward defining the problem and classifying its various forms based on the various cases they had received (Rojas Valverde 2014). The bill was discussed in parliament in 2005 and 2006 and sent to a joint committee to resolve some technical issues.

By 2007, the issue reached the agenda of the Tenth Regional Conference on Women, organized by the United Nations (UN) Economic Commission for Latin America and the Caribbean (ECLAC), in Quito, Ecuador. The meeting's Consensus of Quito contained the first international call to member states "to adopt legislative measures and institutional reforms to prevent, sanction, and eradicate political and administrative harassment against women to accede to elected and appointed decision-making positions" (ECLAC 2007, 5). While continuing to lobby for the bill, ACOBOL joined forces with the UN Population Fund (UNFPA) to develop a handbook of basic definitions and examples to raise awareness of the problem, gain support for legal reforms, and offer guidance on using indigenous justice systems, creating local networks of support, and collecting data on complaints (Yaksic and Rojas 2010).

In 2011, the campaign gained new life with support from women in parliament, the Vice Minister of Equality of Opportunities, an alliance of more than 15 women's organizations, and UN Women. The bill was brought up again in the 2011–2012 session and reworked in light of the new constitution approved in 2009. Key changes included expanding its remit to encompass women in all political-public functions (not just elected women) and changing the language to focus on acts committed against women (rather than acts committed "for reasons of gender") (Restrepo Sanín 2018b, 128). Passed in 2012, the bill defines political harassment and violence, establishes legal sanctions, and enumerates a series of factors that might magnify these penalties. Article 7 defines harassment as "acts of pressure, persecution, harassment, or threats" and violence as "physical, psychological, and sexual actions, behaviors, and/ or aggressions" aimed at restricting the exercise of women's political rights. Article 8 contains a wide-ranging list of examples of harassment and violence,[1] reflecting the inductive work of ACOBOL drawing on more than 4000 testimonies (ACOBOL 2012, 1). This text, in turn, inspired women elsewhere in Latin America to lobby for similar reforms, with varying degrees of success (Restrepo Sanín 2018b).

## SOUTH ASIA: VIOLENCE AGAINST WOMEN IN POLITICS

In South Asia, discussions of "violence against women in politics" began in 2006 as an initiative of South Asia Partnership (SAP) International, with financial support from Oxfam Novib. The project was inspired by findings from an SAP study on women's participation in governance in South Asia, revealing widespread discrimination, exploitation, oppression, and violence against women in politics (SAP International 2003). The first regional gathering was held in 2006 with women involved in national and provincial level politics, as well as female activists, representatives of the media, and staff from SAP offices in Bangladesh, India, Nepal, Pakistan, and Sri Lanka. Based on the testimonies given, participants proposed that violence against women in politics was a problem present across South Asia, with female politicians enduring not only physical attacks but also mental trauma and other offenses to discourage them from entering or continuing in politics. Women faced this violence within and outside political parties, as well as in the home and in society at large (SAP International 2006).

Subsequent regional conferences were organized in 2007, 2008, and 2009. Noting that many victims hesitated to speak openly about this problem, the 2007 conference in Kathmandu, Nepal, sought to "break the silence on the culture of feminized violence in politics which till now remained invisible" (SAP International 2007, vi). With financial support from a wide range of international actors, including the UN Development Fund for Women (UNIFEM),[2] International Institute for Democracy and Electoral Assistance (IDEA), UNFPA, and National Democratic Institute (NDI), participants elaborated a more extensive typology of different forms of psychological and physical violence faced by female politicians.

The 2008 conference in Kathmandu, supported by Oxfam, UNFPA, CARE Nepal, and International IDEA, focused on laws and policies for reducing violence against women in politics, as well as on showcasing best practices from female politicians themselves. The work enumerated three types of violence—physical, sexual, and psychological—and produced the 2008 Kathmandu Declaration calling for zero tolerance for violence against women in politics (SAP International 2009). The third conference in 2009 in Dhaka, Bangladesh, focused on the role of the media and on galvanizing regional and global action on this issue, identifying Article 7 and General Recommendations 12, 19, and 23 of the UN Convention on the Elimination of All Forms of Discrimination against Women (CEDAW) as potential entry points for action.

SAP International continued this work over the next two years, seeking to disseminate its work across as well as beyond South Asia. In 2010, it published a handbook with definitions of 46 terms and concepts related to violence against women in politics. It adapted the language of the UN's 1993 Declaration on the Elimination of Violence against Women to define it as "any act/s of violence that results in, or is likely to result in, physical, sexual or psychological harm or suffering to women politicians, including threats of such actors, coercion or arbitrary deprivation of liberty, whether occurring in public or in private life" (SAP International 2010, 26). SAP International concluded its work with a 2011 book containing a digest of case studies collected over the course of the project, featuring the testimonies of women in politics in five South Asian countries and Afghanistan (SAP International 2011).

## KENYA: ELECTORAL GENDER-BASED VIOLENCE

The concept of "electoral gender-based violence," finally, surfaced in Kenya in the late 2000s in connection with violence targeting female candidates and voters in the 2007 elections. One case featured prominently in the media involved parliamentary candidate Flora Terah, who was nearly killed after being physically assaulted by a gang of five men hired by her political opponent. While not the first violent incident targeting a political woman, Terah was visited in the hospital by politicians, activists, and even the U.S. ambassador, and the case was covered extensively by both local and global media outlets (Kihiu 2007; Terah 2008). Following the attack, an Electoral Gender Based Violence Rapid Response Unit was set up by the Education Centre for Women in Democracy, with support from UNIFEM, to assist survivors in gaining medical attention and trauma counseling, as well as with referring their cases to the police and the Electoral Commission of Kenya. The UNIFEM director also pledged to support female candidates by organizing trainings on personal security. Women in the media contributed by publishing testimonies of women candidates who had been attacked (Nyambala 2007). In early 2008, Terah launched a campaign against electoral gender-based violence, Terah against Terror, taking a caravan across the country to raise awareness.

Rampant violence following the elections led to the establishment of a Commission of Inquiry on Post-Election Violence, which noted that women and children were most at risk of and most affected by sexual violence, loss of property, and displacement. Enlisting the assistance of UNIFEM and UNFPA, as well as local organizations like the Federation of Women Lawyers (FIDA) Kenya, CARE Kenya, and the Center for Rights Education and Awareness, the commission devoted a chapter of its report to victims of post-election sexual violence. The Independent Review Commission examined conduct during the election itself and observed that a common feature of the elections had been the use of "sexist tactics and violence to keep women out of the race," with "violence during party nominations" being a key reason that "there were few women candidates."[3] The Elections Act of 2011, consolidating existing electoral laws into one piece of legislation, subsequently prohibited threatening and abusive language and actions, including on grounds of gender. These developments influenced preparations for the 2013 elections, which included a dedicated SMS hotline set up by FIDA Kenya for both victims and witnesses to report cases of violence against women in elections, which were forwarded to the closest police station for response with, where relevant, offers of legal aid.[4]

These interventions were strengthened ahead of the 2017 elections. In addition to reviving its hotline, FIDA Kenya trained police officers in five counties on how to handle gender-based violence during the elections.[5] The United Nations Development Program (UNDP) in partnership with UN Women and the Secretary-General's UNiTE Campaign to End Violence against Women, with financial support from UK Department for International Development, the U.S. Agency for International Development, the European Union (EU), and the governments of Ireland and Italy, published a pocket-sized booklet distributed to 180,000 polling agents.[6] It defines electoral gender-based violence as "gender-based violence to achieve political gain," taking sexual, physical, emotional, mental, social, and economic forms. Stating that electoral gender-based violence is a human rights issue, the booklet cites applicable laws on elections, electoral offenses, sexual offenses, criminal procedure, and domestic violence. It also outlines what security agents, citizens, and victims should do when faced with electoral gender-based violence and provides contacts for helplines, legal services, rescue shelters, and medical and trauma services.[7] Various UN agencies and civil society organizations subsequently came together to collect data and case studies, with a number of programming guides in development.[8]

## Transnational Networks and the Forging of a Global Concept

The inductive theorizing done by actors in these three contexts did not immediately translate into a global campaign. Their efforts, however, planted important seeds subsequently taken up by a wide range of international practitioners, who in the late 2000s and early 2010s actively worked to craft a global concept of violence against women in politics. For many, this work grew out of prior programming on women's political participation, which had expanded rapidly in the 1990s and 2000s following increased global and regional calls to promote gender-balanced decision-making (Hughes, Krook, and Paxton 2015).

The first cross-regional exchange was the e-discussion "Eliminating Violence against Women in Politics" organized in 2007 by iKNOW Politics, a joint project of International IDEA, the Inter-Parliamentary Union (IPU), NDI, UNDP, and UNIFEM (now UN Women). The opening message of the forum explained that "Violence or the threat of violence has been identified by members of the iKNOW Politics community—as well as through global and regional meetings of women politicians and their supporters sponsored by iKNOW partner organizations—as a significant impediment to women's political participation."

To strengthen the knowledge base on violence against women in politics, the moderators requested information on dimensions, frequency, and sources of violence; the distinction between violence targeting women because of their gender versus their political affiliations or ideologies; and measures that might be put in place to tackle this violence. Developments in Bolivia, South Asia, and Kenya were all explicitly mentioned in the discussion, along with examples from other countries like Ecuador and Iraq. The iKNOW Politics team concluded that, despite a fair amount of press coverage of specific cases of violence, very little research or policy work had to date been conducted (iKNOW Politics 2007).

## INTER-PARLIAMENTARY UNION

Although the topic surfaced in work that various international practitioners were doing at the time on women's political participation, the IPU was one of the first organizations to address it systematically.[9] Since 2006, the IPU had been supporting parliaments in developing policies to combat violence against women. At the same time, it began conducting survey research with male and female MPs, exploring how to attain greater gender equality in politics (IPU 2008). The latter inspired the IPU's subsequent work analyzing the gendered dynamics of parliament as a workplace. Published in 2011, its *Gender-Sensitive Parliaments* report indicated ongoing challenges faced by women, including problems with sexual harassment (Palmieri 2011). A Plan of Action for Gender-Sensitive Parliaments adopted in 2012 in Quebec, Canada, called on parliaments to take steps to foster "a work culture free of discrimination and harassment" (IPU 2012).

In parallel developments, the IPU organized a side event on gender and electoral violence at the UN's Commission on the Status of Women (CSW) meetings in March 2011. In April, the IPU Assembly adopted a resolution on electoral violence in Panama City, Panama, which included paragraphs expressing concern that female voters and candidates were "deterred from participating in the political process by a climate of intimidation" and observing that "gender-based electoral violence occurs prior to, during, and after elections and includes physical violence and verbal abuse" (IPU 2011). From 2014 onward, the IPU's annual reports on progress and setbacks in women's parliamentary representation have included a number of paragraphs on violence. The first report to do so, on elections that had taken place in 2013, noted that gender-based electoral and political violence was receiving greater attention and offered examples from Kenya, Honduras, and Italy (IPU 2014).

These trends led the IPU to carry out a consultative process with female parliamentarians in 2014 and 2015, with the idea of conducting a survey. The resulting brief, published in October 2016, showed that psychological, physical, sexual, and economic violence against women in parliaments was widespread (IPU 2016b). To coincide with its publication, the IPU Assembly approved a resolution noting that "the increasing inclusion of women in political processes around the world has been accompanied by forms of resistance such as stereotyping, harassment, intimidation, and violence," such that "women face an additional obstacle to their engagement in politics that can inhibit their freedom to exercise their mandate as they would wish" (IPU 2016a). A study done in collaboration with the Parliamentary Assembly of the Council of Europe two years later showed that younger women, as well as members of staff, suffered from exceptionally high levels of violence and harassment (IPU 2018).

UNITED NATIONS

These issues began to be taken up within the global UN system in late 2010. In a report on women's participation in peacebuilding, the UN Secretary-General (2010) called for "vulnerability mapping to assess potential violence facing women (as voters, party workers and candidates), as well as action to prevent and respond to such threats" (15). In February 2011, UN Women in New York collaborated with the Institute for Democratic Alternatives in South Africa and UN Women country offices to develop a toolkit for managing and preventing "political violence against women," piloted sequentially in Uganda, Nigeria, and Zimbabwe (UN Women 2011). In early 2011, UN Women also organized a high-level meeting to update UN General Assembly Resolution 58/142 on women and political participation, adopted in 2003. The new Resolution 66/130, approved by member states in December 2011, urged states "To investigate allegations of violence, assault or harassment of women elected officials and candidates for political office, create an environment of zero tolerance for such offences and, to ensure accountability, take all appropriate steps to prosecute those responsible" (UN General Assembly 2011, 4).

Two years later, the UN Secretary-General's (2013a) report on progress made on Resolution 66/130 expanded this discussion to observe that "violence against women in political life discourages or prevents them from exercising their political rights" (15). Acknowledging that recognition of such violence was new, it argued for data and evidence to be collected to prevent violence and hold perpetrators accountable. It also recognized efforts in Bolivia and Mexico to legislate on the issue, as well as the work of various UN agencies to monitor violence against women in elections and include violence prevention in candidate trainings. The following year, UN Women published a study done in collaboration with the Centre for Social Research in New Delhi on violence against women in politics in India, Nepal, and Pakistan. Citing the work of

SAP International, this work provided data on the nature, extent, motives, and effects of this violence (Centre for Social Research and UN Women 2014).

Intersecting with these developments was an initiative at UNDP to develop a handbook on gender and electoral violence. The project began to coalesce in early 2011, after a colleague who had participated in the CSW panel organized by the IPU later attended a joint EU-UNDP meeting on electoral violence where there was no discussion of gender at all. However, the project encountered challenges in framing the concept—namely, whether to add a gender lens to tools designed to prevent and mitigate electoral violence, or alternatively, to expand violence against women frameworks to political and electoral arenas. After the colleague moved to UN Women in 2012, the work became a joint UNDP/UN Women initiative and—with input from UN Women staff—took on a stronger violence against women angle. As a result, the preferred terminology began to evolve from "electoral violence against women" to "violence against women in elections."[10] This language appeared in a subsequent publication, *Inclusive Electoral Processes*, identifying four types of violence: psychological, physical, sexual, and economic (UNDP and UN Women 2015). The original 2011 project was published in 2017 as a programming guide for tackling violence against women in elections (UNDP and UN Women 2017).

INTERNATIONAL FOUNDATION FOR ELECTORAL SYSTEMS

Inspired by conversations at UNDP, in 2011 the International Foundation for Electoral Systems (IFES) revisited data collected in six countries between 2006 and 2010 via its citizen-monitoring initiative, the Electoral Violence Education and Resolution Program. Focusing on three types of violence—physical, economic, and social-psychological—the research noted significant gender differences in the types of election-related violence experienced by women and men (Bardall 2011). IFES did not take up the issue again, however, until 2014. Similar clashes over terminology occurred. Electoral violence experts preferred "electoral violence against women," which would add women to existing election security frameworks, while the gender team favored "violence against women in elections," which would center more expansive feminist definitions of "violence" as well as the survivors of gender-based violence. To better articulate the issue in its work, in 2016 IFES launched a Violence against Women in Elections Assessment Tool (Huber and Kammerud 2016).[11] It has since carried out assessments in various parts of the world, in addition to pilot studies of online violence against women in elections.[12]

ORGANIZATION OF AMERICAN STATES

During this same period, the Inter-American Commission of Women (CIM) of the Organization of American States (OAS) began fielding numerous requests about political harassment and violence from female politicians across the region. This led it to convene a hemispheric expert group meeting in February 2015 to exchange information on the Bolivian experience as well as on ongoing legislative efforts in other Latin American countries. Based on these discussions, CIM developed a Declaration on Political Harassment and Violence against Women, which was approved by state-parties to the 1994 Inter-American Convention on the Prevention, Punishment, and Eradication of Violence against Women (Belém do Pará Convention) at the conference of the Follow-up Mechanism to the Belém do Pará Convention in Lima, Peru, in October 2015.

Applying the convention's definition of violence against women as acts causing "death or physical, sexual, or psychological harm or suffering to women," the declaration called for the adoption of mechanisms and measures, collection of data, introduction of victim services, awareness raising campaigns, and development of media codes of conduct (CIM 2015, 3). To assist countries in developing legislation to this end, CIM subsequently carried out regional consultations to produce an Inter-American Model Law on the Prevention, Punishment and Eradication of Violence against Women in Political Life (CIM 2017). Points of contention in these debates revolved primarily around the language of "violence" versus "harassment," as well as "violence against women" versus "gender-based violence."[13]

The work of the Group of Women Parliamentarians of ParlAmericas, an independent body that cooperates closely with the OAS, intersected with and complemented these efforts. At its annual hemispheric conference in 2014, a Peruvian participant on a panel discussing barriers to gender equality in politics shared her work with a network of locally elected women to pass a bill on political harassment. The contribution resonated strongly with the audience, leading the group to recommend focusing exclusively on this issue during its 2015 meeting, which was also attended by colleagues from NDI, UN Women, and CIM. To facilitate the sharing of experiences beyond the meeting, staff at ParlAmericas began filming testimonies from women across the Americas, which were later posted on its website as a means to map violence against women in politics across the region.[14] In 2016, ParlAmericas held a special event in Saint Lucia for women parliamentarians from the Anglophone Caribbean, where these debates were less advanced than in the Spanish-speaking countries of Latin America.[15]

## NATIONAL DEMOCRATIC INSTITUTE

Around 2012, NDI began informally collecting stories about women's experiences with harassment and violence during elections. Over the next two years, the need to develop a more systematic approach to data collection became increasingly evident.[16] In 2015, the gender team launched the Votes without

Violence project to "gender" NDI's work on electoral violence and the democratic quality of elections by training stakeholders to detect early warning signs and acts of violence against women in elections. As the project was piloted across several countries in Africa and Latin America, the team expanded its original typology—adding economic violence, for example—to better reflect realities on the ground.[17]

The cross-regional nature of this work inspired NDI to pursue the idea of creating a global framework for conceptualizing, raising awareness, and devising solutions to tackle violence against women in politics. In December 2015, it convened a workshop with practitioners, politicians, and academics to consider how to best frame the case for change. In March 2016, NDI launched the #NotTheCost campaign with a global call to action, arguing that violence should not be the price women have to pay to participate in politics.[18] To give voice to—and draw connections across—women's experiences, the event featured testimonies from female politicians and activists from around the world.

Following this event, NDI developed a suite of tools to address different locations and aspects of this phenomenon. The first involved program guidance, which sought to clarify how violence against women in politics was distinct from political violence affecting both women and men. Drawing on global debates, it proposed that violence against women in politics targets women because of their gender, its forms can be gendered, and its impact is to discourage women in particular from being or becoming politically active (NDI 2016). NDI's subsequent projects focused on violence against women in political parties (NDI 2018); online violence against women in politics, including state-based gendered disinformation (NDI 2019); and individual safety planning.[19] From 2016 onward, NDI also played a vital role in lobbying the UN's Special Rapporteur on Violence against Women to take up the issue, contributing centrally to her report to the UN General Assembly in 2018.[20]

## ADDITIONAL INITIATIVES

A variety of other international practitioners have also generated knowledge and raised awareness. To support implementation of the Quito Consensus, UN Habitat published a report theorizing political harassment as a form of discrimination against women (Torres García 2010) and the UN Women's Training Center funded empirical case studies to map political violence and harassment in Costa Rica (Escalante and Méndez 2011), El Salvador (Herrera, Arias, and García 2011), Ecuador (Arboleda 2012), and Bolivia (Rojas Valverde 2012). In 2013, the Friedrich Ebert Foundation published case studies of harassment against women in politics in Colombia, Costa Rica, Ecuador, El Salvador, Guatemala, Honduras, Mexico, Nicaragua, and Panama (Hoyos 2014). Between 2014 and 2017, International IDEA and the Netherlands Institute for Multiparty Democracy collaborated on a project on women's political rights in

Colombia, Kenya, and Tunisia, which included a prominent focus on violence against women in politics.[21] The Commonwealth Women Parliamentarians dedicated their 2016 conference to the theme of political violence against women. And in 2018, the Westminster Foundation for Democracy, in partnership with the British political parties, hosted an international summit to address violence against women in politics, with more than 50 speakers from over 20 countries.

# 3

# Parallel and Related Trends

Inductive development of the concept of violence against women in politics largely proceeded from an activist and practitioner space focused on the global South. Over this same time period, however, a series of testimonies from politically active women in other regions—including the global North—have emerged, showing that this problem affects women across a range of different countries. In late 2017, the #MeToo movement that swept around the world also drew attention to sexual harassment within political institutions, highlighting that gender-based violence was not restricted to election-related events. These episodes have largely been folded into the work done by practitioners in the violence against women in politics field, helping to strengthen its recognition as a universal phenomenon.

## Individual and Collective Testimonies

Over the last two decades, women's opportunities to participate in politics have expanded rapidly, enabling their entry into new political spaces and leadership positions. In recent years, a growing number of women have spoken out about the violence they have faced in the course of seeking to have a political voice. Emerging organically, these accounts reveal that violence against women in politics is not a phenomenon restricted to particular parts of the global South.

### EGYPT AND TUNISIA

Women were a visible force in protests in late 2010 and early 2011 that spread across the Arab world, toppling longstanding authoritarian regimes. In Egypt, sexual violence against women became a regular feature of mass gatherings following the fall of President Hosni Mubarak (Zaki 2017). However, during Mubarak's rule security forces also used sexual assault—either directly or with

*Violence against Women in Politics.* Mona Lena Krook, Oxford University Press (2020). © Oxford University Press.
DOI: 10.1093/oso/9780190088460.001.0001.

the help of hired thugs—as a means to terrorize women and prevent them from participating in protests (Tadros 2015). Despite attempts to protect female protesters, the number and severity of attacks on women grew in 2013 and 2014, committed by a wide range of perpetrators (Zaki 2017). Consultations by Saferworld (2013) with hundreds of women involved in protests in Egypt, Libya, and Yemen explicitly used the term "harassment" to refer to the range of behaviors women experienced in public spaces, from derogatory comments to groping, sexual assault, and rape. Hearings of the Truth and Dignity Commission in Tunisia in 2014 also revealed systematic patterns of rape and sexual assault against female members of the opposition during the rule of Zine El Abidine Ben Ali and his predecessor Habib Bourguiba (Zaki 2017).[1]

## AUSTRALIA

In 2012, Australian journalist Anne Summers gave a speech detailing the vilification of the country's first female prime minister. She argued that if Julia Gillard worked in any other profession, she would have a strong case for sex discrimination and sexual harassment.[2] Providing examples of sexist and highly sexualized words, cartoons, and doctored photographs circulated widely in the media and by citizens via email and social media accounts, Summers observed this "was something we had not seen before in Australian politics." She attributed this trend to the "misogyny factor," or beliefs "predicated on the view that women do not have the fundamental right to be part of society beyond the home" (Summers 2013, 106, 8). Delivered on the same day that shock jock Alan Jones claimed that female leaders were "destroying the joint," Summers's speech garnered widespread attention across Australia.[3]

A few weeks later, Gillard rose in parliament to respond to Tony Abbott, the leader of the opposition, who had submitted a motion to remove the speaker over crude and sexist texts he had sent to an aide. Speaking largely off the cuff, she opened by emphatically declaring: "I will not be lectured about sexism and misogyny by this man. I will not . . . If he wants to know what misogyny looks like in modern Australia, he does not need a motion in the House of Representatives—he needs a mirror." She went on to document Abbott's own vast history of sexism and misogyny, including statements that the under-representation of women was not "a bad thing," as men's minds were "more adapted to exercise authority."[4] The speech went viral in Australia and around the world, resonating with many women and opening up conversations about sexism in Australian society (Donaghue 2015).

The issue returned to the public eye in 2018, when Greens Senator Sarah Hanson-Young (2018) decided to break her "silence on the smears and sexualized bullying" she had endured for years, following an incident when Senator David Leyonhjelm yelled at her to "stop shagging men" during a debate on tackling violence against women (27). Refusing to apologize, he then went on a series of television and radio shows, where he doubled down with statements like: "Sarah is known for liking men. The rumors about her in parliament are well known." He further claimed that his remarks were not sexist but rather "normal Australian behavior" (29–31). Pointing to Gillard's misogyny speech as a factor in her decision to speak out, Hanson-Young called sexist rumors the "oldest trick in the book" and emphatically stated that no one "deserves to show up to work and be harassed, bullied, or intimidated. It's not okay in the workplace, it's not okay in our homes, and our parliament should set a better example" (94).

## ITALY

Similar debates emerged in Italy in 2013 and 2014 in the wake of sexist and racist attacks against Laura Boldrini, president of the Chamber of Deputies, and Cécile Kyenge, the first black cabinet minister. Interviewed by the *Guardian* in 2014, Boldrini disclosed that she had received thousands of misogynistic insults, threats, and images since becoming a candidate, including photos of her faced superimposed on the body of a woman being raped (Davies 2014). Far-right politicians from the Five Star Movement and the Northern League were particularly active in targeting her, using sexist language, inciting violence, and comparing her to a blow-up sex doll (Feder, Nardelli, and De Luca 2018).

Born in the Democratic Republic of Congo, Kyenge migrated to Italy in 1983 and served as minister of integration from 2013 to 2014. Political opponents—mostly belonging to the far-right—called for her to be raped, threw bananas at her during political rallies, compared her to an orangutan, and remarked that "she seems like a great housekeeper" but "not a government minister" (Meret, Della Corta, and Sanguiliano 2013). In 2016, members of the Parliamentary Intergroup on Women, Rights, and Equal Opportunities published a statement in *La Reppublica* condemning "vulgar insults" and "sexist vignettes" targeting women at all levels of Italian politics. They argued such acts "feed and give legitimacy to the debasement and discrimination of women in society, in the world of work, in institutions, in political life, and in the media" (Bianchi et al. 2016).

## FRANCE

A series of events across Europe and North America in 2016 gave further momentum to these discussions. In May 2016, four female politicians in France—Isabelle Attard, Elen Debost, Annie Lahmer, and Sandrine Rousseau—came forward to accuse Denis Baupin, a Green MP and vice president of the French National Assembly, of sexual harassment, involving both physical assaults as well as the repeated and unwelcome sending of lewd text messages (Chrisafis 2016). The next day, 500 activists and elected officials published a manifesto in *Libération* calling for an end to impunity for sexual harassment in French politics (Le Collectif "Levons l'omerta" 2016). These efforts built on a manifesto issued by a group of female journalists a year earlier, calling out harassing behaviors committed by politicians from all parties at all levels of political power (Amar et al. 2015).[5] Within days, 17 former government ministers from across the political spectrum penned an opinion piece in *Le Journal de Dimanche*: declaring that the "law of silence" was over, they argued it was not women's role to adapt, but rather, the behavior of certain men needed to change (Bachelot et al. 2016).

Although Baupin resigned his leadership post, he remained an MP and denied that his behaviors constituted acts of sexual harassment. In March 2017, the deputy attorney-general decided that while many of the acts fit the legal (and criminal) definition of sexual harassment, the statute of limitations had passed and thus no further action could be taken on any of the four cases. In the absence of a legal remedy, Rousseau decided to write a book sharing her account, with a collective preface by Attard, Debost, and Lahmer, who explained why they chose to speak out: "One day, we realized that our silence had made this man believe that he had all the rights . . . Our fears about being humiliated granted him immunity. Continuing to remain silent would have given him the power to do it again—and this would have made us his accomplices" (Rousseau 2017, 15). Rousseau then went on to establish an association, *Parler*, to assist and support women who were victims of sexual violence.[6]

Meanwhile, female staff at the National Assembly noted limited indignation within the political class itself. Instead, male deputies suggested that the women who accused Baupin had ulterior motives against him; portrayed Baupin as a victim, removing any responsibility from him for his behavior; or "jokingly" asked colleagues or staff if women were going to file a complaint if men said they looked nice or touched their shoulders (Julié-Viot 2018). To raise awareness of sexual harassment in French politics, therefore, a group of staffers created Chair Collaboratrice,[7] a group and a website to receive and post anonymous testimonies from women working at all levels of the political system.[8] These accounts revealed a range of sexist behaviors and highlighted factors facilitating these abuses, including precarious work contracts, late working hours, and widespread use of alcohol.[9]

In March 2019, Chair Collaboratrice sent a questionnaire to all staff members, inquiring into incidents of sexist harassment and sexual violence they had experienced or witnessed in the course of their work at the National Assembly. The results indicated that one in two women were victims of "sexist or sexual jokes," one in three experienced repeated and bothersome staring or simulated sexual acts, one in five fielded unwanted sexual advances, and one in six were touched on the breasts, buttocks, or thighs against their will.[10] As part of the group's efforts to secure a commitment to fight against all forms of harassment and discrimination in parliament, Chair Collaboratrice shared these findings with the Working Group on Work Conditions and Staff, which voted in May 2019 to create an independent office to support victims (Paillou 2019).

UNITED KINGDOM

The murder of British MP Jo Cox in June 2016 served as another major crystallizing event for global debates on violence against women in politics. Several months earlier, Muslim Women's Network UK had raised issues of intimidation of female Muslim candidates. In a letter to Labour leader Jeremy Corbyn, they claimed that Muslim male politicians at the local level had displayed "systematic misogyny" and actively "undermined, sabotaged, and blocked [women] from becoming councilors."[11] Appearing on *BBC Newsnight*, one woman recounted how, during her bid to become a local official, she had been subjected to a smear campaign and men had come to her family home attempting to intimidate her mother (Elgot 2016). A subsequent report by the Citizens Commission on Islam, Participation, and Public Life (2017) confirmed these accounts, finding that a "patriarchal" system "led by male community elders" engaged in widespread bullying to pressure women to stay out of politics (46).

Cox, a member of the Labour Party, was assaulted on the street by Thomas Mair, a far-right extremist who reportedly yelled "Britain first!" during the attack. She had previously contacted police after receiving a stream of malicious messages, leading to an arrest in March 2016. Due to this online harassment, at the time of her death police were considering additional security both at her constituency office in Birstall and her houseboat in London. Many female MPs perceived a gendered dimension in her attack, with Diane Abbott stating: "It is hard to escape the conclusion that the vitriolic misogyny that so many women politicians endure framed the murderous attack on Jo" (Hughes, Riley-Smith, and Swinford 2016). Cox's friend, Jess Phillips, wrote at the time of Mair's sentencing that "for me and for many of my colleagues—particularly female MPs—fear has also become real and present" (Phillips 2016b).

In direct response to Cox's murder, the Metropolitan Police established a Parliamentary Liaison and Investigations Team in August 2016 to provide security support to MPs, beyond existing funds for extra locks and security cameras provided by the Independent Parliamentary Standards Authority. The team estimated that approximately 60% of the cases it receives concern female MPs, although women only constituted 32% of MPs overall.[12] Following snap elections in June 2017, Prime Minister Theresa May called on the Committee on Standards in Public Life (CSPL) to undertake a study on abuse and intimidation of parliamentary candidates. In its report, published that December, the CSPL (2017) noted that, while candidates of all political persuasions are affected, those "who are female, BAME [black, Asian, or minority ethnic], or LGBT [lesbian, gay, bisexual, or transgender] are disproportionately targeted in terms of scale, intensity, and vitriol" (28). Making her first public statement on the report on February 6, 2018, the centenary of women's suffrage, May (2018) drew parallels with suffragettes who "had to contend with open hostility and abuse to win their right to vote."

## UNITED STATES

A third event occurring in 2016, the U.S. presidential election, left perhaps the strongest global impression in relation to these debates. Sexism and misogyny characterized the contested primary season as well as the election itself. Within the Democratic Party, the Bernie Sanders campaign attracted a large contingent of young and enthusiastic male supporters known, disparagingly, as "Bernie Bros." They created and circulated misogynistic memes about Hillary Clinton, while also engaging in sexist harassment and denigration of her female supporters in particular (Albrecht 2017). On the Republican side, supporters of Donald Trump often broke into chants of "Lock her up!" during rallies, while vendors at campaign events sold merchandise with highly sexist and misogynistic content (Beinart 2016).

The candidate himself made numerous remarks during the campaign disparaging women. During the primary season, Trump claimed that a female journalist, Megyn Kelly, questioned him aggressively because she was menstruating. He also declared his female Republican rival, Carly Fiorina, not attractive enough to hold public office. At an August 2016 rally, he wondered aloud whether the "Second Amendment people" (gun owners) could do anything about Clinton. In the following months, he asserted that Clinton simply did not have a "presidential look," and during the third and final presidential debate, he famously called her a "nasty woman."

According to Valentino, Wayne, and Oceno (2018), such comments elevated the role of sexism in driving voting choices, the first and only time this factor had affected presidential election outcomes. Bolstering this interpretation, Levey (2018) tracked usage of the word "bitch" on Twitter at various moments in 2016. She found a relatively stable daily average of 400,000 hits, except on days following the three presidential debates when there was a notable increase. On Election Day, this number spiked to more than 900,000, with content analysis showing that the words "Clinton" and "bitch" often appeared together in these tweets (2018, 123–125). Reflecting on these developments, some commentators suggested that the proliferation of misogynistic hate speech during the campaign had a chilling effect on women's free expression, pointing for example to the emergence of the secret Facebook group, Pantsuit Nation (Carlson 2018). What started as a small group of women planning to wear pantsuits (Clinton's famous wardrobe item) on Election Day rapidly grew into a community of more than three million members offering "a troll-free space in which Clinton supporters could enthusiastically support their candidate."[13]

While some observers expressed concerns that Clinton's loss would normalize misogyny and reverse gains in gender equality, many women reacted by mobilizing and running for political office in record numbers the following year.[14] The increased presence of female candidates contributed, in turn, to more frank discussions of violence against women in politics. As one reporter noted: "Harassment is not new for women in politics . . . [but] it has come to the fore this election cycle, partly because so many women are running and partly because more of them are discussing their experiences" (Astor 2018, 14). In November 2017, the Women's Media Center launched a four-minute video to foster greater "public awareness of the daily hostility that women in politics face as the result of being women in public life." Featuring testimonies from eight Democratic and Republican women who had run for office at all levels, the video sought to "recognize the additional risks women take when they run for office and serve in public roles."[15]

### EUROPE

Collectively, these events facilitated increased recognition of violence against women in politics as a global problem, not confined to specific countries or regions (Krook and Restrepo Sanín 2016b). In a telling indication of growing awareness of this problem in the global North, female parliamentarians from Europe were the first to approach the IPU to conduct a regional study on violence against women in parliament.[16] Conducted in close collaboration with the Parliamentary Assembly of the Council of Europe, the study interviewed more than 120 female MPs and staff across 45 member states. Rates of violence were relatively similar to the global sample, although levels of psychological violence were slightly higher and levels of physical violence somewhat lower. The study further discovered that female MPs under the age of 40 were more likely than older MPs to face acts of psychological and sexual violence, and among staffers, more than 40% had experienced sexual harassment (IPU 2018, 2, 6–7). These findings inspired women in the Party of European Socialists to organize a day-long conference on violence against women in politics in Lisbon, Portugal, in December 2018.

### #MeToo and the Political Sphere

These developments coincided with the rise of the global #MeToo movement in October 2017, which drew attention to problems of sexual harassment in all fields, including politics. The hashtag went viral[17] on Twitter after American actress Alyssa Milano posted a screenshot from a friend suggesting: "If all the women who have been sexually harassed or assaulted wrote 'Me too.' as a status, we might give people a sense of the magnitude of the problem." To this, Milano added: "If you've been sexually harassed or assaulted, write 'me too' as a reply to this tweet."[18] Within 24 hours, 500,000 people responded on Twitter and the hashtag #MeToo appeared on Facebook 12 million times (Renkl 2017). Within three weeks, it appeared in 2.3 million tweets by users in 85 countries (Fox and Diehm 2017). Although allegations of sexual misconduct by Hollywood producer Harvey Weinstein served as the immediate catalyst for #MeToo, many commentators argue that the 2016 U.S. presidential campaign—during which a growing number of women came forward to accuse Trump of sexual assault and Trump himself made comments on tape about sexually assaulting women—also served as a precipitating factor (Hillstrom 2019).

UNITED STATES

Less than two weeks after the *New York Times* article breaking the Weinstein story, and the day after Milano's tweet, more than 140 women in California politics published a letter in the *Los Angeles Times* denouncing widespread sexual harassment against (and by) lawmakers, aides, and lobbyists. In their opening sentences, they wrote: "As women leaders in politics, in a state that postures itself as a leader in justice and equality, you might assume our experience has been different. It has not. Each of us has endured, or witnessed, or worked with women who have experienced some form of dehumanizing behavior by men with power in our workplaces." They explained that victim blaming and fear of professional ramifications had prevented them from speaking out before, including to protect their friends from abuse. Referring to their previous perceived powerlessness to stop the cycle, they asserted: "We're done with this. Each of us who signed this op-ed will no longer tolerate the perpetrators or enablers who do."[19] Calling the group "We Said Enough," they posted 20 firsthand accounts on their website[20] and created a Twitter account to monitor developments related to sexual harassment in politics.[21] In December, one of the group's founders, Adama Iwu, was featured on the cover of *Time* magazine as one of "The Silence Breakers," who were collectively recognized as *Time*'s Person of the Year in 2017.

Although the issue of sexual harassment had previously been raised in a number of state legislatures across the United States, the #MeToo movement brought this problem into sharper focus. By the end of 2017, more than 100 people had publicly accused at least 40 lawmakers across 20 states of sexual misconduct or harassment (Ebert 2017). Several prominent leaders, including U.S. Senator Claire McCaskill, disclosed that as state legislators they were told informally that sexual favors would enable their bills to go further (Vock 2017; Wang 2017). In response to this attention, over the next year 32 states introduced over 125 bills to expel members, mandate harassment training, and criminalize sexual harassment in legislatures.[22] By the end of 2018, 75% of the 138 elected or appointment officials publicly accused had left or been ousted from their positions. However, 23 of the 27 who ran for office again were re-elected or elected to a new government position (Williams 2018, 2–3).

In the U.S. Congress, five members resigned as a result of #MeToo allegations, including four representatives—John Conyers, Blake Farenthold, Trent Franks, and Pat Meehan—and one senator, Al Franken. In November 2017, Representative Jackie Speier shared her experiences as a young congressional staffer and launched #MeTooCongress, urging current and former staffers to come forward with their stories. The problem was not new: according to a CQ Roll Call survey in July 2016, 6 in 10 female staffers reported being sexually harassed (Bacon 2017). Although Speier had sought since 2014 to change the onerous complaint process, she finally succeeded in late 2018, aided by pressure from all 22 female senators in an unprecedented bipartisan display of support. Reforming the Congressional Accountability Act of 1995, the law streamlines the process for reporting allegations, stipulates that legislators are financially liable for harassment settlements, and increases transparency regarding the settlements reached.[23]

## UNITED KINGDOM

#MeToo debates also spread to other political bodies around the world. In the UK, the issue was not new. In 2013, the Liberal Democrat chief executive, Chris Rennard, was accused of sexually harassing numerous female party colleagues going as far back as 2007. Although there was insufficient evidence for criminal charges, an internal party report found credible evidence for other claims, and he was suspended from the party in 2014. In the wake of a sexual assault case against former Deputy Speaker Nigel Evans, in 2014 House of Commons Speaker John Bercow established a confidential hotline for anyone working in parliament to report incidents of harassment and bullying (Dixon 2014). Beginning in October 2017, however, a number of male cabinet ministers and MPs suddenly resigned or were suspended from their parties. Some of these offenders came to light via a list developed by parliamentary staff using a private WhatsApp messaging group (Elgot and Mason 2017).

At the end of October, Labour MP Harriet Harman posed an Urgent Question to House of Commons Leader Andrea Leadsom asking for a statement about her plan to tackle sexual harassment in parliament. Liz Saville Roberts, a Plaid Cymru MP, shared that a female staff member for another MP had come to her that day, frustrated that she had reported an incident no less than four times, but the case had gone nowhere. Roberts commented: "You would expect this place to be setting an example and not lagging behind what is normal workplace practice anywhere else in the country."[24]

Leadsom subsequently established a cross-party working group, which was later expanded to include an academic expert on sexual violence,[25] to develop new policies and mechanisms for handling harassment complaints and improving the working culture at parliament (Culhane 2019). As part of its work, the group conducted a survey that found that one of five people working at Westminster had experienced or witnessed sexual harassment or inappropriate conduct in the previous 12 months (Buchan 2018). In March 2018, Dame Laura Cox (2018) led a parallel independent inquiry into bullying and harassment of staff, noting: "No workplace is immune from pervasive misconduct of this kind and it was perhaps not surprising that such allegations had emerged in the world of politics, where the inherent imbalance of power creates obvious vulnerabilities" (8).

Meanwhile, a group of women in the Labour Party formed LabourToo to raise awareness and lobby for policy changes within the party itself.[26] They set up a website "to enable women to share their stories anonymously so that we can build a compendium of the types of abuse women face which all too often are unseen, ignored, or swept under the carpet."[27] At the same time, Bex Bailey, a former youth leader within the party, came forward to reveal she had been raped by a party figure senior to her in 2011: "It took me a while to summon up the courage to tell anyone in the party, but when I did I told a senior member of staff . . . it was suggested to me that I not report it. I was told that if I did it might damage me" (Mason, Asthana, and Weaver 2017). An independent review by lawyer Karen Monaghan confirmed that the issue was rife within the party and called for new complaint procedures and greater support for victims.

## CANADA

Debates in Canada also had a longer history. In 2014, two female MPs from the National Democratic Party accused two male MPs from the Liberal Party of sexual harassment. When seeking redress, the women discovered there were no formal or informal mechanisms in place in parliament for dealing with complaints involving two colleagues. They approached the Liberal Party leader, Justin Trudeau, who suspended the two men, Scott Andrews and Massimo Pacetti, from the party after an independent expert reviewed the complaints (Wingrove, Curry, and Hannay 2014). In 2015, an all-party House of Commons committee proposed a new code of conduct for MPs, together with a new complaint mechanism involving party whips, the House's chief human resources officers and, if necessary, an independent investigator (Watters 2015).

In the wake of #MeToo, the Canadian Press surveyed female MPs of all parties in December 2017 to learn to what extent they had been targets of sexual harassment or assault. Nearly 58% of respondents said they had personally experienced one or more forms of sexual misconduct during their time in elected office, including inappropriate or unwanted remarks, gestures, or text messages of a sexual nature. The perpetrators included lobbyists, as well as colleagues inside and outside their own parties (Smith 2018). A follow-up survey of political staff of MPs, cabinet ministers, and senators revealed that 29% had been sexually harassed at least once while working in parliament and 9% had been sexually assaulted, with the largest share of harassers being MPs other than those for whom they worked. Most incidents were not reported: in addition to being young and possessing less social capital than perpetrators, targets often worked in precarious employment conditions where partisan and personal loyalty were highly valued (Samara Centre 2018).

Over the course of several days in late January 2018, however, four political leaders stepped down in rapid succession in connection with allegations of sexual misconduct: Nova Scotia Progressive Conservative leader Jamie Baillie, Ontario Progressive Conservative leader Patrick Brown, Liberal Minister Kent Hehr, and Ontario Progressive Conservative president Rick Dykstra. That same week a bill to amend the Canada Labour Code, extending labor code protections regarding harassment and violence to parliamentary workplaces, was referred to the House of Commons Standing Committee on Human Resources, Skills, and Social Development. Introduced by Employment Minister Patty Hajdu in November 2017, the bill sought to balance employee protections while preserving parliamentary privileges and immunities guaranteed to MPs, ultimately passing in amended form in October 2018.[28] In February 2018, the House of Commons Procedure and House Affairs Committee unanimously decided to review the sexual harassment code of conduct for MPs.

## EUROPEAN PARLIAMENT

Few debates on these issues, in contrast, had occurred in the European Parliament (EP) prior to the #MeToo movement. After starting work at the EP in 2014, however, parliamentary assistant Jeanne Ponte began making notes about incidents of sexual harassment—ones she had personally experienced as well as others she had witnessed—in a notebook she kept in her purse. Shocked at how often and easily people around her dismissed such acts, she recorded the events to remind herself—if not others—that they were not "normal" or "acceptable."[29] Other women heard and soon approached her with their own stories, which she also recorded in the notebook.

In October 2017, her boss, Member of the European Parliament (MEP) Édouard Martin, asked if he could mention the notebook, which at that point contained more the 80 accounts, in a local radio interview. Shortly after, MEPs passed a resolution on sexual harassment tabled by seven of the EP's eight political groups, noting that it was form of violence against women and calling on all colleagues to support and encourage victims to speak out and report cases of sexual harassment (European Parliament 2017). Some held up #MeToo placards to demonstrate support, shared their experiences, and criticized existing reporting mechanisms (Fallert 2019).

Concerned that little action was taken in the ensuing months, in March 2018 staffers launched MeTooEP, collecting one thousand signatures to support full implementation of the October 2017 resolution.[30] They sought the creation of a task force of independent experts, an upgrading in the status of doctors and psychologists on case committees, and a requirement making sexual harassment training mandatory for MEPs. In October 2018, further delays led the group set up a blog[31] featuring anonymous testimonies, which organizers argued "would not have been necessary if victims felt comfortable to go through the tools of the institution" (Ritzen 2018). Despite these pressures, many MEPs attributed inappropriate comments and behaviors to "cultural differences"—and some Conservative Germans, a powerful group within the EP, argued mandatory training would infringe upon their individual rights (Berthet and Kantola 2019). In the run-up the 2019 EP elections, MeTooEP introduced a pledge for MEP candidates to sign, supporting work to combat sexual harassment during the 2019–2024 mandate.[32]

ADDITIONAL DEBATES

The #MeToo movement's effects were not limited to these legislatures, however. In Iceland, Reykjavík city councilor Heiða Björg Hilmisdóttir created a Facebook group called *Í skugga valdsins* (In the shadow of power), a closed group where over 600 women shared their experiences of sexual harassment in Icelandic politics. More than 100 of these stories were later made public in anonymized form ("Icelandic Women Politicians" 2017).[33] In early 2018, several female journalists came forward anonymously to accuse Russian MP Leonid Slutsky of sexual harassment. When he laughed off the accusations, four reporters from different outlets then came forward without anonymity, one even sharing a recording of the incident. A parliamentary ethics committee reviewed the accusations and found no "violations of behavioral norms," however. In response, nearly 40 media outlets announced a boycott of the parliament, which retaliated by withdrawing their accreditation (Raspopina 2018).

# 4

# An Expanded Vision

The concept of violence against women in politics, as it has emerged, has largely been restricted to actions perpetrated against women in elections and/or within formal political institutions. During this same period, however, parallel campaigns have surfaced to draw attention to violence committed against women human rights defenders and against female journalists, respectively. These efforts take up highly similar issues concerning violence as a barrier to women's participation in the political field. This book advocates for joining these various streams to forge a more comprehensive concept of violence against women in politics, underscoring continuities across challenges faced by politically active women of all types.

## Violence against Women Human Rights Defenders

Article 12 of the UN Declaration on Human Rights Defenders establishes that everyone has the right "to participate in peaceful activities against violations of human rights and fundamental freedoms." It also stipulates the right to be protected "against any violence, threats, retaliation, de facto or de jure adverse discrimination, pressure or any other arbitrary action as a consequence of . . . legitimate exercise of [these] rights" (UN General Assembly 1998, 6). In 2000, the Commission on Human Rights[1] requested that Secretary-General Kofi Annan appoint a Special Representative on the Situation of Human Rights Defenders to gather information, enter into dialogue with governments, and recommend strategies to better protect defenders. He named Pakistani lawyer Hina Jilani to the position later that year.

Jilani's first report to the UN General Assembly in 2002 included a chapter on women. It noted that women defenders "face risks that are specific to their gender and additional to those faced by men," because "they may defy cultural, religious, or social norms about femininity and the role of women

*Violence against Women in Politics.* Mona Lena Krook, Oxford University Press (2020). © Oxford University Press. DOI: 10.1093/oso/9780190088460.001.0001.

in a particular country or society." Jilani (2002) went on to observe that "the hostility, harassment and repression women defenders face may themselves take a gender-specific form, ranging from, for example, verbal abuse directed exclusively at women because of their gender to sexual harassment and rape." She also pointed out specific risks inherent in defending women's rights, "as the assertion of some such rights is seen as a threat to patriarchy and as disruptive of cultural, religious, and societal mores" (22).

Inclusion of women human rights defenders in the report was significant in that it built on and extended the work of women's rights activists in the 1980s and 1990s who had argued "women's rights are human rights" (Bunch 1990). Although activists successfully lobbied to integrate a gender perspective into the major international rights declarations adopted in the 1990s (Friedman 2003), defenders on the ground continued to meet with strong resistance to the recognition of women's human rights. Further, the women advocating and seeking to protect these rights were frequently attacked themselves on gendered grounds.[2]

Growing awareness of this problem led to collaboration between the International Gay and Lesbian Human Rights Commission (IGLHRC) and Center for Women's Global Leadership (CWGL) on a publication entitled *Written Out: How Sexuality Is Used to Attack Women's Organizing*. Launched in 2000 at a public event during the UN's five-year review of the Fourth World Conference on Women (Beijing +5), the book pointed to a growing counter-reaction to "women who dare to assert their leadership and perspectives as public advocates" and "the disparagement and silencing of their identities and political visions through sexuality-based attacks" (Rothschild 2005, 1).

At the Beijing +5 event, as well as at annual meetings of the UN's Commission on the Status of Women (CSW) in the early 2000s, women's rights opponents disrupted events and harassed participants on numerous occasions. These incidents inspired IGLHRC and CWGL to revise and update the publication in preparation for the Beijing +10 meetings in 2005. A new chapter addressed efforts to discredit female leaders, whether or not their work was related to gender and sexuality. A key tactic, the publication observed, involved the continual questioning of these women's sexuality morality—in some cases by suggesting, often erroneously, that they were lesbians.

To turn these insights into coordinated activism, a group of organizations— Amnesty International; the Asia Pacific Forum on Women, Law, and Development (APWLD); CWGL; and International Women's Rights Action Watch Asia Pacific—organized a meeting with Special Representative Jilani in Geneva, Switzerland, in 2004, with the idea of organizing an international conference on women human rights defenders in 2005. Joined by the Asian Forum for Human Rights and Development; Front Line; Information Monitor; IGLHRC; International Service for Human Rights; the International League for Human Rights; and the World Organization against Torture, the

Geneva group established the International Campaign on Women Human Rights Defenders. To ensure balance between women's rights and human rights groups, they subsequently invited ISIS-Women's International Cross-Cultural Exchange, the Latin American and Caribbean Committee for the Defense of Human Rights, and Women Living Under Muslim Laws (WLUML) to join the campaign.

Held in Colombo, Sri Lanka, the 2005 consultation brought together more than 200 activists from over 75 countries, along with current and former UN Special Rapporteurs on Human Rights Defenders; Adequate Housing; Extrajudicial, Summary, or Arbitrary Executions; and Violence against Women. Providing a platform to recognize violence against women human rights defenders, the consultation highlighted abuse emanating from both state and non-state actors, as well as the need to include sexual rights and LGBT defenders under the "women human rights defenders" umbrella. The meeting also offered skills workshops on security; prevention and protection; documentation; and mental and emotional well-being. Participants decided to create a series of resource tools, spearheaded by different partner organizations, building on these topics. They also committed to mobilizing around November 29 as International Women Human Rights Defenders Day (Real 2005).

In 2007, APWLD published *Claiming Rights, Claiming Justice: A Guidebook on Women Human Rights Defenders*, providing an analytical framework for understanding the issues facing women human rights defenders. To incorporate a wide range of perspectives, they organized two consultations, one in Nepal with participants from South Asia and the other in Indonesia with activists from Asia and the Middle East. Based on documentation from organizations as well as personal stories shared during the consultations, the guidebook defined the concept of women human rights defenders to encompass "women active in human rights defense who are targeted for *who they are* as well as those active in the defense of women's rights who are targeted for *what they do*," clarifying that this included LGBT activists (APWLD 2007, 15).

Theorizing violence against women human rights defenders, the book noted that attacks may take gender-specific forms (like sexual harassment and rape) and generate gender-specific repercussions (like pregnancy). In a critique of existing national and international frameworks, the volume pointed out that many abuses faced by women were not classified as rights violations or were ignored in favor of similar atrocities against male defenders. It also criticized the disregard of abuses committed by non-state actors, like family and community members. It attributed these oversights—as well as the perpetration of these acts of violence more generally—to patriarchal imperatives to preserve male and heteronormative privilege.

In a parallel set of initiatives, the Urgent Action Fund (UAF) for Women's Human Rights published a series of books focusing on security strategies for women human rights defenders. Set up in 1997, the UAF provides rapid response grants to women human rights activists around the world to stay safe or respond to a threat.[3] Drawing on stories of more than 100 activists from 45 countries, the first volume explored how activists managed daily physical and emotional stress (Barry and Đorđević 2007). A second book, based on collaboration with Front Line and the Kvinna till Kvinna Foundation, focused on cataloguing strategies women human rights defenders used to cope with and mitigate security threats. These included hyper-vigilance, fatalism, humor, denial, and paranoia, pointing to the enormous emotional, spiritual, and physical costs involved in suppressing fear and facing violence on a daily basis (Barry with Nainar 2008). Working from a protection manual first developed by Front Line in 2005, a final product translated this research into a set of practical and gender-sensitive tools (Barry 2011).

The International Committee—a steering group of the International Campaign on Women Human Rights Defenders—had been dissolved after the final reports of the 2005 consultation in Sri Lanka. In 2008, however, many of the same organizations came together again to formalize a new network, the Women Human Rights Defenders International Coalition (WHRDIC), which by 2019 included 28 member organizations from around the world.[4] Relying on funds, contacts, expertise, staff time, and facilities from member associations, the WHRDIC worked on lobbying human rights organizations, as well as the new Special Rapporteur on Human Rights Defenders, to increase their focus and reporting on women human rights defenders. A survey of members in the first year found that increasing conservatism around the world exposed women human rights defenders to greater risks. This included growing violence perpetrated by non-state actors, like religious fundamentalists, whose acts were—at the same time—often dismissed as "less serious" forms of human rights violations. Documenting acts committed against women was rendered more difficult by the fact that states and organizations usually did not make note of the sex or gender of victims of human rights abuses or include many gender-specific offenses (Real 2009).

In the ensuing years, publications produced by WHRDIC working groups focused on enhancing analytical understandings as well as creating practical tools for responding to and documenting the problem. Facilitated by the Association for Women's Rights in Development (AWID), the Working Group on Urgent Responses mapped existing resources, many of which were not designed specifically for women human rights defenders (Barcia 2011); developed recommendations for strengthening response mechanisms for women human rights defenders at risk (Barcia and Penchaszadeh 2012); and advanced a holistic approach to security recognizing multiple forms, locations, and perpetrators of violence (Barcia 2014).

Coordinated by WLUML, the Documentation Manual Working Group addressed issues related to documenting abuses from a gender perspective. It noted that existing projects often made assumptions about who defenders are (men), where violations take place (public spaces), who perpetrates these abuses (agents of state), what kinds of advocacy are associated with human rights advocacy (ending the death penalty), and what constitutes a human rights violation (torture in prison). Prevailing approaches thus tended to exclude— and thus ignore—the experiences of female defenders, offenses occurring in private spaces, acts committed by non-state actors, individuals engaged in women's rights advocacy, and violations that were gendered or sexual in nature. Adopting a feminist methodology, the WHRDIC framed documentation as a form of empowerment, "a politically-motivated telling of women human rights defenders' stories . . . a thread between our acts of resistance and the abuses we face" (WHRDIC 2015, 2).

In the midst of these developments, UN Secretary-General Ban Ki-moon named Margaret Sekaggya as the (newly renamed) Special Rapporteur on Human Rights Defenders in 2008. In line with a resolution requesting that future special rapporteurs "integrate a gender perspective throughout the work of his/her mandate, paying particular attention to the situation of WHRDs" (UN Human Rights Council 2008, 2), Sekaggya's first report in 2008—outlining her vision and priorities—called attention to the greater risks faced by women defenders, particularly those working in the area of women's rights. Her third report in 2010 was devoted exclusively to the situation of women human rights defenders. In it, she expanded official debates on these issues in several new directions, reflecting changes in activist understandings. First, she expanded the focus to include male defenders working on women's rights and gender issues, as well as abuses perpetrated against spouses, part- ners, and family members of defenders. Second, she specifically mentioned defenders of sexual and reproductive rights, topics often excluded from tra- ditional human rights agendas.[5] Third, she linked a variety of professions to the pursuit of human rights, listing violations against female health workers, lawyers, journalists, trade union leaders, and indigenous and environmental activists (Sekaggya 2010, 7–11).

The year 2013 marked a turning point in terms of broader institutional- ization of these ideas. In March, the Agreed Conclusions emerging from the annual CSW meetings included language on women human rights defenders for the first time. In December, the General Assembly adopted its first resolu- tion on women human rights defenders. Incorporating many of the ideas found in earlier publications by WHRDIC members, Resolution 68/181 expressed "particular concern about systemic and structural discrimination and violence faced by women human rights defenders of all ages" and called on states to "integrate a gender perspective into their efforts to create a safe and enabling environment for the defense of human rights" (UN General Assembly 2013b, 4). Its adoption, however, was not a smooth process, with last minute interven- tions from conservative governments and the Holy See to remove references to sexual and reproductive rights (WHRDIC 2015, 76).

In advance of the 20th anniversary of the Declaration on Human Rights Defenders, in December 2017 the General Assembly adopted Resolution 72/247, reiterating the key points made in Resolution 68/181. The 2019 report of Michel Forst (2019), the Special Rapporteur on Human Rights Defenders since 2014, captured further advances in theorizing violence against women human rights defenders. First, it explicitly recognized the role of intersectionality—or interactions with other facets of identity, like race, ethnicity, age, and sexual orientation—in shaping "stereotypes and deeply held ideas and norms about who women are and how women should be" (2). Second, it expanded the category of women human rights defenders to include lawyers, journalists, union leaders, politicians, judges, academics, humanitarian and development workers, and health workers, among others. Third, it highlighted recent changes in the global political context leading to "greater resistance" to the work of women human rights defenders and a "rise in misogynistic, sexist, and homophobic speech by prominent political leaders . . . normalizing violence against women and gender non-conforming persons" (6). This report thus offered a clear bridge to debates on violence against women in politics, above and beyond the striking parallels in conceptualization across these two phenomena.

## Violence against Female Journalists

Article 19 of the Universal Declaration of Human Rights establishes that "everyone has the right to freedom of opinion and expression . . . and to seek, receive, and impart information and ideas through any media and regardless of frontiers" (UN 1948, 5). In 1997, the United Nations Educational, Scientific and Cultural Organization (UNESCO) passed a resolution condemning violence against journalists. Resolution 29 observed with concern that "over the past ten years an increasing number of journalists have been assassinated for exercising their profession" and that "the majority of these crimes still go unpunished." Pointing to Article 19, the resolution argued that "assassination and any physical violence against journalists" constituted a "crime against society, since this curtails freedom of expression and, as a consequence, the other rights and freedoms set forth in international human rights instruments" (UNESCO 1997, 1–2).

In 2002, the International Federation of Journalists and International Press Institute proposed the creation of a journalism safety body. Launched in 2003, the International News Safety Institute (INSI) provides training, counseling, and support for journalists around the world, particular those reporting in conflict zones. In 2004, it conducted a survey, sponsored by the Swedish International Development Cooperation Agency, to determine whether female war journalists faced specific safety concerns. The survey found that 82% of survey respondents encountered physical attacks or intimidation, 55%

experienced sexual harassment, and 7% faced sexual abuse while covering conflict.[6] At an event organized in early 2005 with the Dart Center for Journalism and Trauma to discuss these findings, female war correspondents and security trainers pointed to widespread ignorance and dismissal of women's safety concerns.[7] As one participant later remarked, leading handbooks on journalist safety included no sections on sexual harassment and assault, an "oversight" which is "staggering" given "the level of detail over protection against other eventualities" (Matloff 2007, 23).

A dramatic shift in awareness occurred, however, following the widely reported mass sexual assault of American news correspondent Lara Logan in Tahrir Square in February 2011. In *The Silencing Crime: Sexual Violence and Journalists*, a report for the Committee to Protect Journalists (CPJ), Wolfe (2011) interviewed more than 50 female journalists about sexual violence experienced either in retaliation for their work or in the course of their reporting. These acts fell into three broad categories: targeted sexual violation of specific journalists in reprisal for their work; mob-related sexual violence against journalists covering specific events; and sexual abuse of journalists in detention or captivity. Risk came not only from strangers on the street, but also from co-workers and the men who guarded their lodging, drove their cars, or helped arrange their appointments. Few had previously disclosed their experiences due to cultural stigmas, widespread impunity for perpetrators, and professional concerns about being denied future assignments. As a result, sexual violence "remained a dark, largely unexplored corner" (9), in contrast to murders, imprisonments, threats of censorship, and other forms of assault regularly documented by CPJ and other press groups worldwide. To fill this gap, CPJ published an addendum to its existing security guide, focusing on ways to minimize the risk of sexual assault.[8]

The following year, UNESCO and the UN Special Rapporteur on the Promotion and Protection of the Right to Freedom of Opinion and Expression incorporated these findings in their Plan of Action on the Safety of Journalists and Report to the Human Rights Council, respectively, calling for a gender-sensitive approach when considering measures to address the issue of violence against journalists in both conflict and non-conflict environments (LaRue 2012; UNESCO 2012). Nearly identical language appeared in UN General Assembly Resolution 68/163 on "The Safety of Journalists and the Issue of Impunity" in 2013 (UN General Assembly 2013a). In his report on women, peace, and security to the Security Council, the UN Secretary-General went further to recommend that "sexual violence, death threats, or murders of women human rights defenders and journalists" be considered when adopting or renewing targeted sanctions in situations of armed conflict (UN Secretary-General 2013b, 30).

During the second half of 2013, INSI and the International Women's Media Foundation (IWMF) collaborated on the first comprehensive study of dangers faced by women working in news media around the world. The project built on *No Woman's Land*, a book inspired by the attack on Logan and published by INSI in 2012, providing testimonies about safety challenges from 40 female media workers around the world (Storm and Williams 2012). The global survey of nearly 1000 women found that two-thirds had experienced intimidation, threats, or abuse in relation to their work. Physical violence tended to be committed by strangers in crowds or public places, while sexual harassment and assaults occurred both in the field and in the workplace, where it was perpetrated by male bosses, supervisors, and co-workers. Roughly one in five respondents experienced phone taps and various types of digital security threats. When state officials were involved, threats of imprisonment and withdrawal of press passes were most common (Barton and Storm 2014).

Over the course of 2015, UN Security Council Resolution 2222 acknowledged the "specific risks faced by women journalists" and the importance of "considering the gender dimension of measures to address their safety in situations of armed conflict" (UN Security Council 2015, 3), while the UN General Assembly (2015) and UN Secretary-General (2015) reiterated their earlier statements regarding gender and journalist safety. In a new initiative, the Representative on Freedom of the Media of the Organization for Security and Cooperation in Europe (OSCE), Dunja Mijatović, issued a communiqué on the growing safety threat to female journalists online. While pointing out that the "female journalists targeted most report on crime, politics, and sensitive—and sometimes painful—issues," she noted that "online attacks tend not to address the content of the articles but instead degrade the journalist as a woman."[9]

After conducting a small qualitative study in English and Russian with female journalists across the OSCE region, Mijatović convened an expert group meeting in Vienna in September 2015 with 80 stakeholders representing governments, the media and communications industries, academia, international organizations, and civil society. The meeting called on OSCE member states to "declare, unequivocally, that any effort to silence women online must be regarded as a direct attack on our fundamental freedoms" (Mijatović 2016, 1). It also led to a report featuring testimonies and strategies to deal with online threats against female journalists. These essays pointed to varied motivations for these threats: intimidation to stop them from pursuing a particular story; efforts to discredit or humiliate them in retaliation for past reporting; antisocial acts with no strategic aims other than personal harm to the target; and workplace aggression—like gender discrimination or sexual harassment—by a co-worker or boss.

Growing awareness of these issues led to stepped-up efforts to collect women's firsthand accounts and to improve existing channels of data collection. For the first time, the CPJ's annual report, *Attacks on the Press*, focused exclusively on gender, violence, and press freedom (Committee to Protect Journalists 2016). In late 2016, the UNESCO governing council invited Director-General Irina Bokova to improve "data disaggregation [on journalist safety] in order to highlight the specific risks faced by women journalists in the exercise of their work."[10] In 2017, the International Federation of Journalists launched a survey of 400 female journalists in 50 countries, which found that nearly half (48%) had suffered gender-based violence at work. Of these, 63% had faced verbal abuse, 44% online abuse, 41% psychological abuse, 37% sexual harassment, 21% economic abuse, and 11% physical violence. Slightly more than half (55%) of the perpetrators were supervisors or colleagues; the other 45% were sources, politicians, readers, or listeners.[11]

Updating its earlier research, the IWMF collaborated with TrollBusters on a survey of nearly 600 female journalists and media workers in 2018, supplemented by 25 in-person interviews in 2017 and 2018. Nearly two-thirds (63%) of the survey respondents reported that they had been threatened or harassed online at least once. Nearly 60% had been threatened or harassed in person, while 26% had been physically attacked and 10% had received death threats. Most felt that the number of threats in general had grown over the last five years; almost all (90%) said that online threats had increased (Ferrier 2018, 22, 25). Looking at the content of these threats, the report noted that many were "sexist in nature, designed to intimidate or shame the journalists," aiming "to discredit women journalists and media workers, damage their reputations, and ultimately silence them" (12). Most of these threats appeared in online comment sections of news articles, followed by professional and personal Twitter accounts.

International organizations began to accelerate their efforts in this area in 2017. In his annual report on the safety of journalists, the UN Secretary-General (2017) observed rising levels of violence, threats, and harassment directed at female journalists. He noted that while women faced many of the same human rights violations experienced by their male counterparts, they were also subject to additional forms of violence motivated by gender discrimination, involving "severe social pressure not to enter the profession, or to leave it" (3). For this reason, women who covered politics or women's rights were particularly likely to become targets of abuse. He expressed concerns that these attacks were causing women to self-censor or leave the profession, resulting in an absence of women's voices and perspectives in the media. These dynamics not only further entrenched inequality and discrimination, but also impoverished democracy by affecting rights to free expression and access to information.

UNESCO, for its part, added a module on gender and safe reporting to its model syllabus for training journalists in physical and digital safety. The 2017 edition of its *Safety Guide for Journalists*, produced together with Reporters without Borders, also included a specific focus on the safety of women journalists. In November 2017, the UNESCO General Conference invited the Director-General to undertake further activities "addressing the specific threats to the safety of women journalists, both online and off-line" (UNESCO 2017, 43).

UNESCO also organized a panel on threats encountered by women journalists at the 2018 CSW meetings in New York.

Continuing the work of his predecessor, the new OSCE Representative on Freedom of the Media Harlem Désir launched the Safety of Female Journalists Online project in late 2017. Via workshops with journalists, academics, and civil society, the project aimed to raise awareness, provide tools and resources for journalists targeted with online abuse, and create a network of support for female journalists across the OSCE region (OSCE Representative on Freedom of the Media 2018). The OSCE Ministerial Council (2018) subsequently took up these themes at its December 2018 meeting, condemning "publicly and unequivocally attacks on women journalists in relation to their work, such as sexual harassment, abuse, intimidation, threats and violence, including through digital technologies" (3). Collaborating with the International Press Institute, the OSCE Representative also published a study in 2019 on best practices used by newsrooms across Europe for addressing online harassment and attacks on female journalists (Trionfi and Luque 2019). Like work on violence against women in politics and women human rights defenders, these initiatives recognize the gender-specific tools employed to exclude women from exercising their rights to participate in political life.

5

# International Recognition

The conversations outlined in previous chapters have resonated across diverse contexts and captured the attention of actors, from local to international levels, concerned about the role of violence as a previously unarticulated barrier to women's political participation. This is not a small achievement. As Kingdon (1984) notes, "Getting people to see new problems, or to see old problems in one way rather than another, is a major conceptual and political accomplishment" (121). Yet similarities across conceptualizations of violence against women in electoral politics, violence against women human rights defenders, and violence against female journalists also suggest that further leverage might be gained by uniting these separate streams into a single broader concept, highlighting how violence may be deployed as an effective tool for excluding and marginalizing women serving in different political roles. This merging has started to occur, to some extent, as the concept of violence against women in politics has become embedded in a growing number of global normative frameworks.

## CEDAW Committee Reports and General Recommendations

CEDAW has provided one entry point for consolidating and gaining recognition of the concept of violence against women in politics. Every year, a selection of member states submits country reports addressing the progress they have made—or not made—toward reaching the goals set out by the convention. The CEDAW Committee—a body of 23 independent women's rights experts who monitor implementation of CEDAW—reviews and provides comments on these reports. Between 2015 and mid-2019, the committee raised the issue of violence against women in politics in concluding observations to five country reports: Bolivia in 2015, Honduras in 2016, Costa Rica in 2017, Italy in 2017,[1] and Mexico in 2018.

*Violence against Women in Politics*. Mona Lena Krook, Oxford University Press (2020). © Oxford University Press.
DOI: 10.1093/oso/9780190088460.001.0001.

In each case, the CEDAW Committee viewed violence as posing a challenge to effective implementation of Article 7, which stipulates that states should "take all appropriate measures to eliminate discrimination against women in the political and public life of the country" (UN 1979, 3). Adopting a broad definition of political engagement, Article 7 mandates that states must "ensure to women, on equal terms with men" the rights to vote and be eligible for election, to hold public office and perform all public functions, and to participate in non-governmental organizations (NGOs) and associations concerned with the public and political life of the country. To fight discrimination, the committee recommended the passage or more effective application of legislation to combat political harassment and violence against women.

General Recommendations are a second tool which the CEDAW Committee can use to raise attention to issues it believes merit further attention from states. Indeed, the problem of violence against women first entered the remit of the committee through this mechanism, as this issue is not mentioned anywhere in the text of the convention itself. In 1989, General Recommendation No. 12 requested statistical data as well as information on laws and other measures adopted to eradicate this violence. Expanding on discussions taking place around the world in the late 1980s and early 1990s, General Recommendation No. 19 in 1992 provided a lengthier treatment of the topic, including defining gender-based violence and how it constituted a form of discrimination against women.

While General Recommendation No. 19 briefly mentions that "gender-based violence" may keep "women in subordinate roles and contribute to their low level of political participation" (CEDAW Committee 1992, 2), the issue was elaborated at greater length for the first time in General Recommendation No. 30, adopted in 2013. Discussing women in conflict prevention, conflict, and post-conflict situations, the recommendation stated that "substantive progress towards the equal participation of women as candidates and voters" would require ensuring that "women voters and female political candidates are not subject to violence by state or private actors." To this end, it recommended that states "adopt a zero-tolerance policy towards all forms of violence that undermine women's participation, including targeted violence by state and non-state groups against women campaigning for public office or women exercising their right to vote" (CEDAW Committee 2013, 19).

General Recommendation No. 35 on gender-based violence against women, adopted in 2017, served to update General Recommendation No. 19. Drawing connections between the various campaigns outlined in the previous chapters of this book, the new recommendation stated that "harmful practices and crimes against women human rights defenders, politicians, activists, or journalists are . . . forms of gender-based violence against women." In a later paragraph, the recommendation further stressed that "gender-based violence against women occurs in all spaces and spheres of human interaction, whether public or private, including . . . politics" (CEDAW Committee 2017, 6–7).

## UN Special Rapporteur Reports

A second mode of institutionalization has occurred via the mandate of the UN Special Rapporteur on Violence against Women. Created in 1994 by the UN Commission on Human Rights (now the UN Human Rights Council, HRC), the Special Rapporteur seeks and receives information on, and recommends measures to eliminate, all forms of violence against women. In 2008, the HRC adopted Resolution 7/24 which, among other provisions, added that the Special Rapporteur should "continue to adopt a comprehensive and universal approach to the elimination of violence against women, its causes and consequences, including causes of violence against women related to the civil, cultural, economic, political, and social spheres" (HRC 2008, 4).

Two reports submitted in 2018 by Dubravka Šimonović, the Special Rapporteur since 2015, take up the question of violence against women in politics. The first report focused on online violence against women and girls, observing that gendered attacks were pervasive on the internet and produced a range of psychological, physical, sexual, and economic harms to women.

Šimonović (2018a) specifically identified "women human rights defenders, women in politics, including parliamentarians, [and] journalists" as groups "directly targeted, threatened, harassed, and even killed for their work," including through generally misogynistic, often sexualized, and expressly gendered online threats. Stating that such abuse was a "direct attack on women's visibility and full participation in public life" (8), she argued that online violence against these actors had an individual and a societal impact, violating women's rights and undermining democracy.

The second report explicitly tackled the topic of violence against women in politics. In a June 2016 press release, the Special Rapporteur referenced the tragic death of Jo Cox and NDI's #NotTheCost campaign to announce her plans to focus on this topic in an upcoming study.[2] In March 2018, the Office of the High Commissioner on Human Rights and UN Women convened a meeting in New York to support her mandate with more than 40 experts, including politicians, academics, gender equality advocates, representatives from regional human and women's rights monitoring mechanisms, electoral management bodies, and various UN agencies.[3]

In her report to the UN General Assembly in October 2018, Šimonović captured the collective contributions of the many actors who have participated in these debates over the last several years. The section on violence against women in parliaments included references to data collection and interventions developed by the IPU and NDI; the section on violence against women in elections pointed to the work of UN Women, UNDP, SAP International, International IDEA, FIDA Kenya, and IFES; and the section on interventions mentioned CIM's model law. The report adopted a slightly expanded definition of "women in politics," however, to include "all women involved in political activities, those elected at the national or local levels, members and candidates of political parties, government and state officials at the local, national, and international levels, civil servants, ministers, [and] ambassadors," with the further examples of "human rights defenders" and "activists" in the following sentence (Šimonović 2018b, 5).

## UN General Assembly Resolutions

A third pathway to rooting the concept of violence against women in politics in global frameworks has been through efforts at the UN to respond to the conversations initiated by the #MeToo movement. In December 2018, the UN General Assembly approved Resolution 73/148, linking sexual harassment to the intensification of efforts to prevent and eliminate all forms of violence against women and girls. In addition to being the first General Assembly resolution to take up sexual harassment, this resolution is significant for at least two reasons.

First, its preamble expressed deep concerns about "all acts of violence, including sexual harassment, against women and girls involved in political and public life, including women in leadership positions, journalists and other media workers, and human rights defenders" (UN General Assembly 2018, 3). In a single sentence, it thus drew together diverse strands of these debates, highlighting broad continuities across the actions and actors forming part of this phenomenon. Second, the resolution encouraged national parliaments and political parties "to adopt codes of conduct and reporting mechanisms, or revise existing ones, stating zero tolerance by these legislative authorities and political parties for sexual harassment, intimidation, and any other form of violence against women in politics" (5), making it the first UN document to specifically invoke this concept following the Special Rapporteur's report.

## ILO Convention on the World of Work

A fourth, and perhaps unexpected, way that violence against women in politics has been integrated into international frameworks is through a recent standard-setting campaign at the International Labour Organization (ILO). The ILO brings together governments, employers, and workers from UN member states to set labor standards, develop policies, and devise programs promoting decent work for all women and men. In 2015, the ILO's governing body decided to place the issue of violence against women and men in the world of work on the agenda for its conference in 2018. An expert group meeting in 2016 suggested replacing the term "violence" with the broader phrase "violence and harassment" to "ensure the range of unacceptable behavior being targeted is adequately understood and addressed" (ILO Director-General 2017, 2). The 2018 International Labour Conference (ILC) approved the agenda item, setting in motion negotiations between representatives of governments, employers, and workers and culminating in the adoption of the finalized instrument in June 2019.

In 2018, the 16 Days Campaign—an international campaign coordinated by CWGL each year calling for the elimination of all forms of gender-based violence[4]—joined the global call for the new ILO convention. To complement advocacy by unions and labor organizations, 16 Days launched the #ILOendGBV hashtag to strengthen global awareness and demand for the new instrument. To bring needed feminist voices to these debates, CWGL developed a Sector Focus Initiative to highlight violence and discrimination faced by women in various labor sectors, using a curated set of reports, videos, and news items to give a human face to gender-based violence in the world of work and build an evidence-based case for the convention. The five sectors included agricultural workers, domestic workers, garment workers, journalists, and women in politics.[5]

The emphasis on the "world of work" rather than the "workplace" in the broader campaign sought to capture all aspects of the work environment, breaking down the false dichotomy between the public world of work and the private sphere of the home.[6] The campaign by CWGL and others lobbied for five core demands within this framework: recognition of violence and harassment against women in the world of work as a human rights violation; a broad definition of "worker" to encompass all female workers, including those overrepresented in unpaid, underpaid, and/or informal jobs; a comprehensive understanding of "the world of work" to provide protection beyond the workplace, such as during commutes or online; a wide scope ensuring protection to those most vulnerable and including intimate partner violence; and strong language recognizing and addressing the gendered nature of violence and discrimination faced by female workers.[7]

On the final day of its 2019 conference, the ILC voted overwhelmingly to adopt the new instrument, known officially as the Convention Concerning the Elimination of Violence and Harassment in the World of Work, which will enter into force 12 months after two member states have ratified it. From the perspective of debates on violence against women in politics, the convention makes two crucial additions. First, it highlights—from a new angle—the larger implications of allowing violence and harassment to continue undisturbed, stating that it "can constitute a human rights violation or abuse" and, as such, is "unacceptable and incompatible with decent work" (ILO 2019, 2).

Second, the convention contains a number of articles that help resolve ambiguities and specificities regarding "politics" as a place of work. Article 2 defines "workers" to include "employees," as well as "persons working irrespective of their contractual status, persons in training, including interns and apprentices," "volunteers," and "individuals exercising the authority, duties or responsibilities of an employer." Article 3 clarifies that the "world of work" encompasses both public and private spaces serving as places of work. It also includes other locations where work occurs, including "work-related trips, travel, training, events or social activities" and "work-related communications, including those enabled by information and communication technologies" (6). These provisions identify and fill gaps that have posed challenges to dealing with issues of sexual as well as online harassment in political spaces.

## Additional Statement and Frameworks

A handful of other global actors have also helped ground the concept of violence against women in politics in international documents and frameworks. In 2010, the HRC established the Working Group on Discrimination against Women in Law and in Practice to help promote and exchange good practices related to eliminating laws that discriminate against women. In its first thematic report, the working group took up the topic of discrimination against women in public and political life, focusing on current achievements and further challenges to women's full and equal participation. Published in 2013, the report includes an entire section on violence against women, building on the report of the Special Rapporteur on Human Rights Defenders in 2010 and UN General Assembly Resolution 66/130 from 2011. Seeing the link between these two strands, the report observes that "stigmatization, harassment and outright attacks have been used to silence and discredit women who are outspoken as leaders, community workers, human rights defenders, and politicians" (UN Human Rights Council 2013, 15).

More recently, members of the Convening Committee for the Declaration of Principles (DoP) for International Election Observation and the Code of Conduct for International Election Observers came together to develop DoP Guidelines on Integrating Gender Considerations in International Observation, including Violence Against Women in Elections. Developed in the early 2000s as a framework for credible international electoral observation, the DoP is currently endorsed by more than 50 intergovernmental and international organizations. Finalized in 2019, the gender guidelines outlined many ways in which women may participate in elections, including as citizen election observers, media representatives, and election workers, emphasizing that they should be able to serve in all these capacities "without fear or threat of violence" (Convening Committee 2019, 6).[8]

6

# A "New" Phenomenon?

The concept of violence against women in politics has only recently arrived on the world stage, but as feminist naming projects suggest, the birth of new vocabulary does not necessarily mean that the experiences it describes are novel. Applying this lens to women's experiences in the past, indeed, reveals stark parallels with present debates, indicating that violence has long served as a tool to exclude women from political life. At the same time, growing attention to this phenomenon coincides with other developments that appear to be caus-ally related: rising levels of incivility in world politics, bolstered by advances in communications technologies, as well as increased levels of female political engagement around the world. The lack of prior benchmarks complicates the task of testing these various explanations. Yet the search for a definitive answer may also be misplaced: these accounts more likely overlap and coexist, collec-tively capturing distinct elements driving this phenomenon.

## Scenario 1: An Old Problem Newly Expressed

One perspective is that violence against women in politics is simply a new expression of an old problem. Drawing on historical examples, this account highlights continuities in resistance to women's political engagement. In some instances, evidence of violence has long existed, but recent events cast a new light on their meaning. In others, current debates have inspired women to speak out about—and problematize—events they experienced in the past. Recent events have thus raised awareness of long-standing dynamics, rather than uncovered an entirely new problem.

### SUFFRAGE CAMPAIGNERS

Centenaries of women's suffrage in some countries have coincided with rising attention to the problem of violence against women in politics. In the UK, an

*Violence against Women in Politics*. Mona Lena Krook, Oxford University Press (2020). © Oxford University Press.
DOI: 10.1093/oso/9780190088460.001.0001.

exhibition at the Museum of London in 2018 highlighted incidents of violence faced by militant suffragettes.[1] In a media interview, the curator, Beverley Cook, shared a postcard addressed to members of the Women's Social and Political Union with the text: "You set of sickening fools. If you have no homes, no husbands, no children, no relations, why don't you just drown yourselves out of the way?" A handwritten letter to another individual advised: "your windows are likely to be broken shortly, as an act of retaliation, so would warn you to take precautions." Cook drew comparisons between this hate mail and threats that female politicians today receive on Facebook and Twitter(Shearing 2018).

The most notorious incident of violence faced by suffragettes occurred in November 1910, when women marched to the House of Commons upon learning that the prime minister was not going to take up a new suffrage bill. The first contingent faced some physical resistance but was able to enter parliament. Later waves of women, however, were pushed back by police, and over the course of six hours, were brutally assaulted leading to numerous physical injuries (Morrell 1981).

A subsequent inquiry by a journalist and a psychologist drew attention to the sexual nature of many of these acts. One woman testified: "One policeman . . . put his arm round me and seized my left breast, nipping it and wringing it very painfully, saying as he did so, 'You have been wanting this for a long time, haven't you?'" Another woman attested: "my skirt was lifted up as high as possible and the constable . . . threw me into the crowd and incited the men to treat me as they wished." The authors concluded that the impression conveyed by this evidence was that the police sought to "inflict upon [the women] a degree of humiliation and pain which would deter them or intimidate them" (Murray and Brailsford 1911, 9–13).

These attacks were not isolated incidents. Women selling suffrage newspapers often faced physical abuse (Shearing 2018). In 1913 and 1914, antisuffrage forces around the country mobbed speakers at suffragist meetings, wrecked local suffrage offices, threw stones and vegetables at suffragist carts in the streets, and broke windows of suffragists' homes (Harrison 1978).

Women in the United States similarly experienced violence in 1913 when taking part in a suffrage parade in Washington, DC, the day before Woodrow Wilson's presidential inauguration. More than 300 people were injured when thousands of spectators rioted (Finnegan 1999, 52), causing parade leaders to call in cavalry officers when police failed to keep order. In addition to attempting to ignite parade flags and banners, spectators "pinched, fondled, spat on, insulted, jostled, kicked, pulled, and trampled" the marchers, with injuries serious enough to require more than 40 women to be hospitalized overnight (Jensen 2008, 5). During a subsequent Congressional hearing, one parade official stated that she had asked a police officer to help an injured woman, but he simply responded: "there would be nothing like this happen if you would stay at home" (U.S. Senate 1913, 70).

FEMALE POLITICIANS

The first women elected to various political offices also faced extensive, and sometimes violent, resistance. Nancy Astor, the first female MP to take her seat[2] in the British House of Commons and a Conservative, faced "hostility—petty, persistent, and often vicious" from her male colleagues, "mostly from her own party." In a campaign to discourage other constituencies from adopting female candidates, these male MPs sought to prove that Astor—and by extension all other women—were unable to stand the work. Their harassment included refusing to give her a seat at the end of the bench so that she was forced to climb over the men's legs, telling her that no women's toilets were available nearby so that she was compelled to search for facilities on the far side of the building, and putting up graphic photographs during a debate on venereal disease in an effort to embarrass her. Recalling this "bullying animosity," she told her biographer: "If I'd known how much men would hate it I never would have dared do it" (Fox 1998, 322).

In 1954, Coya Knutson became the first woman from Minnesota elected to the U.S. Congress. As she was running for re-election in 1958, a letter signed by her estranged husband, Andy, was published in a regional newspaper. Urging her to "come home," he stated in the letter that he was "sick and tired of having [her] run around with other men all the time and not [her] husband" (Beito 1990, 237). Members of her own party had in fact paid Andy to sign the letter which they had written themselves, upset that she had twice prevailed over candidates preferred by party bosses. They also circulated false rumors in her very religious district that she was having an affair with a young male aide. At a time when women's place was believed to be the home, the story was quickly picked up in newspapers nationwide and had a devastating impact on Knutson's re-election campaign. She ultimately lost the race to a Republican challenger whose campaign slogan was, tellingly, "a big man for a man-sized job" (270).

SEXUAL PREDATORS

Revelations of sexual predation by elected officials, similarly, predate the #MeToo movement. In 1992, the *Washington Post* published accusations from 10 women regarding unwanted sexual advances by U.S. Senator Bob Packwood. The women, who had worked for or with Packwood during his tenure in Washington, DC, described instances where he grabbed them without warning, pushed them into rooms, or pulled their hair while forcefully kissing them or trying to take off their clothes. As more women started to come forward with similar accounts, Packwood initially issued an apology—but then quickly backtracked, claiming he was unaware he had done anything wrong (Moore 1996).

Newly elected Senator Patty Murray, who had run for office because of her outrage at how the Senate Judiciary Committee had treated Anita Hill during the Clarence Thomas hearings the year before,[3] responded to the Packwood case by calling for an end to the congressional exemption to federal laws prohibiting sexual harassment.[4] Although Senator Pat Schroeder had attempted in 1976 with Senator Charlie Rose to create a voluntary employee rights committee to investigate complaints, only 15 other members had signed on to their proposal. Packwood's case was therefore referred to the Senate Ethics Committee, which conducted a three-year investigation and found evidence that Packwood had been sexually harassing subordinates since the 1960s (Bingham 1997). In early 1995, both houses passed the Congressional Accountability Act, subjecting legislators to the civil rights, labor, and workplace safety and health laws governing other employers. Later that year, Packwood resigned amid mounting pressures.

In 1993, a similar scandal occurred in Canada, when the Royal Canadian Mounted Police announced they were investigating Gerald Regan, former premier of Nova Scotia and previously a federal cabinet minister, for sexual misconduct. He went on trial in 1998 for eight counts of rape, attempted rape, and sexual confinement committed against three women between 1956 and 1969. Although he was acquitted, the verdict lifted a publication ban on stories told to police by dozens of women—including office staff, job seekers, reporters, party workers, and a legislative page—relating similar attacks committed by Regan over a 40-year period from the 1950s to the 1990s (Kimber 1999).

More recently, as #MeToo debates got underway in the Canadian parliament in early 2018, a veteran journalist published an editorial about her experiences as a young female reporter on Parliament Hill in the 1980s. She recounted being sexually assaulted one night by a senator in front of two male journalists, who were shocked at what they had just witnessed—but advised her to be careful what she did about it. They reminded her of Judy Morrison, a radio host who had been scorned and ridiculed for exposing inappropriate sexual favors demanded by the prime minister's press secretary. When a female MP had stood up in parliament a few days later to demand an explanation, "the House [had] erupted into uproarious laughter, a rare moment of shared mirth among political foes. The mockery spread up into the press gallery above." After watching other women leave journalism as a result of sexual harassment, she reflected: "I often berate myself for not having had the courage to speak out 30 years ago . . . . But we all came to accept that this was a reality we could not alter" (Off 2018).

## Scenario 2: New Technologies and Contexts for Abuse

An alternative view is that violence against women in politics stems from technological advances and rising levels of incivility in world politics. While abuse may have existed before, widespread "nastiness" is a relatively new development, with shifts in the digital and political environments reinforcing one another. These trends are highly gendered: while men are most likely to be attacked on for their ideas and actions, women are disproportionately targeted for being female (Citron 2014). In this view, barriers to expressing misogyny have simply been lowered, resulting in more visible and personalized attacks against politically active women.

## REDUCED INHIBITION

One reason that increased access to social media has enabled and accelerated violence against women in politics stems from what Suler (2004) terms the "online disinhibition effect," whereby online "some people self-disclose or act out more frequently or intensely than they would in person" (321). Some types of disinhibition are benign, with individuals revealing secret wishes and emotions and engaging in unusual acts of kindness and generosity. Other forms are toxic, however, with individuals expressing anger and hatred through harsh language and even threats.

Anonymity is a key factor contributing to the online disinhibition effect, freeing people to defy social norms—including engaging in their worst behavior because their actions cannot be traced back to them. Online environments also remove the possibility of feedback from social cues, like facial expressions indicating disapproval or empathy that are available when people meet face to face. Finally, online networking technologies can bring together like-minded people, enabling extremists to communicate and providing opportunities to coordinate harassment of specific targets. Group dynamics can also embolden individuals to engage in ever more outrageous forms of abuse, expressing hate speech that is no longer seen as acceptable in society, at work, or at home (Citron 2014; Jane 2017; Vickery and Everbach 2018).

Attacking women online is not a unique phenomenon linked to qualities of the internet, however. Rather, Mantilla (2015) suggests, it is an adaptation of offline misogyny, rooted in a much longer history of driving women out of participating in public spaces. Online technologies simply make this process easier and more efficient, reaching broad global audiences in a matter of seconds (Levey 2018). As Jane (2017) observes: "Misogynists have never had so many opportunities to collectivize and abuse women with so few consequences. Female targets have never been so visible and instantly accessible in such large numbers" (51).

## PERSONALIZED ATTACKS

Online attacks are also often deeply personalized. In an editorial, Diane Abbott reflected on her 30-year political career and the growing amount of online abuse she received as a black female MP in the UK. Although sexism and racism had always been part of her experiences, she noted that something had changed: "Once, the pushback was against the actual arguments for equality and social justice. Now the pushback is the politics of personal destruction." She went on to note, however, that this individualized abuse also had broader ramifications, because "other women [may] look at how those of us in the public space are treated and think twice about speaking up publicly, let alone getting involved in political activity" (Abbott 2017).

These effects are exacerbated by the internet's abilities to spread abuse far and wide. Requiring very little effort, re-tweeting, liking, or sharing posts can help spread degrading and humiliating attacks with dramatic speed (Bardall 2013). They can also help extend the life of destructive posts, with images and screenshots displayed elsewhere on the internet, even when the original posts have been taken down (Citron 2014). Harm done to victims' personal images, in turn, may be difficult if not impossible to correct. Combined, these features of new online technologies amplify the possibility of online abuse, as well as its impact and potential for injury.

## POLITICAL POLARIZATION

Intersecting with these developments is growing political polarization in many countries, leading to greater resentment, nastiness, and incivility across ideological divides. Although some argue that politics has always been a "bit rough," Shea and Sproveri (2012) examine words and phrases appearing in books going back to 1800 and find that writing about "nasty politics" (and similar phenomena like mean, bitter, hateful, and filthy politics) has varied greatly across periods of time, occurring typically in 20- to 30-year cycles. However, they find that all of their measures climb after the 1980s, suggesting a prolonged period of partisan polarization.

Other work highlights structural changes in the political media industry rendering "outrage" content increasingly profitable. In this new landscape, political discourse is increasingly uncivil (Mutz 2015). On particular "outrage platforms" like political talk radio, cable news programs, and political blogs, reporting on politics entails ideological selectivity, vilification of opponents, and fear mongering (Berry and Sobieraj 2014). This "politics of resentment," Engels (2015) notes, "does not promote a discussion about what ails society . . . It is a strategy of distraction that focuses attention on the grievance as an excuse to taunt and offend . . . [turning] citizens against one another, making interpersonal violence seem justifiable and at times righteous" (19, 6). Platforms like Twitter have exacerbated these trends, with its character limits—requiring short and streamlined messages—promoting a "public discourse that is simple, impetuous, and frequently denigrating and dehumanizing" (Ott 2017, 60).

RISE OF "FAKE NEWS"

Claims about "fake news" have elevated the stakes behind these debates, especially for journalists. While initially the concept was used to point out misinformation (the inadvertent sharing of false information) and disinformation (the deliberate creation and distribution of information known to be untrue), "fake news" claims are also increasingly invoked as a tool to demonize traditional news organizations (Tandoc, Lim, and Ling 2018). These dynamics have, in turn, contributed to a qualitative change in how members of the public view and communicate with the news media.

As Swedish television anchor Jenny Alversjö noted to a BBC reporter: "For almost 20 years, I have worked as a journalist and I have always been a target for other people's opinions . . . [but] four or five years ago something changed and the tone became much more aggressive and threatening" (Bell 2015). Corroborating her impression, 90% of female journalists surveyed in 2018 stated that online threats had increased over the last five years (Ferrier 2018, 25).

This trope, however, does not simply target the media industry. Emulating Donald Trump, authoritarian rulers around the world increasingly use the term "fake news" to dismiss critique and deny human rights violations (Schwartz 2017). In calling reporters who provide credible coverage the "enemy of the people," these leaders contribute to rising violence against and persecution of journalists as well as enhanced levels of impunity for acts committed against human rights defenders and opposition politicians.

### Scenario 3: Backlash against Women's Political Opportunities

A third explanation is that violence constitutes a backlash against women's increased political presence (Restrepo Sanín 2020). From this perspective, violence is a new phenomenon, motivated explicitly by attempts to undercut and deter women's expanding opportunities to participate. Feminists typically understand the term "backlash" to refer to "a powerful counter-assault on women's rights . . . at once sophisticated and banal, deceptively 'progressive' and proudly backward . . . triggered by the perception—accurate or not—that women are making great strides" (Faludi 1991, xviii-xix). Mansbridge and Shames (2008) argue that backlash occurs when dominant groups perceive a challenge to existing power relations: reacting emotionally to this loss, they resort to various forms of coercive power to restore their previous status. Violence against women, according to Kimmel (2017), is thus "restorative, retaliatory . . . when that entitlement is aggrieved, [men] don't just get mad; they get even" (183).

Although men and women have the same formal political rights, many political arenas continue to be strongly male dominated. Increased opportunities for women to participate in politics, therefore, can pose a serious challenge to existing gender roles. When these changes occur at an accelerated pace, backlash dynamics may be particularly severe, with opponents seeking to interrupt and even reverse the trajectory toward greater gender equality (Rudman and Fairchild 2004; Yoder 1991). Violence against women in politics may thus be a rejection of women's presence in the political sphere and/or part of a broader reaction against feminism itself.

## BACKLASH AGAINST PRESENCE

Early academic theorizing of violence against women in politics connected it to the phenomenon of electoral gender quotas, policies to promote women's representation which began to diffuse rapidly around the world in the mid-1990s (Krook 2006). As part of this global wave, most countries in Latin America adopted legislative quotas, generally requiring that all parties nominate at least 30% female candidates. In the late 2000s, some states expanded these provisions to 50%, mandating gender parity at all levels of government (Piscopo 2015). During this same period, debates on political harassment and violence emerged, first in Bolivia and then spreading to other countries across the region (Albaine 2015; Krook and Restrepo Sanín 2016a; Restrepo Sanín 2018b).

In this context, Latin Americanists framed violence against women in politics as a tool used to undermine the implementation of quota provisions (Archenti and Albaine 2013; Albaine 2015; Cerva Cerna 2014). Violence weakened quotas, they noted, by reducing both the presence and effectiveness of women in political office. Violence committed by members of a woman's own party typically aimed to pressure women elected via quotas to stand down in favor of male alternates, decreasing the share of women in political bodies. Other tactics, involving a wide range of perpetrators inside and outside their parties, sought to prevent women from exercising functions to which they had been elected or appointed (Albaine 2016; Restrepo Sanín 2018b).

Research on politics in North America, where quotas do not widely apply, theorizes this problem in terms of challenges to the presence of women in politics more broadly. Sanbonmatsu (2008) speculates that three situations might provoke backlash: a high proportion of women in office, a rapid change in the share of women in office, and a historic bid by women to achieve a new level of office. These scenarios can generate challenges to women's leadership, with women facing verbal aggression and dismissal of their authority from male colleagues (Hawkesworth 2003; Kathlene 1994); more frequent competition in their efforts to be re-elected (Lawless and Pearson 2008); and greater levels of social media abuse as they become more visible as political leaders (Rheault, Rayment, and Musulan 2019). Backlash can also motivate the deployment of highly sexualized stereotypes of gender to minimize and degrade women aspiring to higher political roles (Anderson 2011; Hipkins 2011; Sawer 2013; Sheeler and Anderson 2013).

## BACKLASH AGAINST FEMINISM

Others situate violence against women in politics within the context of the growing backlash to feminism around the world. Speaking to the online violence she has experienced as a British MP, Jess Phillips—who self-identifies as a feminist—remarked: "The misogyny has got worse in the last five years. I think it was because the equality side was winning. We made some gains and they retaliated" (Sylvester and Thomson 2019). Due to these interconnections with anti-feminism, Biroli (2018) advocates expanding the concept of violence against women in politics to include reactions to increases in the numbers of women elected as well as efforts to counteract feminist activism in both society and the state.

Although anti-feminism is not new (Chafetz and Dworkin 1987), it has taken on renewed force with the global movement against "gender ideology." Championed by religious leaders, far right politicians, and conservative groups, these campaigns oppose women's and LGBT rights on the grounds that they treat gender as socially constructed, rather than as biologically determined—thus undermining, these groups claim, religious morals and values (Corredor 2019; Kuhar and Paternotte 2017). Framing themselves as victims of more inclusive social orders, "rebellious conservatives," more generally, seek to return to an idealized past in which inequalities were normalized (Dietrich 2014). Treating gains for women as a zero sum game, they utilize "public vitriol and violence" to devalue and dehumanize women—and thus restore undisputed male dominance (Banet-Weiser 2018, 5).

# 7

# Debates and Controversies

The collaborative and multi-streamed construction of the concept of violence against women in politics has provided crucial momentum in its development and diffusion. Yet this inclusive, largely non-hierarchical process has also meant that its contours remain vague, giving rise to potentially conflicting understandings of this phenomenon. These disagreements concern terminology, the focus on women versus gender, types of violence, targets and perpetrators, intersectionality, and the importance of context. The ongoing construction of violence against women in politics as a concept, however, provides an opportunity to address these tensions and contradictions and, in turn, develop more robust definitions, typologies, and indicators to inform future academic research and practitioner programming.

## Terminology

Naming does not simply entail articulating a previously overlooked problem. It also raises the question of what to call the new phenomenon. Naming decisions are difficult, given multiple possible interpretations of a problem (Bacchi 1999) and pressures to find a frame that resonates with the public at large (Benford and Snow 2000). For these reasons, debates over categories are not uncommon as advocates struggle to name and define problems (Kingdon 1984). In the case of violence against women in politics, actors on the ground have resolved these dilemmas in various ways, making decisions that adapt to local circumstances or favor particular theoretical perspectives.

One debate concerns the word "violence" as the best or only term to describe the behaviors in question. This ambivalence stems from two very different approaches to thinking about violence (Bufacchi 2005). A minimalistic perspective equates violence with the use of force, restricting its manifestations to physical attacks on people and property. In so doing, it adopts the view of

*Violence against Women in Politics*. Mona Lena Krook, Oxford University Press (2020). © Oxford University Press. DOI: 10.1093/oso/9780190088460.001.0001.

the perpetrator and focuses on ascertaining the motives behind a violent act that is understood as temporally determinate. A comprehensive approach, in contrast, conceives violence as an act of violation, arguing that it entails a wide range of infringements on personal integrity. As such, it prioritizes the survivor and centers the experience of violence, observing that violence may leave traces that never fully disappear, with "ripples of violence" affecting victims, their families, and their communities for years to come (Bufacchi and Gilson 2016).

To permit the unambiguous inclusion of non-physical forms of violence, many advocates have opted for double- or triple-barreled terms to describe this phenomenon. In Bolivia, ACOBOL made the strategic decision to add "harassment," which they did not see so much as a second dimension but as part of broader continuum of violent behaviors (Restrepo Sanín 2018b). To further ensure no misunderstandings, however, they also used Article 8 of the draft law to enumerate a long list of non-physical manifestations of "harassment and/ or violence."[1] In the case of the IPU, this task was even more complex, with national differences to take into account. After considering many alternatives, it ultimately settled on the phrase "sexism, harassment, and violence" as a way to capture a wide array of behaviors.[2] In other contexts, actors simply avoid the word "violence" entirely. Debates in the UK tend to use the terms "abuse and intimidation," which was the name that Theresa May gave to the problem when commissioning the CSPL report. In Peru, advocates use only the word "harassment," due to strong associations between the phrase "political violence" and the country's earlier history of armed conflict.[3]

A second point of contention revolves around the ordering of the words used to describe this phenomenon. Interviewees at numerous practitioner organizations reported struggling with colleagues over whether to call the problem "electoral (or political) violence against women," or alternatively, "violence against women in elections (or politics)."[4] Many observed that these labels were not arbitrary, but instead reflected very different notions about what the phenomenon was—and, in turn, how it should be conceptualized and measured.

The phrase "electoral violence against women," several interviewees noted, privileged existing electoral violence frameworks—most of which focused exclusively on physical acts of violence—and simply extended these existing frameworks to include women. In contrast, the expression "violence against women in elections" placed feminist concepts of violence against women at the center. These are far more expansive in their scope, recognizing the role of power and inequality as well as a broad array of perpetrators, locations, and forms of violence. To date, however, these ideas had not been applied widely to the realm of politics or elections.

A third, more minor debate involves focusing on violence against women "in elections" versus "in politics." Apart from IFES,[5] whose mission revolves around electoral processes, few organizations restrict their focus to violence against women in elections. Some, like UN Women, however, use both concepts, with "politics" referring to any gender-based violence that prevents women from exercising and realizing their political rights and "elections" focusing specifically on these violations in an electoral context (UNDP and UN Women 2017). In an analogous but distinct strategy, NDI treats "violence against women in politics" as the larger category, under which more specific forms can be identified, like "violence against women in political parties" or "online violence against women in politics."[6]

THIS BOOK'S APPROACH

This book uses the term violence against women in politics for three reasons. First, combining "violence" with words like "harassment," or substituting it for terms like "abuse," may reify the notion that violence is strictly physical, as well as imply a hierarchy between more and less serious or severe injuries. Conversely, using a single word helps highlight continuities and interactions across a broad spectrum of harmful acts. Second, beginning with "violence against women" prioritizes a feminist framing of this issue, expanding rather than simply deferring to traditional definitions of political violence. It also invokes a concept that activists used to unify diverse campaigns around the world in the late 1980s and early 1990s, arguing that distinct practices—like female genital mutilation, rape, sexual slavery, and dowry deaths—were in fact manifestations of the same broader phenomenon, affecting women of all backgrounds (Keck and Sikkink 1998). Third, beyond encapsulating both electoral and non-electoral moments, the word "politics" provides a means for expanding how the concept has been utilized to date—largely restricted to the formal political arena of elections and elected office—to incorporate politically active women of all types.

## Women versus Gender

Feminist scholars have long pointed out that "gender" is not a synonym for "women" (Carver 1996). Indeed, the core theoretical contribution of feminism is the distinction between sex, signifying biological differences between women and men, and gender, referring to social constructions of femininity and masculinity (Hawkesworth 2006). Nonetheless, the terms "violence against women" and "gender-based violence" are often used interchangeably in public discourse (Boyle 2019). This slippage has given rise to vigorous methodological debates among scholars as to how to best conceptualize and measure violence against women in politics.

Some argue that activism and research has been over-inclusive, "subsum[ing] general electoral or political violence" into the phenomenon of violence against women in politics, thus erasing any "distinction between gendered and non-gendered violence" (Piscopo 2016, 443). Others decry the exclusive focus on women, arguing that men's experiences should also be examined to "distinguish between instances of violence in which gender is part of the motive versus contexts in which violence is widespread and affects all political actors" (Bjarnegård 2018, 694). While raising some valid points, these critiques lack nuance, portraying the bulk of work in this field as naively assuming that *all* instances of violence faced by politically active women constitute cases of violence against women in politics.

In fact, early analyses—on which subsequent work builds—specifically highlight the role of gendered power relations, arguing that structural inequalities between women and men—motivating the defense of male privilege—give rise to this phenomenon (Albaine 2016; Cerva Cerna 2014; Machicao 2004). This approach is consistent with global advocacy on violence against women which, while recognizing that women sometimes suffer the same abuses as men, points out that "many violations of women's human rights are distinctly connected to being female—that is, women are discriminated against and abused on the basis of gender" (Bunch 1990, 486). The centrality of gender equality to these definitions, indeed, leads Biroli (2018) to argue for a further expansion of the concept to include efforts to discredit and undermine feminist activism in society and within the state. The central feature of this work is thus to illuminate a *specific set* of acts motivated by gender inequalities.

Revisiting international frameworks helps shed light on the origin of these disparities in interpretation. Article 1 of the UN Declaration on the Elimination of Violence against Women defines "violence against women" as "any act of gender-based violence that results in, or is likely to result in, physical, sexual, or psychological harm or suffering to women, including threats of such acts, coercion or arbitrary deprivation of liberty, whether occurring in public or in private life" (UN 1993a, 3). Despite using the word "women," therefore, this concept does not refer to *all* violence experienced by women, but only that which is "gender-based." Addressing this slippage, CEDAW General Recommendation No. 35 thus prefers "gender-based violence against women" as a "more precise term that makes explicit the gendered causes and impacts of the violence," bolstering "understanding of this violence as a social—rather than an individual—problem" (CEDAW Committee 2017, 4).

## THIS BOOK'S APPROACH

This book tackles these issues at greater length in the following chapters. In brief, it argues that these debates elide two distinct phenomena: violence in politics and violence against women in politics. In the first, hostility derives from what Phillips (1995) calls the "politics of ideas," or competition over political views.

Both men and women are potentially vulnerable to this kind of violence, with levels of risk varying depending on rates of violence in society more generally. These acts may take gendered forms, with women facing politically motivated rape, as well as non-gendered forms, with women subjected, like men, to physical injury or displacement (AIDS-Free World 2009; Bardall 2011). Because this type of violence affects what Pitkin (1967) terms "substantive representation," or advocacy of different policy alternatives, the democratic costs of violence in politics are widely recognized (Schwarzmantel 2010).

Violence against women in politics, in contrast, is about the "politics of presence," or the inclusion of members of diverse groups in policymaking (Phillips 1995). Because it is motivated by bias and discrimination, this form of violence is specifically directed at women, including in intersectional ways. Similar to violence in politics, its forms may also be gendered, like sexual objectification, or non-gendered, like death threats. Its defining feature, therefore, is *not gender differentiation but gender motivation* to exclude women *as women* from participating in political life. As such, violence against women in politics seeks to influence what Pitkin (1967) calls "descriptive representation," the degree to which the composition of decision-making bodies reflects diversity within the population at large. Rendered largely invisible until recently, the democratic costs of this type of violence are *not* yet widely recognized and appreciated.

Previous work has struggled to distinguish these phenomena for several reasons. First, politically active women may experience both forms of violence. These incidents may transpire separately, with attacks focusing on a woman's political views at one moment and their female identity at another. Forms of violence may also co-occur, discrediting women's political views by questioning their right as women to participate at all. Second, most of the data collected or available to study these dynamics captures both forms of violence simultaneously. Studies of online violence, for instance, may identify threatening and abusive tweets that are collectively—and individually—both politically motivated and misogynistic. Third, in some cases women are attacked both as women and in response to their women's rights advocacy, placing them at the intersection between violence in politics (which is issue-based) and violence against women in politics (which is identity-based). With clearer concepts, however, it becomes easier to parse out acts simply *directed at women* from those seeking to *exclude them as women*.

## Types of Violence

Expanding the term violence to incorporate more than just physical acts enables the recognition of a broader range of violations and infringements. However, it also raises questions about how to categorize and name those additional forms of violence. A review of legislation, publications, and toolkits on violence against women in politics reveals widely disparate lists. The most parsimonious, from this perspective, appears in the 2017 law on eliminating violence against women in Tunisia. Alongside other forms, it identifies "political violence" as its own specific type, referring to "all actions and practices based on sex discrimination whose author aims to deprive a woman or prevent her from exercising any political, partisan, or associational activity or right or fundamental freedom."[7]

More commonly, practitioners have adopted one of two approaches to developing these typologies. The first is to draw from existing international frameworks and elaborate them in relation to the political sphere. Article 1 of the UN Declaration on the Elimination of Violence against Women identifies three types of violence: physical, sexual, and psychological (UN 1993a). SAP International directly imports this language into its 2010 handbook defining terminologies and concepts related to violence against women in politics. The 2012 Bolivian legislation also makes use of this typology, defining "political violence" as "physical, psychological, or sexual actions, behaviors, and/or aggressions."[8]

Article 3 of the 2011 Istanbul Convention, formally known as the Council of Europe Convention on Preventing and Combating Violence against Women and Domestic Violence, adds economic violence as a fourth type (Council of Europe 2011). In 2017, CEDAW General Recommendation No. 35 did the same. This typology, in turn, appears in IPU's two publications on the topic; indeed, the glossary to IPU (2018) specifically cites the Istanbul Convention definition of violence against women. The 2019 ILO Convention also mentions these four types. Several other frameworks adapt from this prevailing list. An early IFES report eliminates sexual violence, focusing on physical, psychological, and economic violence (Bardall 2011). The Inter-American Model Law includes these four forms but adds moral and symbolic violence (CIM 2017), while NDI instead includes threats and coercion as a fifth type (NDI 2018).

A second, less widespread approach is to theorize inductively from behaviors observed on the ground. In its 2016 Violence against Women in Elections Assessment Tool, IFES identifies the following categories: physical harms, intimidation, verbal harassment, interference with voting, and other (like arbitrary detention and property damage) (Huber and Kammerud 2016). The CIM (2017) and NDI (2018) examples given earlier might be considered to be at least partly in this category as well, as they identify additional types of violence beyond the four most commonly recognized forms. In its work on online violence, NDI (2019) adapts prevailing categories to features of the online world, focusing on insults and hate speech, embarrassment and reputational risk, physical threats, and sexualized distortion.

THIS BOOK'S APPROACH

This book adopts a combined approach. On the one hand, it follows international conventions by considering acts of physical, psychological, sexual, and economic violence. On the other hand, it draws on inductive insights to propose a new, fifth category, semiotic violence, which captures dynamics that intersect with, but cannot be reduced to, the other four types. Semiotic violence, in short, refers to the use of language and images to denigrate women in an attempt to deny their political rights. A defining feature of these acts is their public signification: while perpetrated against individual women, they seek—though their circulation among citizens at large—to send a message that women as a group are unworthy. While semiotic violence is not a new phenomenon, recent technological innovations have dramatically expanded opportunities to create and distribute negative and harmful portrayals, further normalizing these tropes while also reaching new, potentially global audiences.

## Targets and Perpetrators

Women engaged in any number of activities in the political realm are potential targets of violence against women in politics. Because this concept originated among actors operating in the formal political arena, it has primarily been used in reference to women serving as voters, candidates, pre-candidates, elected and appointed officials, party members, campaign workers, electoral administrators and observers, and to a lesser extent, political staffers. Yet analogous campaigns highlight similar dynamics at work beyond the electoral moment, involving violence against human rights defenders, and by extension, other activists, as well as political journalists. While practitioners are limited in their ability to engage with actors beyond their organizational remit, uniting these different streams under the same umbrella underscores broad continuities in the challenges women face in ensuring their full and equal political participation, regardless of their specific political roles.

Adopting a violence against women perspective calls, in turn, for a broader view of perpetrators. While traditional political violence and human rights frameworks focus on public acts committed by political opponents and state officials, Article 2 of the 1993 UN declaration indicates that members of the family, the community, and the state may all commit and condone acts of violence against women, occurring in both the public and the private spheres (UN 1993a). This expansive approach has informed the literature on violence against women in politics from the beginning, pointing to a wide array of actors attempting to suppress women's participation through violent means.

Relatives may resort to violence on the grounds that women's political activities bring shame to the family's honor (APWLD 2007). Some husbands have locked their wives inside the home to prevent them from participating in political events,[9] or threatened to divorce women who do not vote as they instruct (Makoye 2015). Still others have mounted political campaigns to defeat them.[10] Parents and other relatives have also abused and forcibly confined women to the home to stop their political work. After being released from prison, where she was tortured and sexually assaulted, one young human rights activist in Sudan thus noted: "[The security forces] do not need to detain us anymore, the family members can do their jobs for them" (Human Rights Watch 2016, 30). A survey conducted in India, Nepal, and Pakistan show that these cases are not outliers, as between 25% and 40% of respondents identified family members as responsible for violence against female candidates (Centre for Social Research and UN Women 2014, 62).

Diverse actors within the community may also seek to restrain or punish politically active women. Religious and tribal leaders are among the most powerful, drawing on their traditional positions of authority to restrict women's participation in the public sphere and thus reinforce conservative views on gender roles. Religions and tribal edicts against women's right to vote in some parts of Pakistan, for example, included threats to burn homes and impose fines on those who defied the ban (SAP International 2009, 22). Ordinary citizens, however, may also play a role. Sexual and physical violence during demonstrations is one tool, affecting both activists and journalists, although the anonymity provided by crowds makes it difficult to determine whether perpetrators are hired thugs or state security agents dressed in plainclothes (Barton and Storm 2014; Tadros 2016). Online abuse is a second tool which citizens may use to intimidate women, often behind the cloak of anonymity,[11] through direct attacks as well as more indirectly by liking or re-tweeting abusive posts (Bardall 2013, 2018).

Political and work colleagues are perhaps more surprising perpetrators. Data from a wide range of countries, however, indicate that these are among the most frequent offenders. Across three countries in a 2014 study, the largest share of respondents—58% in India, 63% in Nepal, and 40% in Pakistan—mentioned members of a woman's own party as perpetrators of violence against them (Centre for Social Research and UN Women 2014, 62). More than half (55%) of women surveyed by NDI in Côte d'Ivoire, Honduras, Tanzania, and Tunisia reported encountering violence from party colleagues (NDI 2018, 6). Similarly, data from ACOBOL noted that pressures to resign—typically emanating from male rivals within the party who sought those positions for themselves—were the most common act of intimidation experienced by locally elected women (Rojas Valverde 2010, 529). More recently, a network of male journalists in France was exposed in 2019 after 10 years of coordinating the harassment of their female colleagues via anonymous Twitter accounts ("Ligue du LOL," 2019).

State actors, finally, are particularly prominent perpetrators of violence against human rights defenders and other activists (Sekaggya 2010). In 2019, the Armed Conflict Location & Event Data Project (ACLED), which has monitored incidents of political violence around the world since 1997, launched a new tool tracking political violence against women. Focusing on reported acts of physical and sexual violence, its first analysis found that demonstrations featuring women—where women made up the majority or entirety of protesters—were disproportionately more likely than demonstrations not featuring women to meet with excessive force (live fire) and intervention (arrests and tear gas), usually at the hands of the state (Kishi, Pavlik, and Matfess 2019).

THIS BOOK'S APPROACH

This book includes examples from all these arenas, revealing that violence against women in politics can occur in many spaces—including many where their male counterparts, as a rule, are safe (Krook 2017). The book also emphasizes, importantly, that perpetrators may include both men and women. Although men as a group benefit most directly from patriarchy, men and women alike may punish individuals who deviate from gender norms as a means to defend their own status in the existing system of gender hierarchy (Berdahl 2007; Dovi 2018). This fact is perhaps most evident in the case of family members—like mothers and mothers-in-law—who seek to prevent women from participating in political activities. Yet, women in society can also play a central role in sabotaging and denigrating women who seek leadership roles or campaign to expand women's political rights (Chafetz and Dworkin 1987). Violence against women in politics thus does not imply a simplistic scenario of male perpetrators and female targets, but rather, points to the more systematic and structural targeting of women who challenge prevailing gender norms.

## Intersectionality

Proposing that violence against women in politics is directed at women *as women* centers the role of gender, potentially suggesting that it is the main or only source of abuse. Yet one of the most important contributions in recent feminist research is the concept of intersectionality, theorizing the ways in which different facets of identity—like age, class, disability, education, ethnicity, gender identity, race, and sexual orientation—interact to shape life opportunities and experiences (McCall 2005). While intersectionality has not yet been incorporated widely into theorizing about violence against women in politics (Kuperberg 2018), it is strongly present in news coverage and emerging data on this phenomenon. Practitioner conversations on this topic, moreover, have long sought to include diverse groups of women (WHRDIC 2015, consistent with awareness of the intersectional dynamics of violence against women stretching back at least as far as the 1993 UN Declaration on the Elimination of Violence against Women (UN 1993a).

Two forms of intersectionality shape experiences of violence against women in politics. The first concerns aspects of identity, in line with traditional understandings of intersectionality. Analyzing Twitter abuse against female MPs in the UK, Amnesty International found that women of all backgrounds were targeted. Yet nearly half the abusive tweets in the sample were directed at Diane Abbott, the first black woman MP; when she was taken out of the sample, black and Asian women still received 30% more abuse than their white counterparts (Dhrodia 2017). In India, Nepal, and Pakistan, the majority of respondents to a survey identified female candidates who were poor (60–73%), lower caste (52–68%), or under the age of 30 (55–63%) as the most vulnerable to violence (Centre for Social Research and UN Women 2014, 65). Data from the IPU (2018) indicated that female MPs under 40 were more likely than older MPs to experience psychological and sexual violence. Qualitative evidence, finally, points to anti-Semitism, Islamophobia, and homophobia as additional elements driving attacks against politically active women.[12]

A second form of intersectionality involves women's political views and activities. In an interview about online violence, British MP Jess Phillips remarked that the number of threats directed at her "has its peaks and troughs depending on what I'm talking about . . . If you speak from a feminist perspective, which I very frequently do, you will suffer from a huge amount of internet trolling" (Rawlinson 2018). This observation is confirmed by outspoken feminists in other contexts, who note that gender-based attacks often escalate after they have proposed bills or appeared on television in connection with women's issues[13] or written stories supportive of women's and LGBT rights (Trionfi and Luque 2019). In Afghanistan, women vocal on these issues are regularly abused as infidels or Christians (Human Rights Watch 2009).

## THIS BOOK'S APPROACH

In addition to providing cases illustrating intersectional experiences of violence, this book proposes a theoretical framework that can accommodate an intersectional lens. This approach centers the role of bias and discrimination in these acts which, it argues, are rooted in dynamics of structural, cultural, and symbolic violence against women and other marginalized groups. Because women from non-dominant groups challenge multiple forms of inequality, their presence may thus spark an even stronger reaction than the election of women from dominant groups (Sanbonmatsu 2008). As former MP for the Scottish National Party, Tasmina Ahmed-Sheikh,, observed: "I am from a

Scottish-Asian community. I am a Muslim. And I'm a woman. So it's every-thing. It has an exponential effect, so people will pile on for different reasons. Some of them because you are all of these things, and some because you are one of these things, or two of these things, which makes it so much more difficult to deal with, because you just wonder where do I start with this" (Dhrodia 2017).

## Role of Context

A final consideration raised in emerging debates concerns contextual factors and their role in shaping incidents of violence. Critiquing conceptualizations in Latin America, Piscopo (2016) argues that these efforts fail to take into account elements of the broader political and judicial context, including widespread state and criminal violence, weak police and criminal justice systems, and party efforts to deny women access to political power. She therefore calls on scholars to "resist accepting activists' problem definition at face value" and "instead encourage solutions that address the violence and impunity embedded in the state and in society" (438). From this perspective, violence is the cost of engag-ing in politics, especially in societies characterized by high levels of crime and conflict and weak state capacity.

From the very beginning, however, practitioners have been keenly aware of how features of the social, cultural, economic, and political environment might exacerbate vulnerability to acts of violence against women in politics. For Asoka (2012), relevant contextual factors include religious fundamentalism, militarization accompanied by widespread impunity for law enforcement and military officers, and authoritarianism and democratic backsliding, to which IM-Defensoras (2013) add criminal infiltration of public institutions. These features, individually or collectively, weaken state capacity, leading to increased levels of impunity—thus reducing the costs of violence for perpetrators and depressing the likelihood of redress for targets of this violence. In the words of a female MP in Afghanistan: "I've had so many threats. I report them some-times, but the authorities tell me not to make enemies, to keep quiet" (Human Rights Watch 2009, 22).

The rise of social media has created new tools of abuse and impunity. The internet has dramatically expanded opportunities to harass women directly, while technological innovations have facilitated the creation and circula-tion of harmful, degrading, and often doctored images to shame and attack women (Powell and Henry 2017). The decentralized and anonymous nature of the internet, further, lends important protective cover to perpetrators (Citron 2014). While the internet did not invent sexism, as Jane (2017) notes, it is thus amplifying it in unprecedented ways. Given the global reach of online technol-ogies, these developments affect women around the world—and appear likely to grow in their influence over time.

THIS BOOK'S APPROACH

Despite emphasizing that violence against women in politics is a global phenomenon, this book recognizes the importance of context in shaping women's
experiences with violence in the political realm. While it does not explicitly
theorize these contextual elements, the framework developed in this volume
draws on the concept of "cultural violence" to pinpoint how violence against
women is normalized in different environments. In short, cultural violence
invokes tropes justifying acts of violence—which are otherwise condemned—
when perpetrated against members of particular groups. These resources vary
across countries in light of differences in the social, economic, and political
norms surrounding gender. Nonetheless, they share the common thread of
being grounded in structural inequalities between women and men, rationalizing and validating violence against women in the political realm.

# PART II

# A Theoretical Framework

# 8

# Politics as a Hostile Space

Developing a more robust concept of violence against women in politics requires, first, defining what it is *not*. A common criticism of global efforts to recognize this problem is that it is not a distinct phenomenon: rather, violence is merely the cost of doing politics (Piscopo 2016). This perspective helps explain why this issue has remained hidden for so long. As noted in chapter 1, women often do not speak out about experiences of violence in the political realm because they normalize violence as part of the political game. Alternatively, they acknowledge these behaviors as problematic, but believe that others do not see it this way. They thus remain quiet in order to protect their political careers or avoid further derision—or simply because they have no one to tell—because others view such conduct as acceptable in the world of politics.

This cynical understanding of politics as a hostile and dangerous space has deep roots, infusing both the theory and practice of politics. Some work, however, questions the status of all forms of political conflict as equally valid. The literature on political and electoral violence, for example, contends that using force to achieve political ends poses a threat to democracy and, as such, is illegitimate. More recent efforts focus on violence against three types of political actors: politicians, activists, and journalists. Despite running largely in parallel to one another, these debates converge in arguing that violence not only harms democracy—but also violates personal integrity, undermining human rights.

## Politics as War

Metaphors to describe politics often invoke images of war. For some theorists, engaging in war and politics involves identical skill sets. As Machiavelli (1981 [1532]) writes in his influential political treatise, *The Prince*: "A prince . . . must have no other object or thought, nor acquire skill in anything, except war, its organization, and its discipline. The art of war is all that is required of a ruler"

*Violence against Women in Politics.* Mona Lena Krook, Oxford University Press (2020). © Oxford University Press.
DOI: 10.1093/oso/9780190088460.001.0001.

(87). For others, war and politics exist along a continuum and share the same logic, as reflected in Clausewitz's (2018 [1832]) famous dictum, "War is politics by other means" (40), and Foucault's (2003 [1976]) reversal, "Politics is war by other means" (15). Not surprisingly, therefore, for some politicians the experiences are roughly analogous: as Winston Churchill observed, "Politics is almost as exciting as war, and quite as dangerous."[1]

This line of thinking, in turn, informs how political interactions, as well as the nature of politicians as a class, are understood and conceptualized. In the United States, for example, Howe (1988) notes that political metaphors draw heavily and systematically on the terminology of war and sports. While observing that speakers resort to military metaphors "when politics must be portrayed as ruthless or treacherous" (95), he points out that both sets of metaphors are destructive in that they imply that negotiation and compromise are forbidden, requiring that opponents fight it out until the bitter end. According to Puwar (2004), such views institutionalize metaphorical violence as a "normal" part of the political game, with displays of aggression and overt conflict in debates amounting to the "theatrical delivery of violence" to the opposing side (82).

While these interactive conventions are widespread in the political realm, such behaviors would be largely unacceptable in other professional contexts (Harris 2001). As Jess Phillips (2017), a British MP, ironically remarked: "Apparently if you are an MP, you are meant to take abuse and ill-informed vitriol lying down" (187). Seeking to de-normalize these behaviors, Elizabeth May, leader of the Green Party, noted critically: "This is the only workplace in Canada where abuse is routine. It's perfectly accepted to have people yelling at you, making nasty comments to you, while you're on the floor of the House of Commons doing your work" (McIntyre and Campbell 2018). Disadvantaging women as compelling players in the political arena, moreover, war and sports metaphors typically associate power with brute displays of masculinity (Gidengil and Everitt 1999).

From this perspective, however, politics is not simply tough, aggressive, and competitive. It is also not governed by rules of morality, fostering duplicity. As Machiavelli (1981 [1532]) counsels: "A man who wants to act virtuously in every way necessarily comes to grief among so many who are not virtuous. Therefore if a prince wants to maintain his rule he must learn how not to be virtuous, and to make us of this or not according to need" (91). Believing that politics is fraught with "dirty tricks" and "cheap shots" (Cummins 2015) in turn encourages negative campaigning, highlighting weaknesses of an opponent's policy proposals, prior policy failures, or personal failings, rather than one's own policy ideas, past accomplishments, or personal strengths (Lau and Rovner 2009). Although voters perceive some negative information to be useful, like legitimate critiques of policy performance, studies find they are often turned off by shrill, irrelevant, and ad hominem personal attacks (Kahn and Kenney 1999).

Nonetheless, recent shifts in the political media industry have enhanced this negativity by creating information "silos" that insulate viewers from exposure to contrary perspectives (Allcott and Gentzkow 2017). In particular, new "outrage platforms," like political talk radio, cable news programs, and political blogs, vilify political opponents through ideologically selective reporting (Berry and Sobieraj 2014), leading to greater hostility and incivility across political divides (Mutz 2015). Similar dynamics are evident on social media platforms like Facebook and Twitter, which many people use as primary sources of political news. This unfiltered and non-fact-checked environment gives greater traction to "fake news" stories, amplifying the negative views that each side of the political spectrum holds toward the other (Allcott and Gentzkow 2017).

Portraying politics as a cynical, morally empty, and uncivil enterprise fosters views among citizens, in turn, that politics is "synonymous with duplicity, greed, corruption, interference, and inefficiency" (Hay 2007, 160). A poll conducted in the United States showed, for example, that 85% of voters viewed Congress negatively; only 9% saw it in a favorable light.[2] The growing "demonization of politicians" (Flinders 2012, 2) has serious democratic implications, as it does not "promote a discussion about what ails society" or "provide solutions" (Engel 2015, 19). Rather, it erodes citizen trust and mutual respect across political divides and overlooks the majority of political officials who are sincere and committed public servants. By these various means, "dirty tricks" and personal attacks are equated with "politics as usual," rather than seen as serious and unacceptable threats to personal dignity and democratic integrity.

## Political and Electoral Violence

One longstanding exception to the normalization of hostility and aggression in politics is work on political and electoral violence. Recognizing that conflict is a central feature of the political process, this literature argues that clashes become illegitimate when the aim is to "damage a political adversary" to impose political aims (Della Porta 1995, 2). Violence is "political" when its "purpose, choice of targets or victims, surrounding circumstances, implementation, and/or effects have political significance," in that they "modify the behavior of others" with "consequences for the social system" (Nieburg 1969, 13). It is thus "motivated by a desire, conscious or unconscious, to obtain or maintain political power" (Moser and Clark 2001, 29). Such violence threatens democracy if it helps one side get "its way through fear of injury or death, not through a process in which individuals or groups recognize each other in a dialogue or as rational interlocutors" (Schwarzmantel 2010, 222).

Electoral violence is a sub-type of political violence, distinguished by its objective to influence the electoral process before, during, or after election day (Höglund 2009). Staniland (2014) argues that this violence may be intra-systemic, operating within the existing system to take over power, or anti-systemic, seeking to fundamentally alter the political order. It may thus encompass a wide range of behaviors, from incidents carried out by thugs, criminals, and mobs to coups, insurgencies, state crackdown, and local ethnic clashes. Electoral violence may be directed at a wide range of actors, like rival candidates, journalists, voters, and poll workers, as well as at facilities associated with elections, like polling stations. In most cases, perpetrators seek to reduce uncertainty about electoral outcomes by influencing voter turnout, eliminating political rivals, and—in the wake of elections—engaging in revenge attacks against those who voted for the "wrong" candidate (Söderberg Kovacs 2018).

Emerging research nuances these strategic accounts by arguing that—at least in some contexts—electoral violence should also be understood as a political and social practice (Birch, Daxecker, and Höglund 2020). In these cases, violence is widely perpetrated at election time by militia groups and criminal gangs without specific directives given by political leaders—but rather, stemming from a range of other motives like short-term benefits, personal loyalty, or private score settling (Söderberg Kovacs 2018). Leaders may tolerate or simply lack the resources to control this violence, such that it comes to be seen as a "normal" part of the electoral landscape. In some settings, indeed, democratic participation and violent practices may merge, with violent acts being seen as a way of voicing dissatisfaction with the existing order—and thus as a form of political participation itself (Rasmussen 2018).

Most datasets on political and electoral violence restrict their focus to acts of physical violence, defined as attacks on people as well as property (Della Porta 1995; Norris, Frank, and Martínez i Coma 2015). In some countries, casualty numbers during elections may meet the threshold of civil war in a matter of weeks (Birch, Daxecker, and Höglund 2020). Yet physical violence is also a risky strategy, attracting potential retaliation from targets as well as condemnation from citizens and international election observers. Consequently, "harassment, intimidation, and disruption" are often far more common tactics (Straus and Taylor 2012, 24), selectively focusing on groups seen as most likely to respond, least likely to protest, and most likely to deliver the intended outcome, like decreased voter turnout (Söderberg Kovacs 2018).

The vast majority of this literature focuses on "democracy in dangerous places" (Collier 2009), highlighting electoral violence as a problem confined to the global South. Most research to date focuses on Africa, where more than half of states organizing elections in the post–Cold War period have experienced electoral violence (Burchard 2015, 50). Yet most elections around the world feature some violence, whether physical or non-physical, according to a dataset of 136 countries holding competitive elections between 1990 and 2012 (Daxecker, Amicarelli, and Jung 2019, 715). Consolidated democracies were excluded from this study, however, on the grounds that electoral contention and violence is less "feasible" in these cases (716).

Yet Doan (2007) shows that political intimidation is not a strategy limited to the global South. Focusing on anti-abortion activism in the United States, she defines "political harassment" as "persistent verbal or physical collective challenges intended to change the behavior of others, to have political signifi- cance, to create a reasonable fear, and to be directed at nongovernmental actors because of their beliefs" (24). Doan argues that activists find intimidation to be a cheap and effective way of deterring provision of abortion, compared to pur- suing legislative reforms aimed at restricting such services. Political harassment, like acts of physical violence, can thus also serve anti-democratic purposes, undermining the legislative process and preventing citizens from exercising their full legal rights.

## Violence against Politicians

A more recent wave of activism and research also rejects the notion that hostil- ity and violence are merely "the cost of doing politics." Over the last decade, violence against politicians has received growing attention from practitio- ners and scholars in a variety of disciplines. An early forerunner was the IPU Committee on the Human Rights of Parliamentarians. Established in 1976, this committee receives and pursues complaints regarding human rights viola- tions suffered by MPs, from kidnapping and murder to detention and exclusion from political office.

In recent years, the committee has stepped up its global visibility, publish- ing yearly infographics showing the most common violations, the geographic distribution of cases, the political affiliation, and—in a new development— the gender of victims.[3] Meeting three times a year, it consists of 10 MPs from all regions who hold hearings, undertake missions, and observe trials to pres- sure governments to take action, as well as to achieve redress for affected MPs. Although its deliberations are confidential, its decisions—containing calls for action, expressions of concerns, and requests for information—are made pub- lic on the IPU website.[4]

At the country level, high-profile incidents have inspired a number of gov- ernments to begin collecting data on this problem. Efforts in Sweden have been among the most extensive. The 2003 murder of Foreign Minister Anna Lindh, who was stabbed to death while shopping in a department store, sparked a debate on security risks associated with the Swedish style of politics, where politicians remain highly accessible to the general public. At the time of Lindh's murder, cabinet ministers often traveled without bodyguards, despite the 1986 murder of Prime Minister Olof Palme, who was killed on the street while walking home from the cinema with his family (Beckman, Olsson, and Wockelberg 2003).

In early 2005, the newly created Parliamentary Committee on Threats and Violence against Elected Officials conducted a survey of national, regional, and local officeholders. It found that three-quarters of national parliamentarians and one-third of subnational politicians had experienced harassment, threats, and violence in the course of their mandate. Perpetrators expressed hate, attempted to influence policy decisions, or sought to force them to leave politics, leading 53% of MPs and 39% of local and regional politicians to worry about their security (Blom 2005, 8–10). Since 2012, the National Council for Crime Prevention has administered a series of follow-up surveys to all Swedish politicians and found that risk factors for violence and other illicit behaviors include being younger, a committee chair, a member of local or regional government, or active on social media.[5]

In 2011, U.S. Representative Gabrielle Giffords was shot together with 18 constituents—six of whom died—at a political meeting in her district. Following this attempted assassination, the Congressional Research Service published a report on acts of violence committed against members of Congress and their staff, seven instances of which had resulted in a member's death (Petersen, Manning, and Hemlin 2011, 2). The report also listed laws and procedures in place to deal with such threats, pointing out that it was a federal crime to assassinate, kidnap, or assault a member of Congress or member-elect, or to endeavor or conspire to commit such offenses. In 2017, the Congressional Research Service produced an updated report following a shooting that occurred at a congressional baseball game practice, during which one member, Steve Scalise, was critically wounded (Petersen and Manning 2017). After a series of reforms, members of Congress were entitled to increased allowances to improve security at their offices, as well as to apply funds from their political campaigns to update security systems in their homes.

The 2016 murder of British MP Jo Cox spurred parallel developments in the UK. Prior to her death, issues of political violence and harassment had been considered by an All-Party Parliamentary Inquiry into Electoral Conduct, which published reports in 2013, 2015, and 2017.[6] In response to Cox's murder, Parliament and the police established a specialist team to serve as a point of contact and advice for MPs on security matters.[7] In 2017, Prime Minister Theresa May called on the CSPL to conduct a review on abuse and intimidation of parliamentary candidates. Considering submissions from various stakeholders, the CSPL issued a report several months later in which it distinguished between "intimidation" and "legitimate persuasion or influence which takes place as part of the democratic process." In contrast to the latter, the former was "intended and likely to cause an individual to withdraw from a public space" and "have the effect of limiting freedom of expression" (CSPL 2017, 26).

Academic research on violence against politicians has primarily been done by forensic psychiatrists analyzing the stalking, threatening, and attacking of public figures. These behaviors include physical attacks; threats; unwanted approach; loitering; property interference; spurious legal action; distribution of malicious materials; and inappropriate letters, emails, phone calls, and social media contacts (James et al. 2016a). Distinct to the political violence literature, what is "political" about this violence is not its motivation but its target: a person's role as a political official is what draws the attacker's attention. While perpetrators express a variety of grievances, most are believed to suffer from mental illness—interrupting the political process, but for reasons distinct from traditional political confrontations (Meloy, Sheridan, and Hoffman 2008).

Early studies in this vein examined the archives of the U.S. Capitol Police, which receives evidence and investigates cases of threats and harassment directed at members of the U.S. Congress. This research noted that threats were largely uncorrelated with approach (Dietz et al. 1991; Scalora et al. 2002). Subsequent work thus theorized a distinction between "hunters," who seek to physically harm their targets, and "howlers," who seek to frighten their targets but rarely follow through with further action. While the former pose physical risks, the latter inflict mental and emotional distress (Calhoun and Weston 2016). Schoeneman-Morris, Scalora, Chang, Zimmerman, and Garner (2007) also found that people who wrote letters rather than sending emails were more apt to initiate personal contact, most likely because postal communications require more than twice as many discrete steps to complete—indicating a greater degree of fixation on the target.

More recent work expands this focus to legislatures outside the United States and gathers data via questionnaires. Prevalence rates are strikingly similar across studies: between 80% and 90% of respondents reported experiencing at least one form of harassment (Bjørgo and Silkoset 2018; Every-Palmer, Barry-Walsh, and Pathé 2015; James et al. 2016a; Pathé, Phillips, Perdacher, and Heffernan 2014). More than one-quarter of Canadian politicians described these intrusions as "frightening" or "terrifying" (Adams, Hazelwood, Pitre, Bedard, and Landry 2009, 807). More than 40% of British MPs increased security at home and work as a result. One in five changed their daily routines, one in ten reduced social outings, and 6% took time off work. In addition, 8% consulted a health professional regarding mental and physical stress related to the experience (James et al. 2016b, 186). Collectively, these analyses show no major disparities in terms of the sex, age, party, or length of career of the target (James et al. 2016a). Rather, "aggressive/intrusive" behaviors tend to be driven by mental illness, facilitated by the ability of constituents to engage directly with representatives, with contact information and work schedules widely available to the general public (Narud and Dahl 2015).

A distinct but related body of research, conducted mainly by historians, economists, and political scientists, focuses on the determinants and impact of political assassinations. This work problematizes political convictions and mental health as key drivers of violence, arguing that most assassins harbor multiple motives, including bringing attention to a personal or political problem, avenging a perceived wrong, or ending personal pain (Ayton 2017). Examining this phenomenon globally between 1945 and 2013, Perliger (2015) observes that while these events occur across all regions, political conditions—like restricted competition and strong polarization—make assassinations more likely. Although MPs are more likely than other political actors to be killed, this rarely occurs in more established democracies. Heads of state, in contrast, are targeted everywhere as symbols of the existing social, economic, or political order (Iqbal and Zorn 2008).

Individuals with criminal backgrounds, or connections to organized crime, also commit a large share of these assassinations (Perliger 2015). Their reasons for killing politicians are often not political, but economic. According to Daniele and Dippopa (2017), organized crime groups target Italian municipalities to gain lucrative contracts for waste management, quarries, and other public procurements, as well as a wide range of employment, housing, and welfare subsidies. A politician's probability of being a target of violence thus increases after elections, especially with a change in government, as criminal groups attempt to "condition" politicians to their will by sending signals of criminal strength—most commonly through arson and threatening letters, but also potentially escalating to bombings and homicides. In Mexico, criminal fragmentation and political pluralization have destabilized longstanding alliances, increasing pressures on officials to accept illicit money and enhancing the likelihood that politicians will get caught up in intra-cartel battles (Blume 2017). The democratic impact, in turn, is two-fold: in addition to affecting political decision-making, these dynamics discourage well-qualified citizens from seeking public office by making a political career less attractive (Daniele 2019).

## Violence against Human Rights Defenders

Violence against human rights defenders first began to be recognized as an issue in the 1970s. The Helsinki Act, proclaimed at the Conference for Security and Cooperation in Europe in 1975, stipulated human rights as a principle of international relations for the first time, as states-parties confirmed "the right of the individual to know and act upon his rights and duties in [the human rights] field" (Conference on Security and Cooperation in Europe 1975, 7). In 1980, Canada initiated a resolution in the UN Commission on Human Rights[8] to "encourage and support individuals and organs of society exercising their rights and responsibilities to promote the effective observance of human rights" (Wille and Spannagel 2019). A sub-commission presented guiding principles to this effect in 1984, leading to a decision by the commission to set up a working group to prepare a declaration on this topic. The first draft appeared in 1987. However, adoption of the text took more than a decade, with a key point of contention revolving around the rights of states, as sovereign entities, versus individuals, as bearers of human rights.

After a compromise was finally reached in 1998, the UN General Assembly adopted the UN Declaration on Human Rights Defenders, clarifying the applicability of existing human rights norms and standards to human rights defenders themselves. Article 12 confirmed the right to be a defender, stating that "everyone has the right to participate in peaceful activities against violations of human rights and fundamental freedoms." The declaration also articulated two new rights specific to human rights defenders: the right "to develop and discuss new human rights ideas and principles and to advocate their acceptance" (Article 7) and "to solicit, receive, and utilize resources for the express purpose of promoting and protecting human rights . . . through peaceful means" (Article 13). Article 12 also specifically addressed the problem of violence, stipulating the right to be protected "against any violence, threats, retaliation, de facto or de jure adverse discrimination, pressure or any other arbitrary action as a consequence of his or her legitimate exercise of [these] rights" (UN General Assembly 1998, 4, 6).

In 2000, the Commission on Human Rights requested that the Secretary-General appoint a Special Representative on the Situation of Human Rights Defenders to gather information, enter into dialogue with governments, and recommend strategies to better protect defenders. Special Representative Hina Jilani made her first report to the UN General Assembly in 2002. Early on in her mandate, she expressed concerns that some governments were restricting the activities of human rights defenders on grounds of security and counterterrorism—but, in fact, were seeking to conceal their own human rights abuses and punish the defenders who exposed them (UN Secretary-General 2003). These discussions highlighted the politically driven nature of attacks on activists, but also framed these attacks as human rights violations themselves.

In the ensuing years, regional organizations followed suit in creating their own mandates and guidelines regarding human rights defenders. In 2001, the OAS General Assembly passed a resolution creating its own rapporteur on human rights defenders, with the aim of studying the situation of human rights defenders in the region and identifying and developing international standards for their protection. In 2006, the Inter-American Commission on Human Rights issued its first regional report, emphasizing the legal frameworks available for pursuing claims within the inter-American system. The EU adopted guidelines on human rights defenders in 2004 to strengthen its ongoing efforts to promote human rights, focusing on how the EU could intervene to support and promote human rights defenders at risk. That same year, the African Commission on Human and Peoples' Rights established a special rapporteur on human rights defenders to seek and act upon information on the situation of human rights defenders in Africa.

Driving these advances were a number of civil society organizations working on the issue of human rights defenders. Founded in 1961, Amnesty International began as a network seeking the release of political prisoners, but soon expanded to upholding the whole spectrum of human rights defenders. Human Rights Watch (HRW) formed in 1978 as Helsinki Watch to support citizen groups monitoring government compliance with the Helsinki Act. Over the course of the 1980s and 1990s, it expanded globally and also began to focus on a broader range of human rights. Both organizations mobilize public opinion to pressure states, gathering and publishing data to expose government abuses. A third group, Front Line Defenders, was created in 2001 with the specific mandate of protecting human rights defenders at risk via advocacy, trainings, and other forms of practical support, especially related to personal security.

Academic research on human rights defenders is relatively scarce and relies primarily on data and testimonies collected by NGOs. Landman (2006), for instance, analyzes annual reports produced by the Observatory for the Protection of Human Rights Defenders, a joint program of the World Organization against Torture and the International Federation for Human Rights. He counted 3324 documented violations against human rights defenders in over 50 countries between 1997 and 2003 (129). The most common form of abuse was arbitrary arrest and detention, followed by threats, harassments, and summary executions, as well as various forms of judicial harassment. The main perpetrators of abuse were police officers and members of the judiciary, although many were also unknown, according to the reports.

Other scholarly work seeks to map the global emergence of the international protection regime for human rights defenders. It explores how the term "human rights defender" has been used in practice (Nah, Bennett, Ingleton, and Savage 2013). It also identifies gaps in research, for example on the effectiveness of protection mechanisms and the relationship between repression, activism, and risk (Bennett, Ingleton, Nah, and Savage 2015). Some contributions also explore new forms of violence against human rights defenders, including laws aimed at criminalizing defenders, referencing imperatives related to national sovereignty, counterterrorism, and cultural and religious norms (Bennett et al. 2015; Van der Vet and Lyytikäinen 2015).

## Violence against Journalists

Journalists are not often viewed as political actors, but they play a key role in political life and violence against them also poses crucial threats to both democracy and human rights. As established in the Universal Declaration of Human Rights, "everyone has the right to freedom of opinion and expression . . . and to seek, receive, and impart information and ideas through any media and regardless of frontiers" (UN 1948, 5). In 1997, UNESCO recognized violence against journalists as its own specific issue, affecting both individual reporters and society at large. In Resolution 29, it characterized "assassination and any physical violence against journalists" as a "crime against society," as it "curtails freedom of expression" and "other rights and freedoms set forth in international human rights instruments" (1997, 1–2).

The impetus for this work originated with associations of media professionals responding to challenges faced by colleagues around the world. A group of American foreign correspondents formed the CPJ in 1981 in response to the brutal treatment of fellow journalists by authoritarian governments. Monitoring press freedom in more than 120 countries, the CPJ takes action when journalists are censored, harassed, threatened, attacked, jailed, abducted, or killed for their work. Their full-time staff documents cases, publishes reports, conducts advocacy, campaigns on behalf of the journalist, and provides life-saving emergency support. The CPJ also publishes safety advisories and has developed toolkits on physical, digital, and psychological safety.[9]

Other organizations were not initially established to address violence against journalists, but this issue became a logical extension of their earlier work. The International Federation of Journalists (IFJ) was founded in 1926 to promote the economic and human rights of journalists. In 1990, the IFJ began publishing an annual report on the number of journalists and media staff killed each year; in 1992, it set up a Safety Fund to support journalists faced with persecution. The International Press Institute (IPI), in turn, was established in 1950 to protect press freedom and improve the practices of journalism. In 1997, it introduced Death Watch, a listing of media professionals targeted because of their profession or who had lost their lives while on assignment. In 2002, IFJ and IPI joined forces to propose the creation of an international journalism safety body. Launched the following year, INSI provides training, counseling, and support for journalists, particular those reporting in conflict zones.

Data collected by these NGOs subsequently fed into discussions at the UN and beyond. In 2006, UN Security Council Resolution 1738 condemned "acts of violence . . . against journalists, media professionals, and associated personnel in armed conflict," stipulating that journalists reporting in these contexts be considered and protected as civilians (UN Security Council 2006, 2). The following year, a UNESCO (2007) report on press freedom expanded the focus beyond conflict zones, noting that a majority of journalists killed over the past decade worked in non-conflict contexts, and had typically been targeted "for reporting news that is not popular with those who have power, money, or guns" (6). Stating that "being a journalist has never been more dangerous" (4), the report called for an end to impunity for such crimes, which it saw as rooted in a lack of political will to investigate cases—or deliberate efforts to hide the truth.

Following a Decision on the Safety of Journalists and the Issue of Impunity in 2008, subsequently renewed every two years, the UNESCO Director-General convened a series of meetings to develop a UN Plan of Action on the Safety of Journalists and the Issue of Impunity. Adopted in 2012, the plan noted "disquieting evidence of the scale and number of attacks against the physical safety of journalists and media workers" (UNESCO 2012, 1) and called for a coordinated response across international, state, and civil society sectors to prevent, protect against, and prosecute attacks against journalists.

The UN General Assembly took note of the Plan of Action in a resolution the following year. Reflecting an expanded understanding of this phenomenon, it condemned "all attacks and violence against journalists and media workers, such as torture, extrajudicial killings, enforced disappearances and arbitrary detention, as well as intimidation and harassment in both conflict and non-conflict situations." The resolution also proclaimed November 2 as the International Day to End Impunity for Crimes against Journalists and called on member states to "promote a safe and enabling environment for journalists to perform their work independently and without undue interference" (UN General Assembly 2013a, 3).

In 2013 and 2014, UNESCO piloted a set of journalists' safety indicators to monitor journalist safety and impunity at the global and national levels. It also set up a mechanism to monitor the status of judicial inquiries into the killing of journalists, requesting updates from member states for reports published every two years. In 2015, the UN Statistical Commission designated UNESCO as a contributing agency for data on Indicator 16.10.1 of the Sustainable Development Goals, capturing the "number of verified cases of killing, kidnapping, enforced disappearance, arbitrary detention and torture of journalists, associated media personnel, trade unionists and human rights advocates in the previous 12 months."[10] In the ensuing years, these various UN bodies have continued to track fatalities as well as strengthen normative commitments. In 2017, the Secretary-General advanced these efforts by setting up a network of focal points across the UN system, tapping 14 agencies to coordinate their efforts to deal with cases of attacks against journalists.

Other recent innovations in global debates include a growing focus on the problem of online violence. In 2016, IPI launched OnTheLine, a project to monitor online harassment of journalists with the goal of exposing and countering threats against press freedom and free expression in the digital sphere. This initiative identifies four categories of online violence: threats of violence, like death threats; abusive behavior, including sexual and other harassment, smear campaigns, and posting of defamatory or false materials; technical interference, like use of malware or hacking of accounts and personal information; and improper legal threats, including threats of criminal or civil action or spurious takedown requests.[11]

In late 2018, these various issues gained further recognition when *Time* magazine named journalists who had faced violence in the course of their work as the collective Time Person of the Year. Arguing that informed citizens were essential to democratic governance, the editors characterized attacks on journalists as a "war on truth," criticizing attempts by political leaders to frame media professionals as the "enemy of the people." Among other examples, they mentioned Jamal Khashoggi, a Saudi journalist killed in the Saudi embassy in Istanbul in October 2018, and Maria Ressa, editor of the online news site Rappler in the Philippines, who was charged with tax fraud, which carries a lengthy prison sentence, in an effort to prevent her reporting (Vick 2018).

Studies of this topic are largely written by current or former journalists. One exception is an early book by a historian who suggests that violence against the press is a recurring theme in U.S. history—so integral to the "culture of public expression," he argues, that violent acts should be understood as "systemic rather than episodic" (Nerone 1994, 9). He identities four patterns in this violence over time: individual violence, violence against ideas, violence against groups, and violence against the media as an institution. Historically, he finds, these acts tend to surface in attempts to preserve traditional values in the face of change—an example being violence against African-American newspapers after the Civil War and during the civil rights era, as the status of blacks in U.S. society began to improve.

More recent work parallels the development of global practitioner discussions, focusing initially on dangers faced by reporters in war zones—and then expanding to consider challenges encountered by actors within the profession at large. Tumber and Webster (2006) argue that, while frontline journalism has always entailed safety risks, this work is growing more difficult and dangerous, affecting reporters' physical and mental health. This is because most journalists killed today in conflict zones are deliberately targeted, often in reprisal for their reporting, rather than dying as a result of cross-fire. These dynamics are exacerbated by shifts in how journalists are viewed by combatants, especially terrorist groups: previously treated as neutral observers with civilian status, reporters are now often seen as legitimate—and, indeed, desirable—targets. Kidnapping or killing a journalist can attract political attention, while also intimidating others in an attempt to control the news narrative (Cottle, Sambrook, and Mosdell 2016).

Changing digital technologies have spawned new risks. Opportunities to create and spread "fake news" position journalists as even less politically neutral. At the same time, new technologies have made it easier to identify targets and communicate threats and intimidation. Journalists working on sensitive topics—like human rights, war and international affairs, politics, and investigative reporting—are particularly vulnerable to these forms of aggression (Parker 2015). This is especially true in contexts with rising "nationalist sentiment antagonistic to critical journalism" (Ellis 2017, 57), where governments and coordinated armies of trolls may work together to chill online speech. The aim, as Luque Martínez (2015) points out, is not only to intimidate targeted journalists away from covering certain topics—it is also to damage the victim's credibility as a reporter. In these ways, violence against journalists not only threatens freedom of speech and citizens' right to information but also inflicts potentially devastating personal and professional consequences.

9

# A Distinct Phenomenon

A growing body of activism and research challenges the normalization of conflict and hostility in political life, arguing that some forms of antagonism do not promote but in fact undermine democracy and human rights. Despite important overlaps, this literature does not suffice on its own to adequately conceptualize the phenomenon of violence against women in politics. First, most iterations overlook the role of gender and other identities in shaping incidents of violence (Bardall 2011; Bjarnegård 2018). When sex is included as a variable, its importance is typically downplayed as minor or irrelevant (James et al. 2016a). Second, these frameworks tend to limit their focus to one dimension of democracy: the representation of different political parties or policy positions (Staniland 2014).

Prevailing understandings of political violence, however, provide a useful foundation for theorizing various forms of violence experienced by politically active women around the world. Some of these attacks fall squarely within existing frameworks, with women being targeted for their political views in both gendered and non-gendered ways. However, women may also face a second, qualitatively distinct form of violence. Rather than being an incidental feature, gender is central to the logic of this violence, shaping its origins, manifestations, and outcomes. The purpose is not policy marginalization, but group-based political exclusion—affecting a second dimension of democracy, the participation of different social groups in political decision-making. While only recently recognized and named as a problem, this form of violence poses threats to democracy, human rights, *and* gender equality.

## Violence in the Political Sphere

Emerging academic research on violence against women in politics differs sharply on how to theorize and empirically analyze violence experienced by

*Violence against Women in Politics*. Mona Lena Krook, Oxford University Press (2020). © Oxford University Press.
DOI: 10.1093/oso/9780190088460.001.0001.

women in the political sphere. One approach elides these forms of violence, distinguishing only between gendered motives, forms, and impacts (Bardall, Bjarnegård, and Piscopo 2019). This work stresses the need to compare women and men and generally finds few differences in their experiences (Bjarnegård 2018). An alternative perspective theorizes two separate phenomena—violence in politics and violence against women in politics—which can nonetheless overlap and intersect in individual cases (Krook and Restrepo Sanín 2016b, 2020). Contrary to the first account, this approach does not frame these concepts as competing hypotheses; rather, these phenomena can co-exist, both in the broader population of cases and in the context of a specific woman's own experiences.

These debates echo controversies that have long waged within the literature on gender-based violence. Focusing on the lived realities of women in battered women shelters, feminist constructions have largely viewed domestic violence as a form of patriarchal control exercised by male perpetrators over female victims. However, a counter-narrative on family violence soon materialized, reframing the problem as a case of human violence in which men and women were equally likely to be both perpetrators and victims (Berns 2001). A common response on the part of gender scholars has been to criticize the data used to support these latter claims, noting that apparent gender symmetry is rooted in both dubious coding decisions and gendered norms of behavior that lead women and men to under- and over-estimate—in opposite directions—the frequency with which they use or are on the receiving end of violence (Kimmel 2002).

Johnson (1995) takes a different approach, questioning whether—given these divergent findings—researchers are in fact studying the same phenomenon. He points out that the family violence literature analyzes a wide range of domestic conflicts, including occasional violent outbursts from husbands and wives—the vast majority of which do not escalate to become life threatening. Using data from national samples composed of equal numbers of women and men, these studies uncover only small gender differences in both the use and receipt of violence. Most of these incidents, moreover, arise in the context of everyday conflicts, the prevalence of which is shaped by the degree to which they are embedded within a broader violence-prone culture.

In contrast, feminist advocacy and research is concerned with what Johnson (1995) calls "patriarchal terrorism," or systematic violence perpetrated by men to control women. These acts may involve physical violence but also "coercive control," consisting of psychological threats, subordination, and isolation (Stark 2007). Collecting data from domestic violence shelters, this work uncovers highly disproportionate gender ratios, with 97% of victims being female and nearly all perpetrators being male (Johnson 1995, 285). Because the aim of this violence is to control women, targets often live under constant fear of escalation, with little recourse as their mistreatment is rooted and justified by patriarchal traditions of the family.

Although these two approaches are typically framed as alternative hypotheses, Johnson (1995) argues that divergent sampling decisions have given researchers access to two largely non-overlapping populations experiencing distinct forms of violence. While family violence scholars cast conclusions from shelter populations as invalid because they do not constitute a random sample, national studies are also skewed as those affected by patriarchal terrorism—on both the giving and receiving ends—are highly unlikely to participate in such a survey. A single research design, therefore, does not suffice to study these two phenomena at the same time. These insights, in turn, support the notion that there may also be *two types* of violence in the political sphere: violence in politics, targeting male and female political actors in gendered and non-gendered ways; and violence against women in politics, directed specifically at women as a group to drive them out of the political realm.

## VIOLENCE IN POLITICS

Existing frameworks in political science help elaborate how these two phenomena are related but distinct. Pitkin (1967) theorizes four types of political representation, each of which reflects only a partial view. She observes that "substantive representation," however, is often what most thinkers understand by the term, referring to "an activity in behalf of, in the interest of, as the agent of, someone else" (113). Phillips (1995) describes this as the "politics of ideas," where "representation is considered more or less adequate depending on how well it reflects voters' opinions or preferences or beliefs" (1). This concept of representation drives concerns about political and electoral violence, as well as violence against politicians, human rights defenders, and journalists. Such acts are problematic because they use force to enable one set of political preferences to prevail over the others, violating citizens' ability to make free and informed choices about political alternatives.

Violence in politics, proposed here as a collective term for these dynamics, can affect women and men, with gender playing a relatively small role even when women are specifically targeted. The 2007 assassination of Benazir Bhutto, the former prime minister of Pakistan, falls into this category. Killed as she waved from her car while leaving a political rally, circumstances surrounding her death—and the ensuing police investigation—raised questions about who was ultimately responsible. A UN fact-finding mission noted the distinct lack of data for evaluation: the crime scene was hosed down within an hour of the attack, only 23 pieces of evidence were collected, and an autopsy on the body was refused (UN Commission of Inquiry 2010).

Due to the botched police investigation, many theories flourish regarding her assassins and their potential motivations. Government officials attributed the attack to Al-Qaeda. Bhutto did have concerns that Al-Qaeda and members of the Pakistani Taliban might seek to harm her, based on her strong stance against religious extremism, as well as her support for the U.S. approach to combatting terrorism. During her last months in Pakistan, however, she came to view the government and the military and intelligence communities as the main threats to her safety. She was convinced, further, that threat warnings passed to her by these agencies aimed to intimidate her to stop campaigning (Farwell 2011). All of the potential suspects, therefore, appeared to be driven primarily not by gender but by questions of policy and political power.

In terms of the broader context, moreover, Bhutto was not the first political figure in Pakistan to die in an untimely fashion. Her father, Zulfiqar Ali Bhutto, who served as president and as prime minister, was executed in 1979. Even more tellingly, Pakistan's first prime minister, Liaquat Ali Khan, was assassinated in 1951—in the same park Bhutto was leaving as she was killed. When Bhutto arrived at the hospital after the suicide bombing, the staff was busy treating victims of a shooting at a rival candidate's rally earlier that day (UN Commission of Inquiry 2010). Violence is thus a core feature of politics in Pakistan, affecting a wide range of politically engaged actors from ordinary citizens to high-level political leaders.

Violence in politics can also take gender-differentiated forms, with women and men targeted for their political affiliations in different ways (cf. Bardall, Bjarnegård, and Piscopo 2019). In Zimbabwe, members of President Robert Mugabe's party, the Zimbabwe African National Union-Patriotic Front (ZANU-PF), engaged in an organized and sustained rape campaign against supporters of the Movement for Democratic Change (MDC). Testimonies gathered by AIDS-Free World (2009) following the 2008 presidential elections revealed that members of Mugabe's youth militia abducted, beat, and gang raped hundreds, if not thousands, of women associated with the MDC, arriving at their homes singing ZANU-PF songs or wearing party t-shirts. The Research and Advocacy Unit (2011), a local NGO, conducted surveys of women around the country and found that "politically motivated rape" aimed at "instilling fear, humiliating, and effecting total disengagement in politics on the part of women, men, sons, and male relatives who had dared openly or indirectly to express their partisan affiliations" (19–20).

Men can also be attacked in gendered ways. Following the contested 2007 elections in Kenya, a large number of men from the Luo ethnic group, who were presumed to support Raila Odinga of the Orange Democratic Movement, were forcibly circumcised by supporters of Mwai Kibaki, a member of the Kikuyu ethnic group and the Party of National Union. This sexualized violence sought to emasculate members of the opposition and was rooted in a broader context of suspected election rigging by the ruling party (Auchter 2017). Following a different line of attack, the former Malaysian deputy prime minister turned opposition leader, Anwar Ibrahim, was charged and put on trial numerous times for sodomy in an attempt to destroy his reputation (Abbott 2001), culminating in imprisonment in 2015 as part of a broader crackdown on human rights defenders. The aim of these acts, while taking gendered forms, is to punish or exclude on the basis of political opinions.

## VIOLENCE AGAINST WOMEN IN POLITICS

A second major form of political representation, according to Pitkin (1967), is "descriptive representation," which focuses on "being something rather than doing something" (61). Phillips (1995) labels this the "politics of presence," where fairness requires that political institutions reflect "a more adequate representation of the different social groups that make up the citizen body" (6). Protecting the integrity of this form of representation is the purview of efforts to tackle violence against women in politics. These acts infringe upon basic political rights, seeking to exclude members of certain demographic groups from participating in the political process.

Women are not the only group that has experienced violence targeting their descriptive representation. In 1976, the U.S. National Association of Human Rights Workers created a Special Committee on the Status of Minority Elected Officials. Its first task was to examine political harassment in the decade since passage of the Voting Rights Act protecting the political rights of African Americans. The resulting 300-page report found that "over half of the 16 members of the Congressional Black Caucus; three of four Black State Executives; dozens of Black State Legislators; at least 20 Black Mayors; and unknown numbers of other local officials" (Warner 1977, 11) had faced police and intelligence community surveillance, spurious legal investigations and tax audits, false accusations in the media, withholding of funding for their communities, and death threats to themselves or family members.

Interpreting these acts as "resistance to the intrusion of Blacks on the prerogatives of white values, white power, and white control," the report observed that the aim seemed to be "to make the position of an elected official so frustrating, so unattractive, so anguish-filled, and so intolerable that Blacks quit, or refrain from running for re-election, or decline to seek office in the first place" (Warner 1977, 11, 18). In the late 1980s, the issue surfaced again following the growing mobilization of black voters. In surveys, between one-third and one-half of African Americans believed that black leaders were being singled out for repression by government authorities. This claim was backed up by data showing that black officials at all levels of government were five times more likely than white officials to have been investigated by the Department of Justice (Musgrove 2012, 2, 6).

Distinct from efforts to prevent people from participating due to their political opinions, this type of violence aims to exclude individuals based on their descriptive group membership. Rather than suppressing political competition, it expresses bias and discrimination, calling into question the rights of these groups to take part in politics at all. Female politicians have long been aware of this distinction, even when they lacked a word to capture it. As Ross (2002) finds in interviews with political women in Australia, South Africa, and the UK: "Women are more than 'happy' to be targeted as individual members of an opposing side, as fair game in the war of attrition which is regularly carried out on the floors of debating chambers around the world, but object to the use of their sex as the primary weapon of assault" (193). Along similar lines, Diane Abbott, a British MP, explained that, in these cases, "people are not engaging in debate or scrutiny but just showering you with abuse: that you're a nigg*r; that you're a prostitute; threats against your safety. It's just abuse which has no political content" (Dhrodia 2017).

Acts of violence against women in politics, however, need not take obviously gendered forms: gender motivation, not gender differentiation, is the defining feature of this phenomenon. The 2016 impeachment of Dilma Rousseff, the first female president of Brazil, illustrates the diversity of tools that may be mobilized to delegitimize women's rights *as women* to serve as political leaders. On their face, impeachment proceedings do not appear to constitute a form of "violence." In this case, however, a deeper probe reveals a process permeated with expressions of bias against women in political roles.

Signaling that they did not accept a female leader, those who promoted and voted in favor of impeachment, including conservative media outlets, refused to call Rousseff by her preferred form of address, *presidenta*, the feminine form of the word "president." Instead, they persisted in using *presidente*, the masculine form, reinforcing associations between men and leadership—and thus marking her as clear interloper in this realm. News magazines supportive of impeachment, further, portrayed her as hysterical, a common trope used against powerful women, while other opponents placed stickers of Rousseff with her legs spread apart around gas tank openings on their cars, sexually violating her image every time they filled up. On the floor of the Chamber of Deputies, lastly, mainly male legislators held up signs saying *Tchau, Querida!* (Bye-Bye, Sweetheart!), taunting her in degrading and gendered terms as they voted for her impeachment.

Rousseff, for her part, championed gender equality, expanding the government's work to end violence against women and support women's financial autonomy. She also appointed far more women to cabinet positions than previous presidents and elevated the secretariat on policies for women to a full-fledged ministry (Jalalzai and dos Santos 2015). The main protagonists in the impeachment campaign, in contrast, were well-known for their sexism and misogyny, including Eduardo Cunha, who had sponsored numerous bills against women's and LGBT rights, and Jair Bolsonaro, who led a campaign against "gender ideology" and promoted rape culture on the floor of parliament (Biroli 2016). Michel Temer, Rousseff's former vice president who became acting president on her suspension, appointed the first all-white, all-male cabinet since the military dictatorship and discontinued the majority of policies for women initiated under Rousseff and her predecessor (Rubim and Argolo 2018).

The reaction of Brazilian women suggests, moreover, that a substantial portion believed the impeachment was motivated by gender bias. One activist wrote that "almost all feminists agree that her impeachment was sexist and discriminatory," with thousands of women coming together to express solidarity with Rousseff in a "confrontation with the patriarchy, with male chauvinists" (Hao 2016). Female politicians echoed this message. Senator Regina Sousa remarked during the trial that "the message they are sending in this process is also directed at all women" (Amorim 2016). Rousseff acknowledged this support during her speech at the trial: "Brazilian women have been, during this time, a fundamental pillar for my resistance . . . Tireless companions in a battle in which misogyny and prejudice showed their claws" (Rousseff 2016).

Finally, ample evidence indicates that Rousseff was punished according to a gendered double standard. Her stated offense was to use funds from the central bank to conceal a budget deficit before the 2014 elections. This budgetary practice, known as *pedaladas fiscais*, was made illegal in 2000, but was employed by two previous male presidents without penalty. Moreover, many legal experts agreed it did not amount to a "crime of responsibility," the only type of crime that justifies removing an elected president (Encarnación 2017). Further, over 100 deputies were themselves under formal investigation for criminal activity at the time of the impeachment. Rousseff, in contrast, stood out as one of the cleanest politicians in Brazil (Chalhoub, Collins, Lllanos, Pachón, and Perry 2017). Factors driving Rousseff out of office thus stemmed far less from differences of political opinion than views that women are illegitimate participants in the political realm.[1]

## EMPIRICAL OVERLAPS AND INTERSECTIONS

Previous work has struggled to distinguish these phenomena for several reasons. First, politically active women may experience both forms of violence. These incidents may transpire separately, with attacks focusing on a woman's political views at one moment and their female identity at another. Forms of violence may also co-occur, discrediting women's political views by questioning their right as women to participate at all. In July 2019, for example, President Donald Trump went on Twitter to criticize " 'Progressive' Democrat Congresswomen, who originally came from countries whose governments are a complete and total catastrophe" for "viciously telling the people of the United States, the greatest and most powerful Nation on earth, how our government is to be run." He went on to tell them to "go back and help fix the totally broken and crime infested places from which they came."[2] Although he did not mention them by name, most observers believed he was referring to four women of color elected in 2018: Alexandria Ocasio-Cortez, Ilhan Omar, Ayanna Pressley, and Rashida Tlaib. As the "public faces of the shift toward a more diverse Congress," these women have been targeted repeatedly by Trump and conservative media outlets—skeptical of their policies *and* their descriptive backgrounds—with "aggressive and extensive calls to *shut up and go away*" (Chittal 2019).

Attacks against teenage climate activist Greta Thunberg follow a similar logic, mocking her calls to address climate change by criticizing her as "deeply disturbed," an "arrogant child," and a "teenage puppet." Noting that most of her detractors are older, white, conservative men, Gelin (2019) argues that their hostility is rooted in beliefs that the real threat is not to the environment but to "a certain kind of modern industrial society built and dominated by their form of masculinity" (Anshelm and Hultman 2014, 85). Close associations between women and the environment drive—and in detractors' minds, justify—these reactions: "Environmentalists are female and/or effeminate, and therefore can be dismissed out of hand as stupid or crazy or driven by irrational emotion . . . Women are so worthless in their eyes, it appears, that no amount of evidence will ever make women's arguments hold merit" (Marcotte 2019).

Second, most of the available data for studying these dynamics captures both forms of violence simultaneously. Studies of online violence, for instance, typically employ automated algorithms to identify and analyze abusive tweets. Visualizations accompanying a story on the abuse of U.S., Australian, and British politicians show how this data may reflect a mix of political and gender content. Abuse of Hillary Clinton commonly drew on gendered slurs, like bitch, cunt, and whore, but to a lesser extent also included terms like lying, stupid, and corrupt. In contrast, tweets directed at her rival Bernie Sanders tended to call him an idiot or moron, followed by a range of gender-neutral expletives. A side-by-side comparison of tweets sent to Julia Gillard and her opponent Kevin Rudd indicated more qualitative differences, with abusive language directed at Gillard being more "personal, vitriolic, and sexual," even when phrased in a party-political way (Hunt, Evershed, and Liu 2016).

Third, some women are attacked both as women and in response to their women's rights advocacy (Biroli 2018; Mantilla 2015). In Argentina, women supporting decriminalization of abortion have been physically attacked when wearing a green handkerchief—a symbol of the campaign—on their wrists, necks, or bags. In accounts collected by Amnesty International (2018a), one woman described being slashed in the face with a razor by two young men who yanked the green handkerchief off her backpack, while another was surrounded by a group of men who shouted "you are an abortionist, we are all going to rape you and afterwards you will abort it" (15–16). Numerous activists and journalists also reported being harassed online with threats, insults, and derogatory terms like "prostitute," including one whose home was later raided by police who took everything related to the fight for abortion. Amnesty denounced these as methods seeking "to silence, censor, and oppress women human rights defenders" (15).

With clearer concepts, nevertheless, these overlaps and intersections can be disentangled to distinguish acts *directed at women* for political reasons from those seeking to *exclude them as women* from participating in political life. Identifying instances of both phenomena is important, as both involve violations of electoral and personal integrity (Bjarnegård 2018), undermining—in turn—both democracy and human rights. Violence against women in politics, however, also poses a third threat—to gender equality—that is not yet widely recognized or understood. While largely hidden, the denigration of women permeates the origins, manifestations, and outcomes of these acts, providing deep roots for legitimizing and normalizing their political exclusion.

## Defining Violence against Women in Politics

Campaigns to stop violence against women in politics name a phenomenon that, until recently, has largely been ignored or naturalized as the "cost of doing politics" for women seeking to be politically active. These gendered dynamics work at three levels: structural, cultural, and symbolic. Theorized by disparate scholars and corroborated by a wide range of studies, they work together to create, justify, and reinforce women's secondary status. Deeply embedded in the fabric of society, these forces explain why violence against women in politics remains largely hidden from view—and reveals the implications of allowing these exclusionary tendencies to continue unchallenged.

### STRUCTURAL VIOLENCE

Gender inequality begins with structural violence, the stratification of access to basic human needs based on ascriptive group membership. Built into the social structure, it enacts harm in the form of unequal life chances (Galtung 1969), "mark[ing] some people as deserving worse treatment, or even mark[ing] some people as less human" (Price 2012, 6). Creating and legitimating patterns of hierarchy and inequality, structural violence denies marginalized groups opportunities for emotional and physical well-being, effects that are exacerbated for those who are members of multiple marginalized groups (Anglin 1998).

In contrast to direct personal violence, which can be clearly recognized and denounced by victims, structural violence is a "silent" form of injustice which appears "as natural as the air around us," so that the "object of structural violence may be persuaded not to perceive this at all" (Galtung 1969, 173). Frye (1983) describes these dynamics of oppression using the analogy of a bird cage. She notes that an observer looking only at one wire of the cage would be unable to see why a bird could not just fly around it whenever it wanted to go somewhere. Viewing the cage from a distance, however, reveals the system of wires, explaining why the bird is confined and cannot move freely. While structural violence is largely invisible, therefore, it nonetheless "leaves marks not only on the human body but also on the mind and the spirit" (Galtung 1990, 294).

Manne (2018) argues that, in the case of women, these dynamics constitute "sexism," an ideology establishing and rationalizing a patriarchal social order. Like theorists of structural violence, she points out that gendered norms of behavior have a "coercive quality" that seek to remain "implicit," yet engage "a long list of mechanisms in service of this goal," including the socialization of women to accept these norms, narratives about the inherent nature of sex differences, and the depiction of care work as rewarding (as long as it is performed by women). The "seamless appearance" of sexism is "almost inevitably deceptive," however, as "hostile, threatening, and punitive norm-enforcement mechanisms" are always standing by "should these 'soft' forms of social power prove insufficient for upholding them" (46–47).

Structural violence affects the terms of women's political engagement by imposing what feminists call the "public/private divide," associating men with the public sphere of politics and women with the private sphere of the home. This divide informs political theories as well as broader social practices, valorizing men and masculine attributes in public leadership (Katz 2016) while delegitimizing women's rights and opportunities to move around in public spaces (Elshtain 1981; Landes 1988; Pateman 1988). This gender divide is so foundational to existing concepts of politics, according to Okin (1979), that there is no way to "include women, formerly minor characters, as major ones within the political drama without challenging basic and age-old assumptions about the family, its traditional sex roles, and its relation to the wider world of political society" (286).

Consequently, when women do gain access to the public sphere, they confront a set of expectations that cast them as interlopers in a space governed and occupied by men (Puwar 2004). This sense of intrusion is captured by Winston Churchill's response to Nancy Astor, the first female MP, when she asked why he behaved so terribly toward her. Revealing a view of the British parliament as a protected male space, he replied: "When you came into the House I felt that you had entered my bathroom and I had no sponge with which to defend myself."[3] Eagly and Karau (2002) locate the source of this sense of ill ease in a perceived mismatch between traits stereotypically ascribed to women (warm, polite, and yielding) and those associated with men and good leaders (assertive, decisive, and confident). This results in what Lazarus and Steigerwalt (2018) label "gendered vulnerability," leading to ongoing challenges from political opponents and constant calls for women in politics to prove their worth due to their sex.

A sense of male entitlement to public space, however, is not merely a challenge faced by women seeking to enter formal politics. Structural violence restricts women's free movement as well as their voice in the public realm more generally. Data from WomanStats show that women do not enjoy full freedom of movement in public spaces in any country in the world. Women are typically harassed, or need permission from their families or male escorts, to enter and move in public—with restrictions on their movement even regulated by law in some cases. The upshot is that in only a handful of cases do women enjoy high levels of physical security; rather, the vast majority of women globally face low or non-existent levels of physical safety.[4]

Exploring gender dynamics of public harassment, Gardner (1995) thus observes that women are "situationally disadvantaged in public places," lacking the "same sense of freedom, entitlement, and righteousness that men exhibit" (16, 9). She identifies three common abuses that are used as a form of social control: exclusionary practices, which forbid or discourage women from entering some or all public spaces; exploitative practices, which involve freedoms and intrusions—like touching, pointing, and staring—directed at women that deprive them of the privacy that men enjoy; and evaluative practices, which subject women to the opinions of strangers—like sexualized comments, terms of endearment, or assessments of their attractiveness—in contexts where such evaluation is normally not warranted. Because women who move in public spaces violate gender norms governing the public and private spheres, they are viewed as "fair game" for sexual and other forms of gender-based harassment (Mantilla 2015; Segrave 2014).

## CULTURAL VIOLENCE

Cultural violence taps into and justifies structural violence, making "direct and structural violence look, even feel, right—or at least not wrong" (Galtung 1990, 291). It invokes cultural tropes and norms changing "the moral color of an act from red/wrong to green/right or at least to yellow/acceptable." This dynamic creates a double standard tolerating and legitimizing violence—which is otherwise deemed unacceptable—when it is perpetrated against members of particular groups. Through these tools, Galtung explains, "culture preaches, teaches, admonishes, eggs on, and dulls us into seeing exploitation and/or repression as normal and natural, or into not seeing them . . . at all" (295). The exact manifestations of cultural violence vary across contexts, drawing on ideas denigrating women—and other marginalized groups—in religion, language, ideology, and other cultural domains (Galtung 1990; Jenkins 1998). These tools exist, however, in every society, including those that view themselves as "advanced" in areas of gender equality.

System justification tendencies drive members of both dominant and marginalized groups to naturalize and perpetuate cultural violence. According to this perspective, people defend existing social, economic, and political arrangements, even when these conflict with their self-interests, due to widespread beliefs that the prevailing system—by the mere fact that it exists—is good and desirable (Eidelman, Crandall, and Pattershall 2009). Doing so provides emotional benefits by reducing "uncertainty, anxiety, guilt, dissonance, frustration, and moral outrage brought on by social inequality and other potential system deficiencies" (Jost and van der Toorn 2011, 652).

As a result, those who offer alternative accounts testifying to injustice often experience what Stark (2019) terms epistemic and manipulative gaslighting. The first calls into question a speaker's status as a knower, refusing to listen to and discrediting their testimony. The second involves ridiculing or attacking the speaker, attributing their "misinterpretations" to personal failings. By these mechanisms, gaslighting leads individuals "to doubt not only their ability to discern harm but their standing as one who is owed better treatment" (231).

Cultural violence with respect to women in politics is rooted in, and seeks to reinforce, ideas about the public/private divide—and thus the gender norms this divide creates and upholds. Denigrating and disparaging women who enter the public sphere, these cultural tropes warn other women to stay away or else face similar degrading treatment. While cultural violence can vary across countries, many of these tools are—in fact—strikingly similar in content, focusing on the dubious morality, character, and worthiness of women who dare to engage in public life. Invoking these negative frames and stereotypes has implications for women's full and equal participation, as well as their ability to speak out about violence against women in politics.

"Sexuality-baiting" is a common tactic, "using ideas, or prejudices, about women's sexuality to intimidate, humiliate, embarrass, or stifle the expression of women" (Rothschild 2005, 42). It centers on the female body, passing judgment on a woman's presumed sexual behavior, or commenting on her physical appearance, to undermine her credibility or intellectual contributions (Sobieraj 2018; Spender 1982). Sexual shaming slurs like dyke, slut, and whore (Levey 2018) portray women engaged in politics as unattractive creatures who have failed in their feminine roles and want to be men (Gullickson 2014) or as immoral women who have exchanged sexual favors for entry into the public sphere (Hipkins 2011).

Other gendered insults, like bitch and cunt, are silencing slurs, reflecting the idea that women should be seen and not heard (Levey 2018). Analysis of the term bitch suggests that it refers to a woman who is "disposed to be more boisterous, more assertive, more self-concerned . . . *than is appropriate for a woman/ than a woman ought to be*" (Ashwell 2016, 235). Suggesting it is used as a default term for describing ambitious women in public life, Anderson (1999) argues that the term bitch serves as a "tool of containment" in U.S. politics by invoking "the myth of women's power as unnatural and threatening" (602). These slurs tap into broader gender stereotypes framing women as too emotional to be leaders (Brescoll 2016), reinforced by photos frequently published of female politicians showing them with "their mouths open, unrestrained: mid-yell, spittle-flecked, the very act of making a loud noise a sign of their ugly and unnatural personalities" (Traister 2018, 54).

Additional forms of cultural violence are slightly more subtle, yet nonetheless exert a powerful effect in devaluing women as worthy and autonomous human beings. Androcentric grammar rules, for example, relegate women to a secondary and inferior place in society, with false generics like "man" and "mankind" not only reflecting a history of male domination but also actively encouraging its perpetuation (Gastil 1990). In rendering women invisible, gender-exclusive language, moreover, signals that women do not belong in a particular environment (Stout and Dasgupta 2011). Concerned about this dynamic, Laura Boldrini, the new President of the Italian Chamber of Deputies, circulated a letter asking her colleagues to call officeholders by the appropriate gendered forms. When some criticized her efforts as "frivolous," she responded: "Language is not only a semantic issue, it is a concept, a cultural issue . . . When you are opposed to saying *la ministra* or *la presidente* it means that culturally you are not admitting that women can reach top positions"(Feder, Nardelli, and De Luca 2018).

Cultural violence can also include common mechanisms for deflecting scrutiny for sexism, such as characterizing abusive and misogynistic language as "free speech" (Mantilla 2015), "just a joke" (Bemiller and Schneider 2010), or "locker room talk" (Harp 2018). Accepting these excuses at face value further expands the range of gender-based insults and aggressions seen as normal and routine (Phillips 2015). Combined, the various sexist tropes constituting cultural violence against women have a formulaic and even "quasi-algebraic quality" (Jane 2017, 34), derogating women in "overwhelmingly impersonal, repetitive, stereotyped" ways. As a result, perpetrators often "sound like the exact same [person] . . . speaking to the exact same woman."[5]

## SYMBOLIC VIOLENCE

Cultural violence, in turn, produces symbolic violence, "a subtle, euphemized, invisible mode of domination" (Krais 1993, 172), which seeks to put marginalized people who deviate from prescribed norms back "in their place."[6] Although the concept can be applied to understand various axes of inequality, Bourdieu (2001) views masculine domination as the quintessential form of symbolic violence, with "society organized through and through according to the principle of the primacy of masculinity" (82). Symbolic violence both enacts and legitimizes hierarchy via "misrecognition," whereby members of "dominated [groups] apply categories constructed from the point of view of the dominant to the relations of domination" (35). Women, in this case, are socialized to accept a hierarchy between men and women as "common sense," as the "authorized perspective" on the world (Bourdieu 1991, 239–240). Symbolic violence thus reinforces structural inequalities, further naturalizing gender hierarchy.

Manne's (2018) concept of "misogyny" provides insight into how these dynamics work with respect to women in public life. She argues against naïve conceptions presenting misogyny as a property of individuals who hate "any and every woman simply because they are women." Rather, she suggests, misogyny is "a property of social systems" where women "face hostility of various kinds *because they are women in a man's world* . . . failing to live up to patriarchal standards" (32–33). Misogyny thus polices "women quite selectively, rather than targeting women across the board" (34). This system-defending function means that both men and women may harass or demean those who challenge prevailing gender norms in order to "protect or enhance [their] own sex-based status" (Berdahl 2007, 641). Backlash against female leaders thus not only reinforces gender stereotypes, but can also reward male and female perpetrators psychologically, increasing their self-esteem (Rudman and Fairchild 2004).

While symbolic violence against women in politics can be perpetrated by both women and men, some manifestations are clearly driven by "aggrieved entitlement," a sense among some men that, as a result of feminism and feminists, they are "failed patriarchs" or "deposed kings" (Kimmel 2017, 118). According to scholars of masculinity, manhood is a "precarious state requiring continual social proof and validation" (Vandello, Bosson, Cohen, Burnaford, and Weaver 2008, 1325), and displays of aggression form part of "men's cultural script for restoring threatened gender status" (Bosson, Vandello, Burnaford, Weaver, and Wasti 2009, 623). One result is what Sheffield (1989) calls "sexual terrorism," the mobilization of fear by men through both "actual and implied violence" to control and dominate women (483).

Actions to put women back in their place need not be restricted to the physical realm, however. Symbolic violence is also present when women are sexually objectified and degraded through visual images circulated in online and other public spaces (Anderson 2011), which dehumanizes them in an attempt to render them less worthy of respect (Heflick and Goldenberg 2009). Other forms include efforts to silence women's voices and question their right to speak in public more generally. In 2013, Caroline Criado-Perez (2016), a British activist and journalist, received a wave of threats and insults in response to her advocacy. When analyzing the content of the abuse, she observed: "thousands of threats I received . . . focused on my mouth, my throat, my speech. The message was simple and clear: these men very much wanted me to stop talking" (13). This form of backlash does not stem from policy content, according to Beard (2017): "It is not *what* you say that prompts [the abuse], it's simply the fact that you're saying it" (36–37).

Symbolic violence also takes many more subtle guises, undermining women's effectiveness and feelings of acceptance in male-dominated spaces. Ås (1978) identifies five "domination techniques" used against women who enter male-dominated institutions: making invisible, where women are forgotten, overlooked, or ignored; ridiculing, where women's efforts are scorned or women are treated as incompetent or useless at tasks that do not conform with traditional female gender roles; withholding of information, where women are not invited or are denied access to meetings where key decisions are made; double punishing, where women are criticized for being wrong regardless of what they do or do not do; and heaping blame and putting to shame, where women are told that they are not good enough despite being denied the information needed to succeed.[7] These forms of "selective incivility" violate workplace norms of mutual respect, but ambiguity in their intent to harm the target—due to the possibility that offenders may simply be rude individuals—makes it possible to rationalize these behaviors as unbiased, despite disproportionately affecting women and people of color (Cortina, Kabat-Farr, Leskinen, Huerta, and Magley 2013).

Microaggressions perform a similar function in reinforcing gender and other hierarchies, although in some cases, perpetrators may not even be aware they have engaged in a demeaning exchange with the target. Sue (2010) defines these as "brief and commonplace daily verbal, behavioral, and environmental indignities, whether intentional or unintentional, that communicate hostile, derogatory, or negative . . . slights and insults to the target person or group" (5). Their pervasiveness in everyday conversations means that microaggressions are often dismissed as innocent or innocuous, despite their demeaning messages. Examples include sexist language and jokes, as well as automatic assumptions about the inferiority of women—whether intellectual, temperamental, or physical. As Rebecca Solnit observes: "Men explain things to me, and other women, whether or not they know what they're talking about," a dynamic which "trains us in self-doubt and self-limitation just as it exercises men's unsupported overconfidence." Due to symbolic violence, therefore, women often have to fight "simply for the right to speak, to have ideas, to be acknowledged to be in possession of facts and truths, to have value, to be a human being."[8]

# 10

# A Bias Event Approach

Violence against women in politics is fundamentally distinct from violence in politics: whereas the latter entails acts *directed at women* for their political views, the former involves efforts to *exclude women as women* from participating in public life. While both phenomena may take gendered and non-gendered forms, violence against women in politics is specifically motivated by bias against women assuming political roles. It simultaneously justifies and obscures itself by mobilizing structural, cultural, and symbolic violence framing women as second-class citizens who do not—and should not—engage in political activities.

Despite a clear analytical distinction between these two concepts, identifying cases of violence against women in politics is not a straightforward task. Documenting violence against women in general is notoriously difficult, because women often hesitate to report cases of gender-based violence. This under-reporting occurs for many reasons, including feelings of shame and stigma, fears of retaliation, and beliefs about widespread impunity for perpetrators (Palermo, Bleck, and Peterman 2014). Proving that gender is a motivation is also complex, given that men may also experience violence in the political realm (Bjarnegård 2018)—and the fact that women themselves are highly diverse, with their experiences potentially informed by other axes of privilege and discrimination (Kuperberg 2018).

The literature on hate crimes, however, provides a means for overcoming this impasse and, in turn, for developing an empirical strategy for identifying cases of violence against women in politics. Hate crime laws impose a higher class of penalties when a violent crime targets a victim due to perceived social group membership. These crimes are deemed to be more severe because, in addition to the crime in question, they involve group-based discrimination. To facilitate the detection of such cases, existing legal frameworks provide a range of possible actions that could indicate that bias was a driving factor behind a particular incident. Adapted and expanded, these insights point to six criteria

*Violence against Women in Politics.* Mona Lena Krook, Oxford University Press (2020). © Oxford University Press.
DOI: 10.1093/oso/9780190088460.001.0001.

for adjudicating whether a case is, or is not, an instance of violence against women in politics.

## Methodological Challenges

Studying, as well as organizing to address, violence against women is challenging, given that this violence is highly normalized in many societies. Rather than being seen as a problem in need of intervention, violence against women is often framed as a male or familial prerogative, a socially sanctioned way to subjugate and exercise control over women (O'Toole, Schiffman, and Edwards 2007). Interviewed in 2019, Gloria Steinem, a leader of the U.S. feminist movement in the 1960s and 1970s, captured this notion when she observed: "We didn't have the phrase sexual harassment until I was in my 40s—it was just called 'life.'"[1] Various political dynamics, further, disincentivize speaking out in the case of violence against women in politics, including the desire for a political career or feelings of loyalty to a particular political party.

In addition to these challenges, recent advances in scholarship raise questions about the centrality of "gender" in explaining incidents of violence against women. Some scholars argue that robust research requires comparing women's and men's experiences side-by-side in order to establish whether women are in fact being treated differently (Johnson 1995). Other work highlights the role of intersectionality—interactions between gender and other forms of exclusion based on factors like race, class, and sexuality—in shaping women's experiences. This perspective suggests that gender may not be the only, or even the most important, form of bias driving patterns of exclusion (McCall 2005; Weldon 2006).

### UNDER-REPORTING

Data on violence against women in politics has only recently become available because, lacking a "name," the issue remained under-theorized and under-recognized as a "problem." Despite progress, this phenomenon remains hidden from view in many contexts around the world, in great part because many women still hesitate to speak out—and those who do call out violence are often not believed. Reasons for under-reporting are multiple but collectively contribute to ongoing silence around this issue, undermining a fuller understanding of its scope and impact on women's political engagement.

For some women, the barrier is cognitive: they normalize violence as part of the political game and thus do not view themselves as "victims" when targeted for gendered reasons. Rather, like survivors of gender-based violence more generally, they cope with the violence perpetrated against them by rationalizing it, defining it as tolerable or normal, "forgetting" it, or refusing to acknowledge it (Ferraro and Johnson 1983; Kelly 1988). Speaking at the launch of an initiative to support women seeking public roles in 2014, for example, Hillary Clinton endorsed Eleanor Roosevelt's advice that women in politics should toughen up and "grow skin like a rhinoceros."[2]

Other politically active women appreciate that violence is not acceptable, but they opt to stay quiet for strategic reasons. Female politicians in various contexts are frank about the fact that speaking out would be a form of "political suicide" (Krook and Restrepo Sanín 2020, 6). In some cases, this is because the perpetrators are members of a woman's own political party. In pilot studies carried out by NDI in Côte d'Ivoire, Honduras, Tanzania, and Tunisia, more than half of female respondents reported they had experienced at least one form of violence at the hands of their party colleagues (NDI 2018, 21).

One tactic for overcoming these types of under-reporting difficulties is to avoid the word "violence," which can give rise to varied subjective interpretations, in favor of posing questions about a list of specific acts (UN Department of Economic and Social Affairs 2014). Another is to ask about violence experienced by female colleagues, on the intuition that some women might disclose their own lived realities if they can disguise it as belonging to a friend. Alternatively, as part of female political networks, they may be privy to information affecting the broader community of women—even if they themselves are not personally affected (Cerva Cerna 2014).[3] Employing both approaches, the IPU (2016b) finds that violence against female parliamentarians is widespread, both among the women interviewed and across their broader universe of female colleagues.

GENDERED COMPARISONS

A second set of challenges revolves around establishing gender as a motivation for violence. Recent calls to take gender seriously in political analysis propose that a robust and scientific approach requires studying men and women together. One reason is that doing so recognizes that men also have a gender and like women, may experience the world in highly gendered ways (Bjarnegård 2018). Some male politicians, indeed, have been targeted for gender-based attacks. Harvey Milk, the first openly gay man to hold public office in the United States, was assassinated in 1978 by an anti-gay colleague. In Malaysia, opposition leader Anwar Ibrahim was put on trial for sodomy in an effort to destroy his reputation (Abbott 2001). Another reason, according to scholars who endorse this perspective, is that directly comparing men and women is the only way to ascertain gender differences (Bardall, Bjarnegård, and Piscopo 2019). A review by IFES of its electoral violence data finds, for example, that men experience physical violence while women are more likely to face psychological violence (Bardall 2011).

Emphasizing that gender-based political violence also occurs to men, however, risks falling down a slippery slope into theorizing a false symmetry between men's and women's experiences. Normative associations between men and the public sphere mean that men do not face challenges to their presence in politics *as men*. In the two cases just described, Milk and Ibrahim were not targeted in an attempt to exclude all men from political office; cultural tropes were mobilized, rather, to argue that they were not "real men." In contrast, women potentially face two forms of violence in the political sphere: violence in politics, which is issue-based, and violence against women in politics, which is identity-based. Consequently, women may face attacks that are politically motivated as well as those that are gender motivated—and, in some cases, experience both types of violence simultaneously or sequentially.

Gendered comparisons, therefore, can assist in analyzing a subset—but not the full range—of dynamics in focus here. Comparative studies, notably, can provide insight into gendered patterns in the content and prevalence of violence in politics. This might include illuminating the gendered scripts, like rape, which are activated to intimidate women for political reasons. This approach can also reveal whether men or women are equally or differentially targeted for political violence. This could nuance observations like one made in a recent study of mafia assassinations of Italian mayors (Daniele 2019), observing that all victims were male—and, in turn, implying that men were particularly vulnerable to political murder. This disparity more likely stemmed, however, from the fact that women were severely under-represented in these positions, making maleness per se a less-than-decisive factor in instigating this violence.

Juxtaposing men's and women's experiences, in contrast, provides no leverage for understanding violence against women in politics—a problem uniquely faced by women in the political realm. Politicians, at least in some contexts, appear to grasp this difference. During parliamentary debates on abuse and intimidation in public life in 2017, British MP Martin Whitfield—together with several other male MPs—explicitly rejected notions of equivalence. While he had faced political abuse of his own, he stated: "I fully accept that my experience . . . is but a mere toe in the water compared with the vile abuse received by other . . . Members, especially women."[4] Dogmatic insistence on gendered comparisons thus may not advance knowledge, but instead produce potentially confused and misleading results.

Intersectionality

The emphasis on violence against *women* in politics, finally, seems to suggest that gender is the only source of abuse. Yet patriarchy is inextricably embedded in other forms of hierarchy and domination (Hunnicutt 2009), amplifying mistreatment of women who are also members of other socially and politically marginalized groups. Feminists use the term intersectionality to describe these dynamics, theorizing how different facets of identity—including race, ethnicity, class, or sexuality—interact to shape life opportunities and experiences (McCall 2005). These effects are multiplicative, not additive, and thus other dimensions of exclusion cannot simply be subtracted to identify or focus on the gender dimension alone (Hancock 2007).

While the concept of intersectionality has not yet been incorporated widely into theorizing about violence against women in politics (Kuperberg 2018), emerging data on this phenomenon points to the importance of other axes of inequality in determining the types of women who may be particularly targeted. An analysis of Twitter abuse against female MPs in the UK, for example, finds that nearly half of the abusive tweets identified in the sample were directed at Diane Abbott, the first black woman to be elected to the British parliament. When Abbott was taken out of the sample, black and Asian women still received 30% more abusive tweets than their white counterparts (Dhrodia 2017).

These interactions are not limited to gender and race. Survey respondents in India, Nepal, and Pakistan identified female candidates who were poor (60–73%), lower caste (52–68%), or under the age of 30 (55–63%) as the most vulnerable to violence (Centre for Social Research and UN Women 2014, 65). The IPU (2018) similarly finds that female MPs under 40 were more likely than older MPs to experience psychological and sexual violence. Qualitative interviews, as well as news coverage, point further to anti-Semitism, Islamophobia, and homophobia as additional forms of inequality driving attacks against politically active women.[5]

The intersectional nature of this violence, however, does not undermine bias against women as a key driver. Rather, it substantiates the intuition that structural, cultural, and symbolic violence—against women and members of other marginalized groups—lie at the heart of this phenomenon. Because the election of women from non-dominant groups challenges multiple forms of inequality, their political presence may spark an even stronger reaction than the election of women from dominant groups (Sanbonmatsu 2008). Centering these three forms of violence also explains why women who challenge gender roles in multiple ways—by being outspoken feminists[6] or ascending to leadership positions—also appear to be targeted for more numerous and more vitriolic attacks (Davies 2014; IPU 2018; Rheault, Rayment, and Musulan 2019).

## A Bias Event Approach

Concerns about under-reporting, gendered comparisons, and intersectionality suggest that it may be impossible to study—and know the full extent of—violence against women in politics. Further, bias against particular groups is often highly naturalized as a result of the deep roots of structural, cultural, and symbolic violence in everyday habits, expectations, and interactions. As a result, perpetrators may not be consciously aware of their prejudice, and targets may accept mistreatment as simply the normal course of affairs.

Work on hate crimes, however, offers a way forward, as it explicitly seeks to develop tools to ascertain whether bias against particular groups was a motivating factor behind a given crime. Nevertheless, emphasizing only unlawful behaviors is limited, given that not all acts of violence against women in politics constitute crimes. Additionally, as national criminal statutes vary considerably, restricting the focus only to unlawful activities would result in the same act being deemed a case of violence against women in politics in one country, but not in another. Consequently, this book adapts insights from this literature to present an approach centered on "bias events," actions of both a criminal and non-criminal nature driven by bias against women in political roles, drawing and building on existing legal guidance for identifying hate crimes.

## FROM HATE CRIMES TO BIAS EVENTS

The concept of hate crimes offers guidance for thinking in more concrete terms about the origins, means, and effects of violence against women in politics. While people have long been selected as targets of violence due to perceived group membership, in recent decades a growing number of countries have enhanced the criminal penalties for illegal acts motivated by group-based discrimination (Hodge 2011). Because they are group-based, these actions cannot simply be explained away as the actions of "mean-spirited bigots" against a specific individual. Rather, hate crimes target the group as a whole, using "intimidation and control . . . against those who seem to have stepped outside the boxes that society has carefully constructed for them . . . to reaffirm the precarious hierarchies that characterize a given social order" (Perry 2001, 2, 10).

Hate crimes thus send a message about the inferiority of the targeted group to members of the group as well as to society at large (Kauppinen 2015). They also communicate to group members that, because the crime was group- and not individual-based, they could have easily been victims themselves. Corroborating these vicarious effects, Perry and Alvi (2011) find that members of the affected group often experience shock, anger, and fear following hate incidents, prompting them to change their daily behaviors despite not being directly victimized. Although some critics argue that hate crime legislation punishes "improper thinking," violating free speech (Jacobs and Potter 1997), these "message crimes" seek to deny equal rights to group members—including their opportunities to exercise their own free speech (Iganski 2001; Mantilla 2015).

Hate crime laws often list a variety of categories of bias, including race, color, national origin, and religion. Other characteristics appear less frequently, like gender, sexual orientation, gender identity, age, and disability (Hodge 2011). Various reasons explain why gender was excluded at the outset and even today, is less recognized than other forms of identity in hate crime legislation.

One relates to structural and cultural violence naturalizing the mistreatment of women, viewing violence against women in a different, and often less serious, light (McPhail 2002). Some argue, indeed, that violence against women is so pervasive that prosecuting it would overwhelm the court system and make gathering statistics too cumbersome (Hodge 2011). A second justification points to laws on violence against women, asserting on this basis that incorporating gender into hate crimes statutes is unnecessary (Walters and Tumath 2014).

Perhaps the greatest challenge, however, relates to the word "hate." Early work defined "hate" as a form of "animus" expressed toward members of particular groups. Yet perpetrators of violence against women rarely, in fact, hate *all* women (Gerstenfeld 2004). In addition, as work on femicide observes, many emotions fuel gender-based violence, including "hatred, contempt, pleasure, or a sense of ownership of women" (Caputi and Russell 1992, 15). These conceptual difficulties have given way to a complementary "discriminatory selection" model of hate crimes, highlighting that "it is irrelevant *why* an offender selected his victim on the basis of race or group; it is sufficient that the offender did so" (Lawrence 1999, 30).

Following this logic, Weisburd and Levin (1994) advocate using the term "bias crime," arguing that it more accurately captures the discriminatory, group-based, hierarchical component driving these crimes. In these civil rights violations, they argue, the hateful intent of the perpetrator is less important than the discriminatory use of violence against those who are seen as "transgressors" against their "proper role" in society (36). While offenders gain "personal validation and a sense of power and domination . . . from brutalizing those they perceive as worthy of degradation," the attack is ultimately group-based, "stripping [victims] of their individual identities and treating them as a stereotype, a projected image of the attackers' prejudice" (25). As such, individual cases of bias-motivated violence can infringe upon the civil rights of an entire group.

In the case of violence against women in politics, however, retaining a focus on "crimes" is also too limited. One way to resolve this dilemma is to include "hate incidents," which police in England and Wales define as "any non-crime perceived by the victim or any other person, as being motivated by prejudice or hate" (Ask the Police 2018). Putting these elements together, this book proposes "bias events" as an umbrella concept encompassing both criminal and non-criminal forms of violence against women in politics.

This approach has several advantages over existing hate crimes frameworks. First, it avoids unduly restricting the focus to criminal behaviors, recognizing that legal standards vary across countries, as does state capacity to enforce laws. Second, it decenters the state and the police as the only actors involved in making judgments about bias events, opening the way for political parties, civil society, and international organizations, among other actors, to identify and take steps to tackle violence against women in politics. Third, a bias event approach displaces a focus on perpetrator intentions—which can be misunderstood or denied—to give voice to the perspectives and experiences of victims and society at large.

## CRITERIA FOR DETECTING GROUP BIAS

Passage of hate crime legislation raises questions about how to determine whether bias played a role in motivating a particular crime. Offering guidance to local law enforcement, the U.S. Federal Bureau of Investigation (FBI) notes that it is difficult to ascertain an offender's subjective motivation. As such, it counsels that a crime should be deemed to be driven by bias "only if investigation reveals sufficient objective facts to lead a reasonable and prudent person to conclude that the offender's actions were motivated, in whole or in part, by bias" (FBI 2015, 4). To this end, it lists potential sources of evidence that might be collected and analyzed to make these determinations. Reaching a finding of bias does not require that all categories of evidence be satisfied, but rather, that investigators consider the body of evidence as a whole to weigh whether, on balance, bias played a role in motivating the crime. Group-based bias need not be the sole motivation, but simply a substantial factor in victimization (Weisburd and Levin 1994).

Five of these criteria are relevant for establishing the presence of bias against women in political roles.[7] First, *the offender made oral comments, written statements, or gestures indicating bias.* In some cases, this message may be direct. When campaigning for parliament in 2005, for example, Afghan MP Fatima Aziz reported: "I received a night letter [a letter left at her home late at night] that said if you love your life and your children you must remove yourself from politics, it is not right for you, you are a woman" (Human Rights Watch 2009, 27). Other instances might entail using sexist or sexualized language and body language—in-person, in print, or online—objectifying or otherwise denigrating women. As the share of women in the British parliament grew in the late 1990s, men in the Conservative Party reportedly used gestures to ridicule and intimidate their female colleagues, including—in the words of one female MP—"put[ting] their hands out in front of them, as if they were weighing up melons" (Puwar 2004, 87).

Second, *the offender left bias-related drawings, symbols, or graffiti at the scene.* In these cases, perpetrators might post degrading images of politically active women, or paint sexist insults on campaign posters, homes, or offices. Speaking at an event on online harassment in 2016, for instance, former Texas state senator Wendy Davis shared that she decided to delete social media from her phone after digitally altered pictures of her in sexual positions began to flood her Twitter and Facebook streams (Bowles 2016).

Third, *the victim was engaged in activities related to his or her identity group.* Political women in this scenario might be outspoken feminists, but they may also simply have sought to speak up for women. One prominent feminist politician, British MP Jess Phillips, has written extensively about the abuse she faces, particularly online, after seeking to advance feminist issues in parliament. In a recent book, she writes: "Every day I receive threats. They range from death and rape to warnings of unemployment. Plots to deselect me and others like me from our seats in the House of Commons are the most common" (Phillips 2017, 7). Drawing a direct line to her feminist activism, she attributes these threats to "a perceived imbalance in the established power structure . . . . A woman with power is intolerable to them" (8, 213).

Fourth, *the offender was previously involved in a similar incident or is a hate group member*. In this context, the perpetrator might have harassed other politically active women, or might participate in men's rights networks or other groups seeking to defend patriarchy. Members of two far-right political parties in Italy, the Five Star Movement and the Northern League, have been relentless in targeting Laura Boldrini, a feminist MP who served as president of the Italian Chamber of Deputies, and Cécile Kyenge, the first black cabinet minister who had immigrated from the Democratic Republic of Congo to Italy in 1983. In 2019, Kyenge won a defamation suit against Northern League leader Roberto Calderoli, who compared her to an orangutan during a 2013 party rally; in 2017, another League politician, Mario Borghezio, was ordered to pay a fine of 50,000 euros for making other racist remarks against her (Giuffrida 2019).

Fifth, *a substantial portion of the community where the event occurred perceived that the incident was motivated by bias*.[8] Evidence for this might include speeches, opinion pieces, or demonstrations—especially by other women—which explicitly attribute the attack to a woman's gender. Following the death of British MP Jo Cox in 2016, female MPs were quick to view her murder through a gender lens. Diane Abbott stated: "It is hard to escape the conclusion that the vitriolic misogyny that so many women politicians endure framed the murderous attack on Jo" (Hughes, Riley-Smith, and Swinford 2016). Publishing numerous editorials in the ensuing months, Jess Phillips wrote that "for me and for many of my colleagues—particularly female MPs—fear has also become real and present" (Phillips 2016b). These perceptions were echoed by male politicians. Calling for these threats to be taken more seriously, MP Chris Bryant remarked: "I think women MPs, gay MPs, ethnic minority MPs get the brunt of it" (Mason 2016).

Not all acts of bias are so transparent, however. In cases of unconscious bias, people believe they are not prejudiced—but nonetheless think or act in biased ways. Unconscious bias may take the form of microaggressions: everyday indignities that, while often unintentional, may communicate hostile, derogatory, or negative views toward members of certain groups (Sue 2010). In other cases, people may seek to mask prejudiced views by claiming other forms of wrongdoing on the part of the target. One example is "judicial harassment," whereby individuals are targeted with baseless legal charges that divert time, energy, and resources away from their work (Frontline Defenders 2018). To detect these forms of bias, this book adds a sixth and final criterion: *the victim was evaluated negatively according a double standard.*

In the context of violence against women in politics, these double standards might entail attacking politically active women in ways and for reasons not used against men who are politically engaged. Drawing on the concept of "aversive racism," whereby people who explicitly espouse egalitarian principles may also unconsciously harbor negative feelings and attitudes about blacks, Price (2016) theorizes that "aversive sexism" may help explain at least some negative and visceral reactions to Hillary Clinton's presidential campaign. According to her, one scenario fitting this pattern is "holding things against Hillary Clinton for which you have forgiven other politicians, particularly men."

An example she gives is rabid critiques of Hillary's verbal support for Bill Clinton's racially targeted crime bill in the 1990s—a bill not only signed by Bill, but also voted into law by her 2016 primary opponent, Bernie Sanders, and many members of the Congressional Black Caucus. Thus, while the men directly responsible for the law are permitted to move beyond this negative legacy, Hillary Clinton remains tarnished. To avoid aversive sexism, Price recommends asking: "Am I judging this woman candidate in ways that no candidate could ever measure up?" Being more aware of such dynamics, she suggests, will enable female candidates to be judged fairly, rather than based on "ingrained and implicit gender biases."

Applying these six criteria involves placing particular acts in their broader context, using information about their content, targets, perpetrators, and impact. A bias event approach thus reserves judgment until further investigation, rather than assuming that every aggression against a politically active woman does—or does not—stem from bias. While some cases will be straightforward, many will be ambiguous, with potentially conflicting or competing sources of information. Like the FBI framework, however, this approach does not require that all six criteria be met in full: instead, it draws holistically on these six criteria for guidance to consider whether, on balance, the available data would support a finding of bias against women in political roles.

This approach goes far in resolving the three methodological challenges listed earlier. First, conducting the analysis does not call for the perpetrator or victim recognize the act as an instance of violence against women in politics. Second, this approach is case-centered and thus does not require comparisons with other populations to establish that sexism and misogyny played a role.

Third, attention to bias as a larger category enables intersectional experiences to be taken into account, whether this involves acts that are simultaneously sexist and homophobic, for example, or a collection of events that are individually sexist and racist. In so doing, a bias event approach also presents a framework for ascertaining bias against members of other marginalized identity groups. By emphasizing the need for investigation, finally, this approach opens up the possibility that some incidents against politically active women may *not* be attributable to bias.

# 11

# A Continuum of Violence

Research on political and electoral violence focuses on acts of physical violence, defined as attacks on people as well as property (Della Porta 1995; Norris, Frank, and Martínez i Coma 2015). Work on violence against women, in contrast, highlights a broad spectrum of violent behaviors, using the concept of a "continuum" to connect diverse manifestations of aggression against women (Kelly 1988). Addressing these divergent emphases—including the consequences of adopting different definitions of "violence"—is necessary for developing a shared vocabulary on violence against women in politics and, in turn, generating a typology of its various forms.

## Defining "Violence"

The problem of violence is a central concern across the social sciences, but despite being "cardinal to a proper understanding of political life," as a concept it "remains elusive and often misunderstood" (Bufacchi 2005, 199). Some scholars, indeed, deem it "essentially contested," or "notoriously difficult to define because as a phenomenon it is multifaceted, socially constructed, and highly ambivalent" (De Haan 2008, 28). According to Bufacchi (2005), these ambiguities stem from a conflation of the Latin roots for "violence" (*violentia* = vehemence, a passionate and uncontrollable force) and "violation" (*violare* = infringement). Further, most attempts to define "violence" share two assumptions: violence is motivated by hostility and a willful intent to cause harm, and violence is—legally, socially, or morally—deviant human activity (De Haan 2008).

Capturing variations in the "evaluative character" and "emotive meaning" of the concept (De Haan 2008, 36), Bufacchi identifies two approaches. A minimalist conception of violence as *force* focuses on the deliberate infliction of physical injury, highlighting the intentions of agents committing acts of

*Violence against Women in Politics.* Mona Lena Krook, Oxford University Press (2020). © Oxford University Press.
DOI: 10.1093/oso/9780190088460.001.0001.

violence at single moments in time. In contrast, a more comprehensive view of violence as *violation* recognizes a wider range of transgressions, privileging the experiences of victims and the "ripples of violence" affecting survivors, their families, and their communities over time (Bufacchi 2005; Bufacchi and Gilson 2016). Nagengast (1994) develops a related contrast between reifying violence as a category that is either present or absent within a society and theorizing it as a set of practices, discourses, and ideologies involving the exercise of power.

Choosing between these definitions is not a trivial matter. For De Haan (2008), drawing lines around what counts—and does not count—as an instance of violence has "significant normative import because the definitional debate is, in effect, a debate over which borderline cases ought to be subjected to the same sort of negative appraisal as the paradigms" (36). Opting for one conceptualization over another also raises tangible practical concerns regarding how data on violence is collected. It affects, in turn, the quantity and quality of services provided to victims—whose needs may or may not be met, depending on the range of acts recognized as meeting the threshold of "violence" (DeKeseredy 2011).

## MINIMALIST DEFINITIONS

Reviewing approaches taken in a variety of disciplines—measuring politically motivated violence, economically motivated violence, socially conditioned violence, and interpersonal violence—Krause (2009) observes that most scholars select narrow definitions centered on the purposeful or threatened use of physical force to cause death or bodily injury. Coady (1986, 4) prefers a focus on the infliction of physical harm because, he claims, it reflects the "normal or ordinary understanding of 'violence.'" Collecting data on physical violence also permits cross-national comparisons, some scholars suggest, because the meaning of physical acts is universally recognized. In contrast, other forms are more contested, as they may be socially sanctioned, legitimized, and institutionalized (De Haan 2008; Krause 2009).

This perspective places strong emphasis on intentionality, arguing that to be classified as "violent," an act must not only be physically destructive, but must also be done deliberately by the agent and be unwanted on the part of the target (Bufacchi 2005). Psychological violence can be included in this definition, according to Coady (1986), only to the extent that it has "overpowering effects" and could be viewed as involving the application of force (16). Seeking to forge a compromise, Saltzman (2004) lists five forms of maltreatment against women: physical violence, sexual violence, threats of physical and/or sexual violence, stalking, and psychological/emotional abuse. She suggests that the phrase "violence and abuse against women" be used as a collective term for these five elements, with "violence against women" being applied more restrictively to refer to the first three components only.

## COMPREHENSIVE DEFINITIONS

While minimalist conceptions help delineate clear boundaries around what constitutes an act of violence, other scholars argue that limiting the focus to intentional physical acts ignores other important dimensions of violence and trivializes the experiences of many victims (Bufacchi 2005; DeKeseredy 2011). Garver (2009 [1968]) observes that violence cannot simply be equated with the use of force, because "whenever you do something to another person's body without his consent you are attacking not just a physical entity—you are attacking a person" (174). Psychological violence, in his view, is often more injurious than physical violence—and takes longer to heal—because it violates a person's autonomy, dignity, self-determination, and value as a human being.

Bufacchi (2004) develops this account by drawing on Rawls (1971), who proposes that the most important "primary good" is self-respect, consisting of a sense of one's own value and confidence in one's abilities. The reason why violence is "bad," from this perspective, is because it is "degrading, more so than death. It destroys a person's self-confidence, it diminishes the sense of a person as a person, and it deprives a person of their self-esteem" (Bufacchi 2004, 175). "Violation of integrity," in the sense of the wholeness or intactness of the self, "is the essence of an act of violence, not the injury, suffering, or harm" (Bufacchi 2007, 43). Thus, while an attack on a person's self-respect "may be more difficult to perceive than an assault of a more physical nature," Bufacchi (2004, 175) argues, "it is not less real."

Adopting a more comprehensive approach to understanding violence problematizes the importance of intentionality, centers the experiences of survivors, and expands its temporal and personal effects. As discussed in chapter 9, structural, cultural, and symbolic violence serve to normalize the exclusion and mistreatment of women, both promoting and legitimizing gender inequality. Given this context, perpetrators are often not even aware of the inappropriateness of their actions. Focusing on the dynamics of sexual harassment, for example, Bargh and Raymond (1995) note that alleged harassers often acknowledge the behaviors attributed to them, but rarely ascribe them the same meaning or importance. Denying that they intended to cause distress, men who are accused of harassment instead assign their actions more acceptable motives, like paying the woman a compliment. Cognitive processes linking power and sex, they theorize, explain why some men "just don't get it" and assume erroneously—and perniciously—that the women they harass are in fact attracted to them (87).

Bing and Lombardo (1997) address the implications, in turn, of adopting an "initiator frame" rather than a "victim frame" in discussions of sexual harassment. An initiator frame, they propose, tends to privilege the viewpoint of the alleged harasser and shift the responsibility to the recipient. It does so by emphasizing admirable qualities of the harasser and impugning the motives of the accuser or explaining away the incident as a misunderstanding. A victim frame, in contrast, considers the harm done to the target of harassment, regardless of whether a specific legal threshold has been met. The intentions of the harasser—whether conscious or unconscious—are irrelevant to determining the degree of harm. Because victim frames have rarely been applied to legal discussions of sexual violence, however, laws typically reflect and construct very limited definitions, minimizing what targets experience as abusive—and reinforcing perceptions that violence only involves actions resulting in bodily harm (Kelly and Radford 1990).

Adopting the perspective of survivors, in contrast, alters and expands conceptualizations of violence against women. From a series of focus groups with battered women, Smith, Smith, and Earp (1999) find that—distinct from measures focused on discrete events of male behavior—women experienced battering as enduring, traumatic, and multidimensional. As a result, women do not approach partner assault as episodic—but instead view it as an ongoing threat requiring active and continuous coping strategies. Research in social psychology has made a similar shift, noting that most theorizing on prejudice analyzes people holding prejudiced beliefs. Studying the target's perspective, however, permits closer examination of how they perceive they have encountered discrimination, how it influences their feelings and behaviors, and how they act to minimize the impact of prejudice on their lives (Swim and Stangor 1998).

Focusing on experiences of violence, in turn, challenges the notion that acts of violence have discrete temporal and personal boundaries. This experience can encompass what a person feels before, during, and after a violent act, all of which can make targets feel vulnerable and inferior to perpetrators, undermining their sense of self-respect and self-esteem (Bufacchi 2007). Indeed, the traces of a violent act may never fully disappear, with lingering "ripples of violence" affecting survivors, their families, and their communities for years to come (Bufacchi and Gilson 2016, 34). Violations of personal integrity are thus not necessarily limited to individuals either, creating broader human rights challenges within the framework of structural inequalities.

### Violence as a Continuum

Adopting a comprehensive perspective on "violence," feminists have developed a series of analogies to facilitate the recognition of different forms of violence, connecting these diverse manifestations as well as highlighting their interactive effects. In academic research, the most well-known formulation is Kelly's (1988) concept of a "continuum of violence," a term she uses to denote the common character, as well as sometimes indistinguishable nature, of different types of violent events. Feminist activists have developed two main visual representations of this idea: the iceberg, depicting sexual coercion as the "tip" with a broad range of other violent behaviors hidden below the water line; and the power and control wheel, portraying violent behaviors as the spokes of a wheel connecting power and control to acts of physical and sexual violence. Collectively, these models theorize a spectrum of violent acts that not only shade into each another but also inform and reinforce one another.

## LINKED DIMENSIONS

In early work, Stanko (1985) criticizes tendencies to view violence and intimidation against women as separate phenomena, with incidents affecting only individual women. Doing so, she argues, treats "each assault as an aberration or a random occurrence—a 'personal' problem." She highlights the need instead to "link them together" to expose a "flood of common experiences" that are neither "random" nor "isolated" (18). Kelly (1988) proposes thinking about these connections in terms of a "continuum," inspired by women she interviewed who defined a wide range of behaviors as "sexual violence," some reflected neither in legal codes nor in analytical categories used in prior research. The eleven forms emerging in her study comprised threats of violence, sexual harassment, pressure to have sex, sexual assault, obscene phone calls, coercive sex, domestic violence, sexual abuse, flashing, rape, and incest. While linking these acts, Kelly refuses to rank them, arguing that with the exception of violence resulting in death, the "degree of impact cannot be simplistically inferred from the form of sexual violence women experience." Rather, all forms of violence are serious, making it "inappropriate to create a hierarchy of abuse within a feminist analysis" (76).

The limits of legal frameworks in recognizing a spectrum of violence became especially obvious during the #MeToo movement. As Wexler, Robbennolt, and Murphy (2019) note, women use the #MeToo hashtag to testify to a wide range of acts, including "workplace behavior that would not violate criminal or civil laws, workplace conduct that was abusive but not sexual or sexist in nature, and sexually violative or sexist behavior in nonworkplace settings" (5). While legal interpretations have evolved over time in the United States to recognize both quid pro quo and hostile work environment forms of sexual harassment, many instances are deemed "merely offensive" rather than "pervasive" or "severe," the legal threshold required to pursue a claim in court (White 2018). U.S. Senator Kirsten Gillibrand captured limitations in legal definitions when responding to criticisms against her for calling on Senator Al Franken to resign his seat due to allegations of sexual harassment. Consistent with the idea of a continuum of violence, she stated: "I think when we start having to talk about the differences between sexual assault and sexual harassment and unwanted groping, you are having the wrong conversation. You need to draw a line in the sand and say none of it is OK. None of it is acceptable" (Prakash 2017).

Other research challenges the notion that physical attacks are "worse" than other forms of violence. In an early study, 72% of respondents reported that psychological abuse had a more severe impact on them that physical abuse (Follingstad et al. 1990, 114). This is because, while physical wounds may heal, psychological violence can damage victims' self-respect and their ability to relate to others, affecting every aspect of their lives (DeKeseredy 2011). Work on torture corroborates this view, noting that physical pain is not the most important determinant of traumatic stress in survivors: psychological and sexual acts are associated with at least as much as if not more distress (Başoğlu, Livanou, and Crnobarić 2007).

Recent work on online abuse seeks to further expand this spectrum. Online abuse can take numerous forms, including flaming and trolling, harassment, physical threats, sexual harassment, inciting others to abuse, sexual threats, defamation, stalking, electronic sabotage, and impersonation. Powell and Henry (2017) argue that "harms facilitated through digital means"—including online bullying, abuse, and harassment—are "in fact embodied, tangible, and real" (50). Because digital technologies play a growing role in how people work, learn, play, and communicate, the distinction between "online" and "offline" behavior is increasingly blurred, such that "virtual" abuse can have direct and devastating "real world" implications. Although online abuse can range from episodic and unpleasant to more frequent, threatening, and hateful, Lewis, Rowe, and Wiper (2017)—like prior scholars—caution against creating "scales of severity," as experiences of abuse can be "extremely subjective," with even seemingly mundane exchanges being experienced as harmful (1470).

An analogy that feminist activists have used to capture the linked nature of these various acts is through the image of an iceberg.[1] An example focused on sexual harassment places sexual coercion at the tip, as behaviors like promising professional rewards for sexual favors—and, the converse, threatening professional consequences if sexual demands are unmet—would be clearly recognized and condemned by many people as sexual harassment. Incidents of unwanted sexual attention, like rape, sexual assault, and groping, are just below the tip, with many people viewing them as cases of sexual harassment—but not all, often due to victim-blaming. Acts below the water line of public consciousness may entail gender harassment, including relentless pressures for sex or dates, sexual teasing and insults, vulgar name calling and offensive comments about bodies, and sabotage of women's equipment or advancement in their careers. While diverse, these acts—as sections of the iceberg—form part of the same field of behaviors, constituting the broader phenomenon of sexual harassment.

MUTUAL INTERACTIONS

A second dimension of the continuum of violence relates to the collective impact of diverse forms of violence, highlighting how they overlap, intersect, and sometimes substitute for one another as part of a shared architecture supporting women's domination. Criticizing legal approaches adopting an "incident-specific and injury-based definition of violence," Stark (2007) argues that physical abuse against intimate partners often intertwines with three psychological tactics: intimidation, isolation, and control. In these cases of "coercive control," violence is "ongoing rather than episodic" and "cumulative rather than incident-specific" (10, 12). Sue (2010) offers a similar reflection, noting that "any one microaggression alone many be minimally impactful, but when they occur continuously throughout a lifespan, their cumulative nature can have major detrimental consequences" (7). Positioning some acts as individually more harmful than others, therefore, "risks losing how the quieter forms of intrusion . . . rely on the possibilities and realities of the louder, criminal forms, to have the particular impact they do" (Vera-Gray 2017, 21). Indeed, as Henley (1977) points out, physical force is often a "last-ditch" option (189), with more subtle and invisible forms of violence often preferred by perpetrators in the first instance.

These synergies are evident in empirical research on violence against women. Some work observes, for instance, that some acts have multiple effects, cutting across different categories of violence. As DeKeseredy (2011) writes: "it is very hard for anyone to be beaten up physically and not to be simultaneously emotionally battered" (15). Conversely, Coker, Smith, Bethea, King, and McKeown (2000) find that women experiencing psychological intimate partner violence report poor mental as well as physical health, including suffering from chronic pain, ulcers, migraines, and indigestion. Studying online violence, Jane (2018) describes the professional consequences of psychological harassment as a form of "economic vandalism," affecting women's productivity, work opportunities, and work relationships—and thus their economic livelihoods. These problems, in turn, can exacerbate levels of psychological and economic stress, because "the internet is not a discrete workplace that a woman can leave in the way she might be able to leave a factory in which she experiences offline abuse or harassment" (587).

Encapsulating these ideas, the power and control wheel was first developed by staff at a domestic violence shelter in the 1980s as a tool for describing battering for victims, offenders, members of the criminal justice system, and the general public. Convening focus groups with battered women over the course of several months, they identified a range of common abusive behaviors experienced by these women. Using the analogy of a wheel, they placed power and control at the center, with threats, intimidation, and coercion forming the spokes, which are held together by a rim consisting of physical and sexual violence.[2] Modeling violence against women in this way demonstrates how diverse manifestations of violence operate as a system, with—for example—physical and sexual violence being informed by, as well as magnifying, emotional and economic abuse in the service of dominating and controlling women.

## A Typology of Violence

The feminist concept of a continuum of violence points to the need—when developing a typology of violence against women in politics—to consider a spectrum of acts seeking to deter and undermine women's political participation. In its guidelines for statistics on violence against women, the UN Department of Economic and Social Affairs (2014) recommends collecting data on four types: physical, psychological, sexual, and economic violence. The first three appear in Article 2 of the 1993 UN Declaration on the Elimination of Violence against Women, while the fourth is added in Article 3 of the Council of Europe's 2011 Istanbul Convention and CEDAW General Recommendation No. 35 in 2017. World Bank (2016) data from 189 countries indicate that all four categories of violence appear in national legislation on violence against women, albeit with varying degrees of recognition: physical violence is criminalized in 137 countries, psychological violence in 134, sexual violence in 106, and economic violence in 86. Based on inductive insights, this book adds a fifth type—semiotic—not reducible to these four categories.

Physical violence entails bodily harm and injury, but may also include various forms of unwelcome physical contact, as well as involuntary physical confinement. Psychological violence inflicts trauma on a person's mental state or emotional well-being, for example by sending death or rape threats or otherwise insulting, taunting, or scaring the target. Sexual violence involves sexual acts and attempts at sexual acts by coercion, as well as unwelcome sexual comments or advances. Economic violence comprises behaviors aimed at denying, restricting, or controlling women's access to financial resources. Semiotic violence, finally, mobilizes sexist and degrading words and images to injure, discipline, and subjugate women. Distinct from the other types, it focuses on influencing how the public views politically active women as a group.

In line with the notion of a continuum, analytically distinguishing these five types does not necessarily mean that they are clearly distinct in practice. Sexual assault, for example, may have both physical and psychological components. Similarly, when distributed to a larger public, digitally altered images sexualizing a female politician constitute semiotic violence; when sent to the woman in question, they entail psychological and sexual violence. These overlaps, however, do not undermine the notion of different categories of violence. Instead, they bolster the case for thinking about these acts as part of a shared field of practices, where specific incidents may shade into several types of violence at the same time.

Politically active women may also experience multiple forms of violence over the course of their political engagement. Juana Quispe, a local councilor in Bolivia, faced a combination of physical, psychological, and economic violence in the two years that she held office. Almost immediately after winning her seat in 2010, Quispe faced relentless physical and verbal abuse from colleagues who, together with the mayor, pressured her to resign. When she did not, they changed meeting times and refused her entrance to the sessions. After a group of peasants took over the local council hall to demand her resignation, the council president and vice-president suspended her.

Because Quispe had been duly elected by popular vote, they justified their decision by falsely accusing her of corruption. She subsequently undertook a seven-month legal battle, which resulted in her being reinstated to her position on the local council. The mayor, however, denied her the salary she was owed for those seven months, arguing that she had not attended sessions. One month later, in 2012, Quispe was found murdered, showing signs of strangulation. Although the crime still remains officially unsolved, and local police insist she was killed in a robbery, Quispe's death was viewed as a symptom of hostility toward women's political engagement—and, as such, served as a final catalyst for passage of the Bolivian law criminalizing political violence and harassment against women ("Acoso Político" 2012; Corz 2012).

While acknowledging these overlaps and interactions, the next five chapters take up these various forms of violence in turn, drawing on a global dataset of news items, practitioner reports, autobiographies, and original interviews. Each chapter provides an overview of what each form of violence looks like in practice, selecting examples that collectively address various dynamics at work in different parts of the world. Although women's testimonies tend to be anonymized in existing research, the book focuses wherever possible on cases where politically active women have spoken openly about their experiences, or the events affecting them have been covered extensively in the media, to ensure that these cases conform to the criteria set out in chapter 10 for identifying an instance of violence against women in politics.[3] As a result of this approach, most examples center on the experiences of female politicians. Whenever possible, however, the discussion extends to other categories of politically active women, including voters, activists, and journalists. Due to the inductive nature of this investigation, the sub-typologies in each chapter are intended to be not exhaustive but illustrative, offering a sense of the wide range of potential manifestations of each form of violence—and, in turn, serving as a basis for theorizing and elaborating additional forms.

# PART III

# A Typology of Violence

12

# Physical Violence

Physical violence encompasses a wide range of bodily harms involving unwanted contact and confinement resulting in death or injury. Posing a threat to life and/or bodily integrity, forms include—but are not limited to—killing, beating, shoving, slapping, kicking, biting, choking, burning, and brandishing weapons, as well as kidnapping, displacing, "disappearing," and arbitrarily arresting and detaining targets (APWLD 2007; Barton and Storm 2014; Crowell and Burgess 1996; UN Department of Economic and Social Affairs 2014). The tangible nature of these acts makes them the most widely recognized and least contested forms of violence against women. They tend to be relatively rare, however, with offenders opting for "less costly" means of violence before escalating to physical attacks. While legal redress may be a solution for at least some forms of physical violence, politically active women have developed a number of grassroots strategies to respond to and anticipate physical violence. At the same time, individual women and state actors have devised new preventive security arrangements, seeking to avert or mitigate the effects of physical attacks.

## Manifestations of Physical Violence

Physical violence is generally less common than other acts of violence against women in politics. According to the IPU (2016b), of the female parliamentarians interviewed in their global study, 25.5% had personally experienced some form of physical violence in connection with their work as an MP, while 20% had witnessed an act of physical violence against a female colleague (3). In the IPU's (2018) follow-up report on violence in European parliaments, the prevalence of physical violence that women had personally experienced was slightly lower, but still notable at 14.8%—with 55% of these incidents occurring during political meetings and election campaigns (1, 7). Around the world, acts of

*Violence against Women in Politics.* Mona Lena Krook, Oxford University Press (2020). © Oxford University Press.
DOI: 10.1093/oso/9780190088460.001.0001.

bodily harm perpetrated against women in politics include murder, attempted murder, mutilation, beating, arbitrary arrest, and torture.

## MURDER

A number of politically active women have been killed in the course of their work. Some of these cases constitute examples of violence in politics, like the assassination of former Pakistani prime minister Benazir Bhutto in 2007. Others, however, appear to be linked to efforts to stifle their participation based on their ascriptive identities. The 2018 murder of Marielle Franco, a local councilor in Rio de Janeiro, is one recent case in point. Franco was black, lesbian, and grew up in a *favela* (a poor, neglected, and unregulated neighborhood in Brazil). Prior to being elected in 2016, she was—and continued to be—a strong activist for the rights of women, Afro-Brazilians, the LGBT community, and favela residents. Franco thus posed a threat to the political status quo as "an educated, articulate, and capable young woman from a favela: a far cry from the moneyed, middle-aged, white male politicians Brazilians are accustomed to, in a country where more than half the population is black or mixed-race" (Phillips 2018).

In March 2018, Franco and her driver, Anderson Gomes, were shot and killed in their car in a drive-by assassination after leaving a meeting focused on the empowerment of young black women in Brazil. Franco served as the head of the women's rights commission of the Rio local council, and the month prior, had been chosen as speaker of a new commission overseeing police and security forces in the city's favelas. Evidence at the scene suggested, early on, that these forces may have been involved: in addition to bullet casings pointing to ammunition purchased by the federal police in 2006 (King 2018), surveillance cameras at the nearby metro station had been switched off prior to the attack. The sophisticated and coordinated nature of the murder gave rise to speculation that the local military police unit may have been responsible, and one year later, police arrested two former military police officers (Ramalho 2019).

When making the arrests, a police statement acknowledged that it was "uncontestable" that Franco had been "summarily executed for her political activity in the defense of the causes she defended" (Langlois 2019). While she was heavily involved in the movement against militarized police brutality in the Rio favelas, these issues also very much encompassed her work on group-based rights. Her final public words at the meeting she left before being murdered were: "I am not free while any woman is a prisoner, even when her shackles are very different from my own" (Barber 2018). Following her assassination, protests took place around the world—including crowds of thousands in Rio—using the slogans *Marielle, Presente!* (Marielle is here) and *Não vão nos calar* (They are not going to shut us up), reflecting views of her as "a repository of hope for Brazil's traditionally voiceless and excluded groups: its favela residents, its black and poor people, and women" (Greenwald 2018). In January 2019, her close friend Jean Wyllys, the first and only openly gay Congressman, announced he was leaving politics and Brazil, having been under police escort since her murder (Barros 2019).

In addition to being an elected official, Franco was also a human rights defender, as recognized in statements put out following her death by Amnesty International and Human Rights Watch. While fatal violence against women human rights defenders is often linked to state actors, these are not the only potential perpetrators. A Nepalese activist, Laxmi Bohara, died in 2008 after being severely beaten by her husband and mother-in-law, who then forced her to ingest poison. According to witnesses, the two viewed her human rights work as incompatible with her domestic roles as a wife and mother. Frequently criticizing and harassing Bohara, they falsely accused her of "consorting with men" and threw her out of the house 10 days before her death. After she returned home, her daughter said her father beat Bohara all night, only taking her to the hospital after she was poisoned. When she died, her husband initially fled the area, but his cousin then performed the autopsy and claimed it was a suicide, clearing him of any wrongdoing. The national network of women human rights defenders took up the case, staging a 24-day relay hunger strike, rallies, and sit-ins. Many of these women, in turn, were threatened by members of Bohara's husband's family, who warned them they would be killed themselves if they continued to work on her case (Asoka 2012, 10–11).

ATTEMPTED MURDER

One of the best known cases of attempted murder is the shooting of teenage activist Malala Yousafzai by the Pakistani Taliban in 2012. Yousafzai first came to public attention at the age of 11 when writing under a pen name for BBC Urdu about her life and her family's fight for girls' education under the Taliban.[1] She eventually began speaking at events with her father to campaign for every girl's right to an education, generating both national and international attention. As her family had been running a school for girls for a long time, they were used to receiving threats—either published in newspapers or passed along directly as notes from various people.

In early 2012, however, the police showed her father a file detailing death threats made against her specifically. A journalist also informed Yousafzai that the Taliban had called for her and another female activist, Shad Begum, to be killed for spreading secularism. Like Yousafzai, Begum was involved in promoting women's education—prohibited under Taliban rule—as well as other political and health improvement projects aimed at women at the grassroots level. As a result of these threats, Yousafzai began taking a bus to school rather than walking as she had done before. This precaution failed in October 2012, however, when a man leaned into the bus and asked, "Who is Malala?" and then shot her at point-blank range. A bullet went into her left eye and other shots hit her classmates in their hands and arms. After being medically evacuated to the UK, Yousafzai eventually recovered from her wounds.

In a book she published the following year, Yousafzai wrote that she wanted to be known as the "girl who fought for education" and vowed that she would continue to campaign on behalf of "millions of girls around the world who are being denied the right to go to school and realize their potential" (Yousafzai with Lamb 2013, 327). At the UN Youth Assembly, on her sixteenth birthday, she highlighted the gendered motivations behind her attempted assassination, observing that "the power of the voice of women frightens" the Taliban. She stressed, therefore, that peace deals "must protect women's and children's rights" or were otherwise "unacceptable."[2] That same day, UN Secretary-General Ban Ki-moon declared that, in shooting Yousafzai, "extremists showed what they fear most—a girl with a book" (Johnston 2013).

## MUTILATION

Other examples of physical violence involve inflicting serious bodily injuries. Various sources in 2009 reported that members of the Taliban had cut off the fingers of several women who voted in the presidential elections in Afghanistan. According to an official at the Free and Fair Election Foundation, this occurred to two women in the southern province of Kandahar and possibly also a third woman in the eastern part of the country ("Monitors" 2009). In Afghanistan, voters' index fingers are dipped in ink as a measure to prevent election fraud— in this case, helping both election monitors as well as members of the Taliban identify who had voted. Reports from the 2014 elections indicate that these mutilations were not isolated events. The gender neutral nature of subsequent coverage makes it difficult to know the degree to which women in particular were targeted for this practice ("Afghan" 2014).

However, other information regarding the context of the 2009 Afghan elections suggests that, compared to men, female voters faced extensive and disproportionate intimidation intended to stifle their participation. To avoid public mingling between men and women, officials agreed to set up sex-segregated polling stations, although observers later reported that at least 650 of these did not open on election day. At many polling centers that did, few women cast votes, especially in the south and southeast parts of the country. In Kandahar, moreover, only three women ran for the four seats reserved for women on the provincial council (Gall 2009). Other potential candidates were likely dissuaded by the assassination of Sitara Achakzai, a provincial council member known for fighting for women's rights who had been murdered a few months earlier by gunmen in front of her home ("Female Afghan" 2009). The EU observer mission thus concluded that "poor security conditions, widespread cultural opposition to women in public life, and a number of attacks clearly aimed at deterring women's activities all created significant obstacles" to women's participation (Gall 2009).

## BEATING

Numerous women in Kenyan politics have faced physical assault during their campaigns or in the course of their work as members of elected assemblies.[3] In 2019, Rashid Kassim, a male MP, attacked Fatuma Gedi, a female MP, in the parliament parking lot after confronting her about why, as a member of the Budget and Appropriations Committee, she failed to allocate additional money to his constituency. He then called her "stupid" and a "liar" and punched her in the jaw and neck. After another female MP intervened, Gedi was taken to record a statement at the Parliament Police Station, leading to charges against Kassim (Karanja 2019). After a photo circulated on Twitter showed Gedi crying with blood on her mouth,[4] several male MPs began mocking their female colleagues, joking "it was slapping day" and "women needed to have manners" and "know how to treat men." Female MPs then staged a walkout, with one declaring: "We are all members of parliament . . . we are no lesser than them" ("Kenya MP" 2019).[5]

One of the most extensively covered attacks, however, occurred three months before the December 2007 elections. Flora Igoki Terah, a first time candidate for the small Kenya Africa Democratic Development Union party, decided to run for a seat in parliament after years of community organizing on issues like female genital mutilation, inheritance, and child marriage.[6] On a bus back to the city of Meru one evening, she was debating political issues with other passengers when she kept receiving phone calls from unidentified callers asking when she would get home. She did not find this unusual, assuming they were supporters who wanted to meet with her upon her arrival—a pattern that also occurred frequently during her years as a social worker.

Three men greeted her as she entered the long driveway to her mother's home. Punching her in the nose, they grabbed her neck and pushed her to the ground. Scratching her hands and arms with thorns from a nearby hedge, they tore out lumps of her hair and mixed it with feces and forced it into her mouth. When the neighbors' dogs starting barking, the leader of the group went to get his car and told one of the younger assailants to lift her, saying: "Hurry up, we are now going to take her to her father's grave and rape her." As the young man dragged her to the street, she recounted, he began "pleading with me to give up politics because nothing could be compared to my life" (Terah 2008, 101–102). Neighbors soon arrived to help, but the attackers blended into the crowd and slipped away.

In a subsequent interview, Terah attributed the assault to the incumbent MP, David Mwiraria, who at the time was also a cabinet minister. Prior to that night, she explained: "I was pressured many times to quit, harassed, and even told that I could be given better, more lucrative opportunities. The physical attack came when all that failed." She also later recognized one of her attackers as a senior police administrator, who was arrested but released on the same day that she identified him at the police station. When asked what she thought led to her attack, Terah said she thought she was targeted because "in Kenya, and especially in the Ameru community I belong to, women are not supposed to get leadership positions" (IPS Correspondents 2008).

Corroborating this intuition, the assault on Terah did not appear to be an isolated incident. A Nairobi-based NGO, the Education Centre for Women and Democracy, handled more than 250 complaints of electoral violence against women in the run up to the 2007 elections (IPS Correspondents 2008). The U.S. ambassador to Kenya, Michael Ranneberger, announced that the U.S. government would "increase resources to counter gender-based violence" against "female candidates for office as part of our electoral assistance program" (Terah 2008, 70). Determined not to be intimidated, Terah continued her campaign but, having been hospitalized for weeks after the attack, she was not able to canvass properly—and ultimately lost her bid for office. However, a widespread national and international campaign to highlight her case contributed to the defeat of the incumbent MP by another candidate.

ARBITRARY ARREST

The unlawful detention of politically active women is a theme that emerges in diverse contexts. In 2016, supporters of U.S. presidential candidate Donald Trump famously chanted "Lock her up!" during political rallies, suggesting that his Democratic rival, Hillary Clinton, be imprisoned despite the lack of any evidence of criminal wrongdoing. At one event, Trump went further to suggest, falsely, that Clinton wanted to abolish the Second Amendment, a provision in the Constitution guaranteeing the rights of citizens to bear arms. If she were elected president, he cautioned: "nothing you can do, folks. Although the Second Amendment people, maybe there is, I don't know." Many interpreted the statement as instigating physical violence against Clinton (Diamond and Collinson 2016), a call Clinton condemned on Twitter, saying: "A person seeking to be the President of the United States should not suggest violence in any way."[7] The chant crossed national borders in December 2016, when crowds in Edmonton chanted "Lock her up!" at a rally for Chris Alexander, candidate for leadership of the Conservative Party of Canada. The chant began in response to criticisms of Alberta Premier Rachel Notley—for the "crime" of proposing a carbon tax in the oil-dependent province (Ross and Muzyka 2016).

In other countries, women have in fact been arrested in efforts to stop their political work. In March 2015, nine feminist activists in China were detained by police for planning to hand out stickers denouncing sexual harassment on public transport in Beijing, Guangzhou, and Hangzhou on International Women's Day. Four activists were soon released but five—Li Maizi, Wei Tingting, Zheng Churan, Wu Rongrong, and Wang Man—were kept in custody until April. Later sharing her experiences with a reporter, Li Maizi recounted that police interrogated her at a Beijing police station, asking who was funding her organization and why she was "organizing subversive activities about sexual harassment." When she refused to answer their questions, one officer showed her a group of women in the waiting room—bragging they had arrested so many young feminists that night that there were not enough interrogation rooms for them all.

As Li and her colleagues had not done anything to oppose the government, she assumed initially that she would not be held for more than 24 hours. Although they released some women the next day, Li was moved to the Haidian Detention Center, surrounded by so many officers that she sensed that they "were very afraid I would escape. At that moment, I knew there was no way they were letting me go home." Interrogated at least once a day, Li refused to cooperate—and the agents then tried to humiliate her by calling her a "lesbian" and a "whore" and waking her in the middle of the night to scrub floors. They also pressured her father, who wrote to his daughter telling her to give up her activism. When these tactics did not work, Li was taken into a special room where police interrogators shone a bright light in her face, accused her of being a "spy" working for "foreign forces," and threatened her with up to 10 years in prison (Fincher 2016).

Global diplomatic and social media pressure led to the release of the five women in April 2015. The arrests garnered international attention because they coincided with preparations for Chinese President Xi Jinping to co-host a UN summit on women's rights to mark the anniversary of the Fourth World Conference on Women held in Beijing in 1995. Clinton, who provided one of the most memorable moments of the conference with a speech declaring "Women's rights are human rights," personally tweeted in reaction to the arrests: "Xi hosting a meeting on women's rights at the UN while persecuting feminists? Shameless."[8] Additionally, hashtags like #FreeTheFive went viral on Twitter, Instagram, and Facebook (Fincher 2016). However, the women were only released on bail, meaning they remained under surveillance as "criminal suspects" and thus were subject to state detention at any time (Zeng 2015). Acknowledging the "difficult" political environment, Li noted the need "to think very carefully about new methods to push forward China's feminist movement" (Fincher 2016).

TORTURE

Some women who are arbitrarily detained may face acts of physical torture while in custody. In May 2018, the Saudi government arrested a number of activists without charge, including prominent women's rights campaigners. Kept in solitary confinement and denied communications with people outside the prison for the first three months, the activists were eventually able to have contact with family members—but were warned by prison officials against disclosing any accounts of torture or prison procedures. In November, however, Amnesty International obtained three separate testimonies regarding the torture of these activists. They condemned Saudi authorities for having "deprived [the women] of their liberty . . . simply for peacefully expressing their views" and "subjecting them to horrendous physical suffering." Violating the UN Convention against Torture and Other Cruel, Inhuman, or Degrading Treatment or Punishment, measures applied by prison officials reportedly ranged from electrocution to flogging to sexual harassment, leading at least one woman to repeatedly attempt to take her own life inside the prison.[9]

In March 2019, Saudi Arabia's public prosecution agency announced that four women—Loujain al-Hathloul, Hatoon al-Fassi, Eman al-Nafjan, and Aziza al-Yousef—would be charged and put on trial. Some had campaigned to lift the ban on women driving, while others had been in the process of opening up a shelter for abused women. The government claimed that the women had admitted to receiving "financial and moral support" from elements "hostile to the kingdom" (Hubbard 2019). Put on trial later that month, several of the women described for the three-judge panel the mistreatment they had faced while in state custody, including beatings, electric shocks, and sexual assault. The public prosecutor claimed to have investigated these claims and said that he concluded they were false. The fact that the arrests occurred several weeks before the ban on women driving was lifted, however, was interpreted by many activists and diplomats as a message to activists not to challenge the government's agenda (Kalin 2019).

One of the women, Loujain al-Hathloul, was a prominent voice in the campaign for the right to drive. She was also a long-standing critic of the country's guardianship laws requiring women to obtain permission from a male guardian before getting a job, traveling internationally, or getting married. While not mentioning a date when it would enter into force, an August 2019 government decree removed some—but not all—of these requirements for women over the age of 21. Nonetheless, Hathloul remains in prison and members of her family were placed under a travel ban barring them from leaving Saudi Arabia. Relatives abroad, including her sister Lina, have continued to speak out, reporting that Hathloul was offered a deal if she would deny the allegations of torture, but she had refused. Referencing recent changes, Lina stated: "if the Saudi government are sincere about the reforms on women's rights then they should release the women who asked for these reforms" (Oppenheim 2019).

## Solutions to Physical Violence

Survivors of physical violence, in some contexts, can gain justice through legal frameworks. In June 2016, British MP Jo Cox was fatally shot and stabbed while arriving at a weekly walk-in session for constituents at a library in West Yorkshire. After the attack, the assailant Thomas Mair calmly walked away. With the help of eyewitnesses, police officers arrested him approximately one mile from the murder scene (Cobain 2016). Within two days, Mair was brought before a court, and following a series of hearings, he was denied bail and his case was assigned to be handled using terrorism-related protocols. His trial began in November, less than five months later. After nine days, the jury took only 90 minutes to convict him of Cox's murder, grievous bodily harm to a bystander, possession of a firearm with intent, and possession of a dagger. The judge sentenced Mair to life in prison, with no possibility of parole (Cobain and Taylor 2016).[10]

Within the larger universe of acts of violence against women in politics, however, the Cox/Mair case is exceptional. Perpetrators, instead, often enjoy high levels of impunity, even when committing physical assaults that are clearly criminal. Inadequate response from state authorities is typically due to low levels of state capacity to investigate these crimes—and/or to the fact that state actors themselves are responsible. Recognizing these limitations, women in civil society have implemented various strategies to empower women to speak out, anticipate, and circumvent problems with physical violence in the course of their political work. Individual women have also cooperated with security agencies to develop new protocols and measures to prevent and respond to physical attacks.

### AWARENESS-RAISING

After her assault, Kenyan politician Flora Terah received a wide range of visitors—including politicians, activists, diplomats, and ordinary citizens—as well as thousands of emails. As part of this wave of attention, she was invited to participate on a BBC interactive radio program with women around the world who had suffered gender-based violence. The experience was transformative, as she recounted later in her autobiography: "I got to realize that it was not only me. Other women seeking leadership positions in African countries were facing similar predicaments." Further, the people who called into the show "gave me a reservoir of strength I thought I had lost . . . I was determined to help other women stand up to the monster of gender-related election violence" (Terah 2008, 68–69). Terah's resolve grew stronger after her friend Alice Onduto was shot dead while campaigning—and further still when Benazir Bhutto was assassinated on the same day that the 2007 Kenyan election was held.

In January 2008, Terah launched an awareness-raising campaign called Terah against Terror to address the problem of electoral gender-based violence. In an interview, she described "this intimidation [as] not always physical but enough to deter women from taking part in politics, not only at the parliamentary level but also locally" (IPS Correspondents 2008). Her campaign focused in particular on reaching and educating young people, observing that youth were often mobilized by politicians to commit electoral violence. Additionally, she wrote and published a book on her experiences (Terah 2008). Combined, these efforts not only helped inform the public, but also contributed to her own psychological healing, helping her use her experiences positively to effect change.

## SELF-DEFENSE TRAINING

A longer historical view of the problem of violence against women in politics yields a second strategy to combat physical violence: training in self-defense techniques. In the late 19th century, greater numbers of women in U.S. cities began venturing out into public spaces, alone and without chaperones, and confronted what is now known as "street harassment." The slang term "masher" was used to describe men who leered, made sexual remarks, touched, or even followed women as they attempted to go about their day (Segrave 2014). In response, women began organizing self-defense clubs to teach boxing and jiu-jitsu—both in person and through lessons by mail. The martial art of jiu-jitsu was particularly attractive because its techniques use attackers' weight against them, enabling smaller individuals to defeat larger opponents. Newspapers garnered publicity for the cause, publishing articles with illustrations or photos showing women how to fight back physically against an attacker (Rouse 2017).

The British militant suffrage movement explicitly connected these tactics to women's political empowerment. On Black Friday in November 1910, women marching on parliament were physically and sexually assaulted by police and onlookers for more than six hours. Violence from the general public, however, was also common: when going about "their daily business, suffragettes could be heckled, pushed, shoved, kicked, and pelted with rotten fruit and vegetables by bystanders" (Rouse 2017, 127). In 1908, Edith Garrud, who ran a martial arts studio, began working with members of the Women's Social and Political Union (WSPU), teaching them jiu-jitsu in secret locations around London (Williams 2012).

In 1913, the need for self-protection took on additional urgency as the government began releasing suffrage prisoners who were on hunger strike so that they could recover their health before being rearrested. To prevent leaders like Emmeline Pankhurst and other fugitive suffragettes from being recaptured, Garrud helped form a 30-member group known as the Bodyguard. These women engaged in hand-to-hand combat with police on several occasions in

1914 and used disguises and decoys to stage a number of successful escapes and rescues (Ruz and Parkinson 2015).[11] While the press portrayed suffragettes who knew jiu-jitsu as a curiosity, Garrud emphasized that her training was intended only as a form of self-defense against those who had attacked women first, as a way to "invert the violence directed at them" (Rouse 2017, 130).

## VIRTUAL CAMPAIGNING

Founded in 2014, Mina's List is an organization devoted to recruiting and supporting women's rights activists to run for political office. Through their work with women in various countries in the global South, they came to identify two major barriers preventing women from standing and being elected as candidates: money and security. Both obstacles stem from cultural norms passing negative judgment on women speaking to men outside their families, which make it more difficult for women than men to raise funds for political campaigns and campaign openly in public spaces.[12] In 2015, Mina's List partnered with Voatz, a group of U.S.-based developers with expertise in technology, digital security, and mobile payments, to work on an app to make campaigning and fundraising simpler, safer, and more accessible for aspiring women candidates.

Piloted in Nigeria, the Women Influencing Nations (WIN) app was officially launched in 2018 at a workshop in New Delhi for female candidates from Afghanistan. Available in English, Dari, and Pashto, the WIN app enables women to communicate directly with voters without risking their physical safety. Candidates can set up profiles detailing their policy platforms, post campaign videos, and link to their existing social media accounts. They can even create digital polls to learn more about the priorities of their constituents. Voters, in turn, are able to learn about the candidates, as well as donate to their campaigns using a secure money-transfer system linked to the candidate's account. While donors can be verified to ensure compliance with campaign finance laws, the app permits them to remain anonymous in the first instance when public knowledge of such donations might pose a security threat.[13]

## SECURITY SOLUTIONS

Concerns about potential dangers, finally, have led to a variety of ad hoc security solutions to promote the physical safety of politically active women, including provision of bodyguards, distribution of bulletproof vests and vehicles, and identification of safe houses. Following the murder of Jo Cox in 2016, British MPs requested the creation of a dedicated team to investigate threats and abuse directed at parliamentarians. The Parliamentary Liaison and Investigation Team (PLaIT), based at the parliamentary estate, was subsequently established as part of the Parliamentary and Diplomatic Protection Command of the Metropolitan Police. While not focused exclusively on the security of female

MPs, data collected by PLaIT in its first few years of operation indicated that women appear to be disproportionately targeted: while women constituted 32% of MPs, about 60% of the cases PLaIT had handled were directed at women.[14] These dynamics led the team to recruit a dedicated female security advisor in June 2018 to assist female MPs in dealing with threats, abuse, and intimidation by providing tailored personal security advice and liaising with police and security companies on their behalf.[15]

These provisions compliment other security measures offered to MPs both before and in the wake of Cox's murder. The Fixated Threat Assessment Centre (FTAC) was established in 2006 by the British Home Office, the Department of Health, and the Metropolitan Police Service as a joint police/mental health unit to "assess and manage risks from lone individuals who harass, stalk, or threaten public figures."[16] This work, however, focuses on violence against politicians more generally: according to FTAC staff, every MP has a group of resentful constituents who channel their frustrations toward their local MP.[17] Just days after Cox's assassination, the parliamentary Estimates Committee decided to automatically offer enhanced security to all MPs—including panic buttons, extra lighting, and additional locks—without MPs having to apply to have them installed. Previous policies required a risk assessment by local police as well as two written estimates before any work could be carried out ("MPs to Be" 2016). Security expenses for MPs, including extra measures taken in response to specific threats, rose as a consequence from just over £77,000 in the 2014–2015 financial year to more £4.2 million in 2017–2018.[18]

# 13

# Psychological Violence

Psychological violence inflicts trauma on individuals' mental state or emotional well-being. It seeks to disempower targets by degrading, demoralizing, or shaming them—often through efforts to instill fear, cause stress, or harm their credibility. Its varied forms comprise, but are not limited to, death threats, rape threats, intimidation, threats against family members, verbal abuse, bullying, rumor campaigns, illegal interrogation, surveillance, social ostracism, and blackmail (APWLD 2007; SAP International 2010; UNDP and UN Women 2017). These acts may occur inside and outside official political settings and be carried out in person, by telephone, or via digital means like email and social media (SAP International 2010; Sekaggya 2010).

While psychological violence is widely recognized in global declarations and national laws, scholars and practitioners have struggled to define and measure it adequately (Follingstad 2007). This is due at least in part to perceptions that physical violence exacts a greater toll on its victims (O'Leary 1999), although studies find that most survivors rate emotional abuse as having a far more negative impact that physical abuse (Follingstad et al. 1990; Stark 2007). According to Galtung (1969, 169), this is because physical violence "works on the body," while psychological violence "works on the soul." Experiencing it firsthand, targets (and their allies) have taken the lead in devising and sharing coping strategies, empowering individuals and mobilizing groups to call out psychological violence and counteract its pernicious effects.

## Manifestations of Psychological Violence

Studies using a variety of data sources—testimonies of female politicians (SAP International 2011), data on electoral violence (Bardall 2011), and purpose-built surveys (Herrick et al. 2019)—suggest that psychological violence is the most widespread form of violence against women in politics. Prevalence rates

*Violence against Women in Politics*. Mona Lena Krook, Oxford University Press (2020). © Oxford University Press.
DOI: 10.1093/oso/9780190088460.001.0001.

are virtually identical across the IPU's global and European surveys: 81.8% of female parliamentarians in the global sample had faced some form of psychological violence in the course of their political work (IPU 2016b, 3), while this was the case for 85.2% of European MPs (IPU 2018, 1). Among the latter, 46.9% had received threats of death, rape, or other acts of physical violence, while 58.2% had faced sexist attacks online—with these figures rising to 50% and 76.2% for female MPs under the age of 40 (IPU 2018, 6). Opponents employ diverse tactics, ranging from threats and abuse to intimidation both online and offline, to frighten, degrade, and bully women to prevent them continuing their political work.

## DEATH AND RAPE THREATS

Jess Phillips, a British MP since 2015, has been quite open about the death and rape threats she has received in connection with her work as a politician. Prior to entering parliament, Phillips worked for Women's Aid, a domestic violence organization—and thus not only calls herself a "feminist" but also has expertise in recognizing tactics used by abusers. At the launch of NDI's #NotTheCost campaign in 2016, she disclosed that often after speaking in parliament about topics related to women's rights, "I [suffer] daily attacks on Twitter, on my email system, or endless online article articles written about how people wished to see me raped, they wished to come find my sons hanging from a tree" (CSPL 2017, 27). A few months after that event, Phillips helped launch the Reclaim the Internet campaign, a cross-party initiative by female politicians in the UK to raise awareness and address misogynistic bullying online. She received approximately 5000 Twitter notifications in response, as people tagged her in discussions about whether or not they would sexually assault her; more than 600 of these entailed explicit rape threats. Because the abuse was not an isolated incident, she noted to a reporter: "I don't need to contact the police anymore because my local police officers watch what happens on Twitter and they get in touch with me" (Oppenheim 2016b).

Weeks after the assassination of Jo Cox, Phillips posted a photo on Twitter of a man with tools at her home with the caption: "Locksmith spending 6hrs to make my home safe. Think [about] how my kids feel next time you mock up a picture of me dying."[1] Based on their content, many of these attacks appear to come from men's rights activists operating in what Marwick and Caplan (2018) call the "manosphere," a loose online network of anti-feminists and misogynists in the UK and abroad. Other perpetrators include the far-right, including members of the UK Independence Party (UKIP). In 2019, British police announced they would investigate Carl Benjamin, a UKIP candidate, for "malicious communications" against Phillips. Responding to a 2016 tweet in which she decried rape and death threats sent to women online, he replied: "I wouldn't even rape you . . . feminism is cancer." In a later video, he stated: "I suppose with enough pressure I might cave." Benjamin refused to apologize, claiming his comments were meant merely as a "joke" (Walker 2019).

Far-right groups also target women more broadly across the political spectrum. Female MPs in Europe not only receive more abuse than their male counterparts, but this abuse also differs markedly in its content, mainly taking the form of "misogynistic and violent anti-female vitriol" (Spring and Webster 2019). Katharina Schulze, co-leader of the Greens in Bavaria, estimates that, on average, 20% of the emails she receives each day are abusive, frequently containing threats of sexual assault. Spring and Webster (2019) find that in addition to memes posted on far-right platforms like 4chan targeting her appearance and sexual reputation, over a quarter of the abuse directed at Schulze on mainstream social media take aim at her gender and sexuality. In the first four months of 2019, the far-right party Alternative für Deutschland mentioned Schulze on its Facebook page 10 times more than any other individual German political figure or party and four times more than all other references combined. Comments on these posts often sexualized her, with a handful implying they wished she would be raped. Her male party co-leader Ludwig Hartmann, despite sharing the same policy views, was not subjected to similar treatment: the harshest tweets call him a communist appealing to young, inexperienced voters.

In addition to politicians, female journalists also often face sexualized hate speech online. Analyzing 70 million comments left on the *Guardian* website since 2006, editors discovered that, among the 10 most abused writers, eight were women and two were black men—despite the fact that the vast majority of its opinion writers were white men. The findings confirmed "what female journalists have long suspected: that articles written by women attract more abuse and dismissive trolling than those written by men, regardless of what the article is about" (Gardiner et al. 2016). Providing a closer look into these threats, a television show in Sweden, Mission Investigate, broadcast a documentary in 2013 entitled, "Men Who Hate Women on the Net."[2] In the program, a series of well-known female journalists read from letters and emails they had received communicating death threats and sexualized hate speech. One sent to news anchor Jenny Alversjö stated: "Now is the time . . . for us to have sex, I will be waiting for you outside the building. If you say no, I will cut up your body" (Edström 2016, 99). Alversjö noted she had worked for nearly twenty years as a journalist and had "always been a target for other people's opinion." But "when someone threatens to kill you . . . the world stops . . . [a] person who wanted me dead said I had two weeks left to live. It's hard to describe the fear I felt" (Bell 2015).

In 2016, the national Swedish television channel produced a program, "The Threatened," exploring how a range of politically active women—female journalists, opinion-makers, and politicians—received threats and hateful messages online, by letter, or through texts and calls to their mobile phones. Most communications took on a sexual character, with perpetrators often describing how they would rape the target or get an orgasm watching them die (Haraldsson 2016). One politician featured on the program was Rossana Dinamarca, who has served as an MP for the Left Party since 2002. She described the moment she first began to be harassed and threatened by one particular man, while she was at her sister's home in 2014, as a shocking contrast between the "beautiful day" with "kids playing in the garden" and the sexually graphic message she received on her phone: "You don't go and expect that when your phone beeps that you'll pick up a sexual threat . . . But there it is—while you're standing and making pancakes."[3]

Although Dinamarca did not know it at the time, numerous other female politicians in Sweden received similar texts at the same time, communicating sexual threats and signed "Greetings from a Sweden Democrat," referring to the name of a far-right party. While sent from unregistered numbers, police determined that the threats were all coming from the same device. They could only find out the model type, however, and not the identity of the person using the phone. The perpetrator was eventually caught when he topped up credit on the phone at a gas station with a surveillance camera. Court proceedings subsequently revealed that he had harassed 10 female politicians from the Social Democratic Party, the Left Party, and the Green Party using 15 different prepaid phone cards.

Although the man claimed he did not know why he sent the threats, he had previously been charged with unlawful threats against ethnic minorities and analysis of his internet searches revealed he had looked up all 10 women's names. After being sentenced to three months in jail and damages for sexual harassment, the man continued to insist that his messages were not intended as threats—and pointed out that on Facebook, he had seen "people write worse things about her than what I sent as text messages."[4] Far from excusing his behavior, this comment indicates that—at least in some parts of the internet—sexualized abuse of political women is normalized and widespread. The charges also demonstrate that his threats were not a casual, one-time event, but instead involved systematic and ongoing harassment: he texted and called Dinamarca incessantly for seven months, including sending 46 emails in one day.[5]

## INTIMIDATION AND COERCION

Intimidation and coercion may also prevent women from exercising their political rights. During the 2008 elections in Pakistan, threats issued by religious militants in North-West Frontier Province prevented thousands of women from casting their ballots. The day before the election, militants posted signs warning candidates not to bring their female supporters to vote; on election day, elders in one district decided to close 30 polling stations for women. In other districts, women's polling stations were largely deserted, with some poll workers relieved that women had not come: "In a democratic society, everyone should vote. But in this situation, life is more important than voting." Others expressed fears, however, that they themselves would be attacked when carrying the ballot boxes back to central government offices (Rohde 2008). A parallel scenario played out in the province of Lower Dir during a parliamentary by-election in 2015. According to one report, mosques broadcast warnings telling women not to vote, while "baton-wielding men" guarded polling stations to block the few women who attempted to cast their ballots (Boone 2015).

Women in Zanzibar, an autonomous region of Tanzania, faced similar pressures not to vote in 2015. However, this intimidation and coercion came not from religious fundamentalists, but from members of their own families. Mzuri Issa, coordinator of the Tanzania Media Women's Association (TAMWA) in Zanzibar, stated that 47 women were divorced for voting against their husband's orders. One woman recounted: "I thought it was just normal and free in a democracy to differ in politics. But unfortunately, my husband was adamant to the end and decided to divorce me. He has even decided not to bring basic needs to our young children." In response, TAMWA and other women's rights organizations launched a campaign to raise awareness, especially among men, that all citizens have the freedom to make their own political decisions (Makoye 2015).

Analysis by the Tanzania Women Cross-Party Platform finds that these trends are widespread across the country: 40.6% of the women interviewed had heard of women being forced not to participate in politics by relatives (Semakafu 2016, 21). In addition to husbands pressuring their wives, younger women suffered harassment from their parents and older women were subjected to violence from their sons. In some cases, this intimidation resulted in physical and mental scars. One woman shared that, after her husband caught her watching the presidential primaries of another party, he "ordered me to switch off the television . . . he then attacked me and beat me and then went to the bedroom and wrote divorce papers. And that was the end of my marriage." An elderly woman whose sons were not happy with her vote recounted: "my house was stoned every night. I cannot go out to the lavatory for fear of getting injured" (23, 22). Other men confiscated women's voter registration cards to prevent them from voting, while some escorted women to the polls to "assist" them in voting, using the pretext that their wives did not know how to read or write—thus ensuring men's control over their votes.

Anecdotal data from the United States suggests that intimidation and coercion by family members is not limited to the global South. Following the 2018 elections, door-to-door canvassers interviewed by Solnit (2018) shared that it was relatively common that husbands "refused to let the wife speak to canvassers, or talked or shouted over her, or insisted that she was going to vote Republican even though she was a registered Democrat." One man, only half joking, asserted: "if she needs to know how to vote, I'll just take her in the back and beat her." In one particularly memorable account, a woman who opened the door "looked petrified" while her husband stood "menacingly" behind her. As the canvasser made a pitch for Beto O'Rourke, a Democratic candidate in Texas, the woman's husband began yelling, "We're not interested." As the wife quickly closed the door, however, she silently mouthed: "I support Beto." Solnit suggests that while it would be impossible to know how many men in the United States "bully, silence, and control their wives into voting conservative," the growing popularity of voting by mail may deprive some women of the secrecy of their vote—and thus freedom to vote as they wish.

## INTRUSIVE DISRUPTIONS

Intrusive disruptions aim at interrupting—and inducing enough fear to stop women from continuing—their political work. In 2000, two sets of UN women's rights events were held in New York: the CSW meetings, held every year in March, and a special session organized in June to commemorate five years since the Fourth World Conference on Women in Beijing (Beijing +5). Serving as a preparatory conference for Beijing +5, the CSW meetings attracted a particularly large number of participants, including an outsized contingent of conservative organizations that attended with the aim of watering down advances made on gender, sexuality, and human rights in the Beijing Platform for Action.

In 1995, the presence of evangelicals in Beijing, together with the Vatican and leaders of various Muslim-majority nations, had contributed to the striking of language recognizing non-discrimination on the basis of sexual orientation. When proposed language on sexual orientation was provisionally included in the Beijing +5 documents, members of these groups mobilized to attend and disrupt meetings, especially events arranged by the lesbian caucus. In a context where "being 'outed' in their home countries meant great personal danger," members of anti-homosexuality groups "displayed an intimidating interest in discovering not just what lesbian women were strategizing and saying, but exactly who they were." At one workshop, members of conservative groups were observed copying names and contact information from an attendance sheet—and one woman made sure everyone in the room was aware she knew who they were, stating that "it was nice to put a face to all your names" (Rothschild 2005, 104).

These groups also disturbed meetings and sought to intimidate participants. During a lesbian caucus panel, for example, priests read aloud from the Bible during the presentations. After the panel concluded, a former nun who had been a panelist was encircled and taunted by religious extremists until UN security guards were able to intervene. The nun described this as a shift in tactics "from obstruction to intimidation," with priests "waving rosaries as a weapon to ward off evil spirits" and conducting "an exorcism in the room where the lesbian caucus had met." Calling out these actions, a group of four NGOs put out a statement against these "pro-family" forces, noting that their activities had included "removing documents, intimidating NGO representatives, and giving biased information." Similar scenes were repeated at Beijing +5. Due especially to the presence of a very large number of U.S. religious-right groups, many with little knowledge of the UN or sexual rights issues, the special session was characterized by an "overt climate of hostility not previously experienced in UN settings" (Rothschild 2005, 109, 105).

These battles continue to the present day. In 2019, Koki Muli Grignon, the CSW vice-chair and Kenya's deputy ambassador to the UN, was inundated with 3000 text messages in 12 languages—forcing her to suspend the negotiations and leave the UN building to get a new phone number. Sent by CitizenGo, a Spanish NGO, the texts demanded that any references to "abortion, sexual orientation and gender identity, and comprehensive sexuality education" be removed from the final text of the 2019 CSW meetings. Muli Grignon believed she was targeted due to confusion about her role: as a facilitator, she in fact had no influence over the content of the agreed conclusions. As a result of the attack, however, "it was totally impossible to work." She added: "The UN should be a safe space—nobody should be intimidated." Other activists recognized the incident as part of a "strategy of distraction" used by conservative activists to prevent progress at women's rights conferences by attempting to hijack the agenda (Kent 2019).

Other disruptions involve issuing bomb threats against women's homes and places of work. In 2013, *Guardian* columnist Hadley Freeman received a tweet from an anonymous account which claimed: "A bomb has been placed outside your home. It will go off at exactly 10.47 PM on a timer and trigger destroying everything." Identical threats were received by Grace Dent, a columnist for the *Independent*; Catherine Mayer, Europe editor of *Time* magazine; and Anna Leszkiewicz, editor of *Cherwell*, Oxford University's independent student newspaper. The threat against Freeman appeared to be in response to her latest column calling out misogynistic abuse online. She explained: "I get loads of abuse on Twitter. That I should just 'go back to the kitchen,' or someone saying they can't wait until women lose the vote." The disruption posed by a bomb threat, however, convinced her finally to go to the police: "There was that guy arrested for threatening to blow up an airport. If it's illegal to threaten to bomb an airport, it's illegal to threaten to bomb me" (Batty 2013).

## JUDICIAL HARASSMENT

Bringing baseless legal accusations against someone is a further means of causing mental and emotional stress, with the added bonus of potentially harming the target's reputation within the broader community. While spurious legal actions have been taken against various politicians, notably Hillary Clinton and Dilma Rousseff, judicial harassment is perhaps most commonly employed as a tactic to defame and justify imprisoning human rights defenders—while also diverting time, energy, and resources away from their work (Frontline Defenders 2018). While cases of judicial harassment carry the trappings of formal legal frameworks, they are often characterized by irregularities related to due process and fair trial procedures, including lack of access to a lawyer, unacknowledged detention, and wrongful sentencing (Sekaggya 2010).

In May 2018, Egyptian police raided the home of actress Amal Fathy two days after she posted a 12-minute video on her personal Facebook page venting about sexual harassment in Egypt. In the video, she detailed two incidents that had occurred earlier that day, in which a taxi driver groped her and, a couple of hours later, a bank guard grabbed his crotch while making lurid comments about her. She also criticized the government for failing to adequately address harassment in the country. Although Fathy told police that she only posted the video because she "had a very bad day," they carried assault rifles and took her away in the middle of the night on charges of terrorism (Daragahi 2018). Five months later, she was sentenced to two years in prison: one year for "spreading fake news" with the intention of toppling the Egyptian regime and a second year for possessing "indecent materials" (a reference to the video itself). She was also fined 10,000 Egyptian pounds (Malsin 2018).

Recent Egyptian cybercrime laws increased the powers of the government to shut down websites critical of the government, including blogs with more than 5000 followers. However, most "fake news" charges to date have been used to target women (DeGeurin 2018). In a related incident, Lebanese tourist Mona el-Mazbouh was initially sentenced to 11 years in prison for uploading a video to Facebook complaining of sexual harassment—but was ultimately deported and issued a fine instead. Feminist writer Mona Eltahawy recognized these gendered dimensions when she tweeted after the trial that "the sentencing of Amal Fathy aims to terrorize women out of public space and is a green light to men that they can assault women with impunity."[6] In a second tweet, she compared the Egyptian president, Abdel Fattah al-Sisi, to other authoritarian leaders, declaring: "Patriarchy at the highest levels protects & enables misogyny."[7]

### Solutions to Psychological Violence

Some forms of psychological violence are clearly illegal, as in the case of Swedish MP Rossana Dinamarca described earlier. In the UK, a number of female MPs—including Luciana Berger, Stella Creasy, and Anna Soubry—have taken their cases to the courts, leading to jail time for a number of their harassers. However, in general, existing legal frameworks lack robustness and leave many victims unsatisfied—and largely unprotected. Additionally, many forms of psychological violence are not legally prohibited, such that no state-led recourse for justice is available. As a result, targets and their allies have worked among themselves to develop a range of interventions to deal with and call out incidents as they occur—as well as to provide support for victims to resume their political work. These include both individual-level strategies to handle and prevent abuse and collective mechanisms to express solidarity and enhance women's safety in the political world.

## DELETING, BLOCKING, AND REPORTING

The IPU (2016b) identifies online abuse as the most common form of psychological violence against female parliamentarians. As many politically active women around the world point out, simply turning off the computer or logging out of email or social media accounts is not a realistic option. New technologies have become increasingly embedded in people's daily lives, such that politicians, activists, and journalists have come to rely on online platforms to communicate with constituents, elites, and the wider public. Exiting this space can therefore have serious social and economic implications (Committee to Protect Journalists 2016; Dhrodia 2017). Moreover, walking away from these technologies due to harassment effectively cedes these spaces to abusers, permitting perpetrators of violence to control and further isolate women (Henry and Powell 2015).

One way that female politicians have attempted to deal with online harassment on their own is by deleting, blocking, and reporting abuse. The preferred option for many female MPs in the UK is simply to delete or block offensive posts.[8] For the staff of Diane Abbott, the first black woman elected to the British parliament, this task forms part of their daily routine. After a study by Amnesty International showed that Abbott received nearly half of the abusive tweets sent to female MPs between January and June 2017 (Dhrodia 2017), her staffers were invited to give evidence to the CSPL inquiry on abuse and intimidation in British politics. They described the work in plain terms: "The first thing we do in the morning is to block and delete online abuse, usually whilst having breakfast. Porridge with one hand, deleting abuse with the other." They cautioned that this was an imperfect solution because once they blocked or muted an account, they had to rely on others to see and report inappropriate content. Moreover, leaving this abuse online, they recognized, could still have negative effects: "removing it from Diane doesn't stop another black woman from seeing it, or from emboldening someone else" (CSPL 2017, 38).

Some MPs also take advantage of opportunities to report abusive content directly to social media companies. Twitter, for example, explicitly states that users may not threaten violence against an individual or a group of people; engage in targeted harassment of someone; promote violence against, threaten, or harass other people on the basis of race, ethnicity, national origin, sexual orientation, gender, gender identity, religious affiliation, age, disability, or serious disease; or depict sexual violence and/or assault.[9] Many soon become disillusioned with the process, however. In 2016, Jess Phillips penned a piece entitled: "By Ignoring the Thousands of Rape Threats Sent to Me, Twitter is Colluding with My Abusers." She explained that after reporting a message from "someone gloating, in intricate detail, about how they would *not* rape me," Twitter responded that they "reviewed the content and determined that it was not in violation of the Twitter rules" (Phillips 2016a). Seyi Akiwowo, a former local councilor who went on to form Glitch, an NGO to end online abuse, expressed similar vexation: "There's something really infuriating when someone is clearly being hateful and you've reported but Twitter reply claiming there are no violations. It . . . feels like gaslighting."[10]

AWARENESS-RAISING

In the face of psychological violence, other women have taken a different tack: sharing the abuse women have received in hopes of raising awareness and spurring broader action. In January 2018, Baroness Anne Jenkin spoke in a debate in the British House of Lords on social media regulations about the experiences of a Conservative female candidate. Jenkin recounted that, every time this woman left her house, she faced activists "yelling at her, and I quote—and please, my Lords, forgive the unparliamentary language and block your ears if you are sensitive or easily offended—a 'Fucking Tory cunt.'"[11] The speech quickly garnered attention on Twitter, as well as in traditional media outlets, noting that it was the first time this slur had been uttered on the floor of parliament. In a subsequent interview, Jenkin acknowledged there was "a sharp intake of breath" in the chamber—but that she "wasn't out to shock people," but to make them aware that "this sort of abuse happens to women candidates" (Atalanta 2018, 40).

Two months later, Mhairi Black, an MP for the Scottish National Party, made a more extensive intervention during a parliamentary debate on misogyny on the eve of International Women's Day. Both the youngest MP and a lesbian, Black had personally faced a variety of lines of abuse, including being called a "wee boy" and a "cunt." But she continued: "I struggle to see any joke in being systematically called a dyke, a rug muncher, a slut, a whore, a scruffy bint. I've been told you can't put lipstick on a pig, let the dirty bitch each shit and die." While Black noted she could have softened her language "by talking about the C-word . . . the reality is there is no softening when you're targeted with these words and you're left reading them on my screen every day." She said that she felt uncomfortable reading out the insults, "yet there are people who feel comfortable flinging these words around every day." For Black, allowing the abuse to go unchallenged helps normalize it and "when it becomes normalized it creates an environment that allows women to be abused" (Settle 2018).

Canadian politician Sandra Jansen made a similarly impassioned speech on the floor of the Legislative Assembly of Alberta, opening her speech by declaring: "What a traitorous bitch!" Jansen had left her longstanding party, the Progressive Conservatives, in 2016 due to the bullying and harassment she experienced at a 2016 party convention. Subsequently crossing the floor to join the New Democratic Party, she received a torrent of abuse after changing parties, including "Sandra should stay in the kitchen where she belongs" and "Dumb broad, a good place for her to be is with the rest of the queers." She called on colleagues who were "stunned by the words" or "reject[ed] the inherent violence behind them" to recognize that "harassment and abuse, even if it's verbal, even if it's online, and even if it's directed at a political opponent, is poison." She pleaded: "Please oppose it. Don't ignore it. Don't look the other way. Don't excuse it. Because our daughters are watching us." Once she concluded, the speech drew a standing ovation—and was widely discussed across Canada (McConnell 2016).

## COUNTER-SPEECH AND SOLIDARITY

Reviewing her "personal archive of conservative hate mail," Cloud (2009, 471–472) shares that her preferred rejoinder was to post the hate mail on public forums, "turning the tables on cyber intimidators and bringing their violations into the light of day." Many harassers, she was surprised to find, backpedaled and/or apologized for the tone of their letters—because, she surmised, they then became accountable to a larger community. Alexandria Ocasio-Cortez, a member of the U.S. Congress, also employs a form of counter-speech, using Twitter to respond to and/or call out abuse. A tweet on Halloween in 2019 by *Fox News* commentator Tomi Lahren captures many conservative tropes used to denigrate Ocasio-Cortez: "I decided to dress up as the person who scares me most. The Democratic Dimwit Darling, socialist-loving, freedom-hating, former bartender herself @AOC."[12] Responding to the bartender trope on a previous occasion, Ocasio-Cortez inverted her opponents' logic by tweeting: "I find it revealing when people mock where I came from, & say they're going to 'send me back to waitressing,' as if that is bad or shameful . . . But our job is to serve, not to rule."[13]

Jess Phillips (2017) makes a similar suggestion in her memoir, calling on allies of women "in the firing line" to "form a misogyny counter-speech army." She explained: "Sometimes if I am going on the telly or about to do something I think will attract Internet hobgoblins, I put out a request for cat pics and kindness to flood my feed. I can cope with loads of vitriol and hatred when it is interspersed with pictures of people lying on the floor with a hamster" (227–228). Phillips's strategy recalls one employed informally by women in the British parliament in the late 1980s. Dawn Primarolo, a newly elected Labour MP, was the target of so many sexist taunts that other female MPs, even those from other parties, made a point of sitting with her as a way to counteract the "culture of intimidation that some Members of the House, for some strange reason, thought that's how Members of Parliament should behave" (Sones 2005, 67).

An automated version of counter-speech and solidarity is ParityBot,[14] the brainchild of Lana Cuthbertson, co-founder of Parity YEG, a non-partisan, Edmonton-based NGO working toward gender parity in politics and public office, in collaboration with computer developer Kory Mathewson.[15] Using machine learning methods, ParityBot detects abusive and problematic tweets directed at women during an election and then sends out a positive tweet for every bad tweet, with the aim of generating more positive political discourse for women during elections. The bot was deployed during the spring 2019 pro-vincial elections in Alberta and, based on feedback, revised and implemented a second time in the fall 2019 Canadian federal elections. Between September 24 and October 26, ParityBot analyzed a total of 228,225 tweets sent to 314 female candidates and identified 9,987 abusive tweets. To avoid violating Twitter rules, which limit accounts to 100 tweets per hour, the developers set a relatively high threshold of 90% likelihood of being abusive. Despite these strict criteria, ParityBot sent out 2,428 responses in the month leading up to the election, or an average of 74 tweets per day, using 227 messages of encouragement submit-ted online[16] or written by Parity YEG volunteers (Emmanuel 2019).

While many of these strategies entail mobilizing other women for sup-port, research by Munger (2017) suggests that spurring men to participate in these campaigns can be vital. In a study of racist online harassment, he iden-tified a dataset of public Twitter accounts whose users were white men who had employed racist slurs. He assigned these accounts to four conditions, using bots he created in which he varied the race of the apparent account holder as well as their purported number of followers. Each bot was programmed to send a tweet to subjects after they made a racist remark, with a message telling them their behavior was unacceptable. Analyzing the results, Munger discov-ered that subjects significantly reduced their use of racist slurs when they were sanctioned by a white man with high number of Twitter followers. There was no impact when the bots were white men with few followers or black men with many followers. However, subjects increased their rates of harassment after receiving a message from a black man with few followers. These findings point to the importance of high-status allies joining the fight against online harass-ment, not simply leaving the heavy lifting to members of marginalized groups who are disproportionately affected.

INTERNET SAFETY

Other women have been inspired by their own experiences—and those of their colleagues—to develop and offer services to enhance the online safety of other politically active women. In 2017, the International Federation of Journalists and the South Asia Media Solidarity Network joined up to launch the Byte

Back campaign to raise awareness and combat online harassment of women journalists in the Asia-Pacific region. They devised a guide to explain how cyber harassment works—including how users can disguise themselves, mobilize other users to attack, and set up bots to engage in automated trolling—and provide practical information for handling these cyberattacks. In addition to sharing how to set up filters and block or mute certain users, the guide outlined three primary strategies for responding to and tracking online abuse: "name and shame," re-tweeting a screenshot of the post with comments calling out the abuse; "shout it out," refusing to remain quiet and making the media house aware and accountable for abuse received; and "save and document abuse," collecting evidence regarding the messages and the accounts sending them (International Federation of Journalists 2017).

In the United States, former reporter Michelle Ferrier founded TrollBusters in 2015 as a hands-on "rescue service" for female journalists experiencing cyber harassment. As a columnist for the *Dayton Beach News-Journal*, between 2005 and 2007 she regularly received abuse and threats in anonymous letters sent to the newsroom. The communications were so chilling, she recounted: "I would pull the letters I received out of sealed plastic bags with rubber gloves while standing outdoors, so as not to expose my coworkers at the newspaper to any potential toxins—and to preserve any fingerprints that might still be imprinted atop these hateful words" (Ferrier 2016, 46). As the letters became increasingly violent, she went to the newspaper's management, local police, and the FBI and CIA. The CPJ ultimately took her case to the Department of Justice, yet "nothing changed. But I did. I changed as a person. I became angrier. More wary and withdrawn . . . I gave up and quit my job to protect my family and young children."[17]

Leaving journalism for a career in academia, Ferrier came up with the idea for a rescue service at a hackathon for women news publishers in 2014. She subsequently worked with an international team of female journalists to develop the tools and services to "provide a hedge of protection around women so they can persist online and tell the story, and not become the story" (Ricchiardi 2018). The website offers digital security courses, social media monitoring, and digital hygiene lessons.[18] It also provides infographics in English, Hindi, and Spanish, mapping out possible scenarios and providing advice on steps to take in each case. If the problem, for example, is that "someone is posting sexually explicit photographs of me without my consent," the chart recommends reporting the incident to Twitter or Facebook; consulting an attorney; documenting everything; and reporting the incident to the police, TrollBusters, and employers. The infographic lists what to document: number of threats; date, time, picture of threats; number of people involved; and implied/explicit severity of the attack. It also provides guidance on how to change Twitter settings "to ensure you only see what you want," including filtering tweets to see only those from accounts followed; filtering out "lower-quality content" from people not followed or recently interacted with; and muting tweets containing specific words.[19] The aim, according to Ferrier, is to take a proactive stance to online abuse, acting as "first responders online" and sending "positive messages" so women "know they are not alone" (Ricchiardi 2018).

## SAFE SPACES

A further strategy is to create "safe spaces" for women's political expression. On October 20, 2016, Libby Chamberlain, a private citizen, set up Pantsuit Nation, an invite-only Facebook group to follow the third U.S. presidential debate between Hillary Clinton and Donald Trump. Like the red "Make America Great Again" caps that came to symbolize the Trump campaign, the pantsuit refers to the clothing Clinton famously wore during her many years in public life. The group grew from 30 members originally to nearly three million by election day on November 8 (Correal 2016). Adopting the mantra ascribed to First Lady Michelle Obama—"When they go low, we go high"—Pantsuit Nation became what one reporter described as a "troll-free internet oasis for Clinton supporters" (Desmond-Harris 2016). To keep it positive and inspiring, the group remains "secret," meaning that people must be invited to join by another member. All posts must also be approved by administrators before they can appear on the page.

Pantsuit Nation resonated with many female Clinton voters, in particular, because many had experienced vicious sexist online (and offline) harassment from opponents on both the right and the left (Clinton 2017). It thus provided space in an otherwise toxic political environment to express enthusiasm for Clinton's historic campaign, without having "to debate or be harassed or criticized by friends and family" (Desmond-Harris 2016). One woman who lived among Trump supporters explained: "It did sort of revive my spirit. I didn't believe in 'election depression' until I realized it was happening to me. I've cut ties with my family, or rather, they've cut ties with me." She then added: "Someone thanked me, in the comments, for being a strong woman. How often do we say that to one another, in real life? That's been the biggest benefit. This group brings out the supportive side of women" (Correal 2016). In subsequent years, posts focused less on Clinton per se than on promoting political engagement more broadly, with members sharing decisions to run for office, become more politically active, and register and turn out to vote.[20]

## SELF-CARE

In 2010, six organizations came together to form the Mesoamerican Women Human Rights Defenders Initiative (IM-Defensoras) to develop alternative strategies to respond to violence faced by women human rights defenders, particularly in El Salvador, Guatemala, Honduras, Mexico, and Nicaragua.[21] In an initial study, IM-Defensoras (2013) found that existing protection mechanisms focused narrowly on the physical protection of individuals, employing traditional security measures such as bodyguards and bullet-proof jackets. Little attention was paid, in contrast, to broader threats and their impact on women's physical and mental health. According to one female Mexican activist, "constant threats, attacks, sexual harassment, and smear campaigns against activists cause increasingly high levels of stress, fatigue, depression, anxiety, migraines" (Hernández Cárdenas and Tello Méndez 2017, 173). Despite these pressures, many women human rights defenders strongly neglected these aspects of their daily lives as a result of commitment to their causes.

Troubled by these findings, in 2016 IM-Defensoras partnered with a Mexican NGO to create Casa La Serena, offering 10-day stays to women human rights defenders across the five countries. Informed by the model of "integrated security" developed by Barry and Đorđević (2007), the aim of the retreat is to create an opportunity for those "experiencing extreme fatigue, emotional or physical exhaustion, personal crises, mourning, losses, or other impacts derived from the context of violence and patriarchal culture that obstructs their work of defending human rights to recuperate, heal, rest and reflect" (Hernández Cárdenas and Tello Méndez 2017, 177). Self-care, they argue, should thus not be viewed as a luxury, but in a profession that suffers from chronic burnout, as a vital political strategy for individual and collective well-being—and thus for continuing and sustaining women's human rights work in the region.

# 14

# Sexual Violence

Sexual violence comprises a host of unwanted behaviors targeting a person's sexuality and sexual characteristics, ranging from non-consensual physical contact to unwelcome verbal conduct of a sexual nature. Its varied forms include rape, attempted rape, touching, kissing, groping, exposure, sexual jokes, suggestive remarks, and requests for sexual favors (APWLD 2007; Barton and Storm 2014; SAP International 2010; UN Department of Economic and Social Affairs 2014; UNDP and UN Women 2017). Whether involving a single incident or a pattern of behavior, sexual violence violates human dignity, communicating a message of domination and disrespect. Employed to display, gain, or maintain power, sexual violence can also create a hostile work environment, interrupting and potentially undermining women's labors and contributions (Berdahl 2007; Schultz 1998).

If sexual violence is not about sex, but about power, its existence is not surprising in the realm of politics, where "the inherent imbalance of power creates obvious vulnerabilities" (Cox 2018, 8). However, some female politicians observe that the "casual groping of junior staff and volunteers that passed without comment decades ago is increasingly called out and challenged today" (Swinson 2018, 46–47). Recent interventions around the world, especially in the wake of the #MeToo movement, seek to deepen these emerging understandings, with politically active women—and some male allies—working to raise awareness, pursue sanctions, and devise preventative measures to expose and combat sexual violence in its various forms.

## Manifestations of Sexual Violence

Sexual violence is among the least reported forms of violence against women in politics across the two IPU surveys: 21.8% of the MPs in the global sample and 24.7% of those in the European study reported they had personally experienced

*Violence against Women in Politics.* Mona Lena Krook, Oxford University Press (2020). © Oxford University Press.
DOI: 10.1093/oso/9780190088460.001.0001.

sexual violence in the course of their work in parliament. Among the European MPs, 6.2% had experienced sexual assault (IPU 2018, 7). Interestingly, however, the global study also asked respondents whether they had witnessed acts of violence against their female colleagues—and a significantly larger share, 32.7%, said they had (IPU 2016b, 3). A closer look at the results of the European survey—showing that sexual violence was committed by male colleagues, either political opponents or members of their own parties, in 75.9% of cases (IPU 2018, 7)—suggests that cultural stigmas together with political factors may suppress women's willingness to declare themselves victims.

Additionally, data collected in the 2018 survey indicate that MPs under the age of 40 were far more likely to report having faced sexual harassment (36.4%) and assault (13.6%) (IPU 2018, 7). While it may be that young female MPs are targeted more frequently, another possibility is that younger cohorts are more willing to disclose their experiences to researchers. Corroborating both hypotheses, 40.5% of parliamentary staffers, who are often young, report having faced sexual harassment at work—roughly similar to the share (41.5%) who said they had witnessed incidents involving a female colleague (IPU 2018, 8). Yet power disparities clearly play a role in decisions to lodge official complaints: while 23.5% of female MPs reported incidents, only 6% of staffers did (IPU 2018, 9). Despite powerful incentives to remain quiet, politically active women around the world have broken the silence around sexual violence—including rape, sexual assault, sextortion, rape insults, and sexual harassment—they have experienced as women in the political realm.

## RAPE

As the global #MeToo movement got underway in October 2017, British Labour Party member Bex Bailey decided to speak out about being raped at a party event by a senior party figure in 2011 when she was only 19 years old. In an interview on the Radio 4 PM program, Bailey said she had initially tried to pretend the rape had not happened—and therefore did not report it to the police at the time. Two years later, she finally found the courage to go to a senior party staff member. However, that person dissuaded her from reporting the incident, saying it could "damage" her within the party. She was not given any advice on what to do next and said that there did not seem to be procedures to bring up such complaints.[1]

Committed to Labour's politics, Bailey continued to be active within the party in the ensuing years, serving as assistant to a shadow minister, leading the youth wing, and sitting on the party's National Executive Committee for three years. In an opinion piece published in March 2017, she wrote that she was "proud of the work [Labour was] doing for women across the country." The party itself, however, was not free from misogyny: falling into the trap of believing otherwise, she cautioned, "lets women members down and puts the party in danger of not taking them seriously when they report incidents." The irony was thus that "as the Labour party fights for me to feel safer in society, I still feel unsafe in the Labour party" (Bailey 2017). Her motivation in coming forward six months later, therefore, was not to harm the party, but simply to make it better,[2] in the hope that #MeToo disclosures would "result in some sort of change in our parties as well as in Parliament" ("Labour Activist" 2017).

SEXUAL ASSAULT

Egyptian women played an active role in protests toppling the regime of President Hosni Mubarak in February 2011. However, when women returned to Tahrir Square a few weeks later to commemorate International Women's Day, a group of men appeared and began attacking demonstrators. One woman, 20-year-old Salwa Husseini Gouda, stated: "They looked like thugs. They called me a whore and hit me in the face." They dragged her and around 20 other women to the Egyptian Museum, where they handed them over to the military—who, in turn, took them to a military prison. Once there, the soldiers forced the women to undress, and while some searched the women's belongings, one took photographs of them naked—which Gouda feared they would use "to make us look like prostitutes." Held overnight, the women woke to an announcement that a doctor would inspect the unmarried women to determine whether they were virgins, a process Gouda found "horribly humiliating" (Shafy 2011). Three months later, an army general admitted to the tests, but impugned the women's reputations, claiming: "These girls who were detained were not like your daughter or mine. These were girls who had camped out in tents with male protestors in Tahrir Square . . . We didn't want them to say we had sexually assaulted or raped them, so we wanted to prove that they weren't virgins in the first place. None of them were."[3]

A second notable clash, subsequently known as the "blue bra incident," occurred in December 2011, when a video captured a soldier stripping a woman of her veil and black *abaya* (a long robe covering her entire body), revealing her underwear. However, security forces were not the only groups implicated in these assaults. In late 2012, a wave of protests against the new regime of Mohamed Morsi led to attacks from pro-Morsi factions (Tadros 2015). As the number and severity of these assaults escalated in 2013 and 2014, ordinary citizens also joined in (Zaki 2017). Evidence suggests that some attacks were coordinated. Describing what women came to call the "circle of hell," one activist recalled suddenly being "surrounded by hundreds of men in a circle that was getting smaller and smaller around me. At the same time, they were touching and groping me everywhere and there were so many hands under my shirt and inside my pants" (Kingsley 2013). For activist Mariam Kirollos, it appeared that "cases of sexual assault that have happened in Tahrir . . . are trying to

frighten women and marginalize them to the extent that they will not participate in political life." Corroborating her impression, a man interviewed by the
BBC said he had been paid to "go out and sexually harass girls, go out and has-
sle them, and try to touch them, to the point that they'd leave the demonstration" (Langohr 2013, 21). Egyptian anti–sexual harassment groups estimated
that between 80 and 90 women were sexually assaulted in Tahrir Squire during
the week of protests leading to Morsi's departure (Kingsley 2013).[4]

SEXTORTION

In other cases, women face demands from male party members that they perform sexual favors in exchange for political leadership opportunities. NDI
(2018) found that sextortion was present in at least three of the four countries analyzed. One party member in Tanzania stated: "I was not fully aware
of sexual exploitation practices in party politics. Three party leaders asked me
for sex for them to help me win the nomination contest. I refused and I lost."
Another woman described traveling with her party's chief election officer when
he "started touching my thighs and squeezing my private parts. When I tried
to stop him he persisted. I had to open the door and throw myself out of the
car. My decision to jump out of the moving car was the only option I had,
to avoid shame of being raped at old age." A party member in Honduras
shared: "During the campaign, I received invitations from men in the party to
go out at night because 'they wanted to get to know me.' When I told them,
'Okay, I'll come with my husband,' they responded 'No, that is not the way to
get votes.'" In Côte d'Ivoire, finally, a focus group member divulged: "My case
is truly humiliating. The leader was used to having a girlfriend and wanted it
to be me. He therefore said to me: 'If you want to be head of your section, we
must go to bed together.' I asked: 'Are you proposing that I sleep with you?' He
said: 'Yes, if you want to do politics!'"

Keen to ascertain how widespread these practices were, the Tanzania
Women Cross-Party Platform interviewed female candidates and voters in various parts of the country during the 2015 elections. They found that 19% of the
candidates interviewed had faced requests for sexual favors during the nomination process and 24.1% had received them during the campaign. Among female
voters, 12.5% had heard of women in politics being subjected to demands for
sexual corruption (Semakafu 2016, 15, 21). These findings dovetailed with data
collected by the Tanzania Media Women's Association in 2014, revealing that
the problem affected women in public life more broadly. Nearly 90% of women
in the public sector had experienced sexual harassment—including demands
for sexual favors—in the course of their work (Makoye 2015), prompting more
than 70 women's organizations to form an anti-sextortion coalition.[5]

Opponents of female political participation, however, also weaponized
the issue.[6] In 2016, Goodluck Mlinga, a male MP, was speaking during the

budget debates when he alleged that female MPs in the opposition party were "homosexual" and that it was the norm for "a woman to first agree with male leaders of her party to call her 'baby' [a reference to performing sexual favors] in exchange for [a reserved seat for women in parliament]." When called upon to sanction Mlinga, Deputy Speaker Tulia Ackson refused to take any action or retract the words from the record—and when the women protested, she called on the sergeant-at-arms to escort the women out of the chamber. The cross-party women's caucus, in contrast, condemned "abusive language, mockery, contempt, and humiliation of women in and outside Parliament." Several women's rights NGOs concurred, with the head of the Tanzania Gender Networking Program stating: "the incident aimed at humiliating and depriving women of their dignity so that they could not manage to stand strong and fight for their rights" (Mugarula 2016).

RAPE INSULTS

In 2003, Brazilian MP Jair Bolsonaro was giving a television interview after a hearing on a gang-rape case when his colleague Maria do Rosário approached and stated his position amounted to promoting violence. He asked if she was calling him a rapist, and she said yes—to which he replied: "I would never rape you because you don't deserve it." He then called her a slut, told her to "go cry," and pushed her on camera. Bolsonaro repeated the insult during a debate in parliament in 2014 in which Rosário, then Secretary for Human Rights, denounced the military dictatorship (1964–1985)—which Bolsonaro had supported—for using sexual violence against dissidents. As Rosário left the podium, Bolsonaro called out from his seat, telling her to stay and, again, that he would not rape her because she was not worth it (Griffin 2018).

While Bolsonaro was protected by parliamentary immunity for what he said in the chamber, he repeated the comments to a magazine—at which point the attorney general lodged a complaint with the Supreme Court for slander and defamation of Rosário as well as incitement to rape (Biroli 2016). The judges accepted the case and in May 2019, determined that Bolsonaro should pay 10,000 Brazilian reais in damages as well as issue a public letter of apology. Posting on Twitter in June, Bolsonaro portrayed the exchange as an "ideological clash" around human rights.[7] In contrast, Rosário characterized his comments as promoting rape culture. She thus framed the forced apology as a "victory for all women assaulted and offended on a daily basis by machismo in our country" (Maia and Soares 2019). However, she lamented the fact that, as someone who had achieved numerous human rights reforms as a five-term MP and former minister, this rape insult "is what people remember. Bolsonaro has taken that away from me" (Kaiser 2018).

## SEXUAL HARASSMENT

Prior to the #MeToo movement, a number of elected men around the world lost their positions due to allegations of sexual harassment, including Mbulelo Goniwe, chief whip of the African National Congress party in South Africa in 2006; Massimo Pacetti and Scott Andrews, MPs in Canada in 2014; and Silvan Shalom, interior minister of Israel in 2015. However, charges against Denis Baupin, vice president of the French National Assembly, were distinct from these other cases in that they inspired a broader national conversation around sexual violence and harassment in politics. In May 2016, an investigation by Mediapart, an online investigative journal, and France Inter, a radio station, uncovered complaints from at least 14 victims. Four women from the Green Party, Baupin's party until April 2016, went on to file criminal complaints against him for sexual harassment.

Isabelle Attard, an independent MP who left the Green Party in 2013, said that soon after she was elected in 2012, Baupin began sending her a barrage of lewd daily text messages. Sandrine Rousseau, a former party spokesperson, shared that he had cornered her in a hallway, pinned her against the wall, held her breasts, and tried to kiss her by force. Elen Debost, a local politician, alleged he had sent her approximately 100 sexually harassing text messages, including one declaring he wanted to sodomize her "wearing thigh-high boots" (Chrisafis 2016). Annie Lahmer, a rank-and-file party member, said Baupin chased her around a desk until she told him to stop. The next day, she arrived at the office and when he refused to acknowledge her, she said: "Denis, I don't want to sleep with you so you no longer speak to me?" He then pointed his finger at her and stated: "You will never have a position in this party" ("Annie Lahmer" 2016). After the women's cases were dismissed by a judge in 2017 because they exceeded the statute of limitations, Baupin countersued his accusers unsuccessfully for defamation. At the 2019 trial, former Green party leader Cécile Duflot divulged that she, too, had faced an attempted sexual assault by Baupin on the threshold of her hotel room at a conference in Brazil in 2008.

In another pre-#MeToo case, British Labour Party member Ava Etemadzadeh invited MP Kelvin Hopkins to speak at a party event in 2014 at Essex University, where she was the chair of the university's Labour society. After the event, she guided him to the university car park where he hugged her very tightly and rubbed his crotch against her, "which I found revolting" (Hughes 2017). The following year, she accepted an invitation to visit Hopkins in parliament and when she went to have a conversation, he responded: "let's not talk about politics, do you have a boyfriend?" Hopkins then allegedly said to Etemadzadeh that "if nobody was in his office he would've taken me there. I was absolutely shocked." When she later refused to answer his phone calls, he sent a text message saying she was "an attractive, lovely young woman and a man would be lucky to have [her] as a lover" ("Jeremy Corbyn" 2017). In December 2015, she spoke with an MP who urged her to contact the party's chief whip, Rosie Winterton, who told her that to file a claim she would need to waive her anonymity, a prospect which "scared" her. When the party introduced a new policy in November 2017, she filed a formal complaint and Hopkins was temporally suspended from the party pending an investigation (Etemadzadeh 2018).

During this same time period, Lauren Greene was working as communications' director for U.S. Representative Blake Farenthold. In February 2014, another aide, Bob Haueter, told her that Farenthold had "sexual fantasies" about her, and Farenthold himself said he was "estranged from his wife and had not had sex with her in years." When Greene objected to these comments, she was "marginalized and undermined" by Farenthold and fired several weeks later. When Greene took her case to the Office of Compliance (OOC), she was forced to undergo months of mandatory counseling and mediation before she could file suit—which she did in December 2014, alleging gender discrimination, sexual harassment, and a hostile work environment. The case was later dropped, however, when both parties reached a private settlement. In December 2017, details of the agreement became public when House Administration Committee Chairman Gregg Harper told lawmakers that only one office in the past five years had used an OOC account to settle a sexual harassment complaint—and that settlement amounted to $84,000 (Bade 2017). When Farenthold resigned in April 2018, he promised to reimburse the taxpayer money he had used to settle the lawsuit, but later reneged on this pledge (Parkinson 2018).

In 2019, the Japanese newspaper *Asahi Shimbun* conducted a survey of women in local assemblies elected for the first time in 2015. One-quarter reported having been sexually harassed in the course of their political work. Half said the perpetrator was another assembly member, but 40% pointed to a constituent, a perpetrator not often signaled in other accounts. The problem was significant enough for women to coin a specific term for it: *hyo hara*, or "vote harassment." In both instances, colleagues and constituents preyed on women's lack of political experience and/or their need to consolidate a basis of political support. Former MP and current assemblywoman Masae Ido also attributed it to a "male-dominated society" that "has not gotten used to women who are trying to take leadership roles and are speaking their minds" ("Sex Harassment" 2019).

In one case, a male colleague approached a newly elected assemblywoman, proposing to serve as her mentor. He then became obsessive, calling and texting her several times a day, and even pestered her daughter, asking where her mother was. She ultimately felt compelled to install a stronger entryway to her home, as well as to keep her doors locked at all times. Other women said they had been groped at campaign dinners and pressured to go for drinks with constituents. Hoping to gain a stronger profile in the community, one assemblywoman had the habit of announcing via social media the time and location of her upcoming speeches. She soon noticed, however, that the same three or four middle-aged men came to every speech. Some of them later followed her to a restaurant and another sent her messages like: "I'm nearby. Can we meet?" To avoid further harassment, she was forced to stop posting updates ("Sex Harassment" 2019).

Female journalists similarly face harassment inside and outside their news organizations. An early study of women in the U.S. Capitol press gallery found that 80% perceived that sexual harassment was a problem for female journalists, while 60% had personally experienced it while on assignment. Among the latter, 40% had been harassment by coworkers, 40% by news sources, and 20% by both (McAdams and Beasley 1994, 127). According to Lachover (2005), these problems are particularly acute for female journalists reporting on politics and security, as most informants tend to be male. One-third of the female journalists she interviewed reported verbal sexual harassment, including derogatory language and contemptuous behavior. Grace Wattera, a journalist for a newsweekly in Côte d'Ivoire, told the CPJ that the sexual harassment was so constant that it interfered with her work: when required to provide her contact details on sign-in sheets at press conferences, she would receive sexually harassing calls for days (Wolfe 2011).

## Solutions to Sexual Violence

Addressing sexual violence in politics is complicated not only by cultural stigmas surrounding women's sexuality, but also by the fact that most legal mechanisms—where they exist—focus on dynamics in the workplace. However, politics is rarely conceptualized as a "place of work," with regulations in place typically applying only to workers in traditional employment relationships serving non-political roles, like catering, security, or janitorial services (IPU 2018). Moreover, to the degree that parliaments and parties do seek to deal with behavioral complaints, these mechanisms address issues of financial and ethical (not sexual) misconduct. As Laura Dobson-Hughes, a former political staffer in Canada, explained: "there were no formal processes at all really. So even if you wanted to raise it, you probably wouldn't. You wouldn't know where to go. All the incentives were . . . to bury it, to ignore it" (McKeen and Gibson 2018).

This vacuum of accountability stems from two peculiarities of the political work environment. The first is parliamentary privilege. Politicians in many legislatures enjoy legal immunity for statements and actions in the course of their political duties that—if said or done outside parliament—might result in civil or criminal liability. Privilege enables MPs to speak freely during parliamentary debates, as well as confers autonomy to representatives in relation to other aspects of their political work—like decisions to hire and fire members of their own staff. While this privilege ensures that MPs can surround themselves with trusted colleagues,[8] it also creates opportunities for abuse, like unfair dismissal of staff who speak out against sexual harassment (Collier and Raney 2018). Further, due to imbalances of power, public officials often hold a privileged position vis-à-vis staff, constituents, and journalists, all of whom rely on them for professional advancement, political responsiveness, and access to political information—in turn, exacerbating their vulnerability to and silence on incidents of sexual harassment (Cox 2018; Lachover 2005).[9] Criticizing the use of privilege as an excuse for tolerating sexual harassment, however, U.S. Senator Kirsten Gillibrand has suggested that "elected leaders should absolutely be held to a higher standard, not a lower standard" (Goldmacher 2017).

A second feature of politics affecting accountability is partisanship. The drive to prevail over political opponents can result in the "weaponization" of sexual harassment when committed by members of the opposing party, but its minimization when perpetrated by members of one's own.[10] Despite ideological differences on questions of sexual violence, a U.S. survey found that voters were more willing to punish perpetrators from the other party. Among Democrats, 82% believed that a Republican congressman accused of sexual harassment should resign, but only 74% felt that a Democrat should. Similarly, among Republicans, 71% agreed that a Democrat should leave, but only 54% thought a Republican needed to resign (Alter 2017). Concerns about the fate of co-partisans also delayed consensus among members of a cross-party working group on sexual harassment in the British parliament, with some voicing fears that new rules could be exploited to pursue vexatious claims against their parties.[11] Reflecting on her experiences in Canadian politics, Reaume (2018) characterized these tendencies bluntly as a "culture of protecting predators in order to shield a political party from embarrassment or bad news cycle."

As a result of these dynamics, few robust formal options exist to deal with and mitigate sexual violence in the political world. To protect themselves, women have largely filled these gaps with informal, ad hoc solutions. Natasha Kornak, a Canadian activist, spoke about "open secrets in politics [among women] about who to avoid . . . I've been told don't be alone in a room with this individual. Don't be alone in an elevator with this person" (McKeen and Gibson 2018). In 2017, U.S. Senator Claire McCaskill used similar language to describe her strategy as a young political intern in the 1970s: "I learned to avoid elevators, because elevators were when you were captured. After one unfortunate incident in the elevator, I began taking the stairs everywhere . . . I'm not going to comment as to details of it, but suffice it to say that it happened more than once from more than one person" (Ruiz-Grossman 2017). Seeking greater progress, politically active women have developed a variety of tactics to give voice to women's experiences, as well as to disincentivize and pre-empt opportunities to perpetrate sexual violence in the political realm.

## MANIFESTOS AND OPEN LETTERS

Stigma discourages women from speaking out publicly about episodes of sexual violence. When women do disclose, moreover, the collective societal response has often been to treat them as "tainted witnesses," questioning their credibility and discounting the truthfulness of their testimonies (Gilmore 2017). Nonetheless, women often speak with one another, using "whisper networks" as a "form of organizing . . . sharing information quietly, person-to-person" (Jaffe 2018, 81). A female party member in Tunisia stated in an NDI focus group, for example, that "a woman can't go up to a man and confront him for sexual harassment. [But] as women in the political party, we talk amongst ourselves" (NDI 2018, 16).

What made the #MeToo movement so extraordinary, therefore, was that it invited women to share ordinarily silenced stories to "give people a sense of the magnitude of the problem."[12] In its first 48 hours, the hashtag #MeToo was used nearly one million times on Twitter and 12 million times on Facebook, creating—according to an analysis of 1.5 million tweets posted during the first two weeks of its popularity in October 2017—a "counterpublic safe space for disclosure which, subsequently, generated more disclosures" (Gallagher, Stowell, Parker, and Welles 2019, 1). These "choruses of 'me too,'" according to Gersen (2018), helped render "each individual's account that much more believable," making #MeToo "an evidentiary claim of sorts: what you say happened to you happened to me, too, and so it is more likely that we are both telling the truth." Tackling sexual violence thus requires breaking the silence, going beyond the "whisper network in politics," not least because "these whispers don't reach everyone" (Reaume 2018).

The French case is notable for the widespread use of manifestos and open letters to call out sexual violence in politics. In 2015, over 40 female journalists came together to denounce the sexual harassment they had experienced at the hands of politicians. Presenting these accounts anonymously, they sought to highlight a broader cultural problem, rather than to call out certain men or specific incidents.[13] One "rising star," they wrote, "insisted on seeing us at night, away from parliament and outside of working hours," while a "political heavyweight interrupted the interview and proposed to go to a hotel instead." During a factory visit, a minister laughed at the blue overalls everyone had to wear and said suggestively to a journalist: "it would be better if you had nothing on underneath." Still others sent countless text messages, offering "one piece of information [for] one drink." While sexual harassment occurred in other professions, the women felt compelled to come forward because the perpetrators were "elected officials responsible for making policies," further noting that the perpetrators came "from all political parties [and] operate at all levels of politics." Seventeen women then signed their names on behalf of 24 other journalists who remained anonymous, fearing professional repercussions (Amar et al. 2015).

One year later, the sexual harassment scandal involving Denis Baupin spurred further action. The day after the revelations, more than 500 male and female activists and elected officials joined forces to call for "an end to impunity" for sexual harassment in politics. Giving examples of advice women are often given—"If so-and-so proposes dinner at a restaurant, say no"; "Above all, do not take the elevator alone with what's his name"; "Be careful if you find yourself alone at night in the office with x"—they pointed out that women are forced to modify their behavior "to endure, avoid, or go along with" the harassers. The manifesto criticized the silence of politicians on this matter, "which has made it difficult to recognize that [this problem] exists—even if in hushed tones it is known by all." The only way to get men rather than women to adapt their behavior, to put an end to impunity, to shift guilt from one camp to the other, they argued, was "to talk [about it]. This speech, these words must finally become a political topic, rather than being considered an interpersonal one" (Le Collectif "Levons l'omerta" 2016).

The following Sunday, 17 female former government ministers—from parties across the ideological spectrum—published a joint call denouncing sexist remarks and behaviors in French politics. They explained that, while they went into politics for different reasons and to defend different ideas, "we share the belief that sexism has no place in our society." While sexism was not unique to politics, they argued, "the political world has a duty to be exemplary. Those who write laws, vote for them, must respect them and therefore be beyond reproach." They explained they were "taking up the pen to say, this time, it's too much, the *omertà* and the law of silence are no longer possible." The word *omertà*, used by the ministers as well as in the name of the collective of activists and elected officials, is a revealing turn of phrase—invoking the code of silence used by the Mafia, preventing both self-incrimination and giving evidence to authorities regarding the misdeeds of others. The ministers emphasized that it was not up to women to adapt to these conditions, but rather the behaviors of certain men had to change. They declared: "That is enough. Impunity, it's finished. We will no longer shut up" (Bachelot et al. 2016).

Five months after these manifestos and open letters, female staff at the French parliament launched their own awareness-raising collective, Chair Collaboratrice. In early 2019, members of the collective published an editorial in which they reflected on how little had changed despite "two and a half years during which we have not ceased . . . to encourage the liberation of women's words . . . Freeing up victims' ability to speak involves offering them a framework in which they feel free to give witness, without fear that they will be putting their professional careers in danger." Impunity for sexual harassment, however, "had not budged one millimeter" and "we carry the heavy secret of multiple aggressions—not punished!—within these walls." They lamented that many women—both politicians and staff—left politics after sharing their experiences, with "sexist remarks, hands on buttocks, or rape attempts" often minimized as "'generational misunderstandings,' 'malicious behaviors' (on the part of women of course), or a 'gray zone.'" They thus called on the government and both houses of parliament to create an independent office that could "truly welcome women's testimonies, accompany them in their efforts, and provide them with real support in court proceedings" (Gayraud Hebbache, Julié-Viot, and Khoshkhou 2019).

This strategy has also been used outside of France. In October 2017, more than 140 women in California politics—legislators, staff, consultants, and lobbyists, both Democrats and Republicans—signed an open letter published in the *Los Angeles Times*. The idea for the letter was born the day after the Harvey Weinstein sexual harassment scandal broke, inspired by something that happened to political lobbyist Adama Iwu that very day. Iwu contacted a number of female colleagues, who tapped into their networks—who in turn activated their own networks—to spread the word among women in the state capitol community. Over the course of a weekend, the group drafted and re-drafted the letter numerous times. Eventually, women agreed to add their names, believing they were stronger together and, collectively, demonstrated that sexual harassment was an experience common to politically active women of all types.[14] When the *Los Angeles Times* declined to publish a manifesto, Melanie Mason, a journalist in Sacramento who a year earlier had sought to write a story on sexual harassment in the state legislature (but was blocked), suggested embedding the letter within a broader story. Collecting a series of testimonies over the course of a day, she wrote an article that went live at midnight, only three days after the letter was initially conceived (Mason 2017). As in France, no targets or perpetrators were named in either the letter or the story—the aim, again, being to focus attention on the broader culture of harassment, rather than reducing it to a problem limited to particular people.[15]

The letter began: "As women leaders in politics, in a state that postures itself as a leader in justice and equality, you might assume our experience has been different. It has not." Drawing on their various experiences, the women offered examples of men who had "groped and touched us without our consent," communicated "insults and sexual innuendo, frequently disguised as jokes," and "made promises, or threats, about our jobs in exchange for our compliance, or our silence." They explained they had not spoken up earlier because many of those men "hold our professional fates in their hands," causing them to fear the professional ramifications of coming forward about sexual harassment. Yet, by remaining quiet, "many of us feel ashamed that we have failed to protect our friends from abuse." While previously feeling powerless to stop the cycle, the women declared they were "done with this" and would "no longer tolerate the perpetrators or enablers." They ended by calling on "women to speak up and share the stories" and for the "good men, and there are many, to believe us, having our backs, and speak up."[16] Later that day, they launched a website[17] and Twitter account[18] declaring: "We Said Enough."

## ALTERNATIVE REPORTING MECHANISMS

Formal procedures to report sexual violence in politics rarely exist—and the few that do often inspire little confidence (Palmieri 2011). To fill this gap, women's networks have set up alternative reporting mechanisms, enabling women to share their testimonies while also learning about potential services they might access for support. In October 2016, Chair Collaboratrice created a website for female political staff in France to report their stories anonymously, arguing that "together we are stronger" and can "demonstrate the existence of a mass phenomenon." On the same page, staffers also had the option to leave contact details to obtain further information or help.[19] Similarly, in October 2018, EP staff came together to launch the MeTooEP blog to provide a venue for women to share anonymously any incidents of sexual harassment they experienced or witnessed at the parliament.[20] Additionally, the blog explains what sexual harassment is and what to do when faced with it[21]—as well as provides resources for seeking help.[22] The blog would not have been necessary, organizers argued, if victims felt comfortable to go through the tools of the institution (Ritzen 2018).

In the UK, a group of women in the Labour Party had been discussing issues of sexual harassment for some time. As the #MeToo movement began to emerge, they held a meeting with MP Sarah Champion and decided to set up a website called LabourToo to collect stories from women that could, in turn, be developed into a short report for party leader Jeremy Corbyn. The women did not inform the party prior to launching the website, concerned that leaders might seek to block it—a suspicion confirmed when party officials began pressuring Champion and other allies to find out who they were.[23] Appearing online in October 2017, the website offered women an opportunity to "anonymously share your experiences of domestic or sexual abuse, harassment, or discrimination in the Labour Party." The website acknowledged that it was "particularly hard to speak out" about harassment experienced or witnessed "as part of being a member, activist, or elected representative of the Labour Party." However, it explained, the goal was to "build a compendium of the types of abuse women face which all too often are unseen, ignored, or swept under the carpet," emphasizing that the initiative came from "women who love the Labour Party and work hard within it, but who know it has to be better." They specifically instructed women not to include any identifying information on themselves or the perpetrators, as the goal was not to "out" people but simply "to demonstrate the extent of the problem."[24]

Closing the survey on December 19, LabourToo then collated the accounts—but, for the sake of anonymity, decided to pull out broad themes from the 43 testimonies. In February 2018, they sent the report to party leader Jeremy Corbyn, party general secretary Iain McNichol, and the party's National Executive Committee, hoping to convince them to take the issue of sexual harassment more seriously. The report identified six themes: problem individuals were "common knowledge," but no actions were ever taken against them; there was little or no confidence in the party's formal complaint or disciplinary processes; women felt there was little support for pursuing complaints, and sometimes they were actively dissuaded from doing so; members lacked guidance and safeguards; men often had a poor understanding as to what constituted sexual harassment; and women were routinely abused by senior people in positions of trust. LabourToo stressed that "sexual harassment, abuse, and discrimination" was not restricted to parliament, "but is taking place at all levels within the Labour Party, and throughout the country."[25]

## LISTENING SESSIONS

A related strategy is to organize listening sessions, enabling women to share their experiences, as well as their suggestions for dealing with sexual violence in the political sphere. While not their explicit intention, members of LabourToo drew on the testimonies that women submitted—as well as their own discussions—to generate a list of five recommendations for the party. One was a fully independent complaints process, with panels composed of people with no clear link to the party who would uphold the integrity of the process rather than trying to protect the perpetrators or the party itself. LabourToo also called for compulsory training for party staff, elected representatives, and key officials in local party organizations; a comprehensive set of policies covering bullying and harassment, sexual harassment, domestic abuse, abuse, assault and sexual assault; a confidentiality policy requiring members not to share information they learn as part of the complaints process; and mandatory disclosure and barring service checks for those seeking selection as candidates at both the national and local levels.[26]

In Canada, founders of the Young Women's Leadership Network (YWLN) drew on their own experiences as political interns and volunteers to observe that young women were especially affected by sexual violence in politics—yet few political training programs addressed or even acknowledged it as a problem. Concerned that experiences with harassment were causing young women to leave politics just as they were beginning their political careers, YWLN sought to create a space to speak about these issues—and, in turn, prepare and support young women in political life.[27] One of their first projects was a guide for addressing sexual violence in political institutions, with the aim of encouraging "concrete actions toward addressing systemic gender-based sexual violence in politics."[28]

To develop the guide, YWLN interviewed 60 young people across Ontario who had been affected by sexual violence in the course of their political work, adopting a broad definition of "women in politics" that included not only elected officials but also political volunteers, interns, staffers, and lobbyists. While understanding sexual violence as stemming from "normalized misogyny and rape culture," YWLN also stressed its intersectional nature, highlighting the role of ableism, ageism, colonialism, homophobia, and racism in potentially magnifying abuses of power within political institutions. Conducting the interviews in early 2018, they found that the women—with an average age of 25—reported less than 5% of the incidents they experienced. Sexual violence occurred most often during social events (32%), in campaign offices (28%), and during electoral canvassing (18%). The most common forms involved verbal sexual harassment (39%), groping (25%), and rape (15%). Nearly half (49%) of the perpetrators were campaign, party, or political staffers, with the second largest group (27%) being political volunteers.

The interviews also provided a deeper look at the impact of sexual violence, finding that a stunning 80% of those interviewed had left politics (52%) or significantly reduced their involvement in politics (28%) as a result. One former party organizer explained: "They treated me as a liability: the candidate's image was far more important to them than my well-being. It was so disheartening to be treated like that by people I had worked with for years." Another former staffer observed: "At some point, you just have to choose between your health and your career. I had so many plans, but at the end of the day I felt sick and tired of being in the same room as [the perpetrator] and have everyone act as if nothing ever happened."

Based on these experiences, participants offered a number of recommendations for moving forward, including alternative programming at events where alcohol is present to lower the risk of sexual violence; provision of third-party, survivor-centric anti-harassment and sexual violence support advisors at political gatherings; codes of conduct and information about support resources; and adequate funding for lodging to ensure that party convention attendees can have private rooms. To support these strategies, YWLN offers four services for political institutions: sexual violence support training, policy consultation, equity and inclusion training, and anti-harassment support at political events and conferences. As of late 2019, the organization had worked with 100 candidates, politicians, volunteers, and staffers to "help create safer campaigns and civic institutions that foster young women's democratic participation,"[29] seeking to "ensure that sexual violence is not the last interaction young women have with political institutions."[30]

In October 2017, the #MeToo movement inspired numerous women in the United States to open up about problems of sexual harassment in state-level politics. In Illinois, six women, including fundraiser Katelynd Duncan, wrote an open letter subsequently signed by scores of other women, detailing widespread sexual harassment in Illinois politics. Duncan, in turn, helped raise money to form the Illinois Anti-Harassment, Equality, and Access (AHEA) Panel in February 2018, spearheaded by three female politicians: State Senator Melinda Bush, State Representative Carol Ammons, and State Comptroller Susana A. Mendoza. They spent six months collecting surveys, consulting with experts, and holding listening sessions across the state with hundreds of women working in politics (Hall 2018). The resulting report, released in September 2018, aimed to serve as a non-partisan roadmap for all political parties, operations, and campaigns to address what the authors saw as the cultural roots of sexual harassment in political spaces. They wrote that "as a Panel of three female elected officials, including two women of color, we have experienced this toxic culture firsthand, and we recognize that true change and progress requires a fundamental change to the culture of Illinois politics" (Anti-Harassment, Equality, and Access Panel 2018, 5).

While the AHEA Panel had no investigatory powers, its listening sessions focused on what women themselves saw as the solutions—and obstacles—to addressing sexual harassment in the political workplace. The discussions highlighted, in particular, certain structural features of political campaigns facilitating opportunities for sexual harassment while also enhancing the likelihood of impunity. For example, campaigns rely extensively on volunteers, consultants, and contractors, none of whom are protected by federal and state employment discrimination laws. Campaign workers also often do not know who their boss is, making reporting difficult. Working on a campaign also tended to prioritize the candidate over everything else, with loyalty being more important than a positive workplace culture and travel and odd hours blurring lines between private and work communications. Drawing on women's testimonies, the AHEA Panel recommended clear and non-negotiable policies not limited to what the law provided; anti-harassment training for all members of campaigns; party funding to campaigns tied to adopting policies and undergoing training; independent reporting avenues in campaigns, and parties more broadly; prohibitions on retaliation, non-disclosure agreements, and mandatory arbitration; and policies for consensual romantic relationships (like a "one ask rule") and prohibiting alcohol use as an excuse for sexual harassment.[31]

## OFFICIAL INQUIRIES

Most initiatives to address sexual violence in politics have been developed and led by women's networks, usually operating outside of the confines of formal politics. However, in 2017 political fallout associated with the #MeToo movement led the British parliament to set up an official cross-party, bicameral working group—including representatives of parliamentary staff and a sexual violence expert—to develop an Independent Complaints and Grievance Scheme to handle complaints related to bullying and harassment on the parliamentary estate. It met 11 times in November and December, hearing from a variety of stakeholders, and commissioned a short survey of people employed at parliament.[32] In February 2018, the working group published its report and recommended not only introducing an independent complaints procedure, but also a new behavior code on bullying, harassment, and sexual harassment for everyone working or lawfully on the parliamentary estate; procedures for dealing with reports of sexual harassment; and a system of training to support the new code. It also put in place a number of immediate measures like interim human resources support for staff of MPs, including an expanded helpline.

While the working group focused its attention on the staff of MPs, it also reviewed two existing mechanisms for House of Commons employees (for example, those providing catering or janitorial services): the Respect Policy, covering House staff bullied by MPs; and the Valuing Others Policy, governing cases where House staff are bullied by other House staff. Although the Valuing Others Policy was adopted in 2007, the Respect Policy was introduced only in 2011 and even when revised in 2014, did not explicitly address sexual harassment. The working group advised correcting this oversight, but otherwise expressed satisfaction with the measures already in place. In March 2018, however, the House of Commons Commission, which employs House staff, announced an independent inquiry to be led by Dame Laura Cox, a former High Court judge with extensive background in employment and equality law. She was tasked with exploring the nature and extent of bullying, harassment, and sexual harassment of House staff, as well as the robustness of existing procedures for addressing these problems (Cox 2018).

DISSUASIVE SANCTIONS

In its pledge for EP candidates, MeTooEP called for "dissuasive sanctions for acts of sexual harassment."[33] While removing elected officials is rarely possible, parliaments have imposed a range of other penalties on those under investigation or found guilty of sexual violence. In the UK, the sanction used most extensively since October 2017 has been "removal of the whip," or the suspension of an MP from the party caucus—which amounts, in this context, to a statement of severe disapproval of behavior.[34] An MP, in contrast, cannot be removed from office, unless his or her constituents raise a petition and recall the MP, triggering a by-election—a mechanism that, to date, has never been used.[35]

Operating within a different legal system, legislators in France passed a law in September 2017 on "trust in political life," stipulating that anyone found guilty of a crime or misdemeanor, including sexual harassment, receive a compulsory supplementary punishment of ineligibility to hold or run for parliament office for a maximum of 10 years.[36] The clause on "moral and sexual harassment" was added via an amendment by Senator Laurence Rossignol during the bill's first reading in the Senate. It was adopted against the advice of the government, which argued that it fully shared in the aims of the amendment but cautioned the text might not be constitutional.[37] However, the final version was validated by the Constitutional Court, which noted that ineligibility was not automatic but had to be justified by the courts at the time of sentencing.[38]

In the United States, dissuasive sanctions took a different form. In October 2017, Representative Jackie Speier renewed her efforts to reform the Congressional Accountability Act to change the onerous process for workers at Capitol Hill to bring forward complaints of sexual harassment. Prior to reform, victims were required to undergo three months of mandated "counseling" and "mediation," as well as two "cooling off periods," before they could file an official complaint. During the first 30 days, moreover, victims were forbidden from telling anyone else that they were pursuing a complaint against a lawmaker or fellow staffer. Additionally, unlike members of the executive branch, lawmakers and congressional aides were not required to undergo sexual harassment training. When perpetrators were found guilty, finally, no public notice was required—enabling repeat offenders to continue the pattern of harassment with others.

In a video released on the day she introduced the #MeToo Congress bill, Speier shared her own experiences as a congressional staffer in the 1970s when the chief of staff "held my face, kissed me, and stuck his tongue in my mouth."[39] A July 2017 survey found that Speier's experience, even today, was not an isolated one: 40% of female staffers said there was a sexual harassment problem on Capitol Hill, and one in six had personally been harassed in their offices. Only 10% were aware that procedures existed to report misconduct (Bade and Schor 2017). Over the course of 2018, the two houses of the U.S. Congress adopted distinct forms of the bill. Both versions eliminated mandatory counseling and mediation periods and forced legislators to personally pay settlement claims for harassment. They differed, however, in the length of time required to file a complaint, definitions of "harassment," and whether lawmakers paid personally for claims of discrimination as well as harassment (Schor and Bade 2018). In December 2018, an agreement was reached, at least in part due to pressure from all 22 female senators in an unprecedented bipartisan display of support. The revised Congressional Accountability Act improves the process for congressional employees to report allegations of sexual harassment, stipulates that legislators are financially liable for harassment settlements, and increases transparency regarding the settlements reached.[40]

CODES OF CONDUCT

In response to allegations of sexual violence, some political institutions have developed codes of conduct to help reduce ambiguities regarding acceptable versus unacceptable behaviors in a political work context. In November 2014, two female MPs in Canada representing the New Democratic Party accused two male MPs from the Liberal Party, Scott Andrews and Massimo Pacetti, of sexual harassment. After officials realized they did not have procedures in place to deal with cases of MP-to-MP harassment, the House of Commons moved to create a Policy on Preventing and Addressing Harassment applying to all MPs, House officers, research officers, and staff in December 2014.[41] It also tasked the Standing Committee on Procedure and House Affairs with devising recommendations for a Code of Conduct on Sexual Harassment governing sexual harassment claims of a non-criminal nature between MPs. In June 2015, the code was approved, together with a pledge to be taken by all MPs "to contribute to a work environment free of sexual harassment."[42]

The Code of Conduct stipulates that party whips may serve as a first point of contact for complainants and may facilitate informal conversations when the complainant and respondent are members of the same party. In addition to providing training, the Chief Human Resources Officer (CHRO) may also serve as a first point of contact. The CHRO is responsible for guiding the dispute resolution process and retaining, if necessary, the services of an external investigator to conduct a fair and impartial investigation in a timely manner. The external investigator should state in the report if the facts support—or do not support—a finding of sexual harassment, or alternatively, if the complaint appeared to be "frivolous or vexatious or not made in good faith." Collier and Raney (2018) are critical of the policy. First, they point out that the code adopts a narrow definition of sexual harassment as "unwanted conduct of a sexual nature that detrimentally affects the work environment," entirely overlooking gender harassment. Second, parties retain considerable power and influence over the process. Whips thus may privilege quick and quiet resolutions to ensure less damage to their party, potentially at the expense of achieving justice for victims. Third, Collier and Raney condemn the decision to include language on "frivolous or vexatious" claims, arguing that this perpetuates debunked myths about false reporting—while also having a potentially chilling effect on women's willingness to come forward.

A slightly different approach was pursued in Chile, where #MeToo protests and sit-ins paralyzed higher education institutions across the country in April and May 2018. In June 2018, president of the lower house of parliament, Maya Fernández, announced she would review and revise internal protocols regarding sexual harassment. Finding that complaints against MPs were channeled through the Ethics Commission, whose code did not explicit forbid sexual harassment, she led a special committee to draft a new policy (Caro 2018). In January 2019, the Committee on Internal Regulations approved a Protocol on Prevention and Sanction of Sexual Harassment. The policy covers all workers and people visiting the parliamentary estate, including political journalists, and prohibits acts of a "nonconsensual sexual or intimate character that involve exchange of benefits or a threat, or generate an intimidatory, hostile, humiliating, degrading, or offensive work environment, involving an attempt against a person's dignity." Possible penalties ranged from fines to censures or reprimands, depending on the type of aggression (Muñoz 2019).

A final approach is simply to forbid sexual relationships between politicians and their subordinates. In February 2018, Australian prime minister Malcolm Turnbull responded to a scandal involving the deputy prime minister, Barnaby Joyce—whose affair with former staffer Vikki Campion came to light with her pregnancy—by imposing a ban on sexual relationships between ministers and their staff. Saying the incident raised "some serious issues about the culture of this place, of this parliament," Turnbull declared he would add a provision to the ministerial code of conduct to ensure that the standards of behavior spoke "clearly about the values of respect in workplaces, the values of integrity that Australians expect us to have" (Murphy 2018). The U.S. House of Representatives adopted a similar measure that same month, amending Rule 23 of its code of conduct to state that members "may not engage in a sexual relationship with any employee of the House who works under [their] supervision." In addition, members and employees "may not engage in unwelcome sexual advances or conduct" toward other members or employees. "Employee" is defined broadly to include job applicants, paid and unpaid interns (and applicants for internships), and those participating in fellowship programs.[43]

## ANTI-HARASSMENT TRAINING

A common approach to sexual violence scandals is to launch anti-harassment training initiatives. In some cases, these efforts meet with ridicule. After Swiss MP Yannick Buttet was accused of stalking an ex-girlfriend in November 2017, the Christian Democrats suspended him from the party, where he had been serving as vice president. Six women—including four MPs—then came forward with complaints of sexual harassment, and when criminal procedures began against him two weeks later, Buttet officially resigned. In response to these events, female MPs called for the creation of an office where victims of sexual harassment in parliament could seek confidential advice. Among the women disclosing their experiences, Conservative MP Céline Amaudruz shared that she had been sexually harassed on several occasions, involving "really inappropriate gestures that make you think twice about whether you dare take the elevator with certain people." Green MP Lisa Mazzone confirmed that such situations occurred in parliament, with acts "sometimes go[ing] beyond the framework of seduction," which can weigh heavily on women in an "atmosphere where sexist or tendentious remarks are permitted" (Bourget 2017).

In mid-December, parliamentary and party leaders met to discuss the Buttet case and its consequences. They decided to set up an independent complaints office for a year-long trial period. Those working at parliament would be able speak to a male or female officer and get advice in all three official languages. The financing provided for the unit was minimal, however, amounting to only 3600 Swiss francs. As an immediate measure, administrators also produced a leaflet distributed to MPs. It defined sexual harassment as any sexual or gender-related behavior that was unwanted on one side and violated a person's dignity. It provided a checklist, further, to clarify differences between flirting and sexual harassment, emphasizing that the deciding factor was the victim's perception—not that of the perpetrator. While a few left-wing MPs criticized the effort, many right-wing politicians derided it as "satire." According to MP Roger Köppel, there was no "real" sexism or sexual abuse in parliament and "with this monkey theater, they taunt the real victims of sexual assault" (Bühler 2017).

In Canada, interventions were more extensive. In the wake of the 2014 sexual harassment scandal, new frameworks were put in place to govern harassment disputes between the staff of MPs as well as cases of MP-to-MP sexual harassment. As part of these efforts, the human resources office developed an online training course on sexual harassment launched in late 2016. Completely voluntary, the training was completed by 620 MPs and staff over the course of the following year (Rana 2018). According to officials, parties were not willing to make their MPs and staff available for in-person trainings, arguing that an online option would be easier to fit in given their busy schedules.[44] To make sexual harassment training accessible beyond parliament, for example to staff in constituency offices, the website did not require a parliamentary login—which also meant, however, that officials were unable to track who had done and not done the training.

After the #MeToo movement got underway, parties and MPs changed their views on the value of sexual harassment training and began calling the human resources team to request in-person sessions. In late January 2018, these efforts accelerated when a number of high profile male politicians lost their positions in a matter of days due to sexual harassment allegations. The House speaker's communications director, Heather Bradley, announced that the House would spend $50,000 to organize in-person sexual harassment training for all MPs, cabinet ministers, and party leaders, in both official languages (Rana 2018). Parties, in turn, made these trainings mandatory, setting aside time for small groups to do the trainings during the weekly Wednesday caucus meetings.[45] The National Democratic Party and Liberal Party also hired outside experts to provide in-person trainings, focusing in particular on the importance of bystander intervention, at national party conventions in 2018 and 2019.[46]

## SAFETY MEASURES

Other tactics for tackling sexual violence in politics are more individualized, focused on equipping women with the skills to fight back against sexualized attacks. After finding that 14% of female journalists had been sexually assaulted and nearly half had experienced sexual harassment on the job (Barton and Storm 2014, 8), the IWMF sponsored a three-day training in Uganda organized by Global Journalist Security (GJS). Offering "hostile environment and first aid training" for reporters, GJS asserts that "a proactive and candid approach to sexual risk is essential in any security training."[47] While its director Frank Smyth was not sure if sexual violence was on the rise "or if women and men among the press corps have recently brought more attention to the issue by finally talking about it," he noted that female journalists appeared to be "at greater risk of being sexually assaulted than men, both by individual and group male attackers, as well as by sexually aggressive mobs." The aim of GJS is thus to go beyond the military-like training offered in other courses to break the stigma preventing frank discussion and to provide adequate preparation for confronting possible sexual violence in the field (Coates 2016).

In other contexts, women have taken it upon themselves to develop their own ad hoc security strategies. Phoebe Asiyo, one of the longest-serving female MPs in Kenya, stated that the greatest expense incurred by women running for parliament was security, which was necessary given frequent use of rape as an intimidation tactic. Mary Okumu, another Kenyan politician, was physically assaulted when running as a candidate in 2002. Corroborating Asiyo's account, Okumu shared that she and other female candidates "routinely carried concealed knives and wore two sets of tights under their dresses in order to buy more time to scream during an attempted rape" (Hunt 2007, 116).

SECURITY PATROLS

A final tactic involves protection brigades provided by members of civil society. In 2012, the rising number of sexual assaults in Tahrir Square in Cairo, Egypt, inspired several informal, youth-led initiatives to counter threats of sexual violence against women in public spaces. Bassma developed a strategy of "security patrols," whereby groups of young men in uniform walked around and made their protective presence known to deter sexual violence in crowded areas where sexual assaults often took place (Tadros 2015). A second group, the Tahrir Bodyguards, also first involved mainly men—until they realized that women under assault would hesitate to trust an all-male intervention team, often because some assailants would pretend to help women before assaulting them. The Bodyguards then recruited some women to join their teams, mainly to talk to people and hand out flyers (Langohr 2013).

OpAntiSH (Operation Anti Sexual Harassment) developed perhaps the most extensive approach. A confrontation group patrolled the square wearing t-shirts with slogans like "Against Harassment" and "A Square Safe for All," distributing cards with emergency hotline numbers with advice telling people what to do if they witnessed an assault. They also engaged in physical confrontation by entering circles of harassers to rescue victims. A safety group waited, usually in apartments close by, with first aid items and clothing and shoes for survivors, who were often stripped during the assaults. That group was then responsible for bringing the victim to a safe place, such as her home, an ambulance, or a hospital. An operations management group, finally, coordinated the work of the other two groups, responding to and making calls alerting the others as to where assaults were taking place. Together, the various patrols addressed a taboo topic with their conspicuous presence—and largely substituted for police who were absent from the square (Tadros 2015).

# 15

# Economic Violence

Economic violence employs economic hardship and deprivation as a means of control, most often by destroying a person's property or harming their financial livelihood as a form of intimidation. Feminist work typically views this form of violence in an intimate partner context, defining it as denial of access to resources in order to isolate a woman, create dependency on the perpetrator, and—if she refuses to comply—expose her to poverty and hardship (UN Department of Economic and Social Affairs 2014). Electoral violence frameworks often incorporate property damage, but tend to treat it as a manifestation of physical attacks on political opponents (Della Porta 1995; Norris, Frank, and Martínez i Coma 2015). While it is a new concept, the Council of Europe's Istanbul Convention and CEDAW General Recommendation No. 35 both recognize economic violence as a fourth category of violence against women—as does legislation in more than 80 countries around the world (World Bank 2016).

Forms of economic violence include vandalism, property destruction, theft, extortion, raids to remove property, withholding of funds and resources, threats to terminate employment, withdrawal of financial support, and restrictions on access to funding (APWLD 2007; Bardall 2011; UNDP and UN Women 2017). Despite direct links between economic violence and the ability of women to perform political functions, it remains a largely invisible phenomenon. Few women, indeed, appear willing to speak on the record about their experiences for fear of negative effects on their personal and professional livelihoods. A study on racial politics in the United States finds, however, that economic pressures were a common intimidation tactic used against black elected officials in the post–Civil Rights era. These ranged from vexatious civil and criminal tax audits to delaying or withholding state or federal funding for municipal services, filing false charges about misuse of public funds, and causing the failure of personal businesses (Warner 1977). Relative silence on these dynamics means that few measures exist to address economic violence, with

*Violence against Women in Politics.* Mona Lena Krook, Oxford University Press (2020). © Oxford University Press.
DOI: 10.1093/oso/9780190088460.001.0001.

civil society largely filling the gap to provide emergency grants and accounting oversight.

## Manifestations of Economic Violence

To capture economic violence, the IPU asked female parliamentarians whether they had ever been refused funds or resources to which they were entitled as MPs, or if their property had ever been damaged or destroyed in connection with their work in parliament. While economic violence is the least common form of violence experienced by women in European parliaments, affecting 13.5% of MPs (IPU 2018, 5), it is the second most common form in the global study. Nearly one-third of respondents (32.7%) reported facing some form of economic violence, far exceeding rates of physical (25.5%) and sexual (21.8%) violence (IPU 2016b, 3). Of these, more had seen their property damaged or destroyed (18.2%), but a significant share had been denied funds (14.5%) or resources (12.7%), affecting their political work (IPU 2016b, 5). These patterns are repeated among European MPs, with 10% stating their property had been damaged or destroyed and 7.5% revealing they had faced barriers in gaining access to resources to which they were entitled (IPU 2018, 8). News coverage and women's direct testimonies, some given only anonymously, point to tactics like vandalism and property destruction, stealing and other forms of property removal, and withholding of economic resources, including state funding.

### VANDALISM AND PROPERTY DESTRUCTION

Women around the world have experienced various attacks on their property, including campaign materials and political office spaces—as well as their homes and personal belongings. During the 2018 elections in Iraq, the first since the defeat of ISIS, female candidates faced far higher levels of violence than witnessed in previous elections (Tajali and Farhan 2018). Women faced extensive vandalism of their campaign posters, in particular. Both women with "veil-framed faces" and those "with make-up and without the traditional Islamic headscarf" were targeted, with posters "splattered with mud, defaced with beards draw on, or completely torn up" (Abdul-Hassan and Salaheddin 2018). This vandalism—together with wide-ranging online abuse—led the Committee of the Electoral Charter of Honor, a voluntary agreement among parties to respect free and fair elections, and the UN Special Representative in Iraq, Ján Kubiš, to "call upon all state and political leaders to raise their voices and stand against the targeting and defamation of women candidates."[1]

In Canada, staffers arrived at the local constituency office of MP Catherine McKenna in October 2019 to find the word "cunt" spray painted in red letters across a large image of her face on the front window. As McKenna had served as Minister of Environment and Climate Change for the last four years, the incident received extensive attention in the Canadian press. Theresa Kavanagh, Ottawa City Council's special liaison on women's issues, suggested the incident should be treated as a hate crime. When asked by reporters if the vandalism made her think twice about being in politics, McKenna attributed the attack to "people [who] clearly want to chase women out of politics." She noted, however, that leaving would not "make politics any better" and declared "it's just going to make me re-commit to making it a better place for women [and] for diversity of all sorts" (Glowacki and Foote 2019).

Three years earlier, a similar incident occurred at the constituency office of British MP Angela Eagle. In July 2016, as she was running to become leader of the Labour Party, a brick was thrown through the window, breaking the glass.[2] The vandalism formed part of a series of attacks on Eagle during the leadership campaign, including death threats, abusive phone calls, and online abuse, including the hijacking of her Facebook page[3]—leading her staff to cancel events and unplug the phones for a period of time (Riley-Smith and Evans 2016). A subsequent internal investigation by the party found that Eagle, the first openly lesbian MP, had received hundreds of "abusive, homophobic, and frightening" messages from party members. They determined that it was "highly likely" that the brick thrown through the window was related to her leadership bid. The investigation also revealed that her office had suffered from coordinated denial of service attacks on their internet, a further form of vandalism (Mason 2016).

Testimonies from women in other countries indicate that attacks on personal property are not uncommon—and are often devastating. Sarah Mahoka, a parliamentary candidate in Zimbabwe, stated that, in addition to burning her campaign t-shirts, opponents "burn[ed] my fertilizer and maize which I use to assist people in the constituency. My cattle were also targeted" (Langa 2018). In a focus group organized by NDI, a female party member in Tanzania shared: "During the campaign one man told me that if I win my house and everything in it will be set on fire. I was frightened to the point that I thought of withdrawing my candidature." Another in Côte d'Ivoire revealed how this violence had affected her family and professional life: "My house has been attacked several times. My husband left and I was fired from my job. My only hope is the party; otherwise I no longer have anything" (NDI 2018, 24–25). Still other women have faced abuse from family members, like Sakhina, a candidate in Bangladesh, whose husband did not approve of her involvement in politics and "burned all her saris in an attempt to stop her from going for election campaigns" (SAP International 2006, 28).

STEALING AND PROPERTY REMOVAL

A related tactic involves stealing or removing property in order to intimidate as well as obstruct women's political work. In 2007, AWID conducted a global survey of more than 1600 women's rights activists and found that nearly 10% had their workplaces destroyed or equipment stolen by religious fundamentalists (Balchin 2008, 26). Most of these incidents occurred in Latin America and the Caribbean. Female politicians in the region have confronted similar challenges, but in these cases, perpetrators are often party or political colleagues. This has been a particular problem in Bolivia, where elected positions are subject to gender parity as well as "alternate succession," whereby officeholders—should they not be able to serve their full mandates—have alternates of the opposite sex. While the latter provision was adopted to ensure that women were not only nominated as alternates, it had the unanticipated effect of contributing to a growth in the number of cases of violence against women in politics, as male alternates employed a host of means to force women to resign so they could access their seats.

Many women were told falsely, for example, that "alternation" meant they would be in office for the first half of the mandate, followed by the male alternate in the second half. To ensure they left office, women were often pressured to sign resignation letters or even simply blank pieces of paper, or to write promissory notes for two and a half years of salary (half the period of the mandate). The latter would put her in debt to her alternate if she later changed her mind and decided to remain in office (Restrepo Sanín 2018b). In one case, the alternate went further by pressuring the councilor to write a document granting him the same powers and responsibilities and stipulating equal distribution of her salary among the two of them (ACOBOL 2012, 10). These forms of economic coercion were highly effective, resulting in sharp increases in the number of women resigning in 2002, 2008, and 2013, approximately two and a half years after elections were held (Restrepo Sanín 2018b, 111).

A second form of stealing entails identity theft. In 2017, former Breitbart editor Milo Yiannopoulos posted a video on Facebook in which Australian Senator Katy Gallagher accused a male senator, Mitch Fifield, of "mansplaining." Viewed more than a million times, the video quickly mobilized an army of right-wing trolls to attack her. In addition to calling her a bitch, bigot, hypocrite, and "misandrist who is not fit to hold public office," they created numerous fake accounts using the same profile and banner pictures as her own verified account.[4] The fake accounts then pretended to be Gallagher, commenting on posts made on her verified page and swearing at and abusing her supporters. Once her office realized what was happening and began deleting the offending comments, she posted: "Looks like my page was hacked. Apologies to those who were offended by some comments posted in my name—they weren't from me I promise. Thank you to those who alerted me."[5] Her staffers reported and blocked the fake accounts, but—due to the structure of Facebook—were not able to prevent others from setting up similar pages using her name and picture (Workman 2017).

Among human rights defenders, raids by state officials are a more common form of economic violence. During these searches, police may remove various materials from human rights defenders' offices, in turn both obstructing their work and endangering those on whose behalf they work (APWLD 2007). Since coming to power in Poland in 2016, the ruling Law and Justice Party has targeted women's rights groups using various forms of economic intimidation. In 2017, the government sent police to raid the offices of two women's rights groups across four cities simultaneously: the Women's Rights Center in Warsaw, Łódź, and Gdańsk, and BABA in Zielona Góra, both of which work with survivors of gender-based violence. Anna Głogowska-Balcerzak, based in the Women's Rights Center in Łódź, was on the phone with Urszula Nowakowska in Warsaw when they realized police had arrived unannounced at both centers. Głogowska-Balcerzak recounted: "It was scary—it was a coordinated action. You don't use these kinds of methods to deal with non-suspects" (Human Rights Watch 2019, 51).

Police stated that the raids were part of an investigation into alleged misconduct on the part of officials in the Ministry of Justice under the former government. The fact that both groups had received funding from the ministry, police claimed, provided grounds for both the search and seizure of property. Yet the raids occurred just one day after women had staged protests against the country's restrictive abortion law, raising suspicions about their timing. Moreover, as funding recipients, both organizations had already submitted extensive documentation to the government, leading one woman to remark: "They already have all the documentation at the ministry, so [the raids] were also symbolic." Materials removed from the activists' offices included documents as well as computer hard drives, which the women pointed out would hamper their work and create risks for victims of domestic abuse who had sought their help (Associated Press 2017).

Other Polish women's rights activists report being denied space to conduct their activities—a problem that they cannot resolve because pursuing legal action would further deplete their limited resources. Renata Durda, for instance, said her organization, Blue Line, was abruptly removed from its space in 2018 by the local government. Katarzyna Kamecka-Lach, who heads the Center of the East, reported that local officials rescinded an agreement granting them a workplace in a school when they were only halfway through the contract. Although officials claimed it was urgently needed for something else, the space remained unoccupied and, she noted: "They hadn't even taken down the nameplate of [our] organization" (Human Rights Watch 2019, 64).

## WITHHOLDING OF ECONOMIC RESOURCES

A final set of tools entails withholding economic resources from women to coerce them and frustrate and undermine their political participation In these cases, economic violence restricts women's access to resources that are otherwise available to men. Conducting a survey of nearly 200 female local and regional councilors in Peru, Quintanilla Zapata (2012) finds that 14% had experienced some form of "economic control" in the course of their political work (9). For some women, the perpetrators are close to home. One local councilor related that, in addition to resistance from her colleagues at work, her spouse prevented her from accessing the family's money after she was elected: "My husband has cut off money to me since I became a local councilor. I am afraid. I am afraid to complain" (14).

Other acts of economic violence are rooted in omissions on the part of other elected officials, like mayors, regional presidents, and municipal and regional bureaucrats, in fulfilling their legal obligations. In Peru, these include "unjustified suspensions, unpaid expenses, [and] refusal of leaves to which one is entitled" (Quintanilla Zapata 2012, 28). In El Salvador, women report being denied or delayed in receiving the public allowances owed to them for attending sessions of the city council (Herrera, Arias, and García 2012). A local councilor in Costa Rica, similarly, noted that women on the council were refused resources provided to men. One explained how this affected her work and her personal finances: "I have been denied a physical space to attend to the people. I have not been assigned a car or a phone. I use my personal resources" (Escalante and Mendez 2011, 22). This is true even of women holding leadership positions, as one female MP shared: "I had to press to obtain a car, additional financing, and security as enjoyed by my male predecessor. I obtained none of it and just gave up" (IPU 2016b, 5).

Female voters may be vulnerable to other economic pressures. In 2015, citizen election observers in Guatemala discovered that women were sometimes forced to participate in political party rallies or were threatened with the loss of social benefits if they did not register with a party or pledge to vote for a certain candidate. Juana Baca, who coordinates a network of indigenous women, noted that women were often the ones receiving social benefits. Together with women's often more marginalized economic status, this rendered them more susceptible to these forms of coercion. Few questioned these dynamics, Baca observed, because "politicians have used social programs to perpetuate violence against women and women are conditioned to think that this is normal" (Barker 2016).

Related dynamics operate with respect to female activists, for whom an important source of precarity is unpredictable access to funding necessary to carry out their activities. Restricting their ability to fundraise, or removing existing funding streams, can thus be an effective form of economic retribution and control—making it impossible to operate unless conforming to state or donor demands. In 1984, U.S. President Ronald Reagan introduced the Mexico City Policy, or "global gag rule," which requires NGOs to agree—as a condition of receiving any U.S. funding—that they "would neither perform nor actively promote abortion as a method of family planning in other nations." Revoked by Bill Clinton in 1993, the gag rule was re-introduced by George W. Bush, lifted by Barack Obama, and reinstated by Donald Trump. Trump, however, expanded its provisions to ban health funding to NGOs using their own funds to provide counseling, referrals, services or to advocate for safe abortion, amounting to 15 times the reach of previous policies.[6] In a report to the General Assembly, the UN Special Rapporteur on Human Rights Defenders noted with regret its adverse impact on "women defenders working on sexual and reproductive rights, HIV, sexual orientation and gender identity rights, and sex workers' rights" (Forst 2019, 6).

In Poland, the Law and Justice Party declared itself an enemy of "gender ideology," a derogatory term for work to promote gender equality (Corredor 2019). Used by anti-gender movements around the world, the concept enlists extreme rhetoric and tactics to attack and intimidate women human rights defenders, claiming that gender equality poses a threat to families and traditional values, especially when it entails rights and recognition for the LGBT community (Kuhar and Paternotte 2017). In 2017, the new Polish cabinet created a centralized agency to oversee disbursement of government funding to civil society, replacing the system of individual ministries allocating funds to groups related to their mandates. When the bill was still in draft form, the OSCE urged the government to decentralize the process and include safeguards to ensure that funding decisions were free from political interference. It disregarded this advice and its appointments to the new agency included a director and at least one member who had publicly discredited and demonized women's and LGBT rights organizations (Human Rights Watch 2019).

Interviewing 30 activists, supporters, and attorneys in 2018, HRW found that seven organizations that had previously received government funding from three ministries—the Ministry of Justice; the Ministry of Family, Labor, and Social Policy; and the Ministry of National Education—had their funding discontinued or drastically reduced. Groups working on violence against women had been forced to cut staff, restrict their geographic coverage, and reduce essential activities like providing shelter and legal and psychological support for survivors. Those focused on sexual and reproductive health reported that a combination of funding and political pressures had decreased opportunities for collaboration with schools and communities, including the provision of educational workshops. In all but one case, the government did not provide clear explanations of why funding was discontinued (Human Rights Watch 2019, 39–40).

Prior to the creation of the new centralized agency, but after the Law and Justice Party came to power, women faced other government pressures intended at undermining their political work. Renata Durda, the executive director of Blue Line, which provides services to victims of violence, shared that—after she went to the press to complain about funding cuts—government officials invited her to the Ministry of Justice and told her they were certain the organization had something to hide—and they would prove it. They then conducted a three-year-long audit of Blue Line's finances, a process that should have only taken a few months. In another case, the Autonomia Foundation, which conducts anti-violence and anti-discrimination workshops, had its funding rescinded mid-grant, accompanied by a demand for repayment of money already spent on project activities, plus interest, within 15 days of the grant termination. The letter was dated one day after a monitoring visit by officials from the Ministry of Family, Labor, and Social Policy. The visit was prompted by criticisms by MPs Robert Winnicki and Piotr Uściński, who claimed the group's leader was a "lesbian feminist" and called their work a form of "feminist and homosexual agitation" (Human Rights Watch 2019, 48). The ministry finally agreed to drop the demand for repayment after a year of exchanging documents, reports, and information—at which point, Autonomia had already reduced its activities and given up its office space.

## Solutions to Economic Violence

Legal measures to counteract economic violence are few and far between. Law 243 in Bolivia includes economic violations within its list of sample acts of political violence and harassment against women, calling out acts that "apply pecuniary sanctions, arbitrary and illegal deductions, and/or withholding of salaries."[7] The UN Declaration on the Rights of Human Rights Defenders also stipulates in Article 13 that everyone has the right "to solicit, receive and utilize resources for the . . . purpose of promoting and protecting human rights and fundamental freedoms through peaceful means" (UN General Assembly 1998, 6). Despite this provision, a growing number of governments prohibit NGOs from or punish them for receiving funds from abroad (Carothers 2006). Some civil society groups, however, provide economic support or press governments to be accountable for the funding they provide.

### EMERGENCY GRANTS

Several programs exist to support at-risk women human rights defenders with economic resources to continue their work. Some involve awards offering public recognition while also providing significant monetary prizes that can support relocation as well as legal fees. These include the Yayori Award from Japan, focusing on female activists, journalists, and artists, and the International Service for Human Rights Awards, with a specific category for women human rights defenders. Other awards are not limited—but often awarded—to women, like the Martin Ennals Award for Human Rights Defenders and the Roger N. Baldwin Medal of Liberty.

Other grassroots organizations provide emergency grants and relief programs available to a wider array of women. Often approving applications within a matter of days, these groups offer funding that can be used to meet a wide range of needs, including improving security (like hiring security guards and installing surveillance cameras and bars on windows), paying medical or legal costs, or supporting evacuation to safe houses—and, if necessary, temporary relocation (Barcia 2011).

One example is the UAF, based in the United States, which offers "rapid response grants" for women and trans* defenders in urgent situations. The organization accepts applications in any language using online, text, and mobile funding applications for requests up to $8,000. UAF staffers respond to all requests within 24 hours, 365 days a year, and make most decisions within one to ten business days. Arguing that these grants are "a lifeline to women's human rights defenders worldwide," the model enables defenders to "act quickly, take advantage of unexpected opportunities, mitigate threats, and/or prevent back-sliding in their ongoing work."[8] By its 10th anniversary in 2007, UAF had supported more than 100 activists from 45 countries, reviewing 2256 grant requests (Barry with Đorđević 2007, viii).

## ACCOUNTING PRESSURES

A second category of measures is illustrated by efforts of the 2% + More Women in Politics campaign in Mexico. In 2008, a reform to the political party financing law created a new obligation on parties to dedicate 2% of their public financing to the training, promotion, and development of women's political leadership. These programs were required to benefit the largest share of women possible through direct activities engaging their participation. In 2011, however, an audit of party expenses using freedom of information requests revealed that parties rarely applied these funds for the purposes for which they were intended.

The National Action Party, at the time the largest party in parliament, used some money to pay for trainings and other activities for women. A not-insignificant amount, however, was spent on bags, pens, bracelets, and balloons with party logos. The Institutional Revolutionary Party, the next biggest party, did not appear to direct any funds to activities for women. While some money was spent on celebrating the party's founding as well as supporting a youth conference, the bulk was used to pay for general services, like telephone calls, electricity, water, security, equipment and building maintenance, laundry, cleaning, and fumigation. The Party of the Democratic Revolution did not account for how it used the funds and was fined a small amount as a result (Cárdenas Morales 2011, 34–39).

In early 2010, women's groups came together with NDI to launch the 2% campaign to ensure that parties in fact spent these earmarked funds to support women's political participation. The network held a series of workshops and engaged in extensive online activism, both to raise awareness among women in the parties as well as to pressure the accounting unit of the Federal Electoral Institute (IFE) to more carefully scrutinize receipts provided by parties to ensure they complied with the 2% earmark. In working sessions with the parties and IFE, the campaign helped develop a new regulation on accountability for this aspect of party spending, which was approved by the IFE Executive Council in 2011. While parties continue to violate the provision, spending the money on gas, printer paper, toner, and bracelets with party logos (Arteta 2019), the earmark was increased to 3% in 2014 and expenses continue to be monitored closely—marking it as an important advance in ensuring that women are not deprived of economic resources to which they are entitled in the political realm.

# 16
# Semiotic Violence

Case materials around the world provide ample evidence for physical, psychological, sexual, and economic violence against women in politics. However, inductive research reveals that these four categories do not exhaust the spectrum of acts constituting violence against women in the political realm. These dynamics "without a name" involve mobilizing semiotic resources—words, images, and even body language—to injure, discipline, and subjugate women. Unlike other forms of violence against women, these acts are less about attacking particular women directly than about shaping public perceptions about the validity of women's political participation more broadly. Naming these dynamics is not only crucial for recognizing additional points on the continuum of violence, but also for spotlighting how this type of violence interacts with and bolsters the injuries committed through the other four more widely recognized forms.

Although this book introduces the concept of semiotic violence, a wide range of existing literatures—in fields as diverse as law, linguistics, psychology, political science, sociology, and gender studies—lend support to conceptualizing language and images as forms of "violence" when used to inflict harm and injury by communicating a message of group-based inferiority. Analyzed inductively, women's experiences in politics suggest two main modes of semiotic violence: *rendering women invisible*, attempting to "symbolically annihilate" women in the public sphere; and *rendering women incompetent*, emphasizing "role incongruity" between being a woman and being a leader. Emerging solutions seek to counteract these dynamics by revising or reversing prevailing semiotic frames and forging new semiotic tools to defend women's right to participate and create a more inclusive public sphere.

*Violence against Women in Politics.* Mona Lena Krook, Oxford University Press (2020). © Oxford University Press.
DOI: 10.1093/oso/9780190088460.001.0001.

## Semiotic Violence as a Concept

Semiotics is the study of signs. Drawing on the philosophy of language and philosophy of art and aesthetics, semiotic analysis "reads" words and images as "texts" to gain insight into the interpretive frameworks filtering and guiding human perceptions of the world (Chandler 2017). According to Peirce (1994), all experience is mediated by signs, making their role in structuring thought processes, ironically, highly invisible and unconscious. The aim of semiotic analysis for Saussure (2011 [1959]) is thus to search for basic signifying units and regularities that can render these interpretive systems more explicit. Relevant to feminist research, semiotic analysis understands signs to be socially constructed, rather than faithful and straightforward reflections of the external world. These constructs often center the perspectives and experiences of privileged groups, creating and maintaining social hierarchies (Barthes 1957). Deconstructing signs can thus serve to reveal and challenge systems of privilege and oppression (Chandler 2017).

Semiotic analysis, together with theories of structural, cultural, and symbolic violence, suggests that words and images offer important resources for preserving the gendered status quo, including in the political world. In her work on misogyny, Manne (2018, 76) captures this insight when she observes that in response to the "psychic threat posed by powerful women . . . women may be taken down *imaginatively*, rather than literally, by vilifying, demonizing, belittling, humiliating, mocking, lampooning, shunning, and shaming them." This book proposes to call these dynamics "semiotic violence." As a general concept, semiotic violence entails drawing on and reinforcing inequalities by using words and images—and in some cases, body language—to injure, discipline, and subjugate members of marginalized groups. In the current context, it refers specifically to the use of semiotic resources to deny women's political rights. A defining feature of semiotic violence is its public signification: while perpetrated against *individuals*, it seeks to send a message that the *person's group* is unworthy, aiming to affect how the *public at large* views members of that group. Such acts may gain further resonance by tapping semiotic resources for denigrating other groups, creating intersectional manifestations of violence.

The concept of semiotic violence is implicitly present in many bodies of academic research. These literatures explore how language and images may enact violence in the sense used throughout this book, as a *violation of integrity* or attack on the wholeness or intactness of the self (Bufacchi 2007). Critical race scholars in the legal field, for instance, theorize hate rhetoric as "assaultive speech," with "trauma [inflicted] by racist assailants who employ words and symbols as part of an integrated arsenal of weapons of oppression and subordination" (Matsuda, Lawrence, Delgado, and Crenshaw 1993, 7). Through assaultive speech, freedom of expression becomes an instrument of domination: its aim is no longer to discover truth or initiate dialogue, but rather to injure and silence the victim through repeated messages of group-based inferiority. Because such speech seeks to dehumanize, degrade, and humiliate, the resulting "psychic injury is no less an injury than being struck in the face, and it often is far more severe" (74).

Linguistic research, similarly, argues that group-based slurs perpetuate discrimination because they offer "speakers a linguistic resource with which to dehumanize their targets and identify them in 'subhuman,' rather than full human, terms" (Croom 2013, 189). Pejorative slurs about women affront their personal integrity and autonomy by communicating beliefs about men's and women's essential differences, women's inferiority to men, and women's lack of ownership over their own bodies. Epithets like "whore" and "slut" use sexual shaming to deny women basic human dignity, while "bitch" and "cunt" dehumanize and discredit women to silence their voices and stifle their participation in public discourse (Levey 2018).

Psychological studies of sexist humor provide insight into why these wounding words are so pernicious, yet also difficult to challenge. Framing remarks as a "joke," these scholars note, is often a deliberate strategy employed by perpetrators to avoid disapproval normally associated with discriminatory conduct. Yet a sexist joke is not "an isolated event in which a woman is harmlessly teased or ridiculed; it is rather one instance among many in which women are belittled or disparaged" (Bergmann 1986, 76). Corroborating these insights, recurring themes in sexist humor involve sexual objectification of women, devaluation of women's personal and professional abilities, and support for violence against women (Bemiller and Schneider 2010).

In an analogous way, feminist critiques of pornography argue that pornographic images seek to dehumanize, degrade, and subordinate women (Itzin 2002). Like sexist jokes, these images are often viewed as "innocent leisure" (Cawston 2018, 649), but in fact depict or defend sexualized violence against women—including via sexually graphic, digitally altered images of female politicians—as pleasurable, natural, or deserved (Sheeler and Anderson 2013). Some authors go so far as to claim that each creation or use of pornography is "itself a politically gendered oppressive act" (Cowburn and Pringle 2000, 59).

Recent work on online misogyny explores how technological advances generate new opportunities for "image-based sexual abuse" (McGlynn, Rackley, and Houghton 2017). Noting that existing criminal codes are often limited to the protection of physical bodies, this research argues that technology-facilitated sexual violence—like creating and distributing (doctored) sexual and sexual assault images, gender-based hate speech, and virtual rape—should also be recognized as "embodied harms." This is because these harms, although taking place in the virtual domain, can have at least as much impact on a person as traditional injuries against a physical body (Henry and Powell 2015).

Research on some forms of body language, finally, points to ways in which asymmetry in status can be communicated through verbal and non-verbal interactions, including forms of address, norms of touching, and patterns of interruption. These behaviors, Henley (1977) argues, serve as mechanisms of social control, reinforcing relationships of power between different categories of people. Such microaggressions "send denigrating messages to certain individuals because of their group membership" (Sue 2010, 24), yet are often so pervasive that their harmful nature is overlooked or forcefully denied.

The concept of semiotic violence ties together the insights from these various literatures, which collectively illustrate how language and images may be deployed to resist, exclude, and undermine members of marginalized groups, particularly women. One implication of tendencies to "naturalize" semiotic violence, however, is that this form of violence remains invisible as well as trivialized. Further developing this concept can thus serve both a theoretical and a political purpose, giving a shared name to dynamics that, to date, have been analyzed separately—and focusing efforts, in turn, on calling out and dismantling semiotic violence as a widespread and pernicious weapon of harm and exclusion.

## Manifestations of Semiotic Violence

Semiotic analysis highlights the structural nature of signs. This contributes to their invisible but pervasive impact—but also implies that their manifestations are not infinitely variable, but rather, both systematic and predictable. Jane (2017) notes, for example, that gendered vitriol often has a "quasi-algebraic quality," with elements seemingly restricted to a "range of pre-determined parameters" that can be "substituted endlessly without altering the structure of the discourse." As a consequence, searching for themes in online misogyny quickly reaches a "saturation point," after which "antagonists seem to run out of ideas" (36). An inductive analysis of women's experiences reveals similar findings in the political realm, with semiotic attacks on politically active women taking two broad forms: rendering women invisible and rendering women incompetent. Within each mode, recurring sub-types can be identified, illustrating the varied—but also limited number of—ways that language and images may be mobilized to resist, exclude, and undermine women as political actors.

### RENDERING INVISIBLE

The first mode of semiotic violence involves rendering women invisible in the political sphere. These acts attempt to "symbolically annihilate" politically active women by refusing to acknowledge their political presence or contributions to political debates. Reinforcing the male as norm, they imply that men are the only legitimate participants—or, if women are included, that men are the only ones whose presence "counts." As a result of these dynamics, the idea that women can be political actors, especially leaders, produces strong cognitive dissonance among the general public, contributing to women's ongoing secondary status.

The concept of symbolic annihilation emerged in media studies with Gerbner's (1972, 43–44) statement: "representation in the fictional world signifies social existence; absence means symbolic annihilation." The lack of women on television is significant, according to Tuchman (1978), because it suggests to viewers that women do not exist—or, if they do, they do not matter much in society. The treatment of the few women who are included—for example, as sexual objects or through the denigration of working women—strengthens this message, cultivating specific ideas about how the world works and where power resides (Gerbner 1972).[1]

Political scientists theorize an analogous dynamic stemming from women's relative absence in political media. Pointing to the lack of women in British election coverage, Walsh (2001, 94) observes, for example, that "the structured invisibility of women is likely to sustain the damaging myth that politics is primarily a 'man's game.'" Confirming this intuition empirically, research shows a close correlation between the share of women as news subjects and experts and the share of female candidates for parliament (Haraldsson and Wängnerud 2019).

Experiences around the world point to at least seven tactics for symbolically annihilating women in politics. These range from erasure of women as political actors to denial of women's rights to speak and be heard in political debates. At the individual level, many acts are also instances of psychological violence, seeking to obstruct the participation of specific women by affecting their mental states through exclusion and trivialization. By playing out before the eyes of the general public, however, the impact of these acts reach beyond the affected individuals, sending a message to society—via these symbolizing actions—that women are not worthy or equal participants in the political realm.

## Removal

Women can be removed from political spaces in a variety of ways. Legal concepts may deny the full humanity of women, rendering them legally invisible and preventing the exercise of their political rights. In Canada, women gained political rights in most parts of the country by 1922. However, they remained excluded from appointment to the Senate by language in Section 24 of the British North America Act (1867), which restricted this to "qualified persons."[2] Emily Murphy, a magistrate, lobbied three prime ministers, only to be told repeatedly that women were not considered "persons" in the constitution. Turning to the courts, Murphy joined four women in petitioning the Supreme Court, which decided in 1928 that women were "expressly excluded from the class of 'qualified persons.'"[3] The women appealed to the British Privy Council, the highest court, which decided in 1929 that "the world 'persons'. . . includes members both of the male and female sex."[4] This struggle illustrates how legal concepts may deny the full humanity of women, rendering them legally invisible and preventing the exercise of their political rights.

In other cases, appeals to customary practices make women literally invisible in political spaces. Although women gained suffrage in Pakistan in 1947, women were barred from voting in many areas. In Dhurnal, a village in Punjab, elders endorsed a ban on women voting prior to the 1962 elections. By sealing it with a prayer, they prevented any households from violating the ban and subjected any who did to social and religious boycott. While some male politicians argued that "if women are happy to follow local traditions, no one should have any objection to it," one young woman in Dhurnal, speaking on condition of anonymity, told reporters: "I know that voting is my constitutional and fundamental right but still I cannot exercise it since I need the permission of men in my household to do so" (Dastageer and Safdar 2018). As a result, even in recent years some polling stations reported that not a single woman had voted.

### Non-Portrayal

Another tactic is simply not to portray women involved in politics, erasing them from public consciousness as actors in the political realm. On several occasions in Israel, ultra-Orthodox newspapers have digitally altered photos of the national cabinet to remove, replace, or block out women. In 2009, one paper erased the two female ministers, Limor Livnat and Sofa Landver, and put two men in their place; another simply blacked out their faces (Shabi 2009). In 2015, three women—Ayelet Shaked, Miri Regev, and Gila Gamliel—were appointed to the new cabinet. Some ultra-Orthodox news outlets declined to publish the photo, while others opted for various digital editing strategies: pixelating the women's faces, editing the three women out, and removing the three women and adding a man in one of the spots (Goldman 2015).

Using a different medium, in early 2019 a toy company in the United States launched a line of Lego-like mini-figures of the "2020 presidential candidates." The series, however, included only the four men who had announced their presidential runs: Beto O'Rourke, Bernie Sanders, Cory Booker, and Pete Buttigieg. When asked by a reporter why the company had not created figures of any of the women who had launched campaigns—like Elizabeth Warren, Kamala Harris, or Kirsten Gillibrand—the company's CEO replied that these would be added later because "at the moment we do not have female hair for the lady candidates" (Render 2019). Given that the company boasts of selling mini-figures of all U.S. presidents, including Donald Trump, failing to stock such a key item is a telling oversight—reflecting and reinforcing the notion that only men can be presidents.

Misrecognition

When members of marginalized groups gain access to political positions, they are often viewed as "space invaders," as "bodies out of place" inside political institutions (Puwar 2004). This dynamic can give rise to encounters with colleagues and others where their identity as political actors is not recognized— and, indeed, sometimes actively contested—reinforcing their secondary status. By these processes, women become figuratively invisible, despite overcoming literal invisibility associated with explicit exclusion. Being from another politically marginalized group can heighten these effects, creating intersectional manifestations of semiotic violence.

In one incident in Denmark, various party leaders had gathered at a television studio prior to taking part in a panel discussion in 2007. During the preparations, Conservative Party leader Bendt Bendtsen asked a young woman to fetch him some coffee. She turned out to be the 23-year-old leader of the Red-Green Alliance, Johanne Schmidt-Nielsen. Rather than tell him who she was, she replied that, unfortunately, she did not know where the coffee was. As the program began, Bendtsen got the "shock of his life" when he subsequently saw the "office girl" on the party leader panel (Nilsson 2007).

That same year, Iyabo Obasanjo became the youngest senator in Nigeria, elected together with eight other women and 100 men.[5] Despite a badge identifying her as a senator, security guards often refused to let her in, only relenting after verifying all her credentials each time. She then hired a 25-year-old female assistant, and one day guards denied her entry into the Senate building. Because male citizens at the gates were being very aggressive, Obasanjo was forced to leave the chamber, where she was due to speak, to prevent her assistant from being assaulted by the crowds. She learned that the Senate president had given instructions to the guards not to let in any young women, owing to rumors that they would "entice men" who would in turn give them money for sex. The policy assumed, clearly, that young women could not be senators or staffers, in addition to blaming women, rather than men, for demands for sexual favors.[6]

Other women's experiences reflect the dual impact of race and gender. Dawn Butler, the third black woman to be elected to the British parliament, has spoken up about multiple incidents. On one occasion, she was inside a "members only" elevator when a fellow MP reportedly commented, "This lift really isn't for cleaners." Another time, a former minister, David Heathcote-Amory, confronted her in the members' section of the terrace, saying, "What are you doing here? This is for members only." When questioned in the press, Heathcote-Amory answered that "he was simply asking" and that "they are quite sensitive about this kind of thing, they think that any kind of reprimand from anyone is racially motivated" (Oppenheim 2016a). Rather than seeing any problem with his behavior, he thus shifted the fault onto Butler for taking offense—further marginalizing her as an "outsider" in political space.

A final form of misrecognition involves confusing political women for one another. In an interview in 2004, Gillian Shepherd shared that, when she first became an MP in 1987, "there was a Conservative MP who was a backbencher, but rather a prominent one, and he called us all Betty. And when I said, 'Look, you know, my name isn't Betty,' he said, 'Ah but you're all the same, so I call you Betty, it's easier'" (Sones 2005, 77). This problem is not confined to the past. After the 2018 elections, Katie Hill and Katie Porter were elected to the U.S. Congress from Southern California. Despite widely distinct personal and professional profiles, constituents, congressional staffers, reporters, and even colleagues regularly mix them up. "It's constant," said Porter, while Hill commented: "Why is this so hard? We don't look anything alike." Reflecting a sense of being a "space invader," Porter ruminated: "Being constantly confused with another member, it deepens the sense of dislocation and 'Do I belong here?'" (Haberkorn 2019).

### Masculinization

A further way to render women invisible is to appeal to male-centered rules of grammar when referring to politicians, implying these positions cannot—and should not—be feminized. Sensitive to this dynamic, upon becoming president of the Italian Chamber of Deputies in 2013, Laura Boldrini sent a letter to MPs asking them to use the appropriate gender when talking about other MPs. In an interview, she explained: "Language is not only a semantic issue . . . When you are opposed to saying *la ministra or la presidente* it means that culturally you are not admitting that women can reach top positions" (Feder, Nardelli, and Maria De Luca 2018). This problem originates in a tendency in many languages to treat men as the "unmarked" or "generic" category and women, conversely, as the "marked" or "subsumed" category. "Generic masculine" forms not only render women invisible (Pauwels 2003), but also create ambiguity for women, as male-designated terms may or may not actually include them (Spender 1980). In a work context, gender-exclusive language can thus subtly inform women that they do not belong (Stout and Dasgupta 2011).

In France, debates on this issue have waged for more than twenty years. In 1997, the new Socialist government decided to address female politicians with feminine titles, despite protests from the Académie Française, the French language council. Female ministers subsequently had feminine titles printed on official stationery and signs on their office doors replaced (Burr 2003). In 2014, a heated exchange in parliament brought this question back into the public eye. In a session presided over by Vice-President of the National Assembly Sandrine Mazetier, a conservative male deputy, Julien Aubert, addressed her as "Madame le President," using the masculine form. After reminding him that assembly rules stipulated she be addressed as "Madame la Presidente," the feminine form, he refused to yield (Cotteret 2014).

The Real Academia Española (RAE), the official institution of the Spanish language, continues to refuse such reforms. In 2016, it addressed growing trends to "split" noun references—avoiding the generic masculine plural when groups include men and women, thus replacing, for example, *ciudadanos* ([male] citizens) with *ciudadanas y ciudadanos* (female and male citizens)—by arguing that this such a practice was "artificial and unnecessary from a linguistic point of view."[7] In July 2018, the issue reemerged when the government asked the RAE to write a report on how to modify the constitution to make it more gender-inclusive. Deputy Prime Minister Carmen Calvo explained: "We have a constitution in the masculine. It is necessary to begin to have a text that includes women" (Sonnad 2018). The RAE confirmed its position, presenting a style manual whose first chapter rejected calls for more inclusive language.

Official language bodies are not the only ones to draw on their positions of power to police language use. In 2014, Speaker Danis Tzamtzis was taking a roll call vote in the Greek parliament. When a number of female MPs responded by answering "present" using the feminine ending, he responded by "correcting" their statements to "present" using the masculine ending. Afroditi Stambouli challenged the "repair" by requesting that the official record make note that she had used the feminine form. Addressing Tzamtzis, she pointed out that he had changed the sex of all the women. Continuing the roll call, he did not apologize but rebuked her request by telling her to "Learn grammar" (Georgalidou 2017, 39). Although the voting continued, the exchange inspired a larger number of female MPs to use the feminine form in a subsequent vote.

## Silencing

Historically, public speaking has been perceived as a masculine act. Consequently, the simple act of women talking in public can be seen as transgressive (Cameron 2006). Yet denying women the right to speak makes their perspectives invisible, undermining their status as political equals (Beard 2017). Alluding to her experiences in Honduras in the 1990s, Doris Gutiérrez shared: "The president of the congress refused to let me speak. He let all the men express their points and he always left me with my hand raised." Rather than let the issue slide, she adopted a counter-strategy: "I decided to cover my mouth with a handkerchief as a sign of protest. Those photos could be seen in the press, and the commentary vacillated between calling it bravery and craziness" (Hoyos 2014, 63). Silencing can involve, at its extreme, expelling women from their seats. In her biography, Afghan MP Malalai Joya claims that during her two years in parliament she never had the chance to speak without getting cut off at some point. After a controversy surrounding remarks she made in the media, the speaker moved to remove Joya from her seat. Not given an opportunity to defend herself, she was subsequently suspended from parliament for the remainder of her five-year term without a formal count of the votes (Joya 2009).

In the United States, a well-known example involves the silencing of Senator Elizabeth Warren during confirmation hearings for Senator Jeff Sessions, nominated by Donald Trump for the position of attorney general. During the hearings, Democrats highlighted Sessions's ongoing failures to protect the rights of minority communities, pointing out that the Senate had previously rejected him as a federal judge on this basis. When it was Warren's turn to speak, she attempted to read a letter written in 1986 by Coretta Scott King, which included relevant details like his attempts to intimidate elderly black voters. In the middle of her speech, Senate Majority Leader Mitch McConnell invoked an obscure rule to prevent her from continuing. Rarely invoked, the rule states: "no Senator in debate shall, directly or indirectly, by any form of words impute to another Senator or to other Senators any conduct or motive unworthy or unbecoming a Senator."[8] The Senate then voted along party lines, 49–43, that Warren violated the rule, in turn barring her from speaking further in the floor debate on the nomination.

Coverage of the incident highlighted the apparent double standard at work, pointing out that no reprimands were made when Senator Ted Cruz called McConnell a "liar" several times on the Senate floor in 2015, or when Senator Tom Cotton criticized the "cancerous leadership" of Senator Harry Reid in 2016 (Cardona 2017). Further, following the vote, three of Warren's male colleagues—Senators Jeff Merkely, Tom Udall, and Bernie Sanders—all read excerpts from the same letter, uninterrupted (Ebbs 2017). Refusing to be silenced completely, Warren stood outside the doors to the Senate chamber and read King's letter, streaming it live on Facebook where it was viewed 13 million times.[9] Called to account for his decision, McConnell later said: "She was warned. She was given an explanation. Nevertheless, she persisted."

### Not Listening

When women do gain the opportunity to speak, another way to silence their contributions is to reduce the possibility they are actually heard. As Spender (1980) notes in her book on "man-made language," women active in a wide array of arenas perceive they are "not listened to with equal attention (or . . . not listened to at all)" (87). Frigga Haug (1995, 137), for instance, recalls an experience she had when giving a speech on gender quotas at a meeting of the German Social Democratic Party in 1989: "the whole audience was male and stressed this by ostentatiously starting to read newspapers, talk to each other, walk out to get some beer, and so on." She noted that the situation had not improved five years later. A debate on equality and equal status for women in parliament was scheduled during the break, leaving only a handful of politicians to discuss the issue while everyone else (including the journalists) went to lunch.

In 2017, Melissa Hortman, House minority leader in the Minnesota state legislature, made a similar observation when she realized that a large group of men had left the chamber prior to a speech by Ilhan Omar, a woman serving as the first Somali-American legislator. In response, Hortman decided to move for a "call of the House," a mechanism requiring that members return to the floor. As a large group of white male representatives filed back into the chamber, she remarked: "I hate to break up the 100 percent white male card game in the retiring room, but I think this is an important debate." Called on by some Republicans to apologize for what they felt was a "sexist" and "racist" comment, Hortman refused, saying: "I am so tired of watching Representative Susan Allen give an amazing speech, Representative Peggy Flanagan give an amazing speech, watching Representative Jamie Becker-Finn give an amazing speech . . . and looking around, to see, where are my colleagues? And I went into the retiring room, and I saw where a bunch of my colleagues were. And I'm really tired of watching women of color, in particular, being ignored. So, I'm not sorry" (Terkel 2017).

"Manterrupting"

Interruptions offer a final mechanism to "engineer female silence" (Spender 1980, 44) by preventing women from achieving their interactional goals. Zimmerman and West (1975, 103) argue that because interruptions involve "violations of speakers' turns at talk," they serve as "a device for exercising power and control in conversation." Meta-analyses find that men are more likely than women to interrupt, suggesting they feel more entitled to take the conversational floor. Men also engage in "intrusive interruptions," which aim to display dominance, at a far greater rate than women (Anderson and Leaper 1998). The concept of "manterrupting," a recent neologism, captures these gendered dynamics, referring to cases where men interrupt women as they are trying to speak (Bennett 2016).

Aggregate-level data from Australia reveals that during estimates hearings—a process involving scrutiny of the government's proposed budget—between 2006 and 2015, male senators overwhelmingly used interruptions to gain the floor or obstruct other speakers, and most negative interruptions were aimed at women. Female witnesses, moreover, were far more likely than their male counterparts to face attempts to destroy their credibility and authority; they were also 2.5 times more likely to be called "emotional" or "unreasonable" (Richards 2016, 49). Asked to respond, female politicians in Australia concurred with the analysis. Senator Katy Gallagher noted: "Nothing in this study surprises me. It reflects my experiences having sat through various Senate committee hearings over the last 18 months" (Workman 2016).

An individual-level experience that gained national attention occurred in Japan in 2014 when Ayaka Shiomura was giving her first speech after being elected a member of the Tokyo Metropolitan Assembly. As she spoke about the need to do more to support working women who want or have children, one male colleague called out: "You're the one who should get married as soon as possible." Another shouted: "Are you not able to have a baby?" She finished the speech, despite their laughter, and then posted a message about the incident on Twitter, which soon went viral. Less than a day later, the assembly had received more than 1000 complaints; within two days, more than 40,000 people had signed an online petition calling on the Tokyo chapter of the suspected perpetrators' party to identify and punish whoever had been involved in the heckling (Kameda 2014). Shiomura's subsequent comments reveal she interpreted it as a gendered attempt to silence and demean her right to have a political voice: "The male members' offensive remarks indicate they think women who aren't married, or can't bear a child, aren't worth listening to" (McCurry 2014).

## RENDERING INCOMPETENT

The second mode of semiotic violence entails rendering women incompetent as political actors. Casting women as a group as "unfit" for leadership, these acts tap into prescriptive and proscriptive stereotypes about women's inability to serve in public roles. They do so by emphasizing "incongruity" between traits and behaviors ascribed to women (warm, polite, and yielding) and those associated with men and leaders (assertive, decisive, and confident) (Eagly and Karau 2002). When women overcome these gendered beliefs to become leaders, therefore, they continue to confront gendered tropes questioning their intelligence, humanity, and morality as political actors. Cognitive dissonance generated by these stereotypes can also question their status as "women," thus reinforcing ideas about men as "natural" and legitimate political leaders.

Feminist psychologists developed the concept of "role incongruity" to account for divergence in evaluations of male versus female leaders. In a meta-analysis, Eagly, Makhijani, and Klonsky (1992) find that, because gender and leadership stereotypes align for men but conflict for women, female leaders tend to be viewed as less competent than male counterparts with similar credentials. Penalized for perceived "status violations" (Rudman, Moss-Racusin, Phelan, and Nauts 2012), female leaders are also often viewed as illegitimate, with their authority not seen as deserved or justified (Vial, Napier, and Brescoll 2016), as well as "cold," losing the warmth stereotypically attributed to women (Cuddy, Fiske, and Glick 2004).

Literature on gender, politics, and the media vividly illustrates these dynamics. Arguing that media coverage privileges the practice of politics as a male pursuit (Sreberny-Mohammadi and Ross 1996), studies observe that while most stories about male politicians focus on their political ideas, a disproportionately large share of women's coverage fixates on their physical appearance (Falk 2008). Similarly, male politicians tend to be presented as living in an integrated world of work and family life; female politicians, in contrast, are often portrayed as inhabiting two conflicting worlds (Van Zoonen 1998; Thomas and Bittner 2017). Tendencies to highlight that female candidates are the "first woman" to pursue a particular office serves, further, to underscore their status as a "novelty and anomaly" (Heldman, Carroll, and Olson 2005, 325).

Investigating the ways in which the competence, and thus the authority, of women in politics is challenged around the world yields at least six strategies. These acts of semiotic violence seek to belittle women who engage in politics, ranging from insulting portrayals of their temperaments or political knowledge, to aggressive campaigns to sexually objectify and shame them, to judgments insinuating that they are "failed" women. Seeking to undercut women's access to, as well as effectiveness in, the political arena, these tactics aim to dehumanize political women, punishing them for presuming they have the right to participate in political life.

### Emotional Ridicule

A common metaphorical dualism in philosophy associates men with reason and women with emotion (Lloyd 1984), proposing a fundamental—and highly gendered—incompatibility between outward emotional displays and the ability to make objective, rational decisions (Brescoll 2016). Expressions of anger by female leaders are particularly fraught: while men's emotional reactions are often attributed to external factors, making their outbursts seem justified, women's anger tends to be ascribed to internal characteristics, marking them as "angry people" and, in turn, lowering perceptions of their competence (Brescoll and Uhlmann 2008, 268). Derogatory terms used against women in leadership positions thus tend to highlight this anger component, trivializing women's voices as "shrill" and "strident" in order to dismiss out of hand what they have to say (Spender 1980).[10]

Ridiculing women as overly emotional is thus a common trope used against female politicians. When Australian Prime Minister Julia Gillard delivered her famous "misogyny speech" in 2012, many media outlets and conservative politicians framed it as an "uncontrolled emotional outburst." Insinuating she had "lost control of any rational façade she had put on," the speech—in their version of the story—"exposed her true nature as reactive, emotional, irrational, and ultimately unsuitable for and incapable of leadership" (Wright and Holland 2014, 456, 465). A similar trope was used by media in Brazil in the months leading up to the 2016 impeachment of President Dilma Rousseff. The magazine *Isto É* was particularly egregious, with images and stories declaring she was "out of control" and suffering from "nervous explosions" (Biroli 2016, 572). Around the same time, a Chinese Communist Party-linked newspaper published an opinion piece calling Taiwan President Tsai Ing-wen "an excessively 'emotional' single woman without family or children, and therefore prone to take 'extremist political positions'" (Fincher 2016).

Disqualification

In other instances, the aim is to portray women as distinctly unqualified for political activity. One common approach is to foreground aspects of women's descriptive backgrounds as a means for calling into question their preparation to hold political office. While the skills and experiences of candidates should be scrutinized by voters, the reservations expressed in these instances are not rooted in sincere concerns that the "best" candidates be elected or appointed. Rather, as Price (2016) suggests, a woman in (or aspiring to) a political position appears to mobilize efforts to find something that might disqualify her, a form of hyper-scrutiny out of proportion to that faced by male politicians. These trip-up campaigns pose a particularly acute challenge for women who are members of other politically marginalized groups, compounding skepticism about their competence to serve in leadership roles.

In 2013, Cécile Kyenge became the first black cabinet member in Italy when she was appointed minister of integration. Seeking to dehumanize her, Italian Senator Roberto Calderoli of the Northern League party stated: "when I see the pictures of Kyenge, I cannot but think of . . . the features of an orangutan." In a supposed apology, party leader Umberto Bossi reinforced her departure from the traditional profile of Italian politicians by noting that she was "differently white" and "also a woman." Other Northern League attacks presumed a more limited role for (black) women in Italian society. One local councilor explained that "she seems like a great housekeeper" but "not a government minister." MEP Mario Borghezio called her a "shitty choice" who was "totally incompetent" and had "the face of housewife" (Meret, Della Corta, and Sanguiliano 2013).

A second version of this tactic involves generating disinformation about political women, drawing on digital manipulation techniques to create false images and stories casting women's qualifications into doubt. In 2019, distorted videos of U.S. Speaker Nancy Pelosi giving a speech were posted and circulated widely online, "subtly edited to make her voice sound garbled and warped" and possibly drunk. Analysis by digital forensics experts found that to correct for the 75% slowdown in the speed of the video, Pelosi's voice had been altered to modify her pitch to make the video sound more realistic. In addition to being viewed millions of times, the video was shared via Twitter by Rudy Giuliani, former mayor of New York and Donald Trump's personal attorney, who commented: "What is wrong with Nancy Pelosi? Her speech pattern is bizarre." Trump himself posted another version, edited to focus on "moments where she briefly paused or stumbled—that he claimed showed her stammering through a news conference" (Harwell 2019).

Despite growing concern about the phenomenon of "fake news," the gendered potential of "deepfake" technologies has not yet been fully explored (Chemaly 2019). While male public figures have also been the subject of doctored videos, research finds that "deepfake videos are much more likely to be deployed against women, minorities, people from the LGBT community,

[and] poor people" (Hao 2019). Particularly alarming, these tools can do more than simply alter and selectively edit existing clips; they can also combine and manipulate images to create computer-generated videos of people saying and doing things they have not done. In countries like Ukraine and Georgia, these forms of "sexualized disinformation" have already started to appear, mixing "old ingrained sexist attitudes with the anonymity and reach of social media in an effort to destroy women's reputations and push them out of public life" (Jankowicz 2017). Such disinformation can have a staggering reach: the American Mirror, a YouTube channel "almost entirely dedicated to videos crafted to criticize or embarrass female Democratic leaders," has more than 30 million total views (Harwell 2019).

### "Mansplaining"

A third way to communicate women's presumed incompetence is via "mansplaining," referring to instances where a man speaks to a woman in a patronizing manner, on the assumption that he knows more about the topic that the person he is addressing (Kinney 2017). This pattern implies that the best person to explain the topic at hand is a man, training women in "self-doubt and self-limitation" while reinforcing "men's unsupported overconfidence" (Solnit 2014, 4). Growing usage of this term by political women around the world signals that, even once elected, women continue to have their place in politics questioned by their male colleagues.

At an interview at the World Economic Forum in 2018, Norwegian prime minister Erna Solberg spoke about an experience early in her career. First elected to parliament at age 28, she observed: "I have met a lot of people who have maybe underestimated you, because you were a young girl in politics at the time." In one instance, she was serving on the finance committee when a bank CEO tried to tell her "like a child, in a very child-like way, how the interest rate market functions." The committee chair then leaned over to clarify to the CEO that she in fact had the highest-level of education on the committee (Parker 2018).

Such exchanges have also taken place on the floor of national and provincial parliaments. The most extensive debate involved a confrontation in the Australian Senate in 2016. Senator Katy Gallagher was questioning Communications Minister Mitch Fifield about several proposed bills on welfare and families and whether they had the support of the prime minister. Fifield responded with a lengthy explanation of internal government procedures, and before she could follow up with another question, he interrupted: "Let me just stop you so you don't waste a line of questioning." Surprised, she commented: "I love the mansplaining. I'm enjoying it." Confused, he asked: "What's mansplaining, senator?" After Gallagher explained that it referred to the "patronizing and condescending way that you are responding to my questions," Fifield chastised her for "invoking gender in impugning how a senator is responding" and advised her to "take a good look at herself." She stated, not without a little irony: "I am surprised that you do not understand the term 'mansplaining'" (Workman 2017).

### Sexual Objectification

Sexual objectification of women reduces them to their body parts and depicts their individual and collective worth solely in terms of their ability to be sexually attractive. It is therefore a potent tool for denigrating women and, particularly, for attacking women seeking a role in public life. Research on objectification reveals that exposure to such portrayals leads to diminished opinions regarding a woman's competence, morality, and humanity among women and men (Ward 2016). Consequently, this strategy can negatively shape perceptions of women's credibility and suitability for political roles (Funk and Coker 2016). Coinciding with advances in communication technologies enabling "a new era of objectification" (Heldman and Wade 2011, 156), politics has become increasingly "pornified," with images, metaphors, and narratives from pornography entering online spaces as well as mainstream media coverage. This process affects male and female politicians unequally: while men are typically cast in positions of power, female candidates tend to be humiliated, violated, and abused (Sheeler and Anderson 2013).

Conducting an internet search of politicians' names with the word "porn," Chemaly (2016) finds that male names—like Donald Trump, Ted Cruz, and Bernie Sanders—produce relatively "benign lists" of articles, while female names—like Hillary Clinton, Condoleezza Rice, Nancy Pelosi, and Sarah Palin—yield "page after page of actual porn sites, using the women's names and photographs of their faces to portray them in bestial and brutally sexually objectifying videos and photos." She argues these forms of "nonconsensual porn" use "graphic sexualization to comment on a woman candidate's worthiness for office," as a "form of attack intended to degrade and silence women."

In the United States, these trends began in earnest in 2008, after the nomination of Sarah Palin as vice presidential candidate for the Republican Party (Sheeler and Anderson 2013). Her physical appearance was a substantial focus of early media coverage: *Time* magazine referred to her as a "sex symbol," and a clip of Palin wearing a swimsuit during a beauty contest received well over a million views on YouTube (Heflick and Goldenberg 2011). Over the course of the campaign Palin was increasingly sexualized. Entrepreneurs marketed blow-up dolls and pornographic films and, in a widely circulated image, photoshopped Palin's head onto the body of a woman in a bikini holding a rifle (Carlin and Winfrey 2009). Evidence suggests this sexualization was not harmless fun: priming people to focus on her appearance reduced perceptions of her competence, as well as intentions to vote for the Republican ticket (Heflick and Goldenberg 2009).

A distinct strategy of sexual objectification was employed against Kolinda Grabar-Kitarović, the first woman and youngest person ever to serve as president of Croatia. Rather than publishing digitally altered images, online and traditional news outlets more commonly engaged in "false identity attribution,"[11] using videos and photos of other women portrayed in sexually objectifying ways but claiming that the woman was Grabar-Kitarović herself. Soon after her election in 2015, for example, a Serbian tabloid published stills purporting to show her in a porn video (Kumar 2018). In 2016, the *Washington Post* and other international outlets published stories about viral photos purporting to show her in a bikini. Although the images were later determined to be of Coco Austin, an American reality star, photos continued to surface online, featuring a range of different models and porn stars. In an interview, Grabar-Kitarović stated: "It makes you feel like an object, rather than as an actor" (Full Frontal with Samantha Bee 2016).

## Slut Shaming

"Slut shaming" is a related but distinct phenomenon, involving the "shaming of someone due to their sexual behavior—real, imagined, or made up" (Hanson-Young 2018, 55). This type of shaming is directed almost exclusively at women to silence them, often for reasons that have nothing to do with actual sexual activity. In the Philippines, President Rodrigo Duterte accused Senator Leila de Lima, a harsh critic of his administration's policies, of having an affair with her married chauffeur. Claiming she had a "propensity for sex," he declared she was "not only screwing her driver" but "also screwing the nation" (Sherwell 2016). Soon after, representatives in the lower house of parliament loyal to the president proposed screening a sex tape supposedly featuring de Lima with her chauffeur. The five other female senators came together, despite their political differences, to speak out against the plan, calling it "a form of slut-shaming that will not set a good example for the country" (Elemia 2016).

In 2018, female candidates in Iraq faced unprecedented levels of abuse and intimidation in the run-up to parliamentary elections. The problem was so bad, indeed, that UN Special Representative Ján Kubiš issued a statement denouncing the "targeting and defamation of women candidates," including "attacks against the reputation and honor of candidates and their families, pressing them to step down."[12] In at least five instances, purported "sex tapes" surfaced to damage the women's campaigns. In one case, a three-minute clip appeared on social media, showing a woman and a man engaged in intimate acts, alleging that the woman in the video was Intidhar Ahmed Jassim, a candidate for the Victory Coalition of Prime Minister Haider al-Abadi. Jassim denounced the video, calling it "fabricated," but within hours of her statement, Hussein al-Adily, a spokesman for the Victory Coalition, announced she had withdrawn her candidacy. Seemingly siding with her perpetrators, however, he stated: "it is the right of every coalition and party to withdraw any candidate not abiding by the qualifications and characteristics set for all the candidates . . . and this candidate did not abide by the guidelines" (Tajali and Farhan 2018). The Victory Coalition also dropped Antithar Al Shammari, a sitting MP, as a candidate for reelection after a "salacious video" allegedly featuring her was posted online—despite her insistence that the video was fake (Aldroubi 2018).

Another strategy entails "revenge porn," or "nonconsensual pornography" involving "the distribution of sexually graphic images of individuals without their consent" (Citron and Franks 2014, 346). In 2019, a conservative website, RedState.org, and a British tabloid, the *Daily Mail*, published nude photos and a series of damaging articles about U.S. Representative Katie Hill. Weeks before they were published, Hill's estranged husband Kenny Heslep had reportedly reached out to the *Los Angeles Times*, asking if they wanted "the whole story" of their divorce. Joe Messina, an aide to former Representative Steve Knight, informed the National Republican Congressional Committee he was in possession of more than 700 images and texts tied to Hill. Their release into the public domain coincided with allegations that Hill had engaged in affairs with a female campaign aide, which she admitted and apologized for as "inappropriate," as well as her male legislative director, which she denied (Caygle 2019). The House Ethics Committee opened an investigation into the latter, stemming from a rule passed in 2018 banning sexual relationships between Congress members and staffers.

Although Hill vigorously denied the affair with her staffer, she opted a few days later to resign from her position in Congress. The letter announcing her resignation made clear that her decision was driven by the "revenge porn." Expressing anguish that "private photos of personal moments" had been "weaponized" against her, Hill lamented the "pain inflicted by my abusive husband and the brutality of hateful political operatives who seem to happily provide a platform to a monster who is driving a smear campaign built around cyber exploitation." However, she vowed to keep fighting to "defeat this type of exploitation . . . which will keep countless women and girls from running for office or entering public light."[13] In her final speech in Congress, Hill criticized the "misogynistic culture that gleefully consumed my naked pictures, capitalized on my sexuality, and enabled my abusive ex to continue that abuse, this time with the entire country watching." Responding to the forces that had come together to "push a young woman out of power," she concluded: "I yield the balance of my time for now, but not forever."[14]

### Identity Questioning

A final tactic for undermining women as political actors is to intimate that women who do demonstrate political competence are not "real women." In an experimental study, Schneider and Bos (2014) find that female politicians are not seen as sharing qualities stereotypically attributed to women. Perhaps for this reason, a common mode of criticizing them is to accuse them of being lesbians (Rothschild 2005). This trope figures prominently in media coverage and social media representations of high-level politicians like Julia Gillard, Helen Clark (former prime minister of New Zealand), and Tarja Halonen (former president of Finland).

Empirically, female politicians around the world are more likely to be single and childless than they are to be mothers, while male politicians are predominantly family men (Thomas and Bittner 2017). This pattern stems from cultural beliefs that women with children should not run for political office, as well as parliamentary working conditions that make it difficult to balance work and family life, including lack of parental leave, late working hours, and frequent travel (Childs 2015). In 2016, First Minister of Scotland Nicola Sturgeon opened up about a miscarriage she had experienced in 2011 at the age of 40. While she acknowledged in an interview that there were "many reasons why women don't have children," the graphic included with the story not only flattened this nuance, but also reinforced the notion of female leaders as "deviant" by featuring six other women under the caption: "childless politicians" (Rhodes 2016).

Treating political women as an aberration from gendered expectations, however, is perhaps most obvious and acute in the case of Hillary Clinton. During the 2007–2008 U.S. presidential primary campaign, Clinton was frequently depicted as a "monster" or a cyborg. Ritchie (2013, 103) argues that this was not accidental: rather, female political figures "are especially prone to monsterization and the political arena is a fertile site for the creation of monstrous women" because they "destabilize identity categories." Demonizing her, anti-Hillary groups digitally simulated devil horns and the number 666 tattooed across her forehead. They also commonly spliced her head onto a male body or morphed her face together with her husband's. These representations, Ritchie argues, portrayed Hillary Clinton—and her bid for the White House—as "improper and unnatural" (102).

## Solutions to Semiotic Violence

The concept of semiotic violence is new, but its manifestations are not—and some legal frameworks offer recourse for targets of this form of abuse. The primary instrument available is defamation law, which can punish false statements harmful to a person's reputation expressed in either written or spoken form. Other strategies more directly address the semiotic dimensions of this violence. Some pursue change at the structural level of language, while others seek to create new habits and practices, drawing on the inherently interactive nature of speech. Further tactics respond to semiotic violence in the moment, challenging its power by seeking to undermine its effects or standing in solidarity with victims.

## LEGAL REFORMS

A straightforward means to counteract women's invisibility in political spaces is to make them visible. Legal reforms have recognized women's status as autonomous human beings and provided them with full and equal political rights. In some contexts, nevertheless, women have been denied full political recognition until recently. In Mexico, indigenous communities in Oaxaca have the right to follow their own traditions and customs when electing their leaders. In 2007, a woman in one of these municipalities, Eufrosina Cruz, ran to become mayor. However, when town leaders saw her name on some of the ballots, they tore them up, claiming she was not a "citizen" and that, according to the custom, "only the citizens vote, not the women" (Stevenson 2008). Cruz lodged a complaint with the National Commission of Human Rights, which ruled in her favor and recommended changes to Oaxacan laws. In 2010, she stood again as a candidate, this time for local deputy, and two years later, she was elected to the national parliament. Due in part to her efforts, Article 2 of the Constitution was revised in 2015 to stipulate that indigenous people could "elect, in accordance with their traditional rules, procedures, and customs, their authorities and representatives," but must also guarantee "the right to vote and be elected of indigenous women and men under equitable conditions."[15]

Legal measures may also be implemented as a way of changing prevailing community practices, thereby bringing them in line with existing legal rights. In 2017, the parliament in Pakistan approved a new Elections Act that, among other changes, addressed the problem of women being prevented from exercising their right to vote in various parts of the country. In a section on powers to declare a poll invalid, the text includes "implementation of an agreement restraining women from casting their votes" among "grave illegalities" that have "materially affected the result of the poll at one or more polling stations." It mandates, in turn, that "if the turnout of women voters is less than ten percent of the total votes polled in a constituency, the [Election] Commission may presume that the women voters have been restrained through an agreement from casting their votes" and therefore may declare those elections void, requiring voters to "recast their votes in the manner provided for bye-elections."[16]

## LEGAL PROCEEDINGS

Defamation law provides an ongoing legal remedy in many countries, although specific laws vary widely in terms of how defamation is defined, what exemptions are provided, and what standards of evidence exist for proving that defamation in fact occurred. In Italy, former Integration Minister Cécile Kyenge has pursued and won several legal cases related to the sexist and racist abuse she faced during her time in office. In 2017, Mario Borghezio was ordered to pay €50,000 for describing the cabinet, with Kyenge's inclusion, as "bongo-bongo government." In 2019, Roberto Calderoli was found guilty of defamation by racial hatred for likening her to an orangutan, resulting in an 18-month prison sentence. While he attempted to excuse his remarks as "playful banter," Kyenge argued that the verdict was a "very important signal . . . in the name of respect and dignity for people." She continued: "Words are weighty, and when they come from a politician, they risk having a very negative impact" (Giuffrida 2019).

In Australia, Sarah Hanson-Young, a Green Senator, had faced repeated innuendos about her sexual behavior since being elected in 2008, as both the youngest woman ever to win a seat and an unmarried single mother.[17] In 2018, she decided she could no longer stay silent after Senator David Leyonhjelm yelled at her during a debate on violence against women: "You should stop shagging men, Sarah!" Both the Green Party leader and Senate president asked him to apologize, but he refused and then went on a Sky News program in which he said that "Sarah is known for liking men," and "The rumors about her in parliament are well known" (quotes then included in the electronically generated captions posted at the bottom of screen). Leyonhjelm spread the message further on additional television and radio programs, prompting Hanson-Young to sue him for defamation (Hanson-Young 2018, 69).

The lawsuit focused on Leyonhjelm's suggestions that she was a misandrist and hypocrite, rather than the promiscuity allegations. Because his comments in the Senate were protected by parliamentary privilege, the case covered only the interviews he gave outside parliament. His lawyers argued that since the remarks had originated in the Senate, they were also covered by privilege. The judge disagreed, arguing that "he published his claim concerning the applicant to a mass audience with the intention of publicly shaming her" ("Sarah Hanson-Young" 2019). Much of the legal case revolved around his claim that Hanson-Young had said words to the effects of "all men are rapists," a claim she denied and which was backed up by other senators in court. Finding in her favor, the judge ordered Leyonhjelm to pay $120,000 in damages, which Hanson-Young said she would donate to two women's charities. At a press conference following the verdict, she stated it was "important . . . to put a line under this type of behavior," as "it doesn't matter if you work in a shop or a factory floor or the parliament. Every woman deserves to be treated with respect" (McGowan and Karp 2019).

## LANGUAGE ADAPTATIONS

Resistance to feminizing political language continues in many countries. However, steps have been taken in some contexts to consider how to make language more inclusive. In France, the government of François Mitterrand created the first Ministry for Women's Rights in 1981. However, when the minister, Yvette Roudy, sought to be called "Madame la Ministre" (rather than

Madame le Minstre, the masculine form), she was refused ("Yvette Roudy" 2019). In 1983, parliament passed a law on professional equality, leading to the creation in 1984 of a commission to explore the feminization of titles and functions. The commission produced a circular in 1986 prescribing the usage of feminine terms in official documents and offering rules for feminizing professional terms and titles. It had little effect, however, meeting with substantial resistance. Consequently, when Édith Cresson became the first female prime minister in 1991, she was referred to throughout her term as "le premier ministre" (the masculine form).

Over the course of the 1990s, a movement for gender parity emerged, sparking extensive public debate on women's role in public life. When a Socialist government was elected in 1997, six of the eight women in the new cabinet asked to be addressed as "Madame la Ministre." The government published a circular in early 1998 declaring all women would be addressed with feminine titles. The commission appointed to establish the rules on feminization, however, reified the distinction between public space and the private sphere. Arguing that professions were located in the private sphere, the commission accepted the feminization of professional titles. However, they strongly opposed changes to titles used for jobs in the public sphere, like the civil service, arguing that in these spaces the law was indifferent to sex. As such, they proposed the "unmarked" masculine form was required when referring to the role or office, but the "marked" feminine form could be used when referring to particular individuals (Burr 2003).

Throughout these debates, the Académie Française, the official authority on the usages, vocabulary, and grammar of the French language, remained resolutely opposed to any of these reforms. In February 2019, however, it pronounced itself in favor of feminizing all professions and titles, a move that one journalist called "nothing less than a revolution," being "the very first time that the institution, created in 1634, has gone so far in recognizing the feminine nature of words" (Rérolle 2019). A report published by a study commission declared "there existed no obstacle in principle to the feminization of nouns" and noted, indeed, that many professions—apart from those "higher in the professional hierarchy"—had already feminized their functions and titles. While continuing to insist that public roles, when referred to in the abstract, should retain the "unmarked" from, they no long opposed feminization when referring to those holding these positions. Thus, Rérolle (2019) observes, "if France had a woman again as the head of its government, she would be called without a doubt 'première ministre,' and 'présidente' [the feminine forms] if she occupied the highest function."

## LANGUAGE GUIDES

The movement for inclusive language began in earnest during the second wave feminist movement, resulting in efforts to change linguistic practices. In 1987, representatives from Canada and the Nordic countries raised the issue of sexist language at the UNESCO General Conference. The debate led to Resolution 14.1, instructing the director-general to "adopt a policy related to the drafting of all of the Organization's working documents aimed at avoiding, to the extent possible, the use of language which refers explicitly or implicitly to only one sex except where positive measures are being considered."[18] Further resolutions strengthening this stance were passed in 1989, 1991, and 1995, reflecting "a growing awareness that language does not merely reflect the way we think: it also shapes our thinking. If words and expressions that imply that women are inferior to men are constantly used, that assumption of inferiority tends to become part of our mindset; hence the need to adjust our language when our ideas evolve."[19]

To this end, UNESCO published a "Guide to Non-Sexist Language" in 1987; by its third edition in 1999, this title had been changed to "Guidelines on Gender-Neutral Language." In January 2019, the Division on Gender Equality summarized the "underlying principle of gender-inclusive language" as treating and respecting women and men as equals. Linguistically, such efforts entail "overall gender balance, parallel word choices for both men and women, and elimination of terms that stereotype, exclude, or demean women." In the way of alternatives, UNESCO recommended avoiding terms that make irrelevant assumptions about gender and gender roles; replacing masculine generic forms (like "mankind" or "fatherland") with gender-inclusive generics (like "humankind" and "homeland"); altering occupational titles that include irrelevant gender modifiers (like "spokesman" to "spokesperson"); using double pronouns ("he and she" in lieu of "he"), adopting gender-inclusive synonyms ("they"), or eliminating personal pronouns altogether; and avoiding references and titles reflecting a woman's marital status.[20]

Embodying this spirit of reform, the lower house of parliament in Argentina published a *Guide for the Use of Non-Sexist and Egalitarian Language in the National Chamber of Deputies* in 2015. Part of a parliamentary modernization program, the authors described the guide as a "didactic proposal to promote communication that is more democratic and in line with legislative reforms in recent years regarding gender equality." Noting that language use was "not innocent," they argued that male-centered conventions contributed to the "persistence in the collective imagination the perception that women are subsidiary, secondary, and dispensable," thus creating obstacles to the equal rights of women and men as established in Argentine law. Against the RAE, they deemed efforts to defend masculine universals on the grounds of "economy in language" both "abusive and sexist." Giving copious examples of inclusive language, they stressed the semiotic and political importance of using feminine forms: "Female legislators exist, work in both chambers of Congress, and it is correct and essential to render visible their presence and participation" (Honorable Cámara de Diputados de la Nación 2015, 10, 27, 54).

## AMPLIFICATION

Women's contributions in professional discussions can be erased and minimized in many ways. In addition to interruptions, which deny their rights to speak and be heard, women's voices may also not be "heard" when they are able to speak. In some instances, a male colleague may—consciously or unconsciously—express the same idea only minutes later, with others responding by giving him credit for the idea. Work on sexism in the workplace increasingly uses neologisms like "hepeating" and "bropropriation" to refer to these common practices. Bennett (2016) offers five strategies for dealing with this problem: using active words taking ownership of the idea, thanking colleagues for picking up on the idea, enlisting a friend to chime in that the idea was first voiced by the woman, putting the suggestion on the record in an email or other electronic document, and supporting other women in meetings who offer new ideas.

Although President Barack Obama openly called himself a "feminist," women were a minority of his top aides and, during meetings, some found their voices and ideas were being ignored and/or appropriated. The women then adopted a strategy they called "amplification," namely "when a woman made a key point, other women would repeat it, giving credit to its author. This forced the men in the room to recognize the contribution—and denied them the chance to claim the idea as their own." One staffer explained: "We just started doing it, and made a purpose of doing it. It was an everyday thing." Obama then began calling more often on women and junior aides during meetings (Eilperin 2016b). The story, which first appeared in the *Washington Post*, went viral and women in a wide range of arenas—music, the tech industry, and the foreign policy world—began to use the strategy. One bank executive described amplification as: "On the one hand, we want to give voice to women. But on the other hand, we want to make sure men have the skill to listen and to hear" (Eilperin 2016a).

## SEMIOTIC REVERSALS

Another way to counteract semiotic violence is to flip the script, reducing the power of these acts to restrict women's political activity by confronting perpetrators and challenging the cultural signification of these words and images. One strategy is to push those who use these tropes to take responsibility for their actions, de-normalizing semiotic violence in the process as reflecting a shared understanding of women's value as actors in the political realm. In 2017, for example, Canadian MP Gerry Ritz tweeted a link to a news article with the headline, "No major advanced industrialized economy is currently on pace to meeting its Paris commitments," and commented, "Has anyone told our climate Barbie!"

Catherine McKenna, then the minister of environment and climate change, responded to the slur—commonly used against her—by tweeting back: "Do you use that sexist language about your daughter, mother, sister? We need more women in politics. Your sexist comments won't stop us." Ritz deleted his original tweet minutes later and then tweeted an apology for "the use of Barbie" as "it is not reflective of the role the minister plays."[21] Several months later, McKenna similarly called out a reporter after he identified himself as working for the far-right news site, The Rebel. Prior to answering his question, she commented: "So you're the Rebel Media that happens to call me 'climate Barbie.' I certainly hope that you will no longer use that hashtag." While he denied calling her that name personally, she interjected that she was simply asking for a commitment that the site no longer use that type of language: "The reason I'm asking you not to do this is because I have two daughters. There are lots of girls that want to get into politics and it is completely unacceptable that you do this" ("Catherine McKenna" 2017).

A second form of semiotic reversal entails appropriating slurs, which are derogatory in most contexts, to "echo" these uses "in ways and contexts that make manifest the dissociation from the offensive contents" (Bianchi 2014, 35). Serving as "vehicles of rapport" among "in-group speakers" (Croom 2011, 343), these negative words can gain positive, even empowering, connotations for the group in question. This occurred, for instance, when Donald Trump called Hillary Clinton a "nasty woman" during the final U.S. presidential debate in 2016. The reaction on social media was immediate, with #NastyWoman trending on Twitter along with memes and gifs featuring Janet Jackson's 1986 hit "Nasty." *People* magazine described it as a moment in which "what was meant to be a slur against Hillary Clinton swiftly became a battle cry for women everywhere as they embraced Donald Trump's 'nasty woman' comment" (Quinn 2016). Providing insights as to why the term resonated with so many, one woman interviewed by the *Huffington Post* stated: "If she's a nasty woman, I want to be a nasty woman too" (Gray 2016).

A third tactic is to invert portrayals as a form of awareness-raising. In 2011, a group of French women formed a feminist action group called *La Barbe* (The Beard). Their aim, spelled out on their website, is "not to place a few more women in men's clubs ruled by men, created by men. It is to render men's domination visible in high spheres of power, in all sectors of professional, political, cultural, and social life by mocking their codes, their values, their esprit de corps."[22] Their actions entail attending events dominated by men—for example all-male panels—and sitting quietly in the audience. At a given moment, the women pull beards out of their bags, put them on, stand up together, and then read out in unison a prepared speech praising the exclusion of women.[23] At a political event, for example, they drew connections across many generations of men who had "the good taste" to "engrave the rights of man and the citizen in stone" while "carefully discarding the rights of women," who were able to "resist the hysterical claims of the suffragettes," and who have "kept the reins of power without sharing," from the "most modest town hall to the corridors of the [presidential] palace."[24]

A comparable effort in English is the "Man Who Has It All" parody Twitter account,[25] which first appeared in 2015. It features advice from an anonymous "working dad" who offers short messages of advice for "men juggling a successful career and fatherhood." By switching out women for men, the tweets illustrate the unrealistic demands often made on women—but normalized in magazines and everyday life—by highlighting how ludicrous they sound when applied to men. They also highlight sexism in commentary on women and their professional accomplishments that would never be made about men (Wills 2016). Sample tweets related to the political arena include: "'Half the population are male, therefore we want up to a third (max) of politicians to be men.' Claudia, politician";[26] "'Male politician' is NOT an offensive term. It is simply a way to differentiate them from normal politicians. End of story";[27] and "TODAY'S QUIZ: Can you name 3 men politicians?"[28] While the "language of these tweets might seem absurdist to anyone who is not female," Vigo (2015) suggests, it also shows "how ridiculous such representations are and how pervasive these tropes lurk throughout our society."

## SOLIDARITY

Expressing solidarity is a final way to challenge semiotic violence, offering support to targets while also undercutting the power of these acts to denigrate and harm them. In the Philippines, both ordinary citizens and women in the Senate came out to oppose plans by a parliamentary committee to screen a purported sex video of Senator Leila de Lima and her driver. On social media, female activists initiated a campaign of "self-incrimination for solidarity," encouraging users to post the line: "I would like to testify in Congress. It was me in the sex video. #EveryWoman." Others simply used the hashtag #EveryWoman to post tweets linking the act against de Lima to the broader suppression of women's participation in politics (Rappler Social Media Team 2016). A few days later, the five other female senators—Risa Hontiveros, Grace Poe, Nancy Binay, Cynthia Villar, and Loren Legarda—filed Senate Resolution No. 184 condemning the proposal. They noted that screening a private video would violate at least two laws—the Anti Photo or Video Voyeurism Act and the Anti-Wiretapping Law—in addition to breaching the "time-honored principle of inter-parliamentary courtesy" whereby sitting senators should not be "subjected" to "ridicule and ignominy." Most crucially, however, they wrote that showing a sex video in Congress would be "a blow to our collective struggle to uplift the dignity of women, respect her agency and her autonomy over her own body, and is a form of slut-shaming that will not set a good example for the country." [29]

PART IV

# A Call to Action

# 17

# Cross-Cutting Solutions

Naming the problem of violence against women in politics has drawn crucial attention to this phenomenon. While tactics have emerged to counteract particular categories of violence, collective efforts to understand this problem highlight the multifaceted and overlapping nature of its manifestations. Consequently, single-pronged solutions—although powerful in specific instances—may not suffice, on their own, to address the fuller spectrum of acts of violence against women in politics. However, numerous strategies developed by practitioners also cut across different kinds of violence, complementing—and potentially amplifying the effects of—these efforts. Pioneered in various parts of the globe, cross-cutting solutions fall into three categories: awareness-raising initiatives, legal reforms, and safety and support frameworks. As a group, they tackle this problem at various stages, seeking to prevent, sanction, and provide redress for acts of violence against women in politics.

## Awareness-Raising Initiatives

Raising awareness is vital to all other efforts, laying the groundwork for de-normalizing violence against women in politics—and, in turn, inspiring action to address it. MacKinnon (1982) describes consciousness-raising as the "major technique of analysis, structure of organization, method of practice, and theory of social change of the women's movement," driven forward by the "collective speaking of women's experience, from the perspective of that experience" (519–520). The #MeToo movement provides a recent example of the power of this approach, with initial disclosures creating momentum for women around the world to come forward about their own experiences of sexual harassment and assault. Noting that many men—but few women—were "surprised by these stories, or by the sheer, vast numbers of them," Renkl (2017) suggests that "for too long women have not considered them stories worth telling" or have hesitated

*Violence against Women in Politics.* Mona Lena Krook, Oxford University Press (2020). © Oxford University Press.
DOI: 10.1093/oso/9780190088460.001.0001.

to say anything "because too often such stories are not believed." Seeking to break the silence around violence against women in politics, actors around the world have adopted a variety of strategies to raise awareness. These range from waging online campaigns to sharing personal accounts to developing resources to educate the general public about the existence of this phenomenon.

## HASHTAG ACTIVISM

Hashtags are keyword phrases preceded by a pound sign (#) that, when employed on social networks, help other users easily find messages with specific content. With the rising popularity of social media platforms, hashtags have become a crucial new tool for activists, spreading their message while also enabling them to connect with others. Taking advantage of opportunities to engage in collective action online, "hashtag feminism" has become a powerful tactic for fighting gender inequities around the world (Clark 2016). One of the first hashtags to emerge on the current subject was #NotTheCost, coined by NDI and launched in 2016 as part of its global call to action to stop violence against women in politics.[1] The phrase "not the cost" offers a rejoinder to arguments that violence is simply the "cost of doing politics," something to be expected—rather than resisted—if women wish to become politically engaged. In the ensuing years, further hashtags have emerged in global (#DefendHer, #SOFJO), regional (#MeTooEP, #NotInMyParliament), and national (#StopVAWIE, #DestroyTheJoint, #LevonsLOmerta, #LiftHerUp) contexts, with the shared goal of de-normalizing violence against women as an acceptable tactic in the political sphere.

## PERSONAL TESTIMONIES

Skeptical of legal and clinical interventions, Stark (2009) proposes that a more valuable and effective solution to violence against women is to "build an audience" around a "vanguard" of women who have "stood up to domination, given it a name and face, and chosen to talk truth to power at risk of physical harm" (1518). While not explicitly framed as such, this approach has been at the heart of efforts by the international practitioner community to bring attention to the issue of violence against women in politics. The launch of NDI's #NotTheCost campaign in 2016, for example, featured testimonies from female politicians and activists around the world. Their experiences overlapped in notable ways, despite distinct contexts, exposing violence as a shared thread of resistance to women's full and equal political participation.[2] A notable moment at a summit organized by the Westminster Foundation for Democracy in 2018 illustrates how these testimonies may resonate. Following a panel of women active in politics in other countries, a politician from Kosovo stood up and affirmed: "I find my story in your story."[3]

Alongside planned events such as these bringing women together across national borders, individual women have also spoken up more spontaneously, penning opinion pieces or making speeches about their experiences with violence in the political world. In November 2016, Sandra Jansen, a provincial assembly member in Canada, began a statement in the Legislative Assembly of Alberta by declaring, "What a traitorous bitch!" She then went on to read out a slew of other demeaning and hateful messages she had received on Twitter and Facebook, including "Sandra should stay in the kitchen, where she belongs." She called on her colleagues to take a stand against hate speech directed at women in politics, urging them to "stand together against this" if they were "stunned" by these words and "reject the inherent violence behind them." Reminding them that "our daughters are watching us," she pleaded: "Please oppose it. Don't ignore it. Don't look the other way. Don't excuse it." Other members of the chamber immediately rose to their feet, giving her a standing ovation and sustained round of applause (McConnell 2016).

## EDUCATIONAL COURSES

Educating people on the concept of violence against women in politics is another way to raise awareness. In 2017, the Mexican Federal Electoral Tribunal developed an online course, free to anyone who registered, offering "conceptual and contextual tools on issues related to gender, violence, and politics, as well as basic information for identifying and addressing it in Mexico." A self-guided track of study, students are provided with course materials to read and are then asked to take a series of tests for self-evaluation. The correct responses are shown for incorrectly answered questions, after which students are given the opportunity to retake each test. Unit 1 presents an overview of gender and human rights, before moving on to Unit 2 on gender-based violence in the political sphere. Unit 3, the core of the course, addresses practical issues related to identifying and dealing with violence against women politics. Topics include how to differentiate it from other forms of violence, who can be victims, what rights victims have, which state institutions have the competence to provide redress, and what to do—as a magistrate, lawyer, or citizen—when confronted with a potential case.[4] Following a final exam, the online system then issues a certificate verifying completion of the course.[5]

## RESOURCE WEBSITES

A related tactic is to create websites with basic information about violence against women in politics as well as resources for addressing it. State institutions in Mexico have developed several of these types of initiatives. In 2014, the National Institute of Women, the Federal Electoral Tribunal, and the National Electoral Institute came together to create the Observatory on Women's

Political Participation in Mexico, with the objective of coordinating—and creating synergies between—actions aimed at promoting women's participation in decision-making in the public sphere.[6] Meeting four times a year, members of the observatory include parliamentary committees on gender equality, political parties, academic units, international organizations, individual experts, and other state and civil society organizations. A dedicated section of its website contains a series of informative materials including a definition of violence against women in politics; graphics on what to do when confronted with a case of violence; protocols for dealing with violence at the federal, state, and political party levels; actions to denounce violence in non-institutional ways, including through hashtag campaigns or contacting the observatory; and existing legislation at the federal and state levels.[7]

In 2018, the network set up a task force on violence against women in politics headed by the Office of the Special Prosecutor on Electoral Crimes. While incorporating many of the same organizations as the observatory, the task force was expanded to include journalists, academics, and local electoral justice bodies. Meeting monthly to issue press releases and exert ongoing political pressure,[8] one of its other principal aims was to create a "tool box" of materials on violence against women in politics. Posted on a website devoted exclusively to this topic, these tools consist of studies and analyses of violence against women in politics; laws, protocols, and guides to prevent, sanction, and eradicate violence against women in politics; information on forums, roundtables, seminars, and conferences on violence against women in politics; and links to diverse organizations engaged in combating violence against women in politics. One of the most extensive sections of the website provides details on how to bring forward complaints on violence against women in politics, mapping out the process within different state institutions.[9]

## PUBLIC SERVICE ANNOUNCEMENTS

A final strategy combines these approaches, spotlighting women's testimonies in videos shared online. Following the 2016 elections, colleagues at the Women's Media Center (WMC)—a civil society organization based in Washington, DC—met to strategize how they might best address violence against women in U.S. politics.[10] Founded in 2005 to raise the visibility and power of women and girls in the U.S. media, ongoing WMC work includes "Name It. Change It.," a joint project with She Should Run that works to end sexist and misogynistic coverage of female candidates by members of the press,[11] and the "WMC Speech Project," which seeks to raise public and media awareness about online harassment of women and girls.[12] Raising money via Kickstarter, the team produced a public service announcement posted online in November 2017, exactly one year after the election.[13]

Opening with statistics from the IPU (2016b), the video featured the experiences of eight women—Democrats and Republicans—who had run for political office across the country: Wendy Davis, a former state senator who also ran to become governor of Texas; Angela Angel, a state representative in Maryland; Marilyn Mosby, the state attorney for Baltimore; Kim Weaver, a congressional candidate in Iowa; Rina Shah Bharara, a member of the Indian American Advisory Council for the House of Representatives Republican Conference; Stephanie Roman, a high school student body president; Katherine Clark, a Congresswoman from Massachusetts; and Ileana Ros Lehtinen, a Congresswoman from Florida. As of February 2019, the version posted on the WMC website had been viewed more than 30,000 times. A re-edited version by Now This was seen by more than 20 million people. The project also inspired editors at the *New York Times* to produce their own video in August 2018, accompanying a story on violence against women in U.S. politics (Astor 2018).[14]

## Legal Reforms

The value of legal reforms for combatting violence against women in politics is contested (Restrepo Sanín 2018a). On the one hand, the impact of laws is limited to what they specifically proscribe. Sexual harassment legislation in the U.S., for example, does not forbid all unwelcome sexual interactions in the workplace, only those that victims can prove are "pervasive," "severe," and "motivated by sex" (White 2018). Moreover, the mere existence of laws—or workplace policies more generally—may obfuscate the fact that little is actually being done to implement them (Edelman 2016). Aware of these dynamics, some are skeptical of efforts to criminalize violence against women, arguing that reform may preclude opportunities for broader structural transformation by equating legal changes with actual changes in society (Bernstein 2012).

On the other hand, law has "expressive value": it condemns particular types of acts, educates the public about the harms such acts inflict, and identifies acceptable patterns of behavior (Citron 2009). The aim thus is less to send perpetrators to jail than to ask them to "do the work of learning" (Jaffe 2018, 84), acknowledging that certain acts should not be tolerated and taking active steps toward establishing new norms of conduct. In this spirit, actors in various arenas have experimented with new laws and policies that de-normalize violence against women in politics by framing it instead as a violation of core social and political values.

### BILLS AND LAWS

Five countries in Latin America—Bolivia, Peru, Costa Rica, Ecuador, and Honduras—proposed stand-alone bills to criminalize violence against women in politics between 2006 and 2018.[15] Most of these policies have stalled at various stages of the legislative process, however, with the only one to pass both chambers being Law 243 in Bolivia, adopted in 2012 (Restrepo Sanín 2018b, 181–182).[16] Law 243 defines political harassment as "acts of pressure, persecution, harassment, or threats" and political violence as "physical, psychological, and sexual actions, behaviors, and/or aggressions" aimed at restricting the exercise of women's political rights. It establishes legal sanctions: monetary fines and removal from office for civil offenses and prison sentences lasting between two to eight years for criminal offenses. The law also lists a series of factors that might magnify these penalties, including acts committed against pregnant, illiterate, or disabled women, or women over the age of 70; acts involving the children of the victims; acts resulting in abortion; acts involving two or more perpetrators; and perpetrators who are repeat offenders, party leaders, or public officeholders.[17] In October 2016, Law 243 was supplemented by Supreme Decree 2.935, which clarified various aspects of its implementation and designated the Ministry of Justice, through the Vice-Ministry of Equal Opportunities, as the unit responsible for designing and carrying out programs promoting women's political leadership.[18] In May 2017, the national electoral authorities published a regulation to assist women in bringing forward their cases, outlining the process and necessary documentation needed to file a complaint.[19]

Other states in the region have pursued legislative strategies, but instead of stand-alone laws, they have reformed or passed new laws on violence against women incorporating text on violence against women in politics. In some cases, these mentions are quite minimal. Passed in 2011, Law 520 in El Salvador, for instance, includes violence in "spaces of political or citizen participation" among a list of expressions of violence against women.[20] In other cases, the text is more substantial. In Panama, Article 4 of Law 82 from 2013 recognizes an extensive range of forms of violence against women, including "political violence" and "violence in the community sphere." The first encompasses discrimination in access to elected office or similar positions inside political parties, while the second entails "denigration, discrimination, marginalization, or exclusion" from groups and associations in the public sphere, like parties, unions, and civil society organizations.[21] Similarly, Article 6 of Law 5.777 in Paraguay, approved in 2016, lists "political violence" as a form of violence against women. It defines this concept as any action against a woman with the goal of "delaying, hindering, or impeding her participation in political life in whatever form and the exercise of her rights outlined in this Law."[22]

Outside of Latin America, legal initiatives to combat violence against women in politics are rare. One exception is Tunisia. Article 46 of the new constitution promulgated in 2014—written by a constituent assembly elected after the ousting of President Zine El Abidine Ben Ali in January 2011—included a number of women's rights provisions. The final line declared: "The state shall take all necessary measures in order to eradicate violence against women."[23]

After the initial draft by Minister of Women Neila Chabaane was rejected by conservative forces,[24] a wide range of stakeholders—including several ministries, women from different parties, civil society groups, and international organizations—came together to develop a revised version.[25] Introduced in the 2015–2016 session, the new bill was modified in the Committee on Rights and Liberties—following consultation with the women's ministry—to include "political violence" as a form of violence against women, alongside physical, moral, sexual, and economic violence.

Female politicians involved in the process largely explain this change as emerging organically from female MPs, although some participants do acknowledge the role of civil society and international organizations in shaping these debates.[26] Setting the scene, one former minister noted not only "brute sexism in political campaigns," but also incidents among MPs themselves— giving the example of a well-publicized exchange[27] in which a male leader responded to criticism from a female leader by dismissing her as "merely a woman."[28] According to several MPs, such encounters—combined with debates on the violence against women bill—led women in parliament to recognize their own experiences as a "specific form" of "violence" in its own right. One described gender-based violence, indeed, as a point of "common ground" among female MPs.[29] Article 3 of Law 58, passed in 2017, consequently recognizes "political violence" as a form of violence against women, defined as "all violence or practice designed to deprive or hinder the exercise of any partisan, political, or associational activity or fundamental right or liberty based on sex discrimination."[30]

## LEGAL FRAMEWORKS

Proponents of legal reform in Mexico have engaged in multiple attempts to legislate on the issue of violence against women in politics: nine bills were presented in the Senate and five in the Chamber of Deputies between 2012 and 2017. Despite being proposed by legislators from parties across the ideological spectrum, only two of the Senate bills have gained approval, while all the Chamber bills have languished at the committee stage (Hevia Rocha 2017). Despite the lack of legislation, actors in various institutions began receiving complaints related to violence against women in politics during the 2015 elections. Seeking to establish a process for dealing with these cases, members of the Federal Electoral Tribunal reached out to colleagues at related bodies to explore what they might be able to do, individually and collectively, within their existing competencies and in light of prevailing national and international standards (Alanís Figueroa 2017).

In March 2016, the Electoral Tribunal published a Protocol to Address Political Violence against Women in collaboration with the National Electoral Institute, the Office of the Special Prosecutor on Electoral Crimes, the Subsecretariat of Human Rights of the Interior Ministry, the Executive Commission on Attention to Victims, the National Commission on Preventing and Eradicating Violence against Women, the National Institute of Women, and the Office of the Special Prosecutor on Crimes of Violence against Women and Human Trafficking. In its opening pages, the protocol states that its purpose is to identify instances of violence against women in politics; inform the public as to who may put forward complaints and how; avoid grave harms to victims and their families and loved ones; provide guidance on how to address violence at the federal, state, and municipal levels; and generate adequate coordination among institutions with the aim of ensuring that violence does not affect women's political and electoral rights. A second version released later in 2016 offered further legal guidance, including emerging jurisprudence.[31] In November 2017, a third edition was launched in preparation for the 2018 elections, with a slightly revised title, as the Protocol to Address Gender-Based Political Violence against Women.[32] All major parties have followed suit, in turn, by adopting protocols of their own to combat violence against their female members.[33]

## CODES OF CONDUCT

Codes of conduct in various parts of the world stipulate acceptable and unacceptable behaviors during election campaigns. While some of these codes are gender-neutral, a growing number explicitly address violence against women in politics. In 2005, the National Elections Commission in Liberia worked with the parties to develop a code of conduct. Among other aims, it sought to prevent "the marginalization of women through violence, intimidation, and fraud." To this end, parties agreed to "the principle of non-discrimination, not to use abusive language, and not to agitate on the basis of sex and gender" (UN 2007, 52). A similar code of conduct for the 2018 Nigerian elections prohibited "inflammatory language, provocative actions, images, or manifestation [inciting] violence, hatred, contempt, or intimidation against another party or candidate or any person or group of persons on grounds of ethnicity or gender."[34]

One of the most developed codes of conduct on matters of gender, however, appears in the Election Law of Bosnia and Herzegovina. Two articles directly address violence against women in politics. Article 7.2 proscribes the "posting, printing, and dissemination of notices, placards, posters, or other [election] materials . . . on which women or men are presented in stereotype and offensive or humiliating ways." Article 16.14 forbids campaign conduct "by way of electronic and printed media where the contents are stereotype and offensive against men and/or women or which encourages any stereotype and offensive behavior on the grounds of gender or any humiliating attitude against the members of different genders." Additionally, Article 7.3 indirectly addresses violence against women in politics by prohibiting hate speech, establishing that electoral actors may not "use language which could provoke or incite someone to violence or spread hatred, or to publish or use pictures, symbols, audio and video recordings, SMS messages, Internet communications, or any other materials that could have such effect."[35] The Central Election Commission has the power to impose three types of sanctions on those who violate these rules: fines up to 5000 euros, removal of perpetrators standing as candidates, and decertification of political parties.[36]

PERPETRATOR BANS

A last measure—albeit only at the proposal stage—is to impose bans on running for office for perpetrators of violence against women in politics. In May 2019, the Fawcett Society, one of the oldest women's rights organizations in the UK, posted a petition online calling for a lifetime ban from standing for elected office for those promoting violence or rape. Arguing that "anyone who issues threats of rape of violence or who incites hatred is not fit to stand for elected office," the petition lamented the fact that—under existing law—"candidates with a track record of abusive conduct can still end up on the ballot paper," ultimately inviting the electorate to endorse and legitimize their conduct.[37] To accompany the petition, which garnered more than 90,000 signatures, the Fawcett Society published an open letter to Prime Minister Theresa May. The signatories, who included women across the political parties and a host of other equality organizations, noted that violence against women in politics had "risen at an alarming rate" and was "driving some women out of politics and deterring others from coming forward." Calling for an end to the "harassment and abuse of women in politics and public life," they declared it was "time to defend our democracy and promote equality, not hate."[38]

## Safety and Support Frameworks

Violence threatens individuals' sense of security, causing people to develop a host of "safety rituals . . . to reduce their anxiety about danger," whether "in their homes, on the street, or at work." These routines are highly gendered, with women "practicing a wider variety as well as a higher number of safety rituals than men" (Stanko 1990, 13–15). Considering how to adapt this "safety work" to "the reality and possibility of violence" in the political sphere (Vera-Gray 2018, 7), therefore, is paramount for addressing the day-to-day security concerns of politically active women—and in turn, for ensuring more broadly that women can participate in politics on equal terms with men. Emerging strategies address these challenges in highly practical ways, lending support to women through proactive planning, emergency response support, and efforts to foster a more positive political environment.

## SAFETY PLANNING

One way to foster greater safety is to evaluate potential vulnerabilities and identify how to counteract and overcome these challenges. Journalists reporting in conflict zones, for example, often undergo security training to understand and prepare for possible risks they may face in the field (Coates 2016). Conducting a global analysis on violence against women in the news media, however, Barton and Storm (2014) suggest that dangers are not limited to war-related contexts. They thus recommend that female journalists—wherever they are based—carry out risk assessments in order to be aware of potential threats so that, if necessary, they may take active steps to mitigate them. Barton and Storm advocate, for example, taking logistical precautions, like check-in protocols with someone trusted; developing a contingency plan to get out of trouble if a situation deteriorates, including what to do if being followed; and securing first aid training and appropriate equipment like a whistle or rape alarm.

Expanding this approach to other categories of politically active women, NDI developed #think10, a tool to provide women in politics with guidance on how to enhance their personal security. Launched in 2018, the tool involves a confidential self-assessment questionnaire posted online[39]—but also available in mobile app and paper formats—asking about levels and types of political activity, personal experiences with violence in political spaces, existence of support networks, intersectional identities, upcoming political events, presence of women's rights protections, legal safeguards and police responsiveness, and societal views on women's public engagement and acceptability of violence against women. Answers to these questions are then combined with a country score from NDI's Women's Political Participation Risk Index to generate an individual safety plan, based on assessed levels of low, moderate, or high risk.

For a woman based in the United States with a moderate risk of violence, for instance, the tool offers the following list of safety precautions: identifying one or two trusted contacts, as well as memorizing or safely storing their contact details; designating one or two safe places to escape to in an emergency, including how to arrive there by different means; keeping personal information private and de-listing home addresses and personal phone numbers; placing important documents in a secure location; remaining aware of the surroundings when carrying out political activities, checking for easy exits, and reviewing the security of homes, workplaces, and political locations; traveling with a trusted colleague, using safe transportation routes, and letting trusted contacts know about travel plans; managing digital footprints by using precautions with passwords, installing firewalls and anti-virus/malware software, creating separate work and personal email accounts, taking screenshots of malicious communications, and reporting online harassment and abuse to relevant authorities; identifying local support services like shelters, clinics, or influential leaders; and documenting incidents of violence, like saving voice messages, keeping a journal of incidents, and photographing physical injuries. The tool advises sharing the safety plan with a trusted colleague, ensuring that family and friends do not inadvertently undermine the plan, and reviewing the plan every few months and revising it accordingly.

## REPORTING MECHANISMS

Dedicated reporting mechanisms offer another means of keeping women safe. Concerned about the lack of swift action by authorities during a sustained period of pre- and post-election violence in Kenya in 2007 and 2008, in the run-up to the 2012 elections FIDA-Kenya set up an SMS hotline for reporting violence against female candidates and voters. The hotline, named "Sema Usikike" (Speak and Be Heard), enabled ordinary Kenyans—whether they were victims or witnesses of election violence—to send a free text message to 21661 describing the violence witnessed and providing the location of the incident. Working in real time, FIDA-Kenya lawyers would immediately inform the closest police station and then follow-up with victims and, where relevant, offer legal aid.[40] Providing these services via text message limited the amount of detailed advice the lawyers could give, but—on the flipside—using SMS technologies, they hoped, would encourage people to report as only phone numbers, and not names, would be visible to responders. In 2017, FIDA-Kenya offered the same hotline, but augmented their support services. In addition to sending cases to the police, they referred victims in need of medical attention to a gender-based violence recovery center. In the Kisu region, a hotspot of election violence, they set up in-person counseling at the FIDA offices to assist those who wanted to report. In five regions, they also trained police officers on gender-based violence in elections to foster more informed responses to these cases.[41]

## ACTION ALERTS

Among human rights defenders, action alerts constitute a widespread tactic for raising awareness, mobilizing support, and pressuring states to cease perpetrating human rights abuses. Urgent appeals—issued within 24 to 72 hours of learning of the violation and circulated through networks of civil society groups and individuals around the world—can be especially effective in countries receptive to the opinions of the international community. Typical appeals provide key facts surrounding the case and then detail what specific actions might be taken, like contacting authorities through email, fax, or telephone to demand they take a specific action. According to a review by the WHRDIC's Working Group on Urgent Responses for Women Human Rights Defenders at Risk, most alerts are accompanied by a sample letter to be sent to governments, but in some instances, organizations provide an automated system for sending such letters. To raise international visibility, some groups also request that senders copy relevant UN bodies in their correspondence. To make these appeals more effective, the working group recommends including more contextual analysis, explaining in clearer terms the ways in which the defender was seen to be breaching social norms and taboos and how the repression was connected to the defender's human rights work (Barcia 2011).

One organization making extensive use of such alerts is Amnesty International. In 2019, for example, it issued an appeal on behalf of Saudi women who had fought for women's right to drive and now faced up to 20 years in prison for their activism. Concerned that "Saudi authorities have chosen to silence the very women bravely speaking up for human rights," Amnesty noted that while three activists—Loujain al-Hathloul, Iman al-Nafjan, and Aziza al-Yousef—were still being held, three others had been provisionally released, indicating that authorities appeared to be listening to international pressure. The appeal stated, further, that the women in custody were reportedly being "tortured by electric shocks and flogging, leaving some unable to walk or stand properly." Pointing out that there was "still time to act and make a difference," it requested that supporters "write to the Saudi Arabian embassy in London, calling on the authorities to release the activists immediately," using the link provided on the website. By the end of 2019, page statistics showed that more than 40,000 people had contacted the Saudi embassy via Amnesty.[42]

## PARTY REGULATIONS

Policies specifying that abuse will not be tolerated in political spaces can also help foster a safer political environment for women. In the wake of debates on sexual harassment, abuse and intimidation, and bullying in British politics, the three major UK parties introduced or revised their codes of conduct to address these problems. The Liberal Democrats, who experienced a sexual harassment scandal in 2014, adopted a code of conduct later that year stating that all members had the "right to be treated fairly, equally, and within the bounds of party rules" and were expected to "behave in a way that does not negatively impact other members, staff, volunteers, people who interact with the Party in a professional capacity, or the party's reputation." On a checklist of questions that members should ask themselves with regard to their actions both inside and outside the party, the first was "Could what I am intending to do or say or write (in any format) be taken as intimidation, harassment or bullying?"[43]

The Conservative Party introduced a code of conduct in late 2017, specifying that anyone who formally represented the party as an elected or appointed official may "not use their position to bully, abuse, victimize, harass, or unlawfully discriminate against others." Additionally, such officials must take "reasonable steps" to ensure that those wishing to raise concerns about such behaviors feel able to do so, and they must "cooperate fully with any process set down by the Party Board should a grievance process be instigated." In an "interpretation annex," the party defined "harassment" as "any unwanted physical, verbal, or non-verbal conduct that has the purpose or effect of violating a person's dignity or creating an intimidating, hostile, degrading, humiliating, or offensive situation or environment for them." It described "bullying," in turn, as "offensive, intimidating, malicious, or insulting behavior involving the misuse of power that can make a person feel vulnerable, upset, humiliated, undermined, or threatened." Those found to have violated these rules were subject to a number of potential penalties, including provisional expulsion from the party, suspension or non-renewal of party membership, suspension from office or candidature, rebuke or severe rebuke, mandated apology, removal of offending social media material, and obligatory training.[44]

The Labour Party's revised 2018 rule book incorporated several new codes of conduct, including one on sexual harassment and gender discrimination and another on social media usage. The sexual harassment policy stated that, as the "party of equality . . . Labour strongly believes that no one should feel disadvantaged, discriminated against or harassed due to their gender either inside the party or in the wider society." Declaring it "will not tolerate any form of discrimination or harassment," Labour committed itself to ensuring the party is "a welcoming environment for all who share our aims and values to engage in political activity and debate without feeling disadvantaged or unsafe." The social media code of conduct called on party members to "treat all people with dignity and respect," arguing that the party "stands against all forms of abuse and will take action against those who commit it. Harassment, intimidation, hateful language and bullying are never acceptable, nor is any form of discrimination on the basis of gender, race, religion, age, sexual orientation, gender identity or disability." The party encouraged the reporting of abusive behavior online to the party, social media platforms, and—where applicable—to the police. A pledge required of all party members, further, entailed a promise "to act within the spirit and rules of the Labour Party in my conduct both on and offline, with members and non-members and I stand against all forms of abuse."[45]

## ELECTING WOMEN

A common—albeit diffuse—response to the question of how to combat violence against women in politics is to increase the number of women in political roles. The intuition is that seeing more women active in the political sphere would normalize women's leadership—and, in turn, de-normalize and increase accountability for acts of violence against them. Among the 123 female MPs interviewed by the IPU (2018) in its European study, for example, over 90% thought that having more women in parliament could provide "a means of changing the atmosphere at work, gradually modifying the conduct and mindset of male colleagues and ensuring that women are able to fulfil their mandate and serve their electors freely and safely" (17). Together with the other strategies outlined here and in the rest of the book, this long-term strategy suggests that a combination of many strategies—addressing individual categories of violence; cutting across different manifestations of violence; and tackling violence in the short, medium, and long term—will likely be necessary to recognize, problematize, and combat violence against women in the political realm.

# 18

# Data Collection and Documentation Challenges

Data collection has always been central to feminist activism, with testimonies and statistics helping to prove the existence of a problem, as well as to measure progress—and setbacks—in relation to gender equality over time (Berkovitch 1999). In 2013, the UN Human Rights Council Working Group on Discrimination against Women in Law and in Practice noted that "evidence-based knowledge [was] weak on the extent of violence against women in politics" as well as "its impact on women's capacity to exercise their right to political participation" (UN Human Rights Council 2013, 8). Five years later, Ballington (2018) made a similar observation, noting that few global statistics or measures were currently available, due to "a lack of commonly agreed definitions and indicators, a reliance on anecdotal evidence, and underreporting because of the stigma attached to gender-based violence in many societies" (696).

Despite these challenges, a growing number of scholars and practitioners have taken steps in recent years to document and analyze this phenomenon, either modifying existing datasets and approaches or developing new sources and methods of data collection. This work has been crucial in advancing these methodological discussions by exploring multiple modes of theorizing, operationalizing, and measuring these phenomena. It has also been important in raising public awareness, establishing that the problem of violence against women in politics exists—as well as motivating action to address it.

At this nascent stage, studies vary widely in how they operationalize and measure violence against women in politics. Nonetheless, they share a tendency to elide the theoretical distinction between violence in politics and violence against women in politics—affecting, in turn, both theory building and hypothesis testing. Neither comparing the experiences of women and men, as some scholars advocate, nor centering women's lives, as others advise, provides a clear cut methodological solution. A bias event approach offers a potential means forward. Focused on collecting and evaluating evidence on the presence

*Violence against Women in Politics.* Mona Lena Krook, Oxford University Press (2020). © Oxford University Press.
DOI: 10.1093/oso/9780190088460.001.0001.

or absence of gender bias in particular incidents, it can assist both qualitative and quantitative researchers in distinguishing these phenomena in future work.

## Emerging Data

Budding awareness of violence against women in politics has inspired a variety of efforts by scholars and practitioners to document and analyze this phenomenon.[1] Ballington (2018) identifies three possibilities for how evidence might be collected: gendering existing mechanisms for monitoring political and electoral violence; adapting current instruments on violence against women to add a political dimension; and collecting testimonies from women to inform country-level analyses, both quantitative and qualitative. Largely following—but also modifying—this template, available work adopts four main approaches: reexamining existing datasets on political and electoral violence through a gender lens; conducting original surveys informed by work on violence against women; gathering and systematizing testimonies from individual women; and collecting social media data using hand-coding and automated techniques.

### EXISTING DATASETS

Several datasets measure political and electoral violence in both conflict and non-conflict contexts (among others, see Birch and Muchlinski 2017; Daxecker, Amicarelli, and Jung 2019). Gender rarely features as a central category in this work, however, at either the data collection or analysis stages. One exception is the IFES Electoral Violence Education and Resolution dataset, recording incidents between 2006 and 2010 in Bangladesh, Burundi, Guyana, Guinea, Nepal, and Timor Leste. Included by chance rather than design, coders in project countries noted the sex of perpetrators and victims of electoral violence. Reviewing the data, Bardall (2011) found a number of striking gender differences. First, men and women tended to suffer different forms of electoral violence: physical violence typically targeted men, while psychological violence was more commonly perpetrated against women. Second, the location of violence varied: men were attacked in public spaces, while women tended to face violence in private homes. Third, incidents targeting men could often be verified through official sources, including police reports, hospital records, and media stories. In contrast, information on acts committed against women was typically provided by electoral observers, election agents, and community sources. The study thus suggested that existing frameworks—focused on physical violence, public spaces, and official records—privileged men's over women's experiences of electoral violence.

A second method is to revise existing modes of data collection, as the Armed Conflict Location and Event Data (ACLED) Project decided to do in

2018. Updated on a weekly basis, its dataset records the date, location, and actors involved in violent political events around the globe. After a series of conversations with colleagues about incidents targeting women, the team secured funding to recode information already in its dataset and adopted a new template for data collection going forward.[2] In line with its prevailing practices, the team restricted its focus to physical violence (including physical forms of sexual violence) in public spaces. Launched in May 2019, the revised dataset defines "political violence targeting women" as events where individual women, or groups primarily composed of women, are attacked on political grounds.[3] An initial analysis finds that certain acts—sexual violence, abductions/forced disappearances, and mob violence—were more common in violence targeting women. Further, while the overwhelming majority (87%) of demonstrations featuring women were peaceful protests, a higher proportion met with excessive force (live fire) or intervention (arrests and tear gas), usually at the hands of the state, than protests involving men or mixed-sex groups (Kishi, Pavlik, and Matfess 2019, 23–24).

A third approach entails drawing on existing templates for electoral observation but adapting them to focus on tactics to prevent women's participation on equal terms as men. In 2015, NDI's Gender, Women, and Democracy team initiated the Votes without Violence project to bring a gender lens to NDI's longstanding work on electoral violence and the democratic quality of elections.[4] Focused on training citizen observers to detect acts of violence against women in elections, they piloted and refined the methodology during election missions in Côte d'Ivoire, Burma/Myanmar, Guatemala, Tanzania, and Nigeria. The resulting toolkit offers a checklist for monitoring incidents of violence against women before, during, and after elections, tracking women's experiences as voters, candidates, election administrators, and public officials. In addition to publishing the checklist (Hubbard and DeSoi 2016), NDI posted the data collected in the five pilot countries on a dedicated website, later adding data from six further countries—Ghana, Kenya, Liberia, Nicaragua, Timor Leste, and Uganda—whose elections were observed by NDI after publication of the assessment framework. The website provides visualizations, as well as opportunities for researchers to download the original data.[5]

ORIGINAL SURVEYS

The converse strategy is to start with concepts from the gender-based violence literature to design and implement surveys to gauge the prevalence and impact of violence against women in politics. The most well-known of these are the two surveys conducted by the IPU, referenced extensively throughout this book, with 55 female parliamentarians from 39 countries across five world regions (2016b) and 81 female MPs and 42 female staffers from 45 European states (2018). Both surveys ask a series of questions based on the four categories of violence against women identified in the 2011 Istanbul Convention: physical, sexual, psychological, and economic. A variety of other entities, however, have also sought to gather similar individual-level data to gain insight into this phenomenon. Most of this work restricts its focus to women, but collectively, surveys various categories of politically active women.

One of the first such studies was carried out in Japan in 2014 by the Alliance of Feminist Representatives (Femigiren). The project was inspired by an incident involving Ayaka Shiomura, a member of the Tokyo metropolitan assembly, who was heckled relentlessly by male colleagues while trying to participate in a policy debate. After sending the questionnaire to more than 500 women serving as local councilors across the country, Femigiren received 143 responses indicating that female politicians in Japan experienced a wide range of harassment, from sexist heckling and taunts about their marital status to silencing in debates and unwanted touching. Self-identified feminists and those campaigning for gender equality were more likely than other women to report being targeted. Additionally, a roughly inverse relationship emerged between the share of women reporting harassment and the proportion of women on the council: 73% of respondents were harassed where women held less than 10% of local council seats, compared to 58% when women occupied 10% to 20% of seats, 37% when the share of women was 20% to 30%, and 48% when the council had more than 30% women (Dalton 2017, 212).[6]

In the run-up to the 2015 elections, the Tanzania Women Cross-Party Platform (TWCP), a network bringing together the women's wings of all parties with representation in parliament, adopted a related but distinct approach. With technical and financial support from UN Women, DEMO Finland, and NDI, as well as local women's organizations like the Tanzania Women Judges Association and Coalition against Sextortion, TWCP deployed 56 monitors to 14 of the 30 regions of the country to undertake participant observation and conduct structured interviews with female candidates and voters. Attending 530 events and speaking to 1532 respondents, the observers personally witnessed abuse at political meetings, including stones being thrown at women, as well as efforts at rallies to mobilize young men to threaten women who did not support the party.

Their interviews with female candidates revealed that a large majority (69%) had faced abusive language and 17% had experienced physical attacks. An alarming share was asked to perform sexual favors at the nomination stage (19%) and during the campaign itself (24%), while 10% reported that their husbands did not support their decision to run (Semakafu 2016, 15–16). Surveying female voters turned out to be far more difficult, because a significant proportion of women did not turn out to vote—and thus were not present at polling stations on the day of the election. Seeking to understand why, monitors spoke with locals and learned that many women faced intimidation at home that had prevented their participation. Among women interviewed after the election, more than half (53%) stated they did not vote, saying they were afraid (34.6%), were missing their voter registration card (33.9%), their spouse "made trouble" (9.8%), or their husband had voted for them (7.9%). Corroborating this figure, more than 40% of voters reported hearing about women forced not to participate by family members (Semakafu 2016, 14, 21).

In other contexts, journalists have been the ones to initiate surveys. Although they had not conducted such research in the past, the utter lack of information on this topic inspired the Canadian Press, a national news agency, to administer a survey to female MPs across all parties during two weeks in December 2017. Asked about personal experiences with sexual misconduct, more than half (58%) of respondents said they faced incidents of sexual harassment or assault in the course of their work in parliament. These ranged from unwanted remarks and gestures to text messages of a sexual nature, mainly from lobbyists as well as colleagues inside and outside their own parties (Smith 2018). A subsequent survey of political staff was more challenging, given no central body to distribute the survey—and no full census of the staff working at parliament.[7] Of those that were contacted and filled out the survey, 29% said they had been sexually harassed at least once while working in parliament, while 9% had been sexually assaulted. In most cases, the perpetrators were MPs—but not the ones who employed them. Most did not report the incidents, however, because they were young, had little social capital, and faced precarious employment conditions where partisan and personal loyalty were highly valued (Samara Centre 2018).

The HuffPost undertook a similar study in 2018, focused on illuminating the experiences of young female party activists across five major German parties. Combining dozens of personal interviews with anonymous surveys of nearly 100 women, it found that more than 70% of the women sitting on federal, state, and district boards of party youth organizations felt they were taken less seriously than their male counterparts. Nearly half (45%) had witnessed sexual harassment during their political work—and one in three had personally experienced it themselves. Incidents of rape at party events were also not uncommon: one woman revealed that she personally knew of seven cases in her party, including herself. Another explained why it was difficult to speak out, pointing to inequalities of power within the party: "I was raped on a political weekend. It's hard to talk about such things as a woman against a man, because you lose your reputation so quickly, especially when the man is higher." A third young activist disclosed that an employee of a prominent MP had bluntly asked her for sex (Pfahler 2018).

Most existing surveys thus center on women's experiences, seeking to shed light on the largely hidden dynamics at work behind the scenes of political life. Herrick et al. (2019) is one of the few teams to survey both women and men, sending a questionnaire in 2017 to all mayors of U.S. cities with 30,000 or more inhabitants. They find that although male and female mayors faced abuse, women were more likely than men to experience all three forms of violence asked about in the survey: psychological (90.3% of women versus 80.9% of men), physical (22.7% of women versus 10.2% of men), and sexual (21% of women versus 2.5% of men) (8).

NDI (2018) bridges these approaches in studies of violence against women in political parties in Côte d'Ivoire, Honduras, Tanzania, and Tunisia. Combining single- and mixed-sex approaches, they administered surveys to men and women within each party, conducted in-depth interviews with party leaders, and held focus groups with female party members. The pooled results indicate that women are more likely than men to be victims of violence, to witness violence against others in the party, and to perceive a climate of violence within the party itself. Although both women and men report experiencing and witnessing physical violence, women report much higher rates of psychological and sexual violence in their parties.

## CASE-BASED RESEARCH

Gathering and systematizing women's testimonies is a sine qua non of feminist activism. Not surprisingly, therefore, case-based research is generally the method employed by women's groups in civil society to map the problem of violence against women in politics. Because this approach relies fundamentally upon women's willingness to come forward to speak about their experiences, organizations like SAP International (2007) have tackled the culture of silence by attempting to create safe spaces for women to share their experiences anonymously. While not necessarily representative of the larger population of politically active women, these non-random samples give voice to women's lived realities in the political sphere. They also offer important analytical pay-offs in terms of mapping this phenomenon, calling attention to subtle practices of violence that might otherwise be missed (Albaine 2016) and illustrating the "endless creativity of misogyny"[8] and the "staggering" variety of "harassment tactics" that surface when women are asked about their experiences (Cohen and Connon 2015, 15).

ACOBOL was one of the first groups to attempt to collect this data systematically. Formed in 1999, the network receives complaints and provides free legal counseling to affected women as part of its mandate to defend women's political rights. Gathering 117 testimonies between 2000 and 2005, ACOBOL found that 80% of acts against women fell into three main categories: pressures on women to resign from positions as local councilors, other political positions, or political organizations (36%); instances of sexual, physical, and psychological violence and abuse of authority (21%); and interference with councilors' ability to carry out their responsibilities and illegal succession to council (21%). Smaller numbers of cases involved the illegal freezing of salaries and denial of compensation for costs related to their protection (9%); discrimination (7%);

and defamation, slander, and libel (6%). After women's complaints were for-warded to local authorities, 40% went to trial but resulted in impunity for the accused; 32.4% met with no response; and 7.6% involved governments recusing themselves, claiming they did not have jurisdiction over these types of cases (Rojas Valverde 2010, 529, 531).[9]

To resolve this legal vacuum, ACOBOL began working on a bill to define "political harassment and violence against women," as well as to classify these acts as crimes or offenses resulting in legal penalties on perpetrators. Article 8 of the final version passed in 2012 offers a long and fascinating list of what political harassment and violence might look like in practice, drawn from the case files of ACOBOL—in turn, highlighting the benefits of using an inductive approach to gain a fuller understanding of the many potential manifestations of this phenomenon. The list of sample acts includes providing false, erroneous, or vague information to women leading to inadequate exercise of their political functions; stopping women from attending sessions and other activities where decisions are being made, preventing or suppressing their right to speak or vote on conditions equal to men; providing false data on the sex of candidates;[10] imposing unjustified sanctions, impeding or restricting the exercise of politi-cal rights; applying monetary sanctions, arbitrary and illegal discounts, and/or withholding of salaries; pressuring or inducing elected or appointed women to resign their positions; and obliging women, through the use of force or intimi-dation, to sign documents and/or take decisions against their will.[11]

Transnational networks of women human rights defenders have simi-larly sought to generate records of their experiences. A guidebook produced by APWLD suggests that documentation is important for at least three rea-sons: it offers the "first step towards seeking justice," with records being vital for pursuing "redress or remedy"; it preserves and recognizes the experiences of women human rights defenders for the "sake of history and building a col-lective memory"; and it provides a "safe space for victims and survivors to tell their stories," presenting opportunities to "link their experiences with that of others for mutual support and collective action" (APWLD 2007, 87–89). To this end, APWLD outlines a sample case form template, illustrating the infor-mation that defenders should record, like the name and personal circumstances of the alleged victim; the type of human rights the person was defending; the alleged violation and its perpetrator(s); evidence for belief in a link between the violation and human rights; and actions taken by authorities.

In 2015, the WHRDIC followed up by publishing an entire manual on doc-umentation, arguing that prevailing methods for recording abuses in the human rights community reflected limited assumptions about who defenders are (men), where violations take place (public spaces), who commits these violations (agents of the state), what is human rights advocacy (for example, campaigns to end the death penalty), and what constitutes a human rights violation (torture in prison). Existing frameworks thus often tended to ignore female defenders, abuses occurring in private spaces, non-state perpetrators, women's rights activities, and violations of a gendered or sexual nature. Embracing the need for an explicitly feminist approach, the WHRDIC (2015, 2) advocated a "politically motivated telling of women human rights defenders' stories," weaving a "thread between our acts of resistance and the abuses we face." Arguing that documentation was a process as well as a product, they called on defenders to undertake and publicize this research in a variety of ways, from taking pictures, recording stories, and shooting documentaries to organizing exhibitions, producing pamphlets, making legal submissions, and sending reports to international bodies. They emphasized that this work not only had a political dimension, but could also serve as an important form of self-care for activists themselves.

Inspired by these debates, IM-Defensoras created the Mesoamerican Registry of Attacks against Women Human Rights Defenders in 2012. Linking the experiences of women human rights defenders in Mexico and Central America, the registry includes information on the scope and types of attacks, describing their main features as well as identifying gendered components. Each national network designates a point person responsible for receiving and verifying information on presumptive attacks—including undertaking face-to-face meetings with survivors and assessing the seriousness of journalistic sources—and entering the information into a shared regional database. An initial report covering the period 2012–2014 observed a collective increase in attacks over time, with 414 reported in 2012, 512 in 2013, and 762 in 2014, for a total of 1688 attacks across the region as a whole. More than half of these cases were part of a repeated series of attacks, and the vast majority were perpetrated against individual women: 84.2% in 2012, 69.8% in 2013, and 71.5% in 2014 (IM-Defensoras 2015, 30–31).

A gender component could be detected in 37% of recorded assaults—40% in 2012, 46% in 2013, and 30% in 2014 (2015, 39)—although IM-Defensoras notes in the report that information was not always available on gendered aspects of these attacks. The most common gender component entailed threats, warnings, and ultimatums using sexist insults; threats of sexual violence; and threats to one's family. Other widespread gendered acts involved slander, accusations, and/or smear campaigns using gender stereotypes, or attacks on individuals or organizations working on women's rights. Less frequent, but still present, were attacks like sexual assault; intimate partner violence; and physical and verbal abuse referring to the victim's sexual identity. Largely similar patterns were observed in a subsequent report focusing on 2015 and 2016, which included the case of Nicaragua in addition to the four original countries, El Salvador, Guatemala, Honduras, and Mexico.[12]

## ONLINE DATA ANALYSIS

A fourth approach is to focus exclusively on online abuse, using a variety of techniques to collect and analyze data. One set of studies adopts a mixed-method approach, combining online data analysis with some of the self-reporting techniques employed in other research. To investigate the prevalence and content of online abuse against female candidates, Luchadoras, a Mexican NGO, monitored Twitter and Facebook conversations, using keywords and hashtags; conducted in-depth interviews with female candidates who had experienced online violence during campaigns; and requested information from local electoral bodies regarding complaints mentioning online attacks. They found that 72% of the messages on Twitter and 39% of those on Facebook were sexist; threats were largely communicated via more private digital technologies like WhatsApp, phone calls, and text messages; and 85 public complaints had been made by 62 candidates in 24 states. They determined, moreover, that more than half (62%) of the attacks were gender-based, involving judgments of sexual character, sexual objectification, and allusions to proper gender roles (Barrera, Zamora, Domínguez, Aguirre, and Esculloa 2018, 44, 37, 51).

Collaborating with Charitable Analytics International, a data technology company, and a long list of country partners, NDI adopted a similar multipronged approach to explore the nature and impact of online violence on young women's political engagement in Indonesia, Colombia, and Kenya. Researchers surveyed 1000 male and female students at two universities in each country, asking about social media usage and experiences with online violence and collecting individual Twitter handles for subsequent data analysis. Staff also ran three-day workshops with partners in each country to develop lexicons of words and phrases in local languages to capture both gender-based harassing language and the political language of the moment.

The lexicons were then used to scrape data from a sample group of Twitter accounts from the population of college-aged men and women who completed the earlier surveys. After the algorithm identified a violent tweet, human coders verified whether it met the established criteria of "violence." If so, they classified the type of abuse, using NDI's typology adapted to the online world: physical threats, insults and hate speech, sexualized distortion, and embarrassment and reputational risk. Bringing together these sources of data, the study produced two particularly notable findings. One was that politically active women paused, decreased, or completely stopped participating online following violent incidents. A second was a dramatic difference between self-reported and observed levels of online violence—17.6% versus 5.5% in Indonesia, 22.7% versus 3.6% in Kenya, and 50.2% versus 8.3% in Colombia (NDI 2019, 16)—suggesting that much online violence may be more subtle than can be detected using automated algorithms.

A second group of analyses falls on the more qualitative end of the spectrum, undertaking content analysis of social media conversations. The Digital Rights Foundation (2018) scrutinized Facebook comments directed at male and female candidates during the 2018 general elections in Pakistan. Hand-coding comments as neutral, unwelcoming, and abusive, the researchers then recorded whether the unwelcoming and abusive comments referenced targets' identity, ideology, or individual personality. They found that female politicians were more likely than their male counterparts to face objectifying, personal, sexualized, or sexual comments, whereas the men tended to be attacked more than the women on policy or political grounds.

Atalanta (2018) compared tweets about three pairs of politicians, male and female, across three continents: Theresa May and Jeremy Corbyn in the UK, Nkosazana Dlamini-Zuma and Cyril Ramaphosa in South Africa, and Michelle Bachelet and Sebastián Piñera in Chile. They analyzed nearly 28,000 tweets mentioning these politicians between September and November 2017, using a natural language processing algorithm, bringing in human verifiers for a selection of tweets to adjust the automated process as necessary. The analysis looked for signs of five types of gendered conversation: comments on physical appearance, comments on relationship or marital status, comments on children, derogatory or provocative language describing the person rather than their profession, and comments on competence due to the person's gender. It found not only a greater volume of conversation directed at women in the five gendered categories, but also more negative content directed at the three women compared to their male counterparts.

A third set of studies addresses these questions on a much larger scale, using machine learning techniques to collect and analyze millions of tweets. An approach developed by IFES utilizes sentiment analysis software to quantify and categorize opinions expressed on social media to measure their strength, emotions, and "charge" (positive, negative, or neutral). In a first study focused on Zimbabwe, the team selected a sample of 213 politicians and activists ahead of the 2018 elections and created monitors for four types of violent online content: physical, sexual, psychological, and economic. With the help of focus groups, they developed a lexicon of words and phrases in English, Ndebele, and Shona to create the algorithms.

Applying these tools to all publicly visible Twitter, Instagram, YouTube, and Facebook posts, as well as public content on news media websites and blogs, the team found that 60% of all violent discourse was directed at women between 2013 and 2018. Women faced three times as much physically violent discourse as men, as well as 24% more psychological violence. Men were associated with more content on sexual violence, but the measure included accusations of having committed rape, not necessarily threats of rape against them. Additionally, women appeared to be subject to more "viral moments" than men, due most likely to sensationalized attention to breaches of social norms (Bardall 2018, 27, 46).

Another method combines machine learning tools to process large numbers of messages, alongside crowdsourced workers to ensure greater accuracy. During one month in 2017, Rheault, Rayment, and Musulan (2019) gathered 2.2 million tweets about and addressed to a sample of U.S. and Canadian politicians. Classifying messages as "uncivil" if they contained swear words, vulgarities, insults, threats, personal attacks, or hate speech, they checked the precision of this method by randomly selecting 10,000 tweets to be annotated by human workers. They then applied the refined tool to the full dataset and via multivariate analysis, found that women were more heavily targeted by uncivil messages as their political visibility increased.

Undertaking an even more ambitious project, Amnesty International (2018b) collected tweets mentioning 778 female politicians and journalists across the ideological spectrum in the United States and the UK between January and June 2017. Focusing on sample of 288,000 tweets, more than 6,500 digital volunteers scrutinized each message for "abusive" or "problematic" content, with the former defined as content promoting violence or threats against people based on their identity and the latter as content that was hurtful and hostile but did not rise to the level of abuse. Follow-up questions asked about the nature of this content (misogynistic, homophobic, racist, or other). Each tweet was analyzed by multiple people, and in addition to definitions and tutorials to help volunteers recognize abusive or problematic content, an online forum enabled volunteers to discuss tweets they were unsure about with each other and with Amnesty's own researchers. For further quality control, three experts on violence against women also examined and categorized a sample of 1000 tweets.

Applied to the full set of 14.5 million tweets, the refined machine learning tool identified 1.1 million abusive and problematic tweets, with relatively similar patterns among politicians (1.3% abusive and 5.9% problematic) and journalists (1.2% abusive and 5.8% problematic). However, while left-wing politicians received 23% more abusive and problematic mentions than right-wing politicians, the opposite was true of journalists, with right-wing journalists targeted for 64% more abusive and problematic posts than left-wing journalists. Race also played a role, with women of color (black, Asian, Latinx, or mixed-race) being 34% more likely to appear in abusive or problematic tweets than white women—a pattern even more prominent among black women, who were mentioned in 84% more abusive and 60% more problematic tweets than white women.[13] Despite many refinements, the Amnesty researchers note that their tool achieved only 50% accuracy compared to the judgment of experts, pointing to the risks of simply leaving the task to algorithms to determine instances of abuse (Chavez 2018).

## Evaluating Documentation Strategies

Efforts to operationalize the phenomenon of violence against women in politics have thus used a variety of research tools, both quantitative and qualitative, to collect and analyze data. While this literature is still in development, initial contributions point to a variety of emerging approaches to measurement. For some, adding a gender lens simply involves recognizing and studying women as political actors, often—but not always—comparing women's experiences with those of men. For others, gendering the study of political violence entails a much deeper critique of existing approaches, requiring an expanded view of its actors, locations, and manifestations. Much of this work places strong emphasis on women's lived experiences, drawing on these for theoretical and empirical guidance. Despite divergent methodological choices, many of these contributions share a tendency to elide (gendered) violence in politics and violence against women in politics—in turn, undermining efforts to understand and articulate the challenges posed by tactics to exclude women *as women* from participating in political life.

## MALE-FEMALE COMPARISONS

In a symposium on studying violence against women in politics, Bjarnegård (2018) criticizes work "focusing only on women's experiences of violence," which she argues obscures efforts "to distinguish between instances of violence in which gender is part of the motive versus contexts in which violence is widespread and affects all political actors." Lamenting attention to women as a form of "same-gender bias . . . in reverse," she proposes that "comparing the experiences of men and women" is the "only way" to "investigate gender differences in election violence prevalence" (693).

Central to Bjarnegård's critique is her view that "violence against women in politics" is an unfortunate misnomer for research on "gender and political violence" (693). As noted in earlier chapters, however, these concepts in fact capture two distinct phenomena. Violence against women in politics is identity-based, aimed at suppressing women's participation *as women*. It is thus a form of violence directed exclusively at women. In contrast, violence in politics is issue-based, employed to silence an opponent's political views. As such, men and women potentially face this type of violence. While some cases exist at the intersection of these two types of violence, focusing on male-female differences can only give insight into gendered patterns of violence in politics, for example in its form and impact (Bardall, Bjarnegård, and Piscopo 2019). A comparative lens, in contrast, provides no leverage for analyzing violence against women in politics, which—by definition—is only experienced by women.

Other scholars espouse a different line of logic in comparing women and men. They assume—albeit implicitly[14]—that male and female politicians may be attacked similarly as politicians. If women are also attacked as women, the overall volume of abuse they experience should be higher on average—making male-female comparisons appropriate for studying both violence in politics *and* violence against women in politics. While intriguing, this intuition is potentially misleading. First, existing studies indicate that not all individuals are equally vulnerable to attack. Politicians who are more visible (Rheault, Rayment, and Musulan 2019), hold leadership positions (Krantz, Wallin, and Wallin 2012; Maidment 2017), and promote controversial political opinions (Biroli 2018; Warner 1977) tend to attract greater attention and hostility. If men are more likely to occupy highly visible leadership roles, they may be more likely than their female colleagues to face politically motivated attacks—in turn depressing estimations of violence against women in politics as a separate phenomenon.

Second, gender may not be the only factor doing "added work" in shaping experiences of violence. Research on harassment of black elected officials (Musgrove 2012; Warner 1977), as well as on the effects of race, age, class, sexuality, and religiosity in heightening vulnerability to violence against women in politics (Centre for Social Research and UN Women 2014; Dhrodia 2017; IPU 2016b, 2018; Kuperberg 2018), suggest that attempts to exclude may activate multiple categories of political marginalization. These factors, moreover, may operate alternatively and simultaneously (Weldon 2006), collectively obscuring how much of this violence is issue- versus identity-based—as well as which identities, in particular, may be driving the results. Relying on male-female comparisons to ascertain the existence (and extent) of violence against women in politics is thus not an infallible approach—but, instead, one subject to serious estimation errors.

## WOMEN-CENTERED STUDIES

International campaigns of women human rights defenders, in contrast, place women's experiences at the center of documentation efforts. The APWLD (2007) guidebook suggests that telling women's stories is important for political and personal reasons. In contexts where abuses against women are "seldom considered as human rights violations" or "serious enough to merit redress," documentation can serve as a crucial learning tool for both survivors and the broader community, providing a "basis for reflection and evaluation" and giving insight into "specific risks and vulnerabilities" faced by female defenders. In addition to "[breaking] the culture of silence," the process of providing testimony can support a woman's "recovery, reintegration, reconciliation, and healing," enabling her to "[recognize] her own voice in the narration of the incident, and [affirm] her dignity and strength to go on with her life" (87–89).

The data collection efforts of ACOBOL embody this feminist ethos, telling of women's stories as a form of resistance and empowerment (WHRDIC 2015). Along with giving voice to women's realities, they analyzed the accounts they collected to identify shared categories among these experiences, which they subsequently used to mobilize for legal reform (Rojas Valverde 2010). Relying on women to come forward with their testimonies has important limitations, however, from a conventional social science perspective. Convenience sampling—drawing from population members who are available and willing to participate—can only provide insight into trends across the pool of people studied. Making claims about broader prevalence rates, in contrast, requires a random, representative sample of the broader population.

While treated as a tenet of "good science," however, such standards are difficult to achieve with "hard-to-reach populations," where respondents have strong incentives to remain hidden due to stigmas associated with the questions being posed (Johnston and Sabin 2010). This pattern is clearly the case for politically active women, who may hesitate to report incidents of violence against women in politics—or may simply normalize it as part of the political game. In the absence of traditional sampling opportunities, researchers can, nonetheless, aim to make their samples as representative as possible of the diversity of relevant explanatory features within the broader population. To this end, the two IPU surveys (2016b; 2018) sought interviews with female MPs from different regions, political parties, age groups, and other backgrounds to lend greater substance to their findings—even if the true generalizability of these trends may never be known. However, if the goal is consciousness-raising, these concerns are moot—as the aim, then, is less to generalize than to offer an authentic articulation of women's lived experiences.

More problematically, starting from the point of view of women's lives, like engaging in male-female comparisons, does not in itself resolve the issue of distinguishing between incidents of violence in politics and violence against women in politics. As noted earlier in this book, politically active women may experience both forms of violence. These incidents may transpire separately, with attacks focusing on a woman's policy priorities at one moment and their female identity at another. Forms of violence may also co-occur, with efforts to discredit women's political views questioning their right as women to participate at all. Consequently, data collected to study women's experiences may capture both forms of violence simultaneously, as in the case of abusive tweets that may be politically motivated and/or misogynistic. Disentangling these elements is especially challenging where women are attacked both as women and in response to their women's rights advocacy, placing them at the intersection of these two phenomena.

Conscious of these possibilities, some researchers take care to identify gendered content. Such a strategy, however, does not necessarily succeed in differentiating between politically and gender-motivated acts. The registry maintained by IM-Defensoras (2015) collects information on attacks against women human rights defenders, recording—when available—data on gendered components. Yet, without further details, it is not clear whether threats of sexual violence, for example, invoke a gendered trope against an ideological opponent, or alternatively, attempt to degrade and delegitimize women as legitimate participants in the political sphere. Similarly, the work of Luchadoras on online abuse in Mexico notes whether attacks were gender-based (Barrera et al. 2018). Whereas sexual objectification and allusions to proper gender roles could be taken as clear manifestations of bias against women's presence in politics, judgments of sexual character are more ambiguous, requiring further information to ascertain how they are used to criticize women's participation as women or as political rivals. Focusing exclusively on women, therefore, does not automatically resolve the problem of identifying and measuring violence against women in politics—but may also, in fact, lead to significant distortions.

## LESSONS LEARNED AND FUTURE RESEARCH

The emerging literature on violence against women in politics reveals that— at this early stage—scholars and practitioners continue to explore how best to theorize, operationalize, and measure this phenomenon. The remarkable variety of approaches employed indicates that this topic is amenable to examination from many different angles. These studies also provide initial evidence furthering both the academic and political agendas around violence against women in politics. Their divergent conceptual roots and methodological assumptions, however, highlight the need for researchers to be explicit about their choices, as different strategies may generate distinct conclusions about the nature, extent, and impact of violence experienced by politically active women around the world.

A central challenge across all studies involves distinguishing between violence in politics and violence against women in politics. While male-female comparisons can help shed light on gendered forms of violence, they provide limited leverage for discerning gendered motivations for violence—the distinction that divides these two phenomena. Similarly, focusing on women exclusively can illuminate the spectrum of violence they experience—but absent further details, does not suffice to ascertain which of these experiences are politically versus gender-motivated. The bias event approach outlined in this book offers a way forward, however, for researchers in both camps, providing a framework for detecting and assessing evidence of bias against women, amenable to a variety of empirical research strategies.

As elaborated in chapter 10, this approach identifies six possible indicators that bias might have played a role in a particular event: the offender made oral comments, written statements, or gestures indicating bias; the offender left bias-related drawings, symbols, or graffiti at the scene; the victim was engaged in activities related to his or her identity group; the offender was previously involved in a similar incident or is a hate group member; a substantial portion of the community where the event occurred perceived that the incident was motivated by bias; and—to capture potential implicit bias—the victim was evaluated negatively according a double standard. This framework does not require that all six criteria be met, but rather, draws on them holistically to assess whether, on balance, available data would support a finding of bias against women in political roles.

While illustrated in this book via qualitative case studies, a bias event approach could also be translated into quantitative measures. Most existing datasets of electoral and political violence, for example, are based on incident reports regarding the type, location, perpetrators, and targets of violence. Incorporating a bias event lens might entail asking follow-up questions about the content of the incident (did it invoke bias-related tropes?), the actors involved (did the targets or perpetrators have a history of activism for or against the target's identity group?), and how the incident was perceived by the broader community (did citizens or the media interpret the incident as motivated by bias?). Surveys could also integrate this approach into the design of questionnaires. After questions about online violence, for instance, respondents could be asked to estimate how much of the abuse was driven by political or gender reasons. Respondents could also be invited to give examples, which researchers could then analyze for bias-related content. Analyses of social media data, finally, often attempt to devise measures to capture the nature of content. Adapting these approaches in a bias-detection-oriented direction, however, could help develop more nuanced typologies of misogynistic versus political issue content.

While the literature on violence against women in politics is still emerging, its scope is impressively wide, analyzing the experiences of women active in a variety of political spaces. Further, its impact is already tangible, not only giving women opportunities—and a language—to speak about their experiences in the political world, but also serving to pressure actors at numerous levels to enact policy change. Future work should build on these solid foundations to produce more robust and cumulative research findings. However, both scholars and practitioners should take care to ensure that, in the process, "efforts to clarify the concept of violence do not privilege intellectual clarity over the lived experience of fear, loss, and insecurity that are an inextricable part of violent acts" (Krause 2009, 354). Anchoring projects—whether qualitative or quantitative—in women's realities will not only inspire new conversations but also help foster awareness and a will to address violence as a gendered tool of political exclusion.

19

# Political and Social Implications

Violence against women in politics is increasingly recognized around the world as a challenge to women's political participation. The implications of these acts reach far beyond individual victims, however, harming political institutions as well as society at large. First, attempting to exclude women *as women* from participating in political life undermines democracy, negating political rights and disturbing the political process. Second, tolerating mistreatment due to a person's ascriptive characteristics infringes on their human rights, damaging their personal integrity as well as the perceived social value of their group. Third, normalizing women's exclusion from political participation relegates women to second class citizenship, threatening principles of gender equality. Naming the problem of violence against women in politics thus has important repercussions along multiple dimensions, making the defense of women's rights integral to the protection of political and human rights for all.

## Democracy

Violence occurs in a variety of professional sectors, but features of politics as a domain magnify the meaning and impact of violence, while simultaneously reducing accountability for its perpetrators. As an arena of public debate, intimidation in political spaces is not merely a personal or institutional problem, but potentially threatens "the very nature of representative democracy," affecting "the diversity of our public life," "the way in which the public can engage" politically, and the "freedom to discuss and debate issues and interests" (CSPL 2017, 13). As such, politics "is not necessarily 'worse' than other sectors" in terms of violence, according to French staffer and member of Chair Collaboratrice, Assia Hebbache, but harassment there "imposes more problems, because it is a place where laws are made." Moreover, she points out, the unique nature of this space—characterized by legal immunity and the importance of

*Violence against Women in Politics.* Mona Lena Krook, Oxford University Press (2020). © Oxford University Press.
DOI: 10.1093/oso/9780190088460.001.0001.

partisan loyalty—creates "incredible impunity" (Philippe 2019), resulting in a lack of protections from abuse that are often standard in more traditional workplaces (Summers 2013). Using violence to deter women's participation *as women* has consequences, therefore, not only for politically active women, but also for the democratic system at large—jeopardizing political rights, hindering political work, and eroding public confidence in political institutions.

## POLITICAL RIGHTS

The Universal Declaration of Human Rights (UN 1948) outlines a number of political rights, including the right to freedom of expression and the right to receive and impart information (Article 19), the right to peaceful assembly and association (Article 20), and the right to take part in elections as candidates and voters (Article 21). The CEDAW Convention (1979) specifies that women have the right—on equal terms with men—to vote and stand for election, to hold public office and perform all public functions at all levels of government, and to participate in NGOs and associations concerned with the public and political life of their countries (Article 7). Creating obstacles to women's exercise of these rights thus not only has tangible effects on women's political participation but also violates national and international laws—thus hollowing out these rights at both the practical and normative levels.

Events surrounding the resignation of Kiah Morris, the only African-American woman in the Vermont House of Representatives, illustrate what these rights violations might look like in practice. A racial and social justice advocate, Morris was first elected to the state legislature in 2014. Although she experienced a few instances of harassment during her first term, the abuse escalated dramatically after she won the Democrat primary for reelection in 2016. Swastikas appeared on trees along walking trails near her home, her car and home were broken into, and a package with racially charged images were slid under the door of her Democratic Party office. When the primary perpetrator, Max Misch, a self-described white nationalist, showed up at her polling station, she was forced to apply for a restraining order against him.

After that order expired one year later, Misch resumed his campaign of harassment and threats. A report released in early 2019 revealed that police had responded at least 16 times to complaints by Morris or her family over two years, including burglaries, people lurking in their yard, and unknown vehicles parked near their home. Morris also received numerous threatening messages online, including one advising her to "go back to Africa, it's the only place you'll ever be safe." Although police concluded that the evidence "showed a family living in constant fear and suspicion," Vermont Attorney General T. J. Donovan declined to press charges against Misch or others, arguing that that there was insufficient physical evidence to identify any suspects in the burglaries—and that, while "disturbing," the harassment itself did not rise to the level of a crime. Describing the experience as "death by a thousand paper cuts" (Flynn 2019), Morris decided to resign from office after winning her third primary in August 2018. The psychological violence perpetrated by Misch, combined with impunity for his sustained campaign of harassment, thus effectively nullified her political rights to run for and hold political office—as well as the rights of voters, whose decisions in the primary election were negated.

While journalists are not often framed as political actors, attacks against them directly affect political rights to free expression and to receive and impart information. Indeed, OSCE Representative on Freedom of the Media Dunja Mijatović convened an expert group meeting in 2015 framing online abuse of female journalists as a new challenge to freedom of expression. Her 2016 report argued that journalists' safety was a precondition for free speech, such that efforts to silence women should be understood as an attack on the freedoms and rights of society as a whole. Likewise, a CPJ study observes that sexual assaults of female journalists seek to silence the messenger, hoping women will be intimidated into self-censorship. However, the broader impact of these attacks is to block dissemination of news and information to the public, thus also affecting the quality of news production overall (Wolfe 2011).

## POLITICAL WORK

Threats aim to change the target's behavior in order to benefit the intimidator. In a work-related context, this involves attempting to interrupt tasks essential to job performance (Parker 2015). On a day-to-day basis, violence against women in politics can burden targets with extra concerns, drawing time and attention away from their political priorities. In an interview with Amnesty International, British MP Anna Soubry noted the "time-consuming" nature of "death threats," as "there's a big process to go through on each occasion with the police and the House authorities, there's obviously extra security measures you have to put in place each time, and also if your kids see the tweets or it's the first time for new members of staff, you have to do a lot of reassurance with them that they shouldn't worry. Obviously you're partly reassuring yourself as well" (Dhrodia 2017). Along similar lines, in the IPU (2018) survey of parliamentary staffers in Europe, more than half (59.7%) of those subjected to violence said they were badly shaken by the experience. A slightly smaller but still significant share (52.9%) reported it had affected their ability to work normally (10). These patterns square with research on microaggressions finding that repeated exposure to denigrating remarks can sap energy, lower self-esteem, and "deplete or divert energy for adaptive functioning and problem solving" (Sue 2010, 15).

Violence can also have longer-term effects, shaping the behaviors of targets into the future. Politically engaged women are often keenly aware that violence aims to force them to reduce or stop their political activities altogether. In

2016, five female members of the Seattle City Council published a joint letter in the *Seattle Times* after a vote about a sports arena—which pitted the five female members against the four male members—inspired a "bombardment of threats, of sexual and other physical violence, hateful language and, in some cases, racist rhetoric and accusations of incompetence rooted in our gender identity." They portrayed the "misogynistic backlash" as an "attempt to communicate a dangerous message: Elected women in Seattle do not deserve the respect necessary to make tough decisions without the fear of violence and racially and sexually charged retaliation." Recognizing that the intention was to "use fear and shame to silence and control," they felt the need to clarify that they would not be deterred, declaring: "We will not be silenced with threats, not today, not tomorrow, and not ever" (Bagshaw, González, Herbold, Juarez, and Sawant 2016).

Despite the resolve of many women to continue their political work unabated, the reality is that many do feel compelled to take precautions that reduce their previous ability to engage fully with the public and express their opinions freely, especially on controversial issues. Illustrating how violence had changed her daily routines and affected opportunities to interact with constituents, British MP Maria Caulfield told the CSPL (2017): "I now have video entry only into my constituency office. I have panic alarms installed. I only post on social media after I have attended events so people can't track my movements, on the advice of local police. I no longer put anything personal on social media. I no longer hold open surgeries [drop-in meetings with local constituents], they are by appointment only and are not advertised in advance" (77).

This violence, in turn, can affect opportunities for political expression. In an opinion piece following the murder of Jo Cox, British MP Jess Phillips (2016b) writes: "Jo's death has brought about so many emotions . . . I am scared that what I might say or do will make me a target. I wish I weren't, but I am . . . For Jo, her beliefs and her courage to air them cost her her life." A survey of 940 male and female journalists across the 47 COE member states found, similarly, that in the face of threats, 15% stopped covering sensitive topics, 31% toned down their coverage of these issues, and 23% opted to withhold information in their stories.[1] A study by the Committee to Protect Journalists (2016) focused specifically on women discovers that, in addition to abandoning stories, some women moved jobs or locations—or even gave up journalism entirely.

Violence can also impoverish political discourse in more indirect ways. In a subsequent book, Phillips (2017) relates that many young women seek out her support and advice for dealing with misogyny online, telling her "they're going to stop posting blogs and tweeting about their politics and their views" (214). Threats of violence also threaten to erode the fight for social justice, as women human rights defenders are often "the ones who search for disappeared victims, who bring to light cases of military sexual violence, who mobilize to defend the lands and natural resources of indigenous groups, who support incarcerated women who choose abortion, and who defend women working in sweatshops" (IM-Defensoras 2013, 448).

PUBLIC CONFIDENCE

Civility in politics demonstrates mutual respect, permitting reasoned debate with those holding opposite viewpoints, while also nurturing citizens' levels of trust in politicians and the political process more generally. Incivility, by contrast, breeds hostility against opponents and mistrust of the political system (Mutz 2015). Sexual harassment scandals brought to light by the #MeToo movement highlight how allegations of sexual misconduct may affect public opinion, as well as broader faith in political institutions. A survey conducted by the Fawcett Society finds that sexual harassment accusations in the British parliament had a negative impact on political engagement: 29% of respondents were less likely to get involved in politics, while 23% said the allegations made them less likely to vote. Affecting both men and women, these trends were particularly pronounced among younger voters, where 48% of women and 45% of men reported they were less likely to get involved in politics as a result (Culhane 2019, 7, 26). The lack of protections for victims magnified these effects, according to both MPs and staff, who expressed concerns that "the place regarded as the heart of our democracy [was] failing to live up to the standards to be expected of any 21st century workplace" (Cox 2018, 4; cf. Krook 2018).

## Human Rights

Although the Universal Declaration of Human Rights (UN 1948) stipulates that everyone has the right to life, liberty, and security of person (Article 3), women's rights were not explicitly recognized as human rights in international instruments until the Vienna Declaration adopted by the UN World Conference on Human Rights in 1993. Describing the "human rights of women" as "an inalienable, integral, and indivisible part of universal human rights" (Article 18), the declaration called for the "elimination of violence against women in public and private life," arguing that gender-based violence constituted a violation of human rights (Article 38) (UN 1993b). The most recent statement of these principles, CEDAW General Recommendation No. 35, asserts that women's right to a life free from gender-based violence is "indivisible from and interdependent" on other human rights, including rights to life, health, liberty, and security of the person; freedom from torture, cruel, inhumane, or degrading treatment; and freedom of expression, movement, participation, assembly, and association (CEDAW Committee 2017, 6). Violence against women in politics thus constitutes a violation of human rights, affronting women's personal dignity and encumbering their rights as a group to participate in public life.

## PERSONAL DIGNITY

Beyond physical injuries, experiencing violent acts can "assail the self-esteem of recipients, produce anger and frustration, deplete psychic energy, lower feelings of subjective well-being and worthiness, produce physical health problems, shorten life expectancy, and deny minority populations equal access and opportunity in education, employment, and healthcare" (Sue 2010, 6). Flora Igoki Terah, a parliamentary candidate in Kenya, was beaten by a group of men leading to an extensive period of hospitalization. In a later book, she reflected that "many people wondered where I got the courage and strength to go on . . . . [My attackers] had wanted to humiliate me, strip me of all my dignity, and leave nothing of me but a shell" (Terah 2008, 46). Former U.S. Secretary of State Madeleine Albright (2016) captured a similar sentiment in an opinion piece in which she wrote: "When a woman participates in politics, she should be putting her hopes and dreams for the future on the line, not her dignity and not her life."

While no studies track the impact of these affronts to dignity among politically active women, interviews with current and former employees of Cognizant, a company that provides Facebook moderation services, points to the physical and emotional toll of repeated exposure to online abuse. Required to review all content—including text, images, and videos—reported to Facebook for violating community standards, moderators developed serious anxiety while still in training and faced serious trauma symptoms long after they left the company (Newton 2019). It is not difficult to imagine that personalized violent content could have similar if not greater impact on the politically active women to whom it is directed, inducing anxiety and undermining their feelings of self-worth.

## SECURITY BURDENS

Abuse also threatens individuals' sense of security, creating additional mental labor and requiring the adoption of extensive preventative measures in the conduct of their daily lives. Vera-Gray (2018) describes these psychological burdens as "safety work," a "range of modifications, adaptions, decisions that women taken often habitually in order to maintain a sense of safety in public spaces" (14). Limiting women's freedom of movement, concerns about security may lead women to "avoid speaking engagements, close their social media accounts, change email addresses and phone numbers, leave their homes . . . or even stop participating online altogether because of gender-based harassment" (Vickery and Everbach 2018, 16). These safety burdens may be both conscious and unconscious: while female journalists told Peterson (2018) they did not deal with threats on a daily basis, many ended up sharing the intricate—and exhausting—strategies they had developed for shielding themselves from abuse.

Such precautions foster a feeling of "constant external awareness" (Vera-Gray 2018, 87) and may thwart women's pursuit of social justice (Calogero 2013) due to an increased sense of the costs of activism. An NGO study on security barriers to women's participation in protests in Egypt, Libya, and Yemen finds, for example, that "ambitious young women are forced to forego opportunities for development that could make them more effective community and political activists in the future" (Saferworld 2013, 16). Interviews with reproductive rights providers in the United States similarly highlight the role of safety concerns in reducing time spent on defending women's human rights. As one clinic director observed: "Our focus had to shift from the lofty goal of women's liberation to protecting our buildings, protecting our staffs, and protecting our clients" (Baird-Windle and Bader 2001, 14).

## Gender Equality

Violence against women, finally, is widely recognized as a form of gender inequality. Article 1 of CEDAW General Recommendation No. 19 defines gender-based violence as "a form of discrimination that seriously inhibits women's ability to enjoy rights and freedoms on a basis of equality with men" (CEDAW Committee 1992, 1). General Recommendation No. 35 expands this definition, stating that violence serves as "one of the fundamental social, political, and economic means by which the subordinate position of women with respect to men and their stereotyped roles are perpetuated," constituting "a critical obstacle to achieving substantive equality between women and men" (CEDAW Committee 2017, 4). In the political realm, violence against women does not simply reflect views that women do not have same right as men to participate. It also seeks to reinforce these inequalities by deterring individual women—as well as women as a group—from becoming and remaining politically engaged.

INDIVIDUAL EFFECTS

The aim of violence against women in politics, by definition, is to discourage women from participating in political life. Most efforts target individual women who are politically involved, with the intention of coercing them to cease their political activities. In some cases, the impact is immediate. Reviewing 10 years of case files, ACOBOL reported that more than one-third (36%) of the complaints it had received concerned forced resignations, with female local councilors being pressured to hand over their seats to male alternates (Chávez 2009). Online violence, similarly, induced politically active women to modify—pause, decrease, or completely halt—their social media engagement, across three project countries studied by NDI (2019).

In other instances, experiences with violence lead women to think twice about political involvement. A study of female journalists found that, in the wake of threats and attacks, nearly one-third (29%) of respondents thought about leaving the profession. These effects were twice as strong among journalists under the age of 30 (36%) as among reporters over the age of 40 (18%) (Ferrier 2018, 44). Sharing this sentiment, British MP Lisa Cameron reflected: "I wouldn't have given up my job and stood for election if the abuse I would receive had been explained to me. I wouldn't have. I believed I had something to contribute . . . but I have a young family, and I wouldn't have wanted to put them through it. Their wellbeing is the priority" (CSPL 2017, 29).

After enduring such violence, many women around the world appear to share the sentiments of a British suffragette who explained, after being "treated both violently and indecently" on Black Friday in November 1910, she had to withdraw from participating in marches on parliament because "my self-respect prevents me from voluntarily subjecting myself again to similar treatment" (Rosen 1974, 142). According to ACOBOL, few female incumbents run for a second term, believing that holding local office in Bolivia was not worth the physical and psychological violence they had endured (Chávez 2009). An online survey of British MPs revealed, along similar lines, that 86% of female MPs were not confident that appropriate action was being taken to tackle violence against women in politics—leading nearly two-thirds (65%) of female MPs to say they were less willing to stand for re-election as a result.[2]

## GROUP EFFECTS

As with violence against women more generally, however, the impact of violence against women in politics is not limited to the women directly targeted. As Manne (2018) observes, "misogyny directed toward one woman in public life may serve as a warning to others not to follow her lead, or even to publicly lend their support to her" (111). Bradley-Geist, Rivera, and Geringer (2015) describe this dynamic as the "collateral damage of ambient sexism" (29), whereby witnessing sexism aimed at other women negatively affects female bystanders' own self-esteem and career aspirations. Some elected women are keenly aware of this possibility. A candidate in the United States explained that she deleted the sexist comments on her Facebook page, as "a lot of women pay attention to my page. It's important to me that we show a good dialogue about the issues and we don't scare women away from running" (Astor 2018, 14). British MP Luciana Berger offered a related story about a woman she encouraged to run for office who told her: " 'I wouldn't do it, I couldn't do it, I couldn't go through what you experience' " (CSPL 2017, 29).

These demonstration effects need not be experienced firsthand. In a report on the state of women's rights in Afghanistan, Human Rights Watch (2009) notes: "Every time a woman in public life is assassinated, her death has a multiplier effect: women in her region or profession will think twice about their public activities" (5). Referring to the case of Sitara Achakzai, a member of Kandahar's provincial council, for example, one UNIFEM official called the assassination "an attack on the entire women's human rights community," sending a "chilling message [that] makes it even less likely for other women to start participating" (Human Rights Watch 2009, 21–22). In cities like Kandahar, indeed, the deterrent was so strong that in the 2009 elections fewer women ran for office than the number of seats side aside for women by law (5).

Across different sources, however, perhaps the greatest concern is how violence against women in politics might affect the political ambitions of young women. In Australia, surveys by Plan International (2017) revealed that, while 95% of girls aged 10 to 17 believed that girls were just as good at being leaders as boys, more than half (56%) of women aged 18 to 25 thought female politicians were treated unfairly by both the media and their male colleagues, leading more than one third (35%) to view gender as a barrier to a career in politics (8).[3] In the UK, almost all (98%) participants in a program for aspiring women leaders reported witnessing sexist abuse of female politicians online, which over 75% indicated was a concern weighing on their decision to pursue a role in public life (Campbell and Lovenduski 2016, 31). Similar sentiments were expressed by a former political staffer, who shared: "My experiences [of sexual harassment] have completely put me off a career in Parliament or in politics generally, an aspiration that I had nurtured and worked hard to achieve for a long time" (Culhane 2019, 11). Violence against women in politics thus undermines broader prospects for gender equality, not only affecting women directly in the moment—but also influencing how women, indirectly as well as into the future, feel empowered to participate fully in the political world.

# Concluding Thoughts

This book tracks the process of naming the problem of violence against women in politics—and in turn, seeks to strengthen its conceptual foundations in order to support ongoing and future efforts to address and study this phenomenon. These global debates have been informed and driven by the courage of countless women around the world who have come forward to share their experiences—some of whom, in the course of reflecting on incidents in their lives, have themselves contributed to theorizing on this topic. In 2016, Canadian politician Janis Irwin (2016) wrote an essay in the *Huffington Post* sharing her thoughts in the wake of the murder of British MP Jo Cox. Seeking to denormalize violence as the cost of doing politics, she mused: "like me, many women in politics have been told to just not engage—and to just 'let things go' . . . We're told that you 'gotta be tough' in politics, and if you can't handle it, then it's just not for you. 'Grow a thick skin,' they'll often say. But the thickest of skins won't combat threats that are acted upon. The thickest of skins won't stop a bullet." In 2019, U.S. Representative Alexandria Ocasio-Cortez tweeted her thoughts on why politically active women are attacked: "The reason women are critiqued for being too loud or too meek, too big or too small, too smart to be attractive or too attractive to be smart, is to belittle women out of standing up publicly. The goal is to 'critique' into submission. & That applies to anyone challenging power."[1]

Although raising awareness about violence against women in politics may potentially depress the political ambitions of other women by highlighting the dangers inherent in engaging in public life, speaking out about these experiences can also be empowering. Indeed, while fear may demobilize, anger can mobilize—producing positive, rather than negative, effects on political participation (Valentino, Brader, Groenendyk, Gregorowicz, and Hutchings 2011). After speaking out about their experiences, indeed, many women appear instead to be galvanized to continue their political work. Among the female MPs in Europe interviewed by the IPU (2018), for example, 79.2% responded

*Violence against Women in Politics.* Mona Lena Krook, Oxford University Press (2020). © Oxford University Press.
DOI: 10.1093/oso/9780190088460.001.0001.

that, despite experiences with violence, they were determined to remain in office and run for another term (10). A study of online abuse of feminists found, likewise, that more than half (54%) said experiencing abuse made them "more determined in [their] political views," while 33% said it made them feel "motivated to continue to engage in debate" as well as "motivated to do something" (Lewis, Rowe, and Wiper 2017, 1475). After a presentation at the UN on violence against women human rights defenders, one participant reported that "even with the acknowledgment of struggle," the meeting had ended not with a "predominant feeling" of "defeat," but rather a "mood" of "fatigued exhilaration" (Rothschild 2005, 5).

Looking to the future, debates on violence against women in politics appear likely to continue. Referring to sexism and misogyny in the political world, Hillary Clinton (2017) shared: "I can't think of a single woman in politics who doesn't have stories to tell. Not one" (116). The ubiquity of this problem makes it easy to dismiss as simply the cost of doing politics, as an unfortunate and pervasive consequence of women's political activity. Viewed through the lens of the lived experiences of the women profiled in this book, however, demonstrates the many troubling ways in which women may be targeted *as women*, with the specific purpose of violating their personal integrity as well as their equal political rights. British MP Jess Phillips (2017) encapsulates these dynamics succinctly when she writes: "It is dangerous to be a woman with a voice, but it is considerably more dangerous for us to shut up" (236).

This book provides some initial concepts and frameworks for better understanding this problem, but—given the many more stories left to tell—does not presume to offer the final word on this topic. Rather, this volume represents an attempt to begin, rather than end, a broader global conversation on violence against women in politics. In this spirit, a companion website to this book—vawpolitics.org—has been created as a platform for cataloguing the original scholarly and practitioner contributions to these debates, as well as for sharing new resources as they emerge to reflect ongoing developments in this field. Former Australian prime minister Julia Gillard captures the ethos of this ongoing collective project in remarks made in memory of Jo Cox in 2016: "Let us stand in solidarity with the next generation of women and support their right to serve and lead, safely and freely, but most importantly—powerfully."

# NOTES

## Introduction

1. Focus group in Tunisia, cited in NDI (2018, 92).
2. Facebook post by Kim Weaver, June 3, 2017, https://www.facebook.com/KimWeaverIA/posts/884931638314035.
3. Tweet by Steve King, June 4, 2017, https://twitter.com/SteveKingIA/status/871417060894457856.
4. Tweet by Monique Pelletier, May 10, 2016, https://twitter.com/pelletiermoniqu/status/729950025795645440.

## Chapter 2

1. For the full text of the law, see http://www.diputados.bo/leyes/ley-n%C2%B0-243.
2. In 2010, the UN General Assembly merged four organizations, including UNIFEM, to create the United Nations Entity for Gender Equality and the Empowerment of Women (UN Women).
3. See http://www.knchr.org/Portals/0/Reports/Waki_Report.pdf, 24, 58.
4. Interview in Nairobi, June 13, 2018.
5. Interview in Nairobi, June 13, 2018.
6. Interview in Nairobi, June 14, 2018.
7. An electronic version is available at https://www.genderinkenya.org/publication/electoral-gender-based-violence-handbook/.
8. Interviews in Nairobi, June 14, 2018.
9. The information that follows draws on an interviews in New York, March 12 and June 7, 2018, as well as interviews via Skype, February 27 and March 11, 2019.
10. Interview in New York, June 7, 2018.
11. Interview in Washington, DC, May 10, 2018.
12. For links to these resources, see https://www.ifes.org/VAWE.
13. Interview in Washington, DC, May 10, 2018.
14. To view these testimonies, see http://www.parlamericas.org/en/gender-equality/political-harassment-map.aspx.
15. Interview via phone, February 27, 2019.
16. Interview via phone, March 28, 2019.
17. NDI presentation at the Carter Center, Atlanta, GA, February 25, 2018.
18. Project details, as well as the call to action, are available at https://www.ndi.org/not-the-cost.
19. Its online #think10 tool is available at https://think10.demcloud.org/ provides women who participate in politics with a confidential way to assess their individual security and make a plan to increase their safety.

20. Interview via phone, March 13, 2019.

21. Interviews via Skype, July 17 and July 27, 2018.

## Chapter 3

1. Interview in Tunis, July 9, 2018.

2. For the video and full text, see http://legacy.annesummers.com.au/speeches/her-rights-at-work-r-rated-version/.

3. Interview in New York, April 25, 2019.

4. For video of the speech, see https://www.youtube.com/watch?v=SOPsxpMzYw4.

5. Interviews in Paris, January 12 and 13, 2017.

6. See https://www.associationparler.com/.

7. The name is a play on words, sounding like Chère collaboratrice ("Dear female staffer") but actually meaning "Flesh of a female staffer."

8. These testimonies are posted on the group's website at https://chaircollabora-trice.com/, Facebook page at https://www.facebook.com/chaircollaboratrice/; and Twitter account at https://twitter.com/chaircollab.

9. Interview in Paris, January 13, 2017.

10. See video at https://twitter.com/chaircollab/status/1108307193265352704.

11. The letter to Corbyn is posted here: http://www.mwnuk.co.uk//go_files/resources/422693-Labour%20Party%20Complaint%20Letter.pdf.

12. Interview in London, January 18, 2018.

13. See https://www.pantsuitnation.org/mission.html.

14. For election-by-election data, see https://cawp.rutgers.edu/facts/elections/past_candidates.

15. For video and commentary, see http://www.womensmediacenter.com/speech-project/nameitchangeit.

16. Interview via Skype, March 11, 2019.

17. Activist Tarana Burke had been using the phrase "Me Too" on social media since 2006, however, and is widely recognized as the founder of the #MeToo movement.

18. Tweet by Alyssa Milano, October 15, 2017, https://twitter.com/Alyssa_Milano/status/919659438700670976.

19. For the full letter, see https://documents.latimes.com/women-california-politics-call-out-pervasive-culture-sexual-harassment/.

20. Click on each account at https://www.wesaidenough.com/stories.

21. See https://twitter.com/WeSaidEnough.

22. For details on specific policy changes, see http://www.ncsl.org/research/about-state-legislatures/2018-legislative-sexual-harassment-legislation.aspx.

23. For the full text of the final bill, see https://www.congress.gov/bill/115th-congress/senate-bill/3749/text.

24. For the full debate transcript, see https://hansard.parliament.uk/commons/2017-10-30/debates/832D011D-F22E-47EB-A7B2-E5062E84AF91/SexualHarassmentInParliament.

25. Interviews in London, January 9 and 16, 2018.

26. Interview in London, January 10, 2018.

27. See https://labourtoo.org.uk/.

28. The legislative summary is available at https://lop.parl.ca/sites/PublicWebsite/default/en_CA/Research. Publications/LegislativeSummaries/421C65E.

29. Interview via WhatsApp, January 31, 2019.

30. See https://metooep.com/news-about-metooep/.

31. See https://metooep.com/.

32. See https://metooep.com/sign-the-pledge/.

33. These stories were published in Icelandic here https://www.mbl.is/media/08/10508.pdf.

## Chapter 4

1. In 2006, the commission was replaced by the UN Human Rights Council.

2. Interview via phone, February 26, 2019.

3. See further details on types of grants and criteria for selection at https://urgentactionfund.org/apply-for-a-grant/criteriado-i-fit/.

4. See https://www.defendingwomen-defendingrights.org/about/.

5. For more extensive discussion of sexual and reproductive rights as human rights, see Center for Reproductive Rights (2009) and Soohoo and Hortsch (2011).

6. See summary discussion at http://www.newssafety.com/stories/insi/wrw.htm.

7. See summary discussion at https://dartcenter.org/content/women-reporting-war.

8. See the full text at https://cpj.org/reports/2011/06/security-guide-addendum-sexual-aggression.php.

9. See the full text at https://www.osce.org/fom/139186.

10. See http://www.unesco.org/new/en/media-services/single-view/news/unesco_welcomes_report_on_safety_of_journalists_and_the_dang/.

11. See data summary at https://www.ifj.org/media-centre/news/detail/category/press-releases/article/ifj-survey-one-in-two-women-journalists-suffer-gender-based-violence-at-work.html.

## Chapter 5

1. Information from Ruth Halperin-Kaddari, vice chair of the CEDAW Committee, March 9, 2018.

2. See https://www.ohchr.org/EN/NewsEvents/Pages/DisplayNews.aspx?NewsID=21652&LangID=E.

3. For a summary of contributions to this meeting, see UN Women, Office of the High Commissioner on Human Rights, and UN Special Rapporteur on Violence against Women (2018).

4. "16 Days" refers to the period between November 25, International Day for the Elimination of Violence against Women, and December 10, Human Rights Day. See more at https://16dayscampaign.org/about-the-campaign/.

5. See details and links here: https://16dayscampaign.org/campaigns/sector-focus-initiative/.

6. Interview via phone, February 26, 2019.

7. Seehttps://ushrnetwork.org/news/119/100/International-Labor-Conference-negotiates-a-standard-setting-process-to-end-violence-and-harassment-in-the-world-of-work.

8. Interview via phone, March 11, 2019.

## Chapter 6

1. Personal visit to the "Votes for Women" exhibition, Museum of London, March 2018.

2. The first woman to win a parliamentary election was Constance Markievicz in 1918. As a member of Sinn Fein, however, she did not take her seat. Astor won her seat in a by-election in 1919.

3. During hearings to confirm Thomas as a member of the U.S. Supreme Court in 1991, Hill came forward with allegations that Thomas had sexually harassed her while serving as her supervisor at the U.S. Department of Education and the Equal Employment Opportunity Commission.

4. This exemption stemmed from the theory that Congress could not be governed by the executive and judicial branches, making it immune from the very laws it had passed to prevent employment discrimination (Bingham 1997). See Jones (2017) for a discussion of the implications of this exemption in the case of race discrimination.

## Chapter 7

1. See pages 3 and 4 of the law at http://www.diputados.bo/leyes/ley-n%C2%B0-243.

2. Interviews via Skype, February 27 and March 11, 2019.

3. Interview in Lima, July 24, 2015.

4. Interviews in Washington, DC, May 10, 2018, and New York, June 7, 2018.

5. See https://www.ifes.org/VAWE.

6. See https://www.ndi.org/not-the-cost.

7. See page 1 of the law at http://www.legislation.tn/sites/default/files/news/tf2017581. pdf.

8. See page 3 of the law at http://www.diputados.bo/leyes/ley-n%C2%B0-243.

9. Interview in Tunis, September 3, 2015.

10. Interview in Nairobi, June 15, 2018.

11. This can also disguise the fact that perpetrators may not even be located within the country itself, working for "troll farms" or participating in global networks of men's rights activists.

12. Interviews in London, January 10, 16, 17, and 18, 2018.

13. Interview in Stockholm, September 13, 2017.

## Chapter 8

1. This quote, indeed, is so central to Churchill's views on politics that it leads the summary of his political career on the National Churchill Museum website: https://www. nationalchurchillmuseum.org/winston-churchill-the-politician.html.

2. See https://www.publicpolicypolling.com/wp-content/uploads/2017/09/PPP_ Release_Natl_010813_.pdf.

3. See the most recent data at https://www.ipu.org/about-us/structure/governing-council/committee-human-rights-parliamentarians.

4. Decisions going back to 1996 are posted at https://www.ipu.org/decisions-committee-human-rights-parliamentarians.

5. Interview in Stockholm, March 31, 2017. See links to reports and data at https://www.bra.se/statistik/statistiska-undersokningar/politikernas-trygghetsundersokning.html.

6. For links to all these reports, see https://antisemitism.org.uk/the-appg/publications/.

7. Interview in London, January 18, 2018.

8. In 2006, the commission was replaced by the UN's Human Rights Council.

9. See https://cpj.org/about/faq.php.

10. See https://sustainabledevelopment.un.org/sdg16.

11. See https://ipi.media/programmes/ontheline/about-ontheline/.

## Chapter 9

1. For a more detailed analysis of the Bhutto and Rousseff cases, see Krook and Restrepo Sanín (2020).

2. The series of tweets (and responses) can be seen at https://www.vox.com/2019/7/14/20693758/donald-trump-tweets-racist-xenophobic-aoc-omar-tlaib-pressley-back-countries.

3. See https://winstonchurchill.org/publications/finest-hour/finest-hour-162/wit-and-wisdom-true-men-and-women/.

4. See the Mobility Map (2017) and Physical Security Map (2014) at http://www.womanstats.org/maps.html.

5. See http://tigerbeatdown.com/2011/11/10/but-how-do-you-know-its-sexist-the-mencallmethings-round-up/.

6. Many thanks to María Clara Medina for her observation at a workshop in Mexico City in November 2015 that symbolic violence serves as the root of all other types of violence against women in politics.

7. See an English-language translation at http://kjonnsforskning.no/en/five-master-supression-techniques.

8. This essay has been reprinted many times, but the original post is at http://www.tomdispatch.com/blog/175584/.

## Chapter 10

1. See https://www.girlboss.com/identity/gloria-steinem-interview-sexual-harassment-feminism-trump.

2. See https://www.csmonitor.com/USA/Politics/Decoder/2014/0214/Hillary-Clinton-tells-women-to-grow-skin-like-a-rhinoceros.-Good-advice.

3. Interviews in Lusaka, March 2016, and New Delhi, June 2018.

4. See debate record at https://hansard.parliament.uk/commons/2017-09-14/debates/33680E1C-D57C-4071-994D-011ADA9FC721/GeneralElectionCampaignAbuseAndIntimidation.

5. Interviews in London, January 10, 16, 17, and 18, 2018.

6. Interviews in London, January 10, 2017, and Stockholm, September 13, 2017.

7. Other criteria listed by the FBI but less relevant to instances of violence against women in politics include: the offender and victim came from different identity groups; objects indicating bias were used (like white hoods indicating membership in the Ku Klux Klan); the victim was a member of a group overwhelmingly outnumbered by other residents

where they live and the incident occurred; the victim was visiting a neighborhood where previous hate crimes had been committed; several incidents occurred in the same locality and targeted members of the same group; the incident coincided with a holiday or date of significance to the group; a hate group claimed responsibility for the crime; and historical animosity existed between the victim's and offender's groups.

8. Although actors may have incentives to play up or play down bias, this criterion seeks to capture community-based understandings of the incident, recognizing that hate crimes seek to send a "message" about inequality and exclusion.

## Chapter 11

1. For a sample visualization see https://www.nap.edu/visualizations/sexual-harassment-iceberg/.

2. For an image of this wheel see https://www.theduluthmodel.org/wheels/.

3. Individual interview sources—sometimes including but often going beyond the women in question—remain anonymized, however, to conform to university research ethics requirements.

## Chapter 12

1. See http://news.bbc.co.uk/2/hi/south_asia/7834402.stm.

2. See the full text of the speech at https://www.theguardian.com/commentisfree/2013/jul/12/malala-yousafzai-united-nations-education-speech-text.

3. Interviews in Nairobi, June 13, 2018.

4. See https://twitter.com/leemakwiny/status/1139113802656620546.

5. Footage of the walkout is posted here: https://twitter.com/Mnurferuz/status/1139151121644175360.

6. Interview via phone, May 3, 2018.

7. Tweet by Hillary Clinton, August 9, 2016, https://twitter.com/HillaryClinton/status/763103518773436416.

8. Tweet by Hillary Clinton, August 27, 2015, https://twitter.com/HillaryClinton/status/648099640714391552.

9. Seehttps://www.amnesty.org/en/latest/news/2018/11/saudi-arabia-reports-of-torture-and-sexual-harassment-of-detained-activists/.

10. For more details on why the Cox case is an instance of violence against women in politics, versus a case of violence in politics, see Krook and Restrepo Sanín (2020).

11. See excerpts from Katherine Marshall's unpublished manuscript, *Suffragette Escapes and Adventures*, at http://suffrajitsu.com/escapes-and-adventures/.

12. Interview in New York, February 15, 2018.

13. Materials received during in-person attendance at Mina's List/Voatz training session in New Delhi, June 27, 2018.

14. Interview in London, January 18, 2018.

15. Personal communication, October 4, 2018.

16. See http://www.fixatedthreat.com/ftac-welcome.php.

17. Interview in London, January 12, 2018.

18. See https://www.theipsa.org.uk/mp-costs/annual-publication/.

## Chapter 13

1. Tweet by Jess Phillips, July 28, 2016, https://twitter.com/jessphillips/status/758670826732412929.
2. This is a reference to the Swedish-language title of *The Girl with the Dragon Tattoo* by Stieg Larsson, *Men Who Hate Women*.
3. See transcript at https://www.svt.se/nyheter/granskning/ug/referens/de-hotade-1.
4. See transcript at https://www.svt.se/nyheter/granskning/ug/referens/de-hotade-1.
5. Presentation at the UN Expert Group Meeting on Violence against Women in Politics, New York, March 8, 2018.
6. See https://twitter.com/monaeltahawy/status/1046071155793285120.
7. See https://twitter.com/monaeltahawy/status/1046072510054313985.
8. Interviews in London, January 7, 16, and 17, 2018.
9. Twitter Rules as of November 3, 2019, at https://help.twitter.com/en/rules-and-policies/twitter-rules.
10. Tweet by Seyi Akiwowo, May 30, 2019, https://twitter.com/seyiakiwowo/status/1134105938544254978.
11. See https://hansard.parliament.uk/Lords/2018-01-11/debates/6e012cd9-93e2-4449-9425-13f8d7015de9/LordsChamber.
12. Tweet by Tomi Lahren, October 31, 2019, https://twitter.com/TomiLahren/status/1189955946337861632.
13. Tweet by Alexandria Ocasio-Cortez, March 8, 2019, https://twitter.com/AOC/status/1104069510238269440.
14. See https://twitter.com/ParityBOT.
15. See "All about ParityBOT" at http://lanacuthbertson.ca/.
16. The link for submitting suggestions is available at https://docs.google.com/forms/d/e/1FAIpQLScNmkBq_JmMgToEgu442ij611RKV60KSeObG20MOjl9SBfr1g/viewform.
17. See https://yoursosteam.wordpress.com/about/.
18. See http://www.troll-busters.com/.
19. See https://yoursosteam.files.wordpress.com/2017/04/trollbusters_tabloidedit3_01_dm.jpg.
20. Personal observations of Pantsuit Nation content between 2016 and 2019.
21. See https://im-defensoras.org/en/.

## Chapter 14

1. See audio link at https://www.bbc.co.uk/news/av/uk-politics-41824720/bex-bailey-i-was-raped-at-a-labour-party-event-in-2011.
2. This sentiment was expressed by members of LabourToo in an interview in London, January 10, 2018.
3. See press release at https://www.amnesty.org.uk/blogs/press-release-me-let-me-go/not-your-daughter-or-mine-forced-virginity-tests-egypt.
4. See also https://www.hrw.org/news/2013/07/03/egypt-epidemic-sexual-violence.
5. Interviews in Dar es Salaam, August 2, 10, and 11, 2016, and New York, June 7, 2018.
6. Interviews in Dar es Salaam, August 16, 2016.
7. Tweet by Jair Bolsonaro, June 13, 2019, https://twitter.com/jairbolsonaro/status/1139218648894189568.

8. Interview in Ottawa, February 5, 2018.

9. Interviews in Ottawa, February 6 and 8, 2018.

10. Interview in London, January 9, 2018.

11. Interviews in London, January 15 and 16, 2018.

12. Tweet by Alyssa Milano, October 15, 2017, https://twitter.com/Alyssa_Milano/status/919659438700670976.

13. Interviews in Paris, January 12, 2017.

14. Interview in San Francisco, April 6, 2018.

15. Interviews in Sacramento, April 9 and 10, 2018.

16. See the letter at https://documents.latimes.com/women-california-politics-call-out-pervasive-culture-sexual-harassment/.

17. See https://www.wesaidenough.com/home.

18. See https://twitter.com/wesaidenough?lang=en.

19. See https://chaircollaboratrice.com/dis-moi-tout-ma-belle/.

20. See https://metooep.com/share-your-story/.

21. https://metooep.com/about-sexual-harassment/.

22. See https://metooep.com/get-help/.

23. Interview in London, January 10, 2018.

24. See https://labourtoo.org.uk/ (version up on October 20, 2017).

25. Information on the content of the report can be found at https://labourtoo.org.uk/blog/.

26. See https://labourtoo.org.uk/blog/.

27. Interview via phone, February 7, 2018.

28. An electronic copy is available at https://issuu.com/ywln/docs/ywln_itstime_0930/20.

29. See https://www.ywln.ca/itstime1.

30. Presentation by YWLN co-founder Arezoo Najibzadeh at the World Forum for Democracy in Strasbourg, France, November 20, 2018.

31. See https://www.aheapanel.org/.

32. See statement by Andrea Leadsom at https://hansard.parliament.uk/Commons/2017-12-21/debates/52E58FEF-E5AB-4531-A9EC-9F4716491B73/IndependentComplaintsAndGrievancePolicy.

33. See the pledge at https://metooep.com/sign-the-pledge/.

34. Interview in London, January 15, 2018.

35. Interview in London, January 16, 2018.

36. See the full text at https://www.legifrance.gouv.fr/affichTexte.do?cidTexte=JORFTEXT000035567974&categorieLien=id.

37. See the full debate at https://www.publicsenat.fr/article/politique/moralisation-les-senateurs-etendent-l-ineligibilite-aux-elus-condamnes-pour.

38. See https://jean-jaures.org/nos-productions/sept-propositions-pour-lutter-contre-le-harcelement-sexuel-au-parlement.

39. See the video at https://www.youtube.com/watch?v=pCNN4MXhpRQ.

40. For the full text, see https://www.congress.gov/bill/115th-congress/senate-bill/3749/text.

41. Yet a third policy applies for administrative staff and unionized employees.

42. See https://www.ourcommons.ca/About/StandingOrders/Appa2-e.htm.

43. See the full text at https://docs.house.gov/billsthisweek/20180205/HRES___.pdf.

44. Interview in Ottawa, February 6, 2018.

45. Interview in Ottawa, February 6, 2018.

46. Interview in Ottawa, February 6, 2018.

47. See https://www.gjs-security.com/training/.

## Chapter 15

1. See https://reliefweb.int/report/iraq/un-s-kubi-rejects-and-denounces-malicious-acts-against-election-integrity-particular.

2. See images of the damage at https://twitter.com/lorna_hughes/status/752804738 270433280.

3. Interview in London, January 10, 2018.

4. To compare the images, see https://www.buzzfeed.com/aliceworkman/trolled-for-mansplaining.

5. See https://www.facebook.com/SenKatyG/posts/looks-like-my-page-was-hacked-apologies-to-those-who-were-offended-by-some-comme/1497654190305295/.

6. See further details at https://www.icrw.org/news/state-dept-announces-guidance-expanded-gag-rule/.

7. For the full text of the law, see http://www.diputados.bo/leyes/ley-n%C2%B0-243.

8. See https://urgentactionfund.org/what-we-do/rapid-response-grantmaking/.

## Chapter 16

1. While not the focus here, fictional works rarely portray women as political leaders. When they do, these representations break with but also reify existing gendered norms of leadership (Sheeler and Anderson 2013).

2. See http://www.legislation.gov.uk/ukpga/Vict/30-31/3/section/24.

3. See https://scc-csc.lexum.com/scc-csc/scc-csc/en/item/9029/index.do.

4. See https://www.canlii.org/en/ca/ukjcpc/doc/1929/1929canlii438/1929canlii438.html.

5. See http://archive.ipu.org/wmn-e/arc/classif311207.htm.

6. Interview in Williamsburg, October 29, 2018.

7. See https://www.rae.es/consultas/los-ciudadanos-y-las-ciudadanas-los-ninos-y-las-ninas.

8. See Rule 19.2 at https://www.govinfo.gov/content/pkg/SMAN-107/html/SMAN-107-pg18-2.htm.

9. See https://www.facebook.com/senatorelizabethwarren/videos/724337794395383/.

10. Brooks (2013) suggests that both male and female leaders are penalized for emotional outbursts, but also provides compelling evidence for the widespread use of this frame when discussing female candidates.

11. Presentation by Eleonora Esposito at the European Conference on Politics and Gender in Amsterdam, July 2019.

12. See https://reliefweb.int/report/iraq/un-s-kubi-rejects-and-denounces-malicious-acts-against-election-integrity-particular.

13. Tweet by Katie Hill, October 27, 2019, https://twitter.com/RepKatieHill/status/1188591520531779584.

14. See https://www.cnn.com/2019/10/31/politics/katie-hill-farewell-speech-full-text/index.html.

15. See https://www.constituteproject.org/constitution/Mexico_2015.pdf?lang=en.

16. See https://www.ecp.gov.pk/Documents/laws2017/Election%20Act%202017.pdf.

17. Interview in Canberra, August 16, 2018.

18. See http://ulis2.unesco.org/images/0007/000769/076995EO.pdf.

19. See https://en.unesco.org/system/files/ge_guidelines_for_publications_-_annex_4.pdf.

20. See https://en.unesco.org/system/files/guidelines_for_pp_-_annex_3.pdf.

21. For the full exchange of tweets, see: https://www.cbc.ca/news/canada/ottawa/gerry-ritz-catherine-mckenna-climate-barbie-1.4298005.

22. See https://labarbelabarbe.org/Qui-sommes-nous.

23. Interview in Paris, July 5, 2012.

24. See https://labarbelabarbe.org/En-politique.

25. See https://twitter.com/manwhohasitall.

26. Tweet by ManWhoHasItAll, October 3, 2018, https://twitter.com/manwhohasitall/status/1047471374665756672.

27. Tweet by ManWhoHasItAll, September 27, 2016, https://twitter.com/manwhohasitall/status/780754090129186817.

28. Tweet by ManWhoHasItAll, November 20, 2019, https://twitter.com/manwhohasitall/status/1197269649236406273.

29. For the full text of the resolution, see https://www.rappler.com/nation/148077-women-senators-senate-resolution-vs-house-show-de-lima-video.

## Chapter 17

1. See https://www.ndi.org/not-the-cost.

2. Personal notes from the #NotTheCost campaign launch, New York, NY, March 17, 2016.

3. Personal notes from the Violence against Women in Politics Summit, London, United Kingdom, March 19, 2018.

4. See http://www.cecafp.senado.gob.mx:8080/elearning/temarios/3.pdf.

5. A completed certificate can be viewed at http://mlkrook.org/pdf/Constancia.pdf.

6. See https://observatorio.inmujeres.gob.mx/mvc/view/public/index.html?q=MTA0.

7. See https://observatorio.inmujeres.gob.mx/mvc/view/public/index.html?q=OTI=.

8. Interviews in Mexico City, May 22 and 23, 2018.

9. See https://violenciapolitica.mx/denuncia.

10. Interview via phone, December 10, 2018.

11. See http://www.nameitchangeit.org/pages/about.

12. See http://www.womensmediacenter.com/speech-project.

13. See http://www.womensmediacenter.com/speech-project/nameitchangeit.

14. Interview via phone, February 19, 2019.

15. Proposals at the federal level in Mexico are not stand-alone bills but focus on reforming existing legislation.

16. While legal reforms have failed at the federal level in Mexico, they have broadly succeeded at the subnational level: as of October 2017, 28 of the 32 states (including Mexico

City) had approved legislation on violence against women in politics. As a group, these reforms are highly heterogeneous, appearing in state constitutions, laws on violence against women, electoral laws, laws on political parties, and/or penal codes (Hevia Rocha 2017).

17. See http://www.diputados.bo/leyes/ley-n%C2%B0-243.

18. See https://oig.cepal.org/sites/default/files/2016_bol_ds2935.pdf.

19. See https://www.oep.org.bo/wp-content/uploads/2017/05/reglamento_renuncias_denuncias_acoso_politico_2017.pdf.

20. See http://escuela.fgr.gob.sv/wp-content/uploads/Leyes/Leyes-2/ARCHIVO-CORTE-SUP-LIEV-8B435.PDF.

21. See http://www.ficame.org/gaceta%2027403%20Ley%2082%20femicidio.pdf.

22. See http://www.bacn.gov.py/leyes-paraguayas/8356/ley-n-5777-de-proteccion-integral-a-las-mujeres-contra-toda-forma-de-violencia.

23. See https://www.constituteproject.org/constitution/Tunisia_2014.pdf.

24. Interview in Tunis, July 10, 2018.

25. Interviews in Tunis, July 10 and 12, 2018.

26. Interview in Tunis, July 12, 2018, and interview via Skype, July 13, 2018.

27. See https://directinfo.webmanagercenter.com/2014/10/02/video-ce-nest-quune-femme-repond-bce/.

28. Interview in Tunis, July 10, 2018.

29. Interviews in Tunis, July 10 and 12, 2018.

30. See http://www.legislation.tn/sites/default/files/news/tf2017581.pdf.

31. See https://www.te.gob.mx/protocolo_mujeres/media/files/7db6bf44797e749.pdf.

32. See https://www.gob.mx/cms/uploads/attachment/file/275255/Protocolo_para_la_Atencio_n_de_la_Violencia_Politica_23NOV17.pdf.

33. See https://observatorio.inmujeres.gob.mx/mvc/view/public/index.html?l=e4da3b7fbbce2345d7772b0674a318d5.

34. See https://www.inecnigeria.org/wp-content/uploads/2018/10/Code_of_Conduct_For_Political_Parties_Preamble.pdf.

35. See https://www.legislationline.org/download/id/7655/file/Bosnia_Herzegovina_election_law_2001_am2016_en.pdf.

36. Presentation by Irena Hadžiabdić at the UN Women Expert Group Meeting on Data and Violence against Women in Politics in New York, December 5, 2019.

37. See https://www.change.org/p/theresa-may-mp-lifetime-ban-from-standing-for-elected-office-for-those-who-threaten-rape-or-violence.

38. For the text of the letter and list of signatories, see https://www.fawcettsociety.org.uk/news/fawcett-calls-on-government-to-impose-a-lifetime-ban-on-candidates-who-promote-violence-through-open-letter.

39. See https://think10.demcloud.org/.

40. See https://web.archive.org/web/20180519222737/http://fidakenya.org/news/launch-of-the-fida-kenya-sms-hotline-sema-usikike-to-report-cases-of-violence-against-women-during-the-electioneering-period/.

41. Interview in Nairobi, June 13, 2018.

42. See https://www.amnesty.org.uk/actions/free-saudi-women-who-fought-right-drive.

43. See https://www.libdems.org.uk/doc-code-of-conduct.

44. See https://www.conservatives.com/codeofconduct.

45. See https://labour.org.uk/wp-content/uploads/2018/04/2018-RULE-BOOK.pdf.

## Chapter 18

1. Studies not covered in this chapter are discussed at length in other parts of this book.

2. Interview via phone, July 3, 2018.

3. See https://www.acleddata.com/curated-data-files/.

4. Interview via phone, March 28, 2019. See also http://www.voteswithoutviolence.org/methodology.

5. See http://www.voteswithoutviolence.org/.

6. Similar studies of female politicians have been conducted in Colombia (Restrepo Sanín 2016) and Argentina (Martelotte 2018), combining large-scale surveys with follow-up interviews.

7. Interview in Ottawa, February 6, 2018.

8. Remarks by Purna Sen (UN Women) at NDI's #NotTheCost launch, New York, March 17, 2016.

9. Similar efforts were undertaken in Peru by three civil society organizations—Centro Flora Tristán, Diakonia Perú, and Calandria—who worked together to produce a report on political harassment against women, focused on gathering information on and systematizing the experiences of women involved in the National Network of Female Local and Regional Authorities (Quintanilla Zapata 2012).

10. To avoid implementing gender quota requirements, some parties simply feminized some of the male names on their electoral lists—a trend widespread enough to lead to the coining of a new term, "transvestite candidates."

11. See http://www.diputados.bo/leyes/ley-n%C2%B0-243.

12. See http://im-defensoras.org/wp-content/uploads/2018/05/Informe-ejecutivo-2015-2016-english.pdf.

13. See https://decoders.amnesty.org/projects/troll-patrol/findings.

14. Personal communication with Rebekah Herrick, December 10, 2019.

## Chapter 19

1. See summary press release at https://rm.coe.int/16807215ba.

2. See summary statistics at https://www.parliament.uk/documents/commons-committees/women-and-equalities/ComRes-WEC-MPs-Tables-Oct19.pdf.

3. Interview in Melbourne, August 9, 2018.

## Chapter 20

1. Tweet by Alexandria Ocasio-Cortez, May 28, 2019, https://twitter.com/AOC/status/1133383123503321090.

# REFERENCES

Abbott, Diane. 2017. "I Fought Racism and Misogyny to Become an MP. The Fight Is Getting Harder." *Guardian*, February 14. https://www.theguardian.com/commentis-free/2017/feb/ 14/racism-misogyny-politics-online-abuse-minorities

Abbott, Jason. 2001. "Vanquishing Banquo's Ghost: The Anwar Ibrahim Affair and Its Impact on Malaysian Politics." *Asian Studies Review* 25(3): 285–308.

Abdul-Hassan, Ali, and Sinan Salaheddin. 2018. "Despite Challenges, Iraq's Female Candidates Run for Parliament." *Christian Science Monitor*, May 3. https://www.csmonitor.com/World/Middle-East/2018/0503/Despite-challenges-Iraq-s-female-candidates-run-for-parliament

ACOBOL. 2012. *Boletin no. 2 del Observatorio de Género*. La Paz: ACOBOL.

"Acoso Político." 2012. *La Razón*, April 17.

Adams, Susan J., Tracey E. Hazelwood, Nancy L. Pitre, Terry E. Bedard, and Suzette D. Landry. 2009. "Harassment of Members of Parliament and the Legislative Assemblies in Canada by Individuals Believed to be Mentally Disordered." *Journal of Forensic Psychiatry & Psychology* 20(6): 801–814.

"Afghan Election: Taliban 'Removed Voters' Fingers.'" 2014. *BBC News*, July 15. https://www.bbc.com/news/world-asia-27857343

"Agression Sexuelle: L'Ex-Ministre Monique Pelletier Dit Avoir Été la Victime d'un Sénateur." 2016. *Le Parisien*, May 11. http://www.leparisien.fr/laparisienne/societe/agression-sexuelle-l-ex-ministre-monique-pelletier-dit-avoir-ete-la-victime-d-un-senateur-11-05-2016-5786023.php

AIDS-Free World. 2009. *Electing to Rape: Sexual Terror in Mugabe's Zimbabwe*. New York: AIDS-Free World.

Alanís Figueroa, María del Carmen. 2017. "Violence Política hacia las Mujeres: Repuesta del Estado ante la Falta de una Ley en México." In *Cuando Hacer Política Te Cuesta la Vida*, ed. Flavia Freidenberg and Gabriella Del Valle Pérez. Mexico City: UNAM, 231–248.

Albaine, Laura. 2015. "Obstáculos y Desafíos de la Paridad de Género: Violencia Política, Sistema Electoral, e Interculturalidad." *Iconos* 52: 145–162.

Albaine, Laura. 2016. "Paridad de Género y Violencia Política en Bolivia, Costa Rica, y Ecuador: Un Análisis Testimonial." *Ciencia Política* 11(21): 335–363.

Albrecht, Michael Mario. 2017. "Bernie Bros and the Gender Schism in the 2016 U.S. Presidential Election." *Feminist Media Studies* 17(3): 509–513.

Albright, Madeleine. 2016. "A Hidden Reality: Violence against Women in Politics." *CNN*, March 8. https://www.cnn.com/2016/03/07/opinions/madelaine-albright-protect-women-in-politics/index.html

Aldroubi, Mina. 2018. "Iraq's Women Candidates Face Smear Campaigns." *National*, April 19. https://www.thenational.ae/world/mena/iraq-s-women-candidates-face-smear-campaigns-1.723263

Allcott, Hunt, and Matthew Gentzkow. 2017. "Social Media and Fake News in the 2016 Election." *Journal of Economic Perspectives* 31(2): 211–235.

Alter, Charlotte. 2017. "Republicans Are Less Likely Than Democrats to Believe Women Who Make Sexual Assault Accusations: Survey." *Time*, December 6. https://time.com/5049665/republicans-democrats-believe-sexual-assault-accusations-survey/

Amar, Cécile, et al. 2015. "Nous, Femmes Journalistes Politiques et Victimes de Sexisme . . . " *Libération*, May 4. https://www.liberation.fr/france/2015/05/04/nous-femmes-journalistes-en-politique_1289357

Amnesty International. 2018a. *Pañuelos Verdes: Relatos de la Violencia Durante el Debate por la Legalización de l a Interrupción Legal del Embarazo*. Buenos Aires: Amnistía Internacional.

Amnesty International. 2018b. "Troll Patrol Findings." https://decoders.amnesty.org/projects/troll-patrol/findings

Amorim, Felipe. 2016. "'Há Vários Elementos de Machismo e Misoginia no Impeachment,' Diz Dilma." UOL, August 29. https://noticias.uol.com.br/politica/ultimas-noticias/2016/08/29/ha-varios-elementos-de-machismo-e-misoginia-no-impeachment-diz-dilma.htm

Anderson, Karrin Vasby. 1999. "'Rhymes with Rich': 'Bitch' as a Tool of Containment in Contemporary American Politics." *Rhetoric & Public Affairs* 2(4): 599–623.

Anderson, Karrin Vasby. 2011. "'Rhymes with Blunt': Pornification and U.S. Political Culture." *Rhetoric & Public Affairs* 14(2): 327–368.

Anderson, Kristin J., and Campbell Leaper. 1998. "Meta-Analyses of Gender Effects on Conversational Interruption." *Sex Roles* 39(3–4): 225–252.

Anglin, Mary K. 1998. "Feminist Perspectives on Structural Violence." *Identities* 5(2): 145–151.

"Annie Lahmer à Denis Baupin: 'On Ne Veut Pas Coucher Avec Toi, Donc Tu Me Parles Plus.'" 2016. *BMFTV*, May 9. https://www.bfmtv.com/politique/annie-lahmer-a-denis-baupin-on-ne-veut-pas-coucher-avec-toi-donc-tu-ne-me-parles-plus-972742.html

Anshelm, Jonas, and Martin Hultman. 2014. "A Green Fatwa? Climate Change as a Threat to the Masculinity of Industrial Modernity." *NORMA* 9(2): 84–96

Anti-Harassment, Equality, and Access Panel. 2018. *Advancing Women in Politics and Addressing Sexual Harassment in Political Campaigns*. https://static1.squarespace.com/static/5b1ac0062971146aa33a72d9/t/5bab43e0e2c4833a6f80dec9/1537950731631/AHEA+Panel+Report.pdf

APWLD. 2007. *Claiming Rights, Claiming Justice: A Guidebook on Women Human Right Defenders*. Chiangmai: Asia Pacific Forum on Women, Law, and Development.

Arboleda, María. 2012. *Levantado el Velo: Estudio Sobre Acoso y Violencia Política en Contra de las Mujeres Autoridades Públicas Electas a Nivel Local en Ecuador*. Quito: ONU Mujeres and AMUNE.

Archenti, Nélida and Laura Albaine. 2013. "Los Desafíos de la Paridad de Género: Tensión Normativa y Violencia Política en Bolivia y Ecuador." *Revista Punto Género* 3: 195–219.

Arteta, Itxaro. 2019. "Partidos Gastan Dinero para Capacitación de Mujeres en Combustible, Pulseras y Hasta la Biografía de Eruviel Ávila." *Animal Político*, October 14. https://www.animalpolitico.com/2019/10/partidos-gastan-dinero-para-capacitacion-de-mujeres-en-combustible-pulseras-y-hasta-la-biografia-de-eruviel-avila/

Ås, Berit. 1978. "Hersketeknikker." *Kjerringråd* 3: 17–21.

Ashwell, Lauren. 2016. "Gendered Slurs." *Social Theory and Practice* 42(2): 228–239.

Ask the Police. 2018. "What Is a Hate Crime or Hate Incident?" London: Police National Legal Database. https://www.askthe.police.uk/content/Q643.htm

Asoka, Kaavya. 2012. *Global Report on the Situation of Women Human Rights Defenders*. Bangkok: WHRDIC.

Associated Press. 2017. "Police Raid Offices of Women's Groups in Poland After Protests." *Guardian*, October 5. https://www.theguardian.com/world/2017/oct/05/police-raid-offices-of-womens-groups-in-poland

Astor, Maggie. 2018. "Women in Politics Often Must Run a Gantlet of Vile Intimidation." *New York Times*, August 28, 1, 14.

Atalanta. 2018. *(Anti)Social Media: The Benefits and Pitfalls of Digital for Female Politicians*. https://www.atalanta.co/antisocial-media

Auchter, Jessica. 2017. "Forced Male Circumcision: Gender-Based Violence in Kenya." *International Affairs* 93(6): 1339–1356.

Ayton, Mel. 2017. *Plotting to Kill the President*. Lincoln, NE: Potomac Books.

Bacchi, Carol Lee. 1999. *Women, Policy, and Politics*. Thousand Oaks, CA: Sage.

Bachelot, Roselyne, et al. 2016. "Harcèlement Sexuel: 'L'impunité, C'est Fini.'" *Le Journal de Dimanche*, May 15. https://www.lejdd.fr/Politique/Harcelement-sexuel-L-impunite-c-est-fini-785595

Bacon, Erin. 2017. "Predatory Behavior: The Dark Side of Capitol Hill." *Roll Call*, February 2. https://www.rollcall.com/news/predatory-behavior-capitol-hill-sexual-harassment

Bade, Rachael. 2017. "Lawmaker Behind Secret $84K Sexual Harassment Settlement Unmasked." *Politico*, December 1. https://www.politico.com/story/2017/11/22/congress-sexual-harassment-settle-payments-259189

Bade, Rachael, and Elana Schor. 2017. "Capitol Hill's Sexual Harassment Policy 'Toothless,' 'A Joke.'" *Politico*, October 27. https://www.politico.com/story/2017/10/27/capitol-hill-sexual-harassment-policies-victims-244224

Bagshaw, Sally, M. Lorena González, Lisa Herbold, Debora Juarez, and Kshama Sawant. 2016. "Don't Let Hateful Voices Intimidate You into Silence or Inaction." *Seattle Times*, May 11. https://www.seattletimes.com/opinion/seattle-women-dont-let-hateful-voices-intimidate-you-into-silence-or-inaction/

Bailey, Bex. 2017. "Labour is a Pioneer in Fighting Sexism. That Doesn't Mean There's No Sexism in Labour." *New Statesman*, March 24. https://www.newstatesman.com/politics/feminism/2017/03/labour-pioneer-fighting-sexism-doesnt-mean-theres-no-sexism-labour

Baird-Windle, Patricia, and Eleanor J. Bader. 2001. *Targets of Hatred: Anti-Abortion Terrorism*. New York: Palgrave.

Balchin, Cassandra. 2008. *Religious Fundamentalisms on the Rise*. Toronto: AWID.

Ballington, Julie, 2018. "Turning the Tide on Violence against Women in Politics: How Are We Measuring Up?" *Politics & Gender* 14(4): 695–701.

Banet-Weiser, Sarah. 2018. *Empowered: Popular Feminism and Popular Misogyny*. Durham, NC: Duke University Press.

Barber, Sharrelle. 2018. "'Marielle, Presente!' Becomes a Rallying Cry in the Global Fight against Racism." Sojourners, March 22. https://sojo.net/articles/marielle-presente-becomes-rallying-cry-global-fight-against-racism

Barcia, Inmaculada. 2011. *Urgent Responses for Women Human Rights Defenders at Risk: Mapping and Preliminary Assessment.* Toronto: AWID.

Barcia, Inmaculada. 2014. *Our Right to Safety: Women Human Rights Defenders' Holistic Approach to Protection.* Toronto: AWID.

Barcia, Inmaculada, and Analía Penchaszadeh. 2012. *Ten Insights to Strengthen Responses for Women Human Rights Defenders at Risk.* Toronto: AWID.

Bardall, Gabrielle. 2011. *Breaking the Mold: Understanding Gender and Electoral Violence.* Washington, DC: IFES.

Bardall, Gabrielle. 2013. "Gender-Specific Election Violence: The Role of Information and Communication Technologies." *Stability* 2(3): 1–11.

Bardall, Gabrielle. 2018. *Violence against Women in Elections in Zimbabwe: An IFES Assessment.* Washington, DC: IFES.

Bardall, Gabrielle, Elin Bjarnegård, and Jennifer M. Piscopo. 2019. "How is Political Violence Gendered? Disentangling Motives, Forms, and Impacts." *Political Studies,* online first. https://doi.org/10.1177/0032321719881812

Bargh, John A., and Paula Raymond. 1995. "The Naïve Misuse of Power: Nonconscious Sources of Sexual Harassment." *Journal of Social Issues* 51(1): 85–96.

Barker, Sara. 2016. "Indigenous Ixil Women Take a Stand Against Gender-Based Violence in Guatemala." *DemocracyWorks,* April 18. https://www.demworks.org/indigenous-ixil-women-take-stand-against-gender-based-violence-guatemala

Barrera, Lourdes V., Anaiz Zamora, Érika Pérez Domínguez, Ixchel Aguirre, and Jessica Esculloa. 2018. *Violencia Política a través de la Tecnologías en México.* Mexico City: Luchadoras and NDI.

Barros, Carlos Juliano. 2019. "Member Jean Wyllys Gives Up His House Seat and Leaves Brazil." Folha de S. Paulo, January 25. https://www1.folha.uol.com.br/internacional/en/brazil/2019/01/congress-member-jean-wyllys-gives-up-his-house-seat-and-leaves-brazil.shtml

Barry, Jane. 2011. *Integrated Security: The Manual.* Johanneshov: Kvinna till Kvinna Foundation and Urgent Action Fund.

Barry, Jane, with Jelena Đorđević. 2007. *What's the Point of Revolution if We Can't Dance?* Boulder, CO: Urgent Action Fund.

Barry, Jane, with Vahida Nainar. 2008. *Insiste, Resiste, Persiste, Existe: Women Human Rights Defenders' Security Strategies.* Ottawa: Urgent Action Fund, Front Line, and Kvinna till Kvinna Foundation.

Barton, Alana, and Hannah Storm. 2014. *Violence and Harassment against Women in the News Media: A Global Picture.* Washington, DC: IWMF and INSI.

Başoğlu, Metin, Maria Livanou, and Cvetana Crnobarić. 2007. "Torture vs. Other Cruel, Inhuman, and Degrading Treatment." *Archives of General Psychiatry* 64(3): 277–285.

Barthes, Roland. 1957. *Mythologies.* Trans. Annette Lavers. New York: Hill and Wang.

Batty, David. 2013. "Bomb Threats Made on Twitter to Female Journalists." *Guardian,* July 31. https://www.theguardian.com/technology/2013/jul/31/bomb-threats-twitter-journalists

Beard, Mary. 2017. *Women & Power: A Manifesto.* London: Profile Books.

Beckman, Ludvig, Stefan Olsson, and Helena Wockelberg. 2003. *Demokratin och Mordet på Anna Lindh*. Uppsala: Krisberedskapsmyndigheten.

Beinart, Peter. 2016. "Fear of a Female President." *The Atlantic*, October. https://www.theatlantic.com/magazine/archive/2016/10/fear-of-a-female-president/497564/

Beito, Gretchen Urnes. 1990. *Coya Come Home: A Congresswoman's Journey*. New York: Pomegranate Press.

Bell, Bethany. 2015. "Twitter Abuse: Women Journalists Get More Threats." BBC Inside Europe Blog, February 6. https://www.bbc.com/news/blogs-eu-31162437

Bemiller, Michelle L., and Rachel Zimmer Schneider. 2010. "It's Not Just a Joke." *Sociological Spectrum* 30(4): 459–479.

Benford, Robert D., and David A. Snow. 2000. "Framing Processes and Social Movements." *Annual Review of Sociology* 26(1): 611–639.

Bennett, Jessica. 2016. *Feminist Fight Club*. London: Penguin.

Bennett, Karen, Danna Ingleton, Alice M. Nah, and James Savage. 2015. "Critical Perspectives on the Security and Protection of Human Rights Defenders." *International Journal of Human Rights* 19(7): 883–895.

Berdahl, Jennifer L. 2007. "Harassment Based on Sex: Protecting Social Status in the Context of Gender Hierarchy." *Academy of Management Review* 32(2): 641–658.

Bergmann, Merry. 1986. "How Many Feminists Does It Take to Make a Joke? Sexist Humor and What's Wrong with It." *Hypatia* 1(1): 63–82.

Berkovitch, Nitza. 1999. *From Motherhood to Citizenship*. Baltimore, MD: Johns Hopkins University Press.

Berns, Nancy. 2001. "Degendering the Problem and Gendering the Blame: Political Discourse on Women and Violence." *Gender & Society* 15(2): 262–281.

Bernstein, Elizabeth. 2012. "Carceral Politics as Gender Justice? The 'Traffic in Women' and Neoliberal Circuits of Crime, Sex, and Rights." *Theory & Society* 41(3): 233–259.

Berry, Jeffrey M., and Sarah Sobieraj. 2014. *The Outrage Industry*. New York: Oxford University Press.

Berthet, Valentine, and Johanna Kantola. 2019. "Gender, Violence, and Political Institutions: Struggles over Sexual Harassment in the European Parliament." Paper presented at the ECPR Joint Sessions of Workshops, Mons, Belgium, April 8–12.

Bianchi, Claudia. 2014. "Slurs and Appropriation: An Echoic Account." *Journal of Pragmatics* 66: 35–44.

Bianchi, Dorina, et al. 2016. "Basta Congli Insulti alle Donne in Politica." *La Repubblica*, March 18. https://www.repubblica.it/politica/2016/03/18/news/_basta_con_gli_insulti_per_le_ donne_in_politica_-135798110/

Bing, Janet M., and Lucien X. Lombardo. 1997. "Talking Past Each Other about Sexual Harassment: An Exploration of Frames for Understanding." *Discourse & Society* 8(3): 293–311.

Bingham, Clara. 1997. *Women on the Hill: Challenging the Culture of Congress*. New York: Random House.

Birch, Sarah, Ursula Daxecker, and Kristine Höglund. 2020. "Electoral Violence: An Introduction." *Journal of Peace Research*.

Birch, Sarah, and David Muchlinski. 2017. "The Dataset of Countries at Risk of Electoral Violence." *Terrorism and Political Violence*. DOI: 10.1080/09546553. 2017.1364636

Biroli, Flávia. 2016. "Political Violence against Women in Brazil: Expressions and Definitions." *Direito & Práxis* 7(15): 557–589.

Biroli, Flávia. 2018. "Violence against Women and Reactions to Gender Equality in Politics." *Politics & Gender* 14(4): 681–685.

Bjarnegård, Elin. 2018. "Making Gender Visible in Election Violence." *Politics & Gender* 14(4): 690–695.

Bjørgo, Tore, and Emilie Silkoset. 2018. *Threats and Threatening Approaches to Politicians: A Survey of Norwegian Parliamentarians and Cabinet Ministers*. Oslo: Politihøgskolen.

Blom, Agneta. 2005. "En Het Fråga." In *I Mediernas Våld*. Stockholm: Kommittén om Hot och Våld mot Förtroendevalda, 7–16.

Blume, Laura Ross. 2017. "The Old Rules No Longer Apply: Explaining Narco Assassinations of Mexican Politicians." *Journal of Politics in Latin America* 9(1): 59–90.

Boone, Jon. 2015. "Women Barred from Voting in Parts of Pakistan." *Guardian*, May 29. https://www.theguardian.com/world/2015/may/29/women-barred-voting-pakistan-khyber-pakhtunkh

Bosson, Jennifer K., Joseph A. Vandello, Rochelle M. Burnaford, Jonathan R. Weaver, and S. Arzu Wasti. 2009. "Precarious Manhood and Displays of Physical Aggression." *Personality & Social Psychology Bulletin* 35(5): 623–634.

Bourdieu, Pierre. 1991. *Language and Symbolic Power*. Trans. Gino Raymond and Matthew Adamson. Cambridge, MA: Harvard University Press.

Bourdieu, Pierre. 2001. *Masculine Domination*. Trans. Richard Nice. Stanford, CA: Stanford University Press.

Bourget, Linda. 2017. "'J'ai Subi des Gestes Inappropriés de Parlementaires.'" SwissInfo, December 1. https://www.swissinfo.ch/fre/harc%C3%A8lement-sexuel_-j-ai-subi-des-gestes-inappropri%C3%A9s-de-parlementaires-/43719810

Bowles, Nellie. 2016. "Former Lawmaker Wendy Davis: 'Trolls Want to Diminish and Sexualize You.'" *Guardian*, March 12. https://www.theguardian.com/culture/2016/mar/12/wendy-davis-sxsw-2016-texas-trolls-online-abuse

Boyle, Karen. 2019. "What's In a Name? Theorising the Inter-Relationships of Gender and Violence." *Feminist Theory* 20(1): 19–36.

Bradley-Geist, Jill C., Ivy Rivera, and Susan D. Geringer. 2015. "The Collateral Damage of Ambient Sexism: Observing Sexism Impacts Bystander Self-Esteem and Career Aspirations." *Sex Roles* 73(1–2): 29–42.

Brescoll, Victoria L. 2016. "Leading with Their Hearts? How Gender Stereotypes of Emotion Lead to Biased Evaluations of Leaders." *Leadership Quarterly* 27(3): 415–428.

Brescoll, Victoria L., and Eric Luis Uhlmann. 2008. "Can An Angry Woman Get Ahead? Status Conferral, Gender, and Expression of Emotion in the Workplace." *Psychological Science* 19(3): 268–275.

Brooks, Deborah Jordan. 2013. *He Runs, She Runs*. Princeton, NJ: Princeton University Press.

Buchan, Lizzy. 2018. "Westminster Scandal: Report Shows One in Five People in Parliament Have Experienced Sexual Harassment." *Independent*, February 7. https://www.independent.co.uk/news/uk/politics/westminster-sexual-harassment-one-five-report-leaked-mps-lords-staff-a8199401.html

Bufacchi, Vittorio. 2004. "Why Is Violence Bad?" *American Philosophical Quarterly* 41(2): 169–180.

Bufacchi, Vittorio. 2005. "Two Concepts of Violence." *Political Studies Review* 3(2): 193–204.

Bufacchi, Vittorio. 2007. *Violence and Social Justice*. New York: Palgrave.

Bufacchi, Vittorio, and Jools Gilson. 2016. "The Ripples of Violence." *Feminist Review* 112(1): 27–40.

Bühler, Dennis. 2017. "Flirten Leichtgemacht: Merkblatt Sorgt Für Spott und Ärger." *Aagauer Zeitung*, December 14. https://www.aargauerzeitung.ch/schweiz/flirten-leichtgemacht-merkblatt-sorgt-fuer-spott-und-aerger-kaelin-legt-sich-mit-koeppel-an-132000960

Bunch, Charlotte. 1990. "Women's Rights as Human Rights: Toward a Re-Vision of Human Rights." *Human Rights Quarterly* 12(4): 486–498.

Burchard, Stephanie M. 2015. *Electoral Violence in Sub-Saharan Africa*. Boulder, CO: Lynne Rienner.

Burr, Elisabeth. 2003. "Gender and Language Politics in France." In *Gender across Languages*, ed. Marlis Hellinger and Hadumod Bussman. Amsterdam: Benjamins, 119–139.

Calhoun, Frederick S., and Stephen W. Weston. 2016. *Threat Assessment and Management Strategies: Identifying the Howlers and Hunters*. New York: Taylor & Francis.

Calogero, Rachel M. 2013. "Objects Don't Object: Evidence That Self-Objectification Disrupts Women's Social Activism." *Psychological Science* 24(3): 312–318.

Cameron, Deborah. 2006. "Theorising the Female Voice in Public Contexts." In *Speaking Out*, ed. Judith Baxter. London: Palgrave, 3–20.

Campbell, Rosie, and Joni Lovenduski. 2016. *Footprints in the Sand: Five Years of the Fabian Women's Network Mentoring and Political Education Programme*. London: Fabian Society.

Caputi, Jane, and Diana E. H. Russell. 1992. "Femicide: Sexist Terrorism against Women." In *Femicide: The Politics of Woman Killing*, ed. Jill Radford and Diana E. H. Russell. New York: Twayne, 13–21.

Cárdenas Morales, Natividad. 2011. *El Financimiento Público de los Partidos Políticos Nacionales para el Desarrollo del Liderazgo Político de las Mujeres*. Mexico City: TEPJF.

Cardona, Maria T. 2017. "Warren Silenced: A Sexist GOP Tells a Woman to Shut Up and Sit Down." *The Hill*, February 8. https://thehill.com/blogs/pundits-blog/national-party-news/318512-warren-silenced-a-sexist-gop-tells-a-woman-to-shut-up

Carlin, Diana B., and Kelly L. Winfrey. 2009. "Have You Come a Long Way, Baby? Hillary Clinton, Sarah Palin, and Sexism in 2008 Campaign Coverage." *Communication Studies* 60(4):326–343.

Carlson, Caitlin R. 2018. "Misogynistic Hate Speech and its Chilling Effect on Women's Free Expression during the 2016 U.S. Presidential Election." *Journal of Hate Studies* 14(1): 97–111.

Caro, Isabel. 2018. "Congreso Moderniza Protocolos de Acoso Sexual." *La Tercera*, July 16. https://www.latercera.com/politica/noticia/congreso-moderniza-protocolos-acoso-sexual/244984/

Carothers, Thomas. 2006. "The Backlash against Democracy Promotion." *Foreign Affairs* 85(2): 55–68.

Carver, Terrell. 1996. *Gender is Not a Synonym for Women*. Boulder, CO: Lynne Rienner.

"Catherine McKenna Takes on Rebel Reporter over Outlet's 'Climate Barbie' Nickname." 2017. *Global News*, November 4. https://globalnews.ca/news/3843773/catherine-mckenna-rebel-climate-barbie/

Cawston, Amanda. 2018. "The Feminist Case against Pornography." *Inquiry* 62(6): 624–658.

Caygle, Heather. 2019. "Katie Hill Delivers Fiery Farewell Speech on 'Double Standard' Facing Women in Power." *Politico*, October 31. https://www.politico.com/news/2019/10/31/katie-hill-farewell-speech-resignation-063075

CEDAW Committee. 1992. *General Recommendation No. 19 on Violence against Women.* Geneva: CEDAW Committee.

CEDAW Committee. 2013. *General Recommendation No. 30 on Women in Conflict Prevention, Conflict, and Post-Conflict Situations.* Geneva: CEDAW Committee.

CEDAW Committee. 2017. *General Recommendation No. 35 on Gender Based Violence against Women, Updating General Recommendation No. 19.* Geneva: CEDAW Committee.

Center for Reproductive Rights. 2009. *Defending Human Rights: Abortion Providers Facing Threats, Restrictions, and Harassment.* New York: Center for Reproductive Rights.

Centre for Social Research and UN Women. 2014. *Violence against Women in Politics: A Study Conducted in India, Nepal, and Pakistan.* New Delhi: CSR/UN Women.

Cerva Cerna, Daniela. 2014. "Participación Política y Violencia de Género en México." *Revista Mexicana de Ciencias Políticas y Sociales* 59(222): 117–140.

Chafetz, Janet Saltzman, and Anthony Gary Dworkin. 1987. "In the Face of Threat: Organized Antifeminism in Comparative Perspective." *Gender & Society* 1(1): 33–60.

Chalhoub, Sidney, Cath Collins, Mariana Lllanos, Mónica Pachón, and Keisha-Khan Y. Perry. 2017. *Report of the LASA Fact-Finding Delegation on the Impeachment of Brazilian President Dilma Rousseff.* Pittsburgh, PA: Latin American Studies Association.

Chandler, Daniel. 2017. *Semiotics: The Basics.* New York: Routledge.

Chávez, Franz. 2009. "Bolivia: Politics, a Risky Business for Women." Inter Press Service, October 27. http://www.ipsnews.net/2009/10/bolivia-politics-a-risky-business-for-women/

Chavez, Halie. 2018. "Twitter Is Indeed Toxic for Women, Amnesty Report Says." *Wired*, December 18. https://www.wired.com/story/amnesty-report-twitter-abuse-women/

Chemaly, Soraya. 2016. "The Shocking Sexualization of Female Politicians in Porn." *Establishment*, March 30. https://theestablishment.co/2016/03/29/the-shocking-sexualization-of-female-politicians-in-porn/

Chemaly, Soraya. 2019. "Katie Hill, Deepfakes, and How 'Political Risk' Is Defined." *WMC News*, November 7. http://www.womensmediacenter.com/news-features/katie-hill-deepfakes-and-how-political-risk-is-defined

Childs, Sarah. 2015. *The Good Parliament.* Bristol, UK: University of Bristol.

Chittal, Nisha. 2019. "Ilhan Omar, AOC, and the Silencing of Women of Color in Congress." *Vox*, April 11, https://www.vox.com/policy-and-politics/2019/4/8/18272072/ilhan-omar-rashida-tlaib-alexandria-ocasio-cortez-racism-sexism

Chrisafis, Angelique. 2016. "'We Can No Longer Stay Silent': Fury Erupts over Sexism in French Politics." *Guardian*, May 13. https://www.theguardian.com/world/2016/may / 13/we-can-no-longer-stay-silent-fury-erupts-over-sexism-in-french-politics

CIM. 2015. *Declaration on Political Harassment and Violence against Women.* Washington, DC: OAS.

CIM. 2017. *Inter-American Model Law on the Prevention, Punishment and Eradication of Violence against Women in Political Life.* Washington, DC: OAS.

Citizens Commission on Islam, Participation, and Public Life. 2017. *The Missing Muslims*. London: Citizens UK.

Citron, Danielle Keats. 2009. "Law's Expressive Value in Combating Cyber Gender Harassment." *Michigan Law Review* 108(3): 373–416.

Citron, Danielle Keats. 2014. *Hate Crimes in Cyberspace*. Cambridge, MA: Harvard University Press.

Citron, Danielle Keats, and Mary Anne Franks. 2014. "Criminalizing Revenge Porn." *Wake Forest Law Review* 49: 345–391.

Clark, Rosemary. 2016. "'Hope in a Hashtag': The Discursive Activism of #WhyIStayed." *Feminist Media Studies* 16(5): 788–804.

Clausewitz, Carl von. 2018 [1832]. *On War*. Trans. J. J. Graham. Overland Park, KS: Digireads.

Clinton, Hillary Rodham. 2017. *What Happened*. New York: Simon & Schuster.

Cloud, Dana L. 2009. "Foiling the Intellectuals: Gender, Identity Framing, and the Rhetoric of the Kill in Conservative Hate Mail." *Communication, Culture, & Critique* 2(4): 457–479.

Coady, C. A. J. 1986. "The Idea of Violence." *Journal of Applied Philosophy* 3(1): 3–19.

Coates, Karen. 2016. "Preparing for the Worst." In *Attacks on the Press: Gender and Media Freedom Worldwide*. New York: CPJ, 27–35.

Cobain, Ian. 2016. "Jo Cox Killer Walked Away Calmly after Brutal Attack, Court Told." *Guardian*, November 17. https://www.theguardian.com/uk-news/2016/nov/17/jo-cox-killer-walked-away-calmly-after-brutal-attack-court-told

Cobain, Ian, and Matthew Taylor. 2016. "Far-Right Terrorist Thomas Mair Jailed for Life for Jo Cox Murder." *Guardian*, November 23. https://www.theguardian.com/uk-news/2016/nov/23/thomas-mair-found-guilty-of-jo-cox-murder

Cohen, David S., and Krysten Connon. 2015. *Living in the Crosshairs: The Untold Stories of Anti-Abortion Terrorism*. New York: Oxford University Press.

Coker, Ann L, Paige H. Smith, Lesa Bethea, Melissa R. King, and Robert E. McKeown. 2000. "Physical Health Consequences of Physical and Psychological Intimate Partner Violence." *Archives of Family Medicine* 9(5): 451–457.

Collier, Cheryl N., and Tracey Raney. 2018. "Canada's Member-to-Member Code of Conduct on Sexual Harassment in the House of Commons: Progress or Regress?" *Canadian Journal of Political Science* 51(4): 795–815.

Collier, Paul. 2009. *Wars, Guns, and Votes: Democracy in Dangerous Places*. New York: Random House.

Committee to Protect Journalists. 2016. *Attacks on the Press: Gender and Media Freedom Worldwide*. New York: CPJ.

Conference on Security and Cooperation in Europe. 1975. *Final Act*. Helsinki: OSCE.

Convening Committee. 2019. *Declaration of Principles Guidelines on Integrating Gender Considerations in International Observation, including Violence against Women in Elections*. Washington, DC: NDI.

Copps, Sheila. 2014. "I Was Sexually Assaulted When I Was an MPP, and I've Been Raped." *Hill Times*, November 10. https://www.hilltimes.com/2014/11/10/i-was-sexually-assaulted-when-i-was-an-mpp-and-ive-been-raped-copps/30214

Correal, Annie. 2016. "Pantsuit Nation, a 'Secret' Facebook Hub, Celebrates Clinton." *New York Times*, November 8. https://www.nytimes.com/2016/11/09/us/politics/facebook-pantsuit-nation-clinton.html

Corredor, Elizabeth S. 2019. "Unpacking 'Gender Ideology' and the Global Right's Antigender Countermovement." *Signs* 44(3):613–638.

Cortina, Lilia M., Dana Kabat-Farr, Emily A. Leskinen, Marisela Huerta, and Vicki J. Magley. 2013. "Selective Incivility as Modern Discrimination in Organizations: Evidence and Impact." *Journal of Management* 39(6): 1579–1605.

Corz, Carlos. 2012. "Juana Quispe Fue Impedida de Ejercer 20 Meses la Concejalía." *La Razón*, April 16. http://www.la-razon.com/ciudades/seguridad_ciudadana/Juana-Quispe-impedida-ejercer-concejalia_0_1597040308.html

Cotteret, Jean-Marie. 2014. "'Madame le Président': Faut-Il Dissoudre l'Académie Française?" *Le Figaro*, October 14. http://www.lefigaro.fr/vox/societe/2014/10/14/31003-20141014ARTFIG00377-madame-le-president-faut-il-dissoudre-l-academie-francaise.php

Cottle, Simon, Richard Sambrook, and Nick Mosdell. 2016. *Reporting Dangerously: Journalist Killings, Intimidation, and Security*. New York: Palgrave.

Council of Europe. 2011. *Convention on Preventing and Combating Violence against Women and Domestic Violence*. Strasbourg: COE.

Cowburn, Malcolm, and Keith Pringle. 2000. "Pornography and Men's Practices." *Journal of Sexual Aggression* 6(1–2): 52–66.

Cox, Laura. 2018. *The Bullying and Harassment of House of Commons Staff. Independent Inquiry Report*. London: House of Commons Commission.

Criado-Perez, Caroline. 2016. "'Women That Talk Too Much Need to Get Raped': What Men Are Really Saying When They Abuse Women Online." In *Countering Online Abuse of Female Journalists*. Vienna: OSCE, 13–16.

Croom, Adam M. 2011. "Slurs." *Language Sciences* 33(3): 343–358.

Croom, Adam M. 2013. "How to Do Things with Slurs: Studies in the Way of Derogatory words." *Language & Communication* 33(3): 177–204.

Crowell, Nancy A., and Ann W. Burgess, eds. 1996. *Understanding Violence against Women*. Washington, DC: National Research Council.

CSPL. 2017. *Intimidation in Public Life*. London: CSPL.

Cuddy, Amy, Susan T. Fiske, and Peter Glick. 2004. "When Professionals Become Mothers, Warmth Doesn't Cut the Ice." *Journal of Social issues* 60(4): 701–718.

Culhane, Leah. 2019. *Sexual Harassment in Parliament: Protecting MPs, Peers, Volunteers, and Staff*. London: Fawcett Society.

Cummins, Joseph. 2015. *Anything for a Vote: Dirty Tricks, Cheap Shots, and October Surprises in U.S. Presidential Campaigns*. Philadelphia: Quirk Books.

Dalton, Emma. 2017. "Sexual Harassment of Women Politicians in Japan." *Journal of Gender-Based Violence* 1(2): 205–219.

Daniele, Gianmarco. 2019. "Strike One to Educate One Hundred: Organized Crime, Political Selection, and Politicians' Ability." *Journal of Economic Behavior & Organization* 159: 650–662.

Daniele, Gianmarco, and Gemma Dipoppa. 2017. "Mafia, Elections, and Violence against Politicians." *Journal of Public Economics* 154: 10–33.

Daragahi, Borzou. 2018. "Sexually Harassed—and Arrested—in Egypt: The Cruel Fate of Amal Fathy." *Daily Beast*, May 22. https://www.thedailybeast.com/sexually-harassedand-arrestedin-egypt-the-cruel-fate-of-amal-fathy

Dastageer, Ghulam, and Rizwan Safdar. 2018. "Why Bans Persist on Women Voting across Pakistan." *Herald*, October 4. https://herald.dawn.com/news/1154065

Davies, Lizzy. 2014. "Laura Boldrini: The Italian Politician Rising Above the Rape Threats." *Guardian*, February 9. https://www.theguardian.com/politics/2014/feb/09/laura-boldrini-italian-politician-rape-threats

Daxecker, Ursula, Elio Amicarelli, and Alexander Jung. 2019. "Electoral Contention and Violence (ECAV): A New Dataset." *Journal of Peace Research* 56(5): 714–723.

DeGeurin, Mack. 2018. "Egypt's 'Fake News' Laws Are Being Used to Silence Online Dissent." *New York*, October 9. http://nymag.com/developing/2018/10/egypt-fake-news-laws-amal-fathy-mona-el-mazbouh-facebook.html

De Haan, Willem. 2008. "Violence as an Essentially Contested Concept." In *Violence in Europe*, ed. Sophie Body-Gendrot and Pieter Spierenburg. New York: Springer, 27–40.

DeKeseredy, Walter S. 2011. *Violence against Women: Myths, Facts, Controversies*. Toronto: University of Toronto Press.

Della Porta, Donatella. 1995. *Social Movements, Political Violence, and the State*. New York: Cambridge University Press.

Desmond-Harris, Jenée. 2016. "Pantsuit Nation, the Giant, Secret Hillary Facebook Group, Explained." *Vox*, November 7. https://www.vox.com/policy-and-politics/2016/11/7/13546830/pantsuit-nation-hillary-clinton-election-secret-private-facebook-group

Dhrodia, Azmina. 2017. "Unsocial Media: Tracking Twitter Abuse against Women MPs." *Medium*, September 3. https://medium.com/@AmnestyInsights/unsocial-media-tracking-twitter-abuse-against-women-mps-fc28aeca498a

Diamond, Jeremy, and Stephen Collinson. 2016. "Donald Trump: 'Second Amendment' Gun Advocates Could Deal with Hillary Clinton." *CNN*, August 10. https://www.cnn.com/2016/08/09/politics/donald-trump-hillary-clinton-second-amendment/index.html

Dietrich, David R. 2014. *Rebellious Conservatives: Social Movements in Defense of Privilege*. New York: Palgrave.

Dietz, Park E., Daryl B. Matthews, Daniel Allen Martell, Tracy M. Stewart, Debra R. Hrouda, and Janet Warren. 1991. "Threatening and Otherwise Inappropriate Letters to Members of the United States Congress." *Journal of Forensic Science* 36(5): 1445–1468.

Digital Rights Foundation. 2018. *Online Participation of Female Politicians in Pakistan's General Elections 2018*. https://digitalrightsfoundation.pk/wp-content/uploads/2019 / 01/Booklet-Elections-Web-low.pdf

Dixon, Hayley. 2014. "Anti-Bullying Hotline Set Up for House of Commons Workers." *Telegraph*, April 8. https://www.telegraph.co.uk/news/politics/10751358/Anti-bullying-hotline-set-up-for-House-of-Commons-workers.html

Doan, Alesha E. 2007. *Opposition and Intimidation: The Abortion Wards and Strategies of Political Harassment*. Ann Arbor: University of Michigan Press.

Donaghue, Ngaire. 2015. "Who Gets Played By 'The Gender Card'?" *Australian Feminist Studies* 30(84): 161–178.

Dovi, Suzanne. 2018. "Misogyny and Transformations." *European Journal of Politics and Gender* 1(1–2): 131–147.

Eagly, Alice H., and Steven J. Karau. 2002. "Role Congruity Theory of Prejudice Toward Female Leaders." *Psychological Review* 109(3): 573–598.

Eagly, Alice H., Mona G. Makhijani, and Bruce G. Klonsky. 1992. "Gender and the Evaluation of Leaders." *Psychological Bulletin* 111(1):3–22.

Ebbs, Stephanie. 2017. "Supporters Tweet #LetLizSpeak After Elizabeth Warren Silenced on Senate Floor." *ABC News*, February 9. https://abcnews.go.com/Politics/supporters-tweet-letlizspeak-elizabeth-warren-silenced-senate-floor/story?id=45351634

Ebert, Joel. 2017. "Sexual Harassment Troubles Mount in Statehouses around the Country." *USA Today*, November 20. https://www.usatoday.com/story/news/nation-now/2017/11/20/sexual-harassment-statehouses/882874001/

ECLAC. 2007. *Consenso de Quito*. Santiago: ECLAC.

Edelman, Lauren B. 2016. *Working Law*. Chicago, IL: University of Chicago Press.

Edström, Maria. 2016. "The Trolls Disappear in the Light: Swedish Experiences of Mediated Sexualized Hate Speech in the Aftermath of Bering Breivik." *International Journal for Crime, Justice, and Social Democracy* 5(2): 96–106.

Eidelman, Scott, Christian S. Crandall, and Jennifer Pattershall. 2009. "The Existence Bias." *Journal of Personality & Social Psychology* 97(5): 765–775.

Eilperin, Juliet. 2016a. "How a White House Women's Office Strategy Went Viral." *Washington Post*, October 25. https://www.washingtonpost.com/news/powerpost/wp/2016/10/25/how-a-white-house-womens-office-strategy-went-viral/

Eilperin, Juliet. 2016b. "White House Women Want to Be in the Room Where It Happens." *Washington Post*, September 13. https://www.washingtonpost.com/news/powerpost/wp/2016/09/13/white-house-women-are-now-in-the-room-where-it-happens/

Elemia, Camille. 2016. "Women Senators Unite, File Resolution vs 'De Lima' Video." *Rappler*, October 3. https://www.rappler.com/nation/148077-women-senators-senate-resolution-vs-house-show-de-lima-video

Elgot, Jessica. 2016. "Corbyn to Examine Claims of Labour Bias against Muslim Women." *Guardian*, February 7. https://www.theguardian.com/politics/2016/feb/07/jeremy-corbyn-examine-claims-labour-bias-against-muslim-women

Elgot, Jessica, and Rowena Mason. 2017. "Sexual Harassment Claims Still Not Being Taken Seriously, Say MPs." *Guardian*, October 27. https://www.theguardian.com/politics/2017/oct/27/mps-complain-sexual-harassment-claims-still-not-being-taken-seriously

Ellemers, Naomi, and Manuela Barreto. 2009. "Collective Action in Modern Times: How Modern Expressions of Prejudice Prevent Collective Action." *Journal of Social Issues* 65(4): 749–768.

Ellis, Steven M. 2017. "Shooting the Messengers." *British Journalism Review* 28(1): 57–62.

Elshtain, Jean Bethke. 1981. *Public Man, Private Woman*. Princeton, NJ: Princeton University Press.

Emmanuel, Rachel. 2019. "Twitter Bot Averages 74 Tweets-Per-Day to Combat Abuse to Female Candidates." *iPolitics*, October 31. https://ipolitics.ca/2019/10/31/twitter-bot-averages-74-tweets-per-day-to-combat-abuse-to-female-candidates/

Encarnación, Omar. 2017. "The Patriarchy's Revenge: How Retro-Macho Politics Doomed Dilma Rousseff." *World Policy Journal* 34(1): 82–91.

Engels, Jeremy. 2015. *The Politics of Resentment*. University Park: Pennsylvania State University Press.

Escalante, Ana Cecilia, and Nineth Méndez. 2011. *Sistematización de Experiencias de Acoso Político que Viven o Han Vivido las Mujeres que Ocupan Puestos de Elección Popular en el Nivel Local*. Santo Domingo: ONU Mujeres and INAMU.

Etemadzadeh, Ava. 2018. "Labour's Sexual Harassment Complaints Procedure is Unfit for Purpose." *Guardian*, June 26. https://www.theguardian.com/commentisfree/2018/jun/26/labours-sexual-harassment-complaints-procedure-inadequate

European Parliament. 2017. *Resolution 2897 on Combating Sexual Harassment and Abuse in the EU*. Strasbourg: EP.

Every-Palmer, Susanna, Justin Barry-Walsh, and Michele Pathé. 2015. "Harassment, Stalking, Threats, and Attacks Targeting New Zealand Politicians." *Australian & New Zealand Journal of Psychiatry* 49(7): 634–641.

Falk, Erika. 2008. *Women for President: Media Bias in Eight Campaigns*. Champaign: University of Illinois Press.

Fallert, Nicole. 2019. "Inside the Fight to Make the European Parliament Take Sexual Harassment Seriously." *Vox*, March 22. https://www.vox.com/2019/3/22/18234860/me-too-european-parliament-leads-to-sexual-harassment-pledge

Faludi, Susan. 1991. *Backlash*. New York: Crown Publishers.

Farwell, James P. 2011. *The Pakistan Cauldron*. Washington, DC: Potomac Books

FBI. 2015. *Hate Crime Data Collection Guidelines and Training Manual*. Washington, DC: FBI.

Feder, J. Lester, Alberto Nardelli, and Davide Maria De Luca. 2018. "Meet The Politician Getting Death Threats for Campaigning for Women's Rights in Italy." *BuzzFeed News*, February 24. https://www.buzzfeednews.com/article/lesterfeder/italian-elections-racism-sexism

"Female Afghan Official Is Slain." 2009. *Philadelphia Inquirer*, April 13. https://www.inquirer.com/philly/news/nation_world/20090413_In_the_World.html

Ferraro, Kathleen J., and John M. Johnson. 1983. "How Women Experience Battering: The Process of Victimization." *Social Problems* 30(3): 325–339.

Ferrier, Michelle. 2016. "The Progression of Hate." In *Attacks on the Press: Gender and Media Freedom Worldwide*. New York: CPJ, 45–52.

Ferrier, Michelle. 2018. *Attacks and Harassment: The Impact on Female Journalists and Their Reporting*. Washington, DC: TrollBusters and IWMF.

Fincher, Leta Hong. 2016. "China's Feminist Five." *Dissent*, Fall. https://www.dissentmagazine.org/article/china-feminist-five

Finnegan, Margaret. 1999. *Selling Suffrage*. New York: Columbia University Press.

Finnemore, Martha, and Kathryn Sikkink. 1998. "International Norm Dynamics and Political Change." *International Organization* 52(4): 887–917.

Flinders, Matthew V. 2012. "The Demonisation of Politicians: Moral Panic, Folk Devils, and MPs' Expenses." *Contemporary Politics* 18(1): 1–17.

Flynn, Meagan. 2019. "A White Nationalist's Harassment Helped Force a Black Female Lawmaker to Resign." *Washington Post*, January 15. https://www.washingtonpost.com/nation/2019/01/15/white-nationalists-harassment-helped-force-black-female-lawmaker-resign-he-wont-face-charges/

Follingstad, Diane R. 2007. "Rethinking Current Approaches to Psychological Abuse: Conceptual and Methodological Issues." *Aggression and Violent Behavior* 12(4): 439–458.

Follingstad, Diane R., et al. 1990. "The Role of Emotional Abuse in Physically Abusive Relationships." *Journal of Family Violence* 5(2): 107–120.

Forst, Michel. 2019. *A/HRC/40/60: Situation of Women Human Rights Defenders*. New York: United Nations.

Foucault, Michel. 2003 [1976]. *Society Must Be Defended*. Trans. David Macey. New York: Picador.

Fox, James. 1998. *The Langhorne Sisters*. London: Granta Books.

Fox, Kara, and Jan Diehm. 2017. "#MeToo's Global Moment: Anatomy of a Viral Campaign." *CNN*, November 9. https://www.cnn.com/2017/11/09/world/metoo-hashtag-global-movement/index.html

Friedan, Betty. 1963. *The Feminine Mystique*. New York: W. W. Norton.

Friedman, Elisabeth Jay. 2003. "Gendering the Agenda: The Impact of the Transnational Women's Rights Movement at the UN Conferences of the 1990s." *Women's Studies International Forum* 26(4): 313–331.

Frontline Defenders. 2018. "#JudicialHarassment." https://www.frontlinedefenders.org/en/violation/judicial-harassmentb

Frye, Marilyn 1983. *The Politics of Reality*. Berkeley, CA: Crossing Press.

Full Frontal with Samantha Bee. 2016. "OK Ladies Now Let's Get Information." *Full Frontal with Samantha Bee*, October 24. https://www.youtube.com/watch?v=I0AhzLEXWgY

Funk, Michelle E., and Calvin R. Coker. 2016. "She's Hot, for a Politician: The Impact of Objectifying Commentary on Perceived Credibility of Female Candidates." *Communication Studies* 67(4): 455–473.

Gall, Carlotta. 2009. "Intimidation and Fraud Observed in Afghan Election." *New York Times*, August 22. https://www.nytimes.com/2009/08/23/world/asia/23afghan.html?em

Gallagher, Ryan J., Elizabeth Stowell, Andrea G. Parker, and Brooke Foucault Welles. 2019. "Reclaiming Stigmatized Narratives: The Networked Disclosure Landscape of #MeToo." *Proceedings of the ACM on Human-Computer Interaction* 3 (CSCW). https://doi.org/10.1145/3359198

Galtung, Johan. 1969. "Violence, Peace, and Peace Research." *Journal of Peace Research* 6(3): 167–191.

Galtung, Johan. 1990. "Cultural Violence." *Journal of Peace Research* 27(3): 291–305.

Gardiner, Becky, Mahana Mansfield, Ian Anderson, Josh Holder, Daan Louter, and Monica Ulmanu. 2016. "The Dark Side of *Guardian* Comments." *Guardian*, April 12. https://www.theguardian.com/technology/2016/apr/12/the-dark-side-of-guardian-comments

Gardner, Carol Brooks. 1995. *Passing By: Gender and Public Harassment*. Berkeley: University of California Press.

Garver, Newton. 2009 [1968]. "What Violence Is." In *Violence: A Philosophical Anthology*, ed. Vittorio Bufacchi. New York: Palgrave, 170–182.

Gastil, John. 1990. "Generic Pronouns and Sexist Language: The Oxymoronic Character of Masculine Generics." *Sex Roles* 23(11–12): 629–43.

Gayraud, Alice, Assia Hebbache, Mathilde Julié-Viot, and Andrea Khoshkhou. 2019. "Le Sexisme Sévit Toujours dans les Couloirs de l'Assemblée." *Libération*, February 8. https://www.liberation.fr/debats/2019/02/08/le-sexisme-sevit-toujours-dans-les-couloirs-de-l-assemblee_1708026

Gelin, Martin. 2019. "The Misogyny of Climate Deniers." *New Republic*, August 28. https://newrepublic.com/article/154879/misogyny-climate-deniers

Georgalidou, Mariathi. 2017. "Addressing Women in the Greek Parliament: Institutionalized Confrontation or Sexist Aggression?" *Journal of Language Aggression and Conflict* 5(1): 30–56.

Gerbner, George. 1972. "Violence in Television Drama." In *Television and Social Behavior*, ed. G.A. Comstock and E. Rubinstein. Washington, DC: U.S. Government Printing Office, 28–65.

Gersen, Jeannie Suk. 2018. "Bill Cosby's Crimes and the Impact of #MeToo on the American Legal System." *New Yorker*, April 27. https://www.newyorker.com/news/news-desk/bill-cosbys-crimes-and-the-impact-of-metoo-on-the-american-legal-system

Gerstenfeld, Phyllis B. 2004. *Hate Crimes: Causes, Controls, and Controversies*. Thousand Oaks, CA: Sage.

Gidengil, Elisabeth, and Joanna Everitt. 1999. "Metaphors and Misrepresentation: Gendered Mediation in News Coverage of the 1993 Canadian Leaders' Debates." *Press/Politics* 4(1): 48–65.

Gillard, Julia. 2014. *My Story*. London: Bantam Press.

Gillard, Julia. 2016. "Julia Gillard Speaks in London in Memory of Jo Cox MP," October 11. http://juliagillard.com.au/articles/julia-gillard-speaks-in-memory-of-jo-cox-mp/

Gilmore, Leigh. 2017. *Tainted Witness: Why We Doubt What Women Say about Their Lives*. New York: Columbia University Press.

Giuffrida, Angela. 2019. "Senator Convicted over Racist Remark about Italy's First Black Minister." *Guardian*, January 14. https://www.theguardian.com/world/2019/jan/14 /league-senator-convicted-for-racist-remark-about-italy-first-black-minister-roberto-calderoli-cecile-kyenge

Glowacki, Laura, and Andrew Foote. 2019. "Vulgar Slur Painted across MP Catherine McKenna's Office." *CBC News*, October 24. https://www.cbc.ca/news/canada/ottawa/catherine-mckenna-vandalism-office-1.5333420

Goldmacher, Shane. 2017. "On Sexual Misconduct, Gillibrand Keeps Herself at the Fore." *New York Times*, December 6.

Goldman, Paul. 2015. "Ultra-Orthodox Israeli Press Edits Out Female Lawmakers From Photograph." *NBC News*, May 21. https://www.nbcnews.com/news/world/ultra-orthodox-israeli-press-edits-out-female-lawmakers-photograph-n362571

Gray, Emma. 2016. "How 'Nasty Woman' Became a Viral Call For Solidarity." *Huffington Post*, October 21. https://www.huffpost.com/entry/nasty-woman-became-a-call-of-solidarity-for-women-voters_n_5808f6a8e4b02444efa20c92

Greenwald, Glenn. 2018. "Marielle Franco: Why My Friend was a Repository of Hope and a Voice for Brazil's Voiceless, Before her Devastating Assassination." *Independent*, March 16. https://www.independent.co.uk/news/world/americas/marielle-franco-death-dead-dies-brazil-assassination-rio-de-janeiro-protest-glenn-greenwald-a8259516.html

Griffin, Tamerra. 2018. "This Congresswoman Had to Watch the Man Who Said She's Not Worth Raping Become President." *BuzzFeedNews*, November 20. https://www.buzzfeed-news.com/article/tamerragriffin/maria-do-rosario-interview-jair-bolsonaro-brazil

Gullickson, Gay L. 2014. "Militant Women: Representations of Charlotte Corday, Louise Michel, and Emmeline Pankhurst." *Women's History Review* 23(6): 837–852.

Haberkorn, Jennifer. 2019. "Is That Katie Porter or Katie Hill? New California Congresswomen Keep Getting Mixed Up." *Los Angeles Times*, April 15. https://www.latimes.com/politics/la-na-pol-congress-katie-hill-porter-name-confusion-20190415-story.html

Hall, Gaynor. 2018. "#MeToo: Report Outlines Ways to Change Culture in Illinois Politics." *WGN9 News*, September 26. https://wgntv.com/2018/09/26/state-report-elect-women-change-campaign-culture-to-end-abuse/

Hancock, Ange-Marie. 2007. "When Multiplication Doesn't Equal Quick Addition: Examining Intersectionality as a Research Paradigm." *Perspectives on Politics* 5(1): 63–79.

Hanson-Young, Sarah. 2018. *En Garde*. Melbourne: Melbourne University Press.

Hao, Ani. 2016. "In Brazil, Women Are Fighting against the Sexist Impeachment of Dilma Rousseff." *Guardian*, July 5. https://www.theguardian.com/global-development/2016/jul/05/in-brazil-women-are-fighting-against-the-sexist-impeachment-of-dilma-rousseff

Hao, Karen. 2019. "Deepfakes Have Got Congress Panicking. This Is What It Needs to Do." *MIT Technology Review*, June 12. https://www.technologyreview.com/s/613676/deepfakes-ai-congress-politics-election-facebook-social/

Haraldsson, Amanda, and Lena Wängnerud. 2019. "The Effect of Media Sexism on Women's Political Ambition: Evidence from a Worldwide Study." *Feminist Media Studies* 19(4): 525–541.

Haraldsson, Sara. 2016. "Känslomässig Köttfärs—De Hotade." Maktsalongen [blog], February 11. http://maktsalongen.se/kanslomassig-kottfars-de-hotade/

Harp, Dustin. 2018. "Misogyny in the 2016 U.S. Presidential Election." In *Mediating Misogyny*, ed. Jacqueline Ryan Vickery and Tracy Everbach. New York: Palgrave, 189–207.

Harris, Sandra. 2001. "Being Politically Impolite: Extending Politeness Theory to Adversarial Political Discourse." *Discourse & Society* 12(4): 451–472.

Harrison, Brian. 1978. *Separate Spheres: The Opposition to Women's Suffrage in Britain.* New York: Routledge.

Harwell, Drew. 2019. "Faked Pelosi Videos, Slowed to Make Her Appear Drunk, Spread Across Social Media." *Washington Post*, May 24. https://www.washingtonpost.com/technology/2019/05/23/faked-pelosi-videos-slowed-make-her-appear-drunk-spread-across-social-media/

Haug, Frigga. 1995. "The Quota Demand and Feminist Politics." *New Left Review* 209: 136–145.

Hawkesworth, Mary. 2003. "Congressional Enactments of Race-Gender: Toward a Theory of Raced-Gendered Institutions." *American Political Science Review* 97(4): 529–550.

Hawkesworth, Mary E. 2006. *Feminist Inquiry*. New Brunswick: Rutgers University Press.

Hay, Colin. 2007. *Why We Hate Politics*. London: Polity.

Heflick, Nathan A., and Jamie L. Goldenberg. 2009. "Objectifying Sarah Palin: Evidence that Objectification Causes Women to Be Perceived as Less Competent and Less Fully Human." *Journal of Experimental Social Psychology* 45(3): 598–601.

Heflick, Nathan A., and Jamie L. Goldenberg. 2011. "Sarah Palin, A Nation Object(ifie)s: The Role of Appearance Focus in the 2008 U.S. Presidential Election." *Sex Roles* 65(3–4): 149–155.

Heldman, Caroline, and Lisa Wade. 2011. "Sexualizing Sarah Palin." *Sex Roles* 65(3–4): 156–164.

Heldman, Caroline, Susan J. Carroll, and Stephanie Olson. 2005. "'She Brought Only a Skirt': Print Media Coverage of Elizabeth Dole's Bid for the Republican Presidential Nomination. *Political Communication* 22(3): 315–335.

Henley, Nancy M. 1977. *Body Politics: Power, Sex, and Nonverbal Communication.* Englewood Cliffs, NJ: Prentice-Hall.

Henry, Nicola, and Anastasia Powell. 2015. "Beyond the 'Sext': Technology-Facilitated Sexual Violence and Harassment against Adult Women." *Australian & New Zealand Journal of Criminology* 48(1): 104–118.

Hernández Cárdenas, Ana María and Nallely Guadalupe Tello Méndez. 2017. "Self-Care as a Political Strategy." *Sur* 14(26): 171–180.

Herrera, Morena, Mitzy Arias, and Sara García. 2011. *Hostilidad y Violencia Política: Develando Realidades de Mujeres Autoridades Municipales.* San Salvador: INSTRAW and ISDEMU.

Herrick, Rebekah, et al. 2019. "Physical Violence and Psychological Abuse against Female and Male Mayors in the United States." *Politics, Groups, & Identities*, online first. https://doi.org/10.1080/21565503.2019.1629321

Hevia Rocha, Teresa. 2017. *Diagnóstico sobre las Causas de la Violencia Política contra las Mujeres en México.* Mexico City: PRI.

Hillstrom, Laurie Collier. 2019. *The #MeToo Movement.* Denver, CO: ABC-CLIO.

Hipkins, Danielle. 2011. "'Whore-ocracy': Show Girls, the Beauty Trade-Off, and Mainstream Oppositional Discourse in Contemporary Italy." *Italian Studies* 66(3): 413–430.

Hodge, Jessica P. 2011. *Gendered Hate.* Boston: Northeastern University Press.

Höglund, Kristine. 2009. "Electoral Violence in Conflict-Ridden Societies: Concepts, Causes, and Consequences." *Terrorism & Political Violence* 21(3): 412–427.

Honorable Cámara de Diputados de la Nación. 2015. *Guía para el Uso de un Lenguage No Sexist e Igualitario en la HCDN.* Buenos Aires: HCDN.

Howe, Nicholas. 1988. "Metaphor in Contemporary American Political Discourse." *Metaphor & Symbolic Activity* 3(2): 87–104.

Hoyos, María Paula, ed. 2014. *Mujeres Muy Políticas, Mujeres Muy Públicas: Crónicas de Acoso a Mujeres Políticas.* Buenos Aires: Fundación Friedrich Ebert.

Hubbard, Ben. 2019. "Saudi Arabia Moves Toward Trials of Women's Rights Activists." *New York Times*, March 2. https://www.nytimes.com/2019/03/02/world/middleeast/saudi-arabia-trial-rights-activists.html

Hubbard, Caroline, and Claire De Soi. 2016. *Votes without Violence.* Washington, DC: NDI.

Huber, Jessica, and Lisa Kammerud. 2016. *Violence against Women in Elections.* Arlington, VA: IFES.

Hughes, Laura. 2017. "Labour MP Suspended after Alleged Victim Tells The Telegraph He Sexually Harassed Her." *Telegraph*, November 2. https://www.telegraph.co.uk/news/2017/11/02/labour/

Hughes, Laura, Ben Riley-Smith, and Steven Swinford. 2016. "Female MP Warned of 'Fatal Attack' before Jo Cox Murder." *Telegraph*, June 17. https://www.telegraph.co.uk/news/2016/06/17/female-mp-warned-of-fatal-attack-before-jo-cox-murder/.

Hughes, Melanie M., Mona Lena Krook, and Pamela Paxton. 2015. "Transnational Women's Activism and the Global Diffusion of Gender Quotas." *International Studies Quarterly* 59(2): 357–372.

Human Rights Watch. 2009. *"We Have the Promises of the World": Women's Rights in Afghanistan.* New York: HRW.

Human Rights Watch. 2016. *"Good Girls Don't Protest": Repression and Abuse of Women Human Rights Defenders, Activists, and Protesters in Sudan.* New York: HRW.

Human Rights Watch. 2019. *"The Breath of the Government on My Back": Attacks on Women's Rights in Poland*. New York: HRW.

Hunnicutt, Gwen. 2009. "Varieties of Patriarchy and Violence against Women: Resurrecting 'Patriarchy' as a Theoretical Tool." *Violence against Women* 15(5): 553–573.

Hunt, Swanee. 2007. "Let Women Rule." *Foreign Affairs* 86(3): 109–120.

Hunt, Elle, Nick Evershed, and Ri Liu. 2016. "From Julia Gillard to Hillary Clinton: Online Abuse of Politicians Around the World." *Guardian*, June 26. https://www.theguardian.com/technology/datablog/ng-interactive/2016/jun/27/from-julia-gillard-to-hillary-clinton-online-abuse-of-politicians-around-the-world

"Icelandic Women Politicians Publish Stories of Sexual Harassment." 2017. *Iceland Monitor*, November 24. https://icelandmonitor.mbl.is/news/politics_and_society/2017/11/24/ icelandic_women_politicians_publish_stories_of_sexu/

Iganski, Paul. 2001. "Hate Crimes Hurt More." *American Behavioral Scientist* 45(4): 626–638.

iKNOW Politics. 2007. *Consolidated Reply—E-Discussion: Eliminating Violence against Women in Politics (10–14 December 2007)*. http://iknowpolitics.org/sites/default/files/evawip-ediscussion-iknowpolitics2007-summary.pdf

ILO. 2019. *Convention Concerning the Elimination of Violence and Harassment in the World of Work*. Geneva: ILO.

ILO Director-General. 2017. *Fifth Supplementary Report: Outcome of the Meeting of Experts on Violence against Women and Men in the World of Work*. Geneva: ILO.

IM-Defensoras. 2013. "A Feminist Alternative for the Protection, Self-Care, and Safety of Women Human Rights Defenders in Mesoamerica." *Journal of Human Rights Practice* 5(3): 446–459.

IM-Defensoras. 2015. *Violence against Women Human Rights Defenders in Mesoamerica: 2012–2014 Report*. http://im-defensoras.org/wp-content/uploads/2016/04/286224690-Violence-Against-WHRDs-in-Mesoamerica-2012-2014-Report.pdf

International Federation of Journalists. 2017. *Byte Back: A Journalist's Guide to Combat Cyber Harassment in South Asia*. Brussels: IFJ.

IPS Correspondents. 2008. "Q&A: 'But They Never Killed My Spirit.'" Inter Press Service, May 29. http://www.ipsnews.net/2008/05/qa-quotbut-they-never-killed-my-spiritquot/

IPU. 2008. *Equality in Politics: A Survey of Women and Men in Parliaments*. Geneva: IPU.

IPU. 2011. *Resolution on Providing a Sound Legislative Framework Aimed at Preventing Electoral Violence, Improving Electoral Monitoring, and Ensuring the Smooth Transition of Power*. Geneva: IPU.

IPU. 2012. *Plan of Action for Gender-Sensitive Parliaments*. Geneva: IPU.

IPU. 2014. *Women in Parliament in 2013: The Year in Review*. Geneva: IPU.

IPU. 2016a. *Resolution on the Freedom of Women to Participate in Political Processes Fully, Safely, and Without Interference*. Geneva: IPU.

IPU. 2016b. *Sexism, Harassment, and Violence against Women Parliamentarians*. Geneva: IPU.

IPU. 2018. *Sexism, Harassment, and Violence against Women in Parliaments in Europe*. Geneva: IPU and Council of Europe.

Iqbal, Zaryab, and Christopher Zorn. 2008. "The Political Consequences of Assassination." *Journal of Conflict Resolution* 52(3): 385–400.

Irwin, Janis. 2016. "The Thickest Of Skins Won't Stop a Bullet." *Huffington Post*, June 17. https://www.huffingtonpost.ca/janis-irwin/slain-british-mp-jo-cox_b_10518686.html

Itzin, Catherine. 2002. "Pornography and the Construction of Misogyny." *Journal of Sexual Aggression* 8(3):4–42.

Jacobs, James B., and Kimberly A. Potter. 1997. "Hate Crimes: A Critical Perspective." *Crime and Justice* 22: 1–50.

Jaffe, Sarah. 2018. "The Collective Power of #MeToo." *Dissent* 65(2): 80–87.

Jalalzai, Farida, and Pedro G. Dos Santos. 2015. "The Dilma Effect? Women's Representation under Dilma Rousseff's Presidency." *Politics & Gender* 11(1): 117–145.

James, David V., Frank R. Farnham, Seema Sukhwal, Katherine Jones, Josephine Carlisle, and Sara Henley. 2016a. "Aggressive/Intrusive Behaviours, Harassment, and Stalking of Members of the United Kingdom Parliament." *Journal of Forensic Psychiatry & Psychology* 27(2): 177–197.

James, David V., Seema Sukhwal, Frank R. Farnham, Julie Evans, Claire Barrie, Alice Taylor, and Simon P. Wilson. 2016b. "Harassment and Stalking of Members of the United Kingdom Parliament: Associations and Consequences." *Journal of Forensic Psychiatry & Psychology* 27(3): 309–330.

Jane, Emma A. 2017. *Misogyny Online: A Short (and Brutish) History*. Washington, DC: Sage.

Jane, Emma A. 2018. "Gendered Cyberhate as Workplace Harassment and Economic Vandalism." *Feminist Media Studies* 18(4): 575–591.

Jankowicz, Nina. 2017. "How Disinformation Became a New Threat to Women." *Coda Story*, December 11. https://codastory.com/disinformation/how-disinformation-became-a-new-threat-to-women/

Jenkins, Janis H. 1998. "The Medical Anthropology of Political Violence: A Cultural and Feminist Agenda." *Medical Anthropology Quarterly* 12(1): 122–131.

Jensen, Kimberly. 2008. *Mobilizing Minerva*. Urbana: University of Illinois Press.

"Jeremy Corbyn 'Warned over Promoting Harassment Claim MP.'" *BBC News*, November 3. https://www.bbc.com/news/uk-politics-41857136

Jilani, Hina. 2002. *2002/106: Promotion and Protection of Human Rights: Human Rights Defenders*. Geneva: Commission on Human Rights.

Johnson, Ann. 2007. "The Subtleties of Blatant Sexism." *Communication and Critical/Cultural Studies* 4(2): 166–183.

Johnson, Michael P. 1995. "Patriarchal Terrorism and Common Couple Violence: Two Forms of Violence against Women." *Journal of Marriage and Family* 57(2): 283–294.

Johnston, Ian. 2013. "Malala Yousafzai: Being Shot by Taliban Made Me Stronger." *NBC News*, July 12. https://www.nbcnews.com/news/world/malala-yousafzai-being-shot-taliban-made-me-stronger-flna6C10612024

Johnston, Lisa G., and Keith Sabin. 2010. "Sampling Hard-to-Reach Populations with Respondent Driven Sampling." *Methodological Innovations Online* 5(2): 38–48.

Jones, James R. 2017. *Black Capitol: Race and Power in the Halls of Congress*. Ph.D. Diss., Columbia University.

Jost, John T., and Jojanneke van der Toorn. 2011. "System Justification Theory." In *Encyclopedia of Power*, ed. Keith Dowding, 650–653. Thousand Oaks: Sage.

Joya, Malalai. 2009. *A Woman among Warlords*. New York: Simon and Schuster.

Julié-Viot, Mathilde. 2018. "L'Assemblée Nationale Fait L'Autruche." In *Violences Sexistes et Sexuelles en Politique*, ed. Esther Benbassa. Paris: CNRS, 21–25.

Kahn, Kim Fridkin, and Patrick J. Kenney. 1999. "Do Negative Campaigns Mobilize or Suppress Turnout?" *American Political Science Review* 93(4): 977–989.

Kaiser, Anna Jean. 2018. "Woman Who Bolsonaro Insulted: 'Our President-Elect Encourages Rape.'" *Guardian*, December 23. https://www.theguardian.com/world/2018/dec/23/maria-do-rosario-jair-bolsonaro-brazil-rape

Kalin, Stephen. 2019. "Saudi Women Activists Detail Torture Allegations in Court." *Reuters*, March 27. https://www.reuters.com/article/us-saudi-arrests/saudi-women-activists-detail-torture-allegations-in-court-idUSKCN1R80M6

Kameda, Masaaki. 2014. "Assembly Member Loses Bid to Punish Sexist Hecklers." *Japan Times*, June 20. https://www.japantimes.co.jp/news/2014/06/20/national/politics-diplomacy/assembly-member-loses-bid-to-punish-sexist-hecklers/

Karanja, Faith. 2019. "MP Called Me Stupid, Liar Then Punched Me, Woman Rep Fatuma Gedi Testifies." *Eve Digital*, October 23. https://www.standardmedia.co.ke/evewoman/article/2001346497/mp-called-me-stupid-liar-then-punched-me-woman-rep-fatuma-gedi-testifies

Kathlene, Lyn. 1994. "Power and Influence in State Legislative Policymaking." *American Political Science Review* 88(3): 560–576.

Katz, Jackson. 2016. *Man Enough? Donald Trump, Hillary Clinton, and the Politics of Presidential Masculinity*. Northampton, MA: Interlink.

Kauppinen, Antti. 2015. "Hate and Punishment." *Journal of Interpersonal Violence* 30(10): 1719–1737.

Keck, Margaret E., and Kathryn Sikkink. 1998. *Activists beyond Borders: Advocacy Networks in International Politics*. Ithaca, NY: Cornell University Press.

Kelly, Liz. 1988. *Surviving Sexual Violence*. Minneapolis: University of Minnesota Press.

Kelly, Liz, and Jill Radford. 1990. "'Nothing Really Happened': The Invalidation of Women's Experiences of Sexual Violence." *Critical Social Policy* 10(30): 39–53.

Kent, Melissa. 2019. "U.S. Investigates Spam Barrage on UN Diplomat at Women's Rights Conference." *CBC News*, Mary 5. https://www.cbc.ca/news/world/un-kenya-abuse-women-diplomacy-us-abortion-1.5122382

"Kenya MP Arrested 'For Slapping Female Colleague.'" 2019. *BBC News*, June 13. https://www.bbc.com/news/world-africa-48629678

Kihiu, Wambui. 2007. "Electoral Violence is an Abuse of Human Rights." *The Dawn*, November–December, 5.

Kimber, Stephen. 1999. *"Not Guilty": The Trial of Gerald Regan*. Toronto: Stoddart.

Kimmel, Michael. 2002. "'Gender Symmetry' in Domestic Violence." *Violence against Women* 8(11): 1332–1363.

Kimmel, Michael. 2017. *Angry White Men*. New York: Nation.

King, Shaun. 2018. "The Assassination of Human Rights Activist Marielle Franco Was a Huge Loss for Brazil—and the World." *Intercept*, March 16. https://theintercept.com/2018/03/16/marielle-franco-assassination-brazil-police-brutality/

Kingdon, John W. 1984. *Agendas, Alternatives, and Public Policies*. Boston: Little, Brown, and Company.

Kingsley, Patrick. 2013. "80 Sexual Assaults in One Day—The Other Story of Tahrir Square." *Guardian*, July 5. https://www.theguardian.com/world/2013/jul/05/egypt-women-rape-sexual-assault-tahrir-square

Kinney, Alison. 2017. "Your Global Mansplaining Dictionary in 34 Languages." *The Establishment*, March 9. https://theestablishment.co/your-global-mansplaining-dictionary-in-34-languages-a5e44bf682ba-2/

Kishi, Roudabeh, Melissa Pavlik, and Hilary Matfess. 2019. *'Terribly and Terrifyingly Normal': Political Violence Targeting Women.* https://www.acleddata.com/wp-content/uploads/2019/05/ACLED_Report_PoliticalViolenceTargetingWomen_5.2019.pdf

Klatch, Rebecca E. 2001. "The Formation of Feminist Consciousness among Left- and Right-Wing Activists of the 1960s." *Gender & Society* 15(6): 791–815.

Krais, Beate. 1993. "Gender and Symbolic Violence: Female Oppression in the Light of Pierre Bourdieu's Theory of Social Practice." In *Bourdieu: Critical Perspectives*, ed. Craig Calhon, Edward LiPuma, and Moishe Postone. Chicago: University of Chicago Press, 156–177.

Krantz, Joakim, Lisa Wallin, and Sanna Wallin. 2012. *Politikernas trygghetsundersökning.* Stockholm: Brottsförebyggande rådet.

Krause, Keith. 2009. "Beyond Definition: Violence in a Global Perspective." *Global Crime* 10(4): 337–355.

Krook, Mona Lena. 2006. "Reforming Representation: The Diffusion of Candidate Gender Quotas Worldwide." *Politics & Gender* 2(3): 303–327.

Krook, Mona Lena. 2017. "Violence against Women in Politics." *Journal of Democracy* 28(1): 74–88.

Krook, Mona Lena. 2018. "Westminster Too: On Sexual Harassment in British Politics." *Political Quarterly* 89(1): 65–72.

Krook, Mona Lena, and Juliana Restrepo Sanín. 2016a. "Gender and Political Violence in Latin America: Concepts, Debates, and Solutions." *Política y Gobierno* 23(1): 125–157.

Krook, Mona Lena, and Juliana Restrepo Sanín. 2016b. "Violence Against Women in Politics: A Defense of the Concept." *Política y Gobierno* 23(2): 459–490.

Krook, Mona Lena, and Juliana Restrepo Sanín. 2020. "The Cost of Doing Politics? Analyzing Violence and Harassment against Female Politicians." *Perspectives on Politics*, online first. https:// doi.org/ 10.1017/ S15375927190013

Kuhar, Roman, and David Paternotte, eds. 2017. *Anti-Gender Campaigns in Europe.* New York: Rowman & Littlefield.

Kumar, Anil. 2018. "Viral Test: 'Croatian President in Bikini' Setting Internet on Fire." *India Today*, July 13. https://www.indiatoday.in/fact-check/story/viral-test-croatia-president-bikini-kolinda-grabar-kitarovic-fifa-1285348-2018-07-13

Kuperberg, Rebecca. 2018. "Intersectional Violence against Women in Politics." *Politics & Gender* 14(4): 685–690.

"Labour Activist 'Warned' About Pursuing Rape Claim." 2017. *BBC News*, October 31. https://www.bbc.co.uk/news/uk-politics-41821671

Lachover, Einat. 2005. "The Gendered and Sexualized Relationship between Israeli Women and Their Male News Sources." *Journalism* 6(3): 291–311.

Landes, Joan B. 1988. *Women and the Public Sphere in the Age of the French Revolution.* Ithaca, NY: Cornell University Press.

Landman, Todd. 2006. "Holding the Line: Human Rights Defenders in the Age of Terror." British Journal of Politics & International Relations 8(2): 123–147.

Langa, Veneranda. 2018. "Women Bear Brunt of Political Violence." *NewsDay Zimbabwe*, June 18, https://www.newsday.co.zw/2018/06/women-bear-brunt-of-political-violence/

Langohr, Vickie. 2013. "'This Is Our Square': Fighting Sexual Assault at Cairo Protests." *Middle East Report* 268: 18–25.

Langlois, Jill. 2019. "Who Ordered the Assassination of Marielle Franco?" *Los Angeles Times*, March 13. https://www.latimes.com/world/mexico-americas/la-fg-brazil-marielle-franco-20190313-story.html

LaRue, Frank. 2012. *HRC/20/17: Report of the Special Rapporteur on the Promotion and Protection of the Right to Freedom of Opinion and Expression.* New York: UN.

Lau, Richard R., and Ivy Brown Rovner. 2009. "Negative Campaigning." *Annual Review of Political Science* 12: 285–306.

Lawless, Jennifer L., and Kathryn Pearson. 2008. "The Primary Reason for Women's Underrepresentation? Reevaluating the Conventional Wisdom." *Journal of Politics* 70(1): 67–82.

Lawrence, Frederick M. 1999. *Punishing Hate.* Cambridge, MA: Harvard University Press.

Lazarus, Jeffrey, and Amy Steigerwalt. 2018. *Gendered Vulnerability: How Women Work Harder to Stay in Office.* Ann Arbor: University of Michigan Press.

Le Collectif "Levons l'omerta." 2016. "Harcèlement et Politique: 'Pour que l'Impunité Cesse.'" *Libération*, May 9. https://www.liberation.fr/france/2016/05/09/harcelement-et-politique-pour-que-l-impunite-cesse_1451542

Levey, Tania G. 2018. *Sexual Harassment Online: Shaming and Silencing Women in the Digital Age.* Boulder, CO: Lynne Rienner.

Lewis, Ruth, Michael Rowe, and Clare Wiper. 2017. "Online Abuse of Feminists as an Emerging Form of Violence against Women and Girls." *British Journal of Criminology* 57(6): 1462–1481.

"Ligue du LOL: Secret Group of French Journalists Targeted Women." *BBC News*, February 12. https://www.bbc.com/news/world-europe-47206248

Lloyd, Genevieve. 1984. *Man of Reason.* London: Methuen.

Luque Martínez, Javier. 2015. "Trolled By the State." *British Journalism Review* 26(4): 61–66.

Machiavelli, Niccolò. 1981 [1532]. *The Prince.* Trans. George Bull. New York: Penguin.

Machicao, Ximena. 2004. *Acoso Político: Un Tema Urgente que Afrontar.* La Paz: PADEP-GTZ.

MacKinnon, Catharine A. 1982. "Feminism, Marxism, Method, and the State: An Agenda for Theory." *Signs* 7(3): 515–544.

Magley, Vicki J., Charles L. Hulin, Louise F. Fitzgerald, and Mary DeNardo. 1999. "Outcomes of Self-Labeling Sexual Harassment." *Journal of Applied Psychology* 84(3): 390–402.

Maia, Gustavo, and Jussara Soares. 2019. "Cumprindo Decisão Judicial, Bolsonaro Pede Desculpas a Maria do Rosário em Rede Social." *O Globo*, June 13. https://oglobo.globo.com/brasil/cumprindo-decisao-judicial-bolsonaro-pede-desculpas-maria-do-rosario-em-rede-social-23737390

Maidment, Jack. 2017. "Male Tory MP Candidates Received Highest Percentage of Twitter Abuse during Election Campaign." *Telegraph*, July 24. https://www.telegraph.co.uk/news/2017/07/24/male-tory-mp-candidates-received-highest-percentage-twitter/

Makoye, Kizito. 2015. "Tanzanian Lawyers Say Up to 50 Women Divorced for Defying Husbands in Vote." *Thomson Reuters*, December 7. http://news.trust.org/item/20151207183849-12z13/

Malsin, Jared. 2018. "Egypt Sends Actress to Jail for Spreading 'Fake News' Over Sexual Harassment." *Wall Street Journal*, September 29. https://www.wsj.com/articles/egypt-sends-actress-to-jail-for-spreading-fake-news-over-sexual-harassment-1538222090

Manne, Kate. 2018. *Down Girl: The Logic of Misogyny*. New York: Oxford University Press.

Mansbridge, Jane, and Shauna L. Shames. 2008. "Toward a Theory of Backlash: Dynamic Resistance and the Central Role of Power." *Politics & Gender* 4(4): 623–634.

Mantilla, Karla. 2015. *Gendertrolling*. Denver, CO: Praeger.

Marcotte, Amanda. 2019. "Misogyny, Meet Hypocrisy: Climate Deniers Go after AOC, Greta Thunberg with Sexist Attacks." *Salon*, August 30. https://www.salon.com/2019/08/30/misogyny-meet-hypocrisy-climate-deniers-go-after-aoc-greta-thunberg-with-sexist-attacks/

Martelotte, Lucía. 2018. *Violencia Política contra las Mujeres en Argentina*. Buenos Aires: Equipo Latinoamericano de Justicia y Género.

Marwick, Alice E., and Robyn Caplan. 2018. "Drinking Male Tears: Language, the Manosphere, and Networked Harassment." *Feminist Media Studies* 18(4): 543–559.

Mason, Melanie. 2017. "Female Lawmakers, Staffers, and Lobbyists Speak Out on 'Pervasive' Harassment in California's Capitol." *Los Angeles Times*, October 17. https://www.latimes.com/politics/la-pol-ca-women-harassment-capitol-20171017-story.html

Mason, Rowena. 2016. "Angela Eagle Received Hundreds of Homophobic Messages from Labour Members." *Guardian*, October 19. https://www.theguardian.com/politics/2016/oct/19/angela-eagle-abusive-homophobic-messages-labour-members

Mason, Rowena, Anushka Asthana and Matthew Weaver. 2017. "Labour Activist Says She Was Raped at Party Event and Told Not to Report It." *Guardian*, November 1. https://www.theguardian.com/world/2017/oct/31/labour-activist-says-she-was-raped-at-party-event-and-told-not-to-report-it

Matloff, Judith. 2007. "Unspoken: Foreign Correspondents and Sexual Abuse." *Columbia Journalism Review* 46(1): 22–23.

Matsuda, Mari J., Charles R. Lawrence III, Richard Delgado, and Kimberle Williams Crenshaw. 1993. *Words that Wound*. Boulder, CO: Westview.

May, Theresa. 2018. "Speech on Standards in Public Life." February 6. https://www.gov.uk/government/speeches/pm-speech-on-standards-in-public-life-6-february-2018

McAdams, Katherine C., and Maurine H. Beasley. 1994. "Sexual Harassment of Washington Women Journalists." *Newspaper Research Journal* 15(1): 127–139.

McCall, Leslie. 2005. "The Complexity of Intersectionality." *Signs* 30(3): 1771–1800.

McConnell, Rick. 2016. "Impassioned Sandra Jansen Calls on Legislature to Stand against Misogyny." *CBC News*, November 22. https://www.cbc.ca/news/canada/edmonton/impassioned-sandra-jansen-calls-on-legislature-to-stand-against-misogyny-1.3863097

McCurry, Justin. 2014. "Tokyo Assemblywoman Subjected to Sexist Abuse from Other Members." *Guardian*, June 20. https://www.theguardian.com/world/2014/jun/20/tokyo-assemblywoman-sexist-abuse

McGlynn, Clare, Erika Rackley, and Ruth Houghton. 2017. "Beyond 'Revenge Porn': The Continuum of Image-Based Sexual Abuse." *Feminist Legal Studies* 25(1): 25–46.

McGowan, Michael, and Paul Karp. 2019. "Sarah Hanson-Young Awarded $120,000 Damages in Defamation Case against David Leyonhjelm." *Guardian*, November 25. https://www.theguardian.com/australia-news/2019/nov/25/sarah-hanson-young-awarded-120000-damages-defamation-david-leyonhjelm

McIntyre, Catherine, and Meagan Campbell. 2018. "Sexual Harassment Has Long Festered on the Hill. Now Female MPs from All Parties are Saying 'Enough.'" *Chatelaine*, March 8.

McKeen, Alex, and Victoria Gibson. 2018. "Young Women Face 'Pervasive' Culture of Sex Harassment in Canadian Politics." *Toronto Star*, January 25. https://respect-groupinc.com/ 2018/03/06/young-women-face-pervasive-culture-of-sex-harassment-in-canadian-politics/

McKinnon, Rachel. 2017. "Allies Behaving Badly: Gaslighting as Epistemic Injustice." In *The Routledge Handbook of Epistemic Injustice*, ed. Ian James Kidd, José Medina, and Gaile Pohlhaus Jr. New York: Routledge, 167–174.

McPhail, Beverly A. 2002. "Gender-Bias Hate Crimes: A Review." *Trauma, Violence, & Abuse* 3(2): 125–143.

Meloy, J. Reid, Lorraine Sheridan, and Jens Hoffmann, eds. 2008. *Stalking, Threatening, and Attacking Public Figures*. New York: Oxford University Press.

Meret, Susi, Elisabetta Della Corte, and Maria Sanguiliano. 2013. "The Racist Attacks against Cécile Kyenge and the Enduring Myth of the 'Nice' Italian." *Open Democracy*, August 28. https://www.opendemocracy.net/en/can-europe-make-it/racist-attacks-against-cecile/

Mijatović, Dunja. 2016. *New Challenges to Freedom of Expression: Countering Online Abuse of Female Journalists*. Vienna: OSCE Representative on Freedom of the Media.

"Monitors: Taliban Cut Off fingers of Afghan Voters." 2009. *CNN*, August 22. https://www.cnn.com/2009/WORLD/asiapcf/08/22/afghanistan.election/index.html

Moore, Mark P. 1996. "Rhetorical Subterfuge and 'The Principle of Perfection': Bob Packwood's Response to Sexual Misconduct Charges." *Western Journal of Communication* 60(1): 1–20.

Morrell, Caroline. 1981. *"Black Friday" and Violence against Women in the Suffragette Movement*. London: Women's Research and Resources Centre.

Moser, Caroline, and Fiona Clark. 2001. *Victims, Perpetrators, or Actors? Gender, Armed Conflict and Political Violence*. New York: Palgrave.

"MPs to Be Offered Extra Security After Jo Cox's Death." 2016. *BBC News*, July 19. https://www.bbc.com/news/uk-politics-36836980

Mugarula, Florence. 2016. "MP Skips Debates to Trade Insults." *The Citizen*, May 15. https://www.thecitizen.co.tz/news/MP-skips-debates-to-trade-insults/1840340-3204332-gdkxga/index.html

Munger, Kevin. 2017. "Tweetment Effects on the Tweeted: Experimentally Reducing Racist Harassment." *Political Behavior* 39(3): 629–649.

Muñoz, Ariela. 2019. "Aprueban Protocolo de Acoso Sexual para la Cámara de Diputados." *BioBio*, January 16. https://www.biobiochile.cl/noticias/nacional/chile/2019/01/16/aprueban-protocolo-de-acoso-sexual-para-la-camara-de-diputados-bromas-y-piropos-estan-incluidos.shtml

Murphy, Katharine. 2018. "Australia Bans Ministers from Having Sex with Staff after Barnaby Joyce Scandal." *Guardian*, February 15. https://www.theguardian.com/australia-news/2018/feb/15/australia-bans-ministers-having-sex-with-staff-barnaby-joyce-malcolm-turnbull

Murray, Jessie, and H. N. Brailsford. 1911. *The Treatment of Women's Deputations by the Metropolitan Police*. London: The Women's Press.

Musgrove, George Derek. 2012. *Rumor, Repression, and Racial Politics: How the Harassment of Black Elected Officials Shaped Post-Civil Rights America*. Athens: University of Georgia Press.

Mutz, Diana C. 2015. *In-Your-Face Politics: The Consequences of Uncivil Media*. Princeton, NJ: Princeton University Press.

Nah, Alice M., Karen Bennett, Danna Ingleton, and James Savage. 2013. "A Research Agenda for the Protection of Human Rights Defenders." *Journal of Human Rights Practice* 5(30): 401–420.

Nagengast, Carole. 1994. "Violence, Terror, and the Crisis of the State." *Annual Review of Anthropology* 23(1): 109–136.

Narud, Kjersti, and Alv A. Dahl. 2015. "Stalking Experiences Reported by Norwegian Members of Parliament Compared to a Population Sample." *Journal of Forensic Psychiatry & Psychology* 26(1): 116–131.

NDI. 2016. *#NotTheCost: Stopping Violence against Women in Politics: Program Guidance*. Washington, DC: NDI.

NDI. 2018. *No Party to Violence: Analyzing Violence against Women in Political Parties*. Washington, DC: NDI.

NDI. 2019. *Tweets That Chill: Analyzing Online Violence against Women in Politics*. Washington, DC: NDI.

Nerone, John. 1994. *Violence against the Press*. New York: Oxford University Press.

Newton, Casey. 2019. "The Trauma Floor: The Secret Lives of Facebook Moderators in America." *The Verge*, February 25. https://www.theverge.com/2019/2/25/18229714/cognizant-facebook-content-moderator-interviews-trauma-working-conditions-arizona

Nieburg, H. L. 1969. *Political Violence: The Behavioral Process*. New York: St. Martin's Press.

Nilsson, Kirsten. 2007. "Bendtsen Bad Enhedslistens Spidskandidat Hente Kaffe." *Politiken*, November 13. https://politiken.dk/indland/politik/art5030718/Bendtsen-bad-Enhedslistens-spidskandidat-hente-kaffe

Norris, Pippa, Richard W. Frank, and Ferran Martínez i Coma, eds. 2015. *Contentious Elections*. New York: Routledge.

"Norway PM Opens Up about Online Abuse." 2015. *The Local*, December 1. https://www.thelocal.no/20151201/norway-pm-opens-up-about-online-abuse

Nyambala, Marceline. 2007. "Unit to Address Gender Violence Launch." *The Dawn*, November–December, 8.

O'Leary, K. Daniel. 1999. "Psychological Abuse: A Variable Deserving Critical Attention in Domestic Violence." *Violence & Victims* 14(10): 3–23.

O'Toole, Laura L., Jessica R. Schiffman, and Marge L. Edwards, eds. 2007. *Gender Violence: Interdisciplinary Perspectives*. New York: New York University Press.

Off, Carol. 2018. "It's the Same as It Ever Was for Women in Politics." *Globe and Mail*, February 2. https://www.theglobeandmail.com/opinion/its-the-same-as-it-ever-was-for-women-inpolitics/article37829238/

Okin, Susan Moller. 1979. *Women in Western Political Thought*. Princeton, NJ: Princeton University Press.

OAS. 1994. *Inter-American Convention on the Prevention, Punishment, and Eradication of Violence against Women*. Washington, DC: OAS.

Oppenheim, Maya. 2016a. "Black MP Dawn Butler Reveals She Was Victim of Racism in Parliament after Fellow MP Assumed She Was a Cleaner." *Independent*, February 28. https://www.independent.co.uk/news/people/black-mp-dawn-butler-reveals-she-was-victim-of-racism-in-parliament-after-fellow-mp-assumed-she-was-a6901261.html

Oppenheim, Maya. 2016b. "Labour MP Jess Phillips Receives '600 Rape Threats in One Night.'" *Independent*, May 31. https://www.independent.co.uk/news/people/labour-mp-jess-phillips-receives-600-rape-threats-in-one-night-a7058041.html

Oppenheim, Maya. 2019. "Sister of Jailed Saudi Women's Rights Activist Says She is Forced to Endure 'Emotional Rollercoaster' due to Authorities' Silence." *Independent*, September 23. https://www.independent.co.uk/news/world/middle-east/loujain-al-hathloul-saudi-arabia-prison-jail-sister-lina-activist-a9117361.html

OSCE Ministerial Council. 2018. *Decision 3/18: Safety of Journalists*. Milan: OSCE.

OSCE Representative on Freedom of the Media. 2018. *#SOFJO: Safety of Female Journalists Online*. Vienna: OSCE.

Ott, Brian L. 2017. "The Age of Twitter: Donald J. Trump and the Politics of Debasement." *Critical Studies in Media Communication* 34(1): 59–68.

Paillou, Sarah. 2019. "Les Députés Votent la Création d'une Cellule Contre le Harcèlement à l'Assemblée." *Le Journal de Dimanche*, May 16. https://www.lejdd.fr/Politique/les-deputes-veulent-creer-une-cellule-contre-le-harcelement-a-lassemblee-3898784

Palermo, Tia, Jennifer Bleck, and Amber Peterman. 2014. "Tip of the Iceberg: Reporting and Gender-Based Violence in Developing Countries." *American Journal of Epidemiology* 179(5): 602–612.

Palmieri, Sonia. 2011. *Gender-Sensitive Parliaments: A Global Review of Good Practice*. Geneva: Inter-Parliamentary Union.

Parker, Ceri. 2018. "Even the Prime Minister of Norway Has Been Mansplained To." *World Economic Forum*, January 25. https://www.weforum.org/agenda/2018/01/even-the-prime-minister-of-norway-has-been-mansplained-to/

Parker, Kelsey N. 2015. *Aggression against Journalists*. Ph.D. Diss., University of Tulsa.

Parkinson, John. 2018. "Disgraced Former Congressman Blake Farenthold Won't Repay $84K Sexual Harassment Settlement." *ABC News*, May 15. https://abcnews.go.com/Politics/disgraced-congressman-blake-farenthold-wont-repay-84k-sexual/story?id=55175396

Pateman, Carole. 1988. *The Sexual Contract*. Stanford, CA: Stanford University Press.

Pathé, Michele, Jane Phillips, Elke Perdacher, and Ed Heffernan. 2014. "The Harassment of Queensland Members of Parliament: A Mental Health Concern." *Psychiatry, Psychology & Law* 21(4): 577–584.

Pauwels, Anne. 2003. "Linguistic Sexism and Feminist Linguistic Activism." In *The Handbook of Language and Gender*, ed. Janet Holmes and Miriam Meyerhoff. Oxford: Blackwell, 550–570.

Peirce, Charles Sanders. 1994. *Peirce on Signs*. Ed. James Hoopes. Chapel Hill: University of North Carolina Press.

Perliger, Arie. 2015. *The Rationale of Political Assassinations*. West Point, NY: Combating Terrorism Center.

Perry, Barbara. 2001. *In the Name of Hate: Understanding Hate Crimes*. New York: Routledge.

Perry, Barbara, and Shahid Alvi. 2011. "'We Are All Vulnerable': The *In Terrorem* Effects of Hate Crimes." *International Review of Victimology* 18(1): 57–71.

Petersen, R. Eric, and Jennifer E. Manning. 2017. *Violence Against Members of Congress and Their Staff: Selected Examples and Congressional Responses*. Washington, DC: Congressional Research Service.

Petersen, R. Eric, Jennifer E. Manning, and Erin Hemlin. 2011. *Violence Against Members of Congress and Their Staff: Selected Examples and Congressional Responses.* Washington, DC: Congressional Research Service.

Peterson, Anne Helen. 2018. "The Cost of Reporting while Female." *Columbia Journalism Review*, Winter. https://www.cjr.org/special_report/reporting-female-harassment-journalism.php

Pfahler, Lennart. 2018. "95 Junge Politikerinnen Berichten über Sexismus in Ihren Parteien." *HuffPost*, January 15. https://lennartpfahler.exposure.co/95-junge-politikerinnen-berichten-ueber-sexismus-in-ihren-parteien

Philippe, Barthélémy. 2019. "Violences Sexuelles à l'Assemblée Nationale: 'Nous Avons Sonné l'Alarme, Mais Rien Ne Bouge!'" *Capital*, March 13. https://www.capital.fr/economie-politique/violences-sexuelles-a-lassemblee-nous-avons-sonne-lalarme-mais-rien-ne-bouge-1331326

Phillips, Anne. 1995. *The Politics of Presence*. New York: Oxford University Press.

Phillips, Dom. 2018. "Marielle Franco: Brazil's Favelas Mourn the Death of a Champion." *Guardian*, March 17. https://www.theguardian.com/world/2018/mar/18/marielle-franco-brazil-favelas-mourn-death-champion

Phillips, Jess, 2016a. "By Ignoring the Thousands of Rape Threat Sent to Me, Twitter is Colluding with My Abusers." *Telegraph*, June 1. https://www.telegraph.co.uk/women/politics/by-ignoring-the-thousands-of-rape-threats-sent-to-me-twitter-is/

Phillips, Jess. 2016b. "Jo Cox's murder Has Left Us MPs More Fearful to Speak Our Minds." *Guardian*, November 23. https://www.theguardian.com/commentisfree/2016/nov/23/jo-cox-murder-mps-abuse-threats-female-democracy

Phillips, Jess. 2017. *Everywoman: One Woman's Truth about Speaking the Truth.* London: Hutchinson.

Phillips, Whitney. 2015. *This Is Why We Can't Have Nice Things: Mapping the Relationship between Online Trolling and Mainstream Culture*. Cambridge, MA: MIT Press.

Piscopo, Jennifer M. 2015. "States as Gender Equality Activists: The Evolution of Quota Laws in Latin America." *Latin American Politics & Society* 57(3): 27–49.

Piscopo, Jennifer M. 2016. "State Capacity, Criminal Justice, and Political Rights: Rethinking Violence against Women in Politics." *Política y Gobierno* 23(2): 437–458.

Pitkin, Hanna Fenichel. 1967. *The Concept of Representation*. Berkeley: University of California Press.

Plan International. 2017. *She Can Lead*. Melbourne: Plan International.

Powell, Anastasia, and Nicola Henry. 2017. *Sexual Violence in a Digital Age*. New York: Palgrave.

Prakash, Nidhi. 2017. "More Than Two Dozen Democratic Senators Have Called For Al Franken To Resign." *BuzzFeed News*, December 6. https://www.buzzfeednews.com/article/nidhiprakash/calls-for-franken-to-resign

Price, Joshua M. 2012. *Structural Violence: Hidden Brutality in the Lives of Women*. Albany, NY: SUNY Press.

Price, Melanye. 2016. "3 Ways to Tell if Your Distaste For Hillary Clinton is Sexist." Ms. Blog, March 17. https://msmagazine.com/2016/03/17/3-ways-to-tell-if-your-distaste-for-hillary-clinton-is-sexist/

Puwar, Nirmal. 2004. *Space Invaders*. New York: Berg.

Quinn, Dave. 2016. "Nasty Women! Thousands Turn Trump's 'Nasty' Debate Diss of Hillary Clinton into a Battle Cry." *People*, October 20. https://people.com/politics/nasty-women-thousands-turn-trumps-nasty-debate-diss-of-hillary-clinton-into-a-battlecry/

Quintanilla Zapata, Tammy. 2012. *Estudio Sobre el Acoso Político hacia las Mujeres en el Perú*. Lima: Centro Flora Tristán, Diakonía Perú, and Calad.

Ramalho, Sérgio. 2019. "Who Killed Marielle Franco?" *Intercept*, January 17. https://theintercept.com/2019/01/17/marielle-franco-brazil-assassination-suspect/

Rana, Abbas. 2018. "House Spending $50,000 on In-Person Sexual Harassment Training for MPs, PM, Cabinet Ministers, Opposition Party Leaders; All Caucuses Say It's 'Mandatory.'" *Hill Times*, January 30. https://www.hilltimes.com/2018/01/30/house-spending-50000-person-sexual-harassment-training-mps-caucuses-declare-mandatory-including-cabinet-prime-minister-opposition-party-leaders/132858

Rappler Social Media Team. 2016. "#EveryWoman: No to Slut-Shaming in the Philippine Congress." *Rappler*, September 30. https://www.rappler.com/technology/social-media/147791-everywoman-campaign-against-slut-shaming-philippines

Rasmussen, Jacob 2018. "Parasitic Politics: Violence, Deception, and Change in Kenya's Electoral Politics." In *Violence in African Elections*, ed. Mimmi Söderberg Kovacs and Jesper Bjarnesen. New York: Zed, 176–196.

Raspopina, Sasha. 2018. "Disgrace in the Duma: Russia's High Profile Sexual Harassment Case is Not Just about #MeToo." *Calvert Journal*, March 31. https://www.calvertjournal.com/ articles/show/9812/duma-disgrace-leonid-slutsky-me-too

Rawlinson, Kevin. 2018. "Labour MP Calls for End to Online Anonymity After '600 Rape Threats.'" *Guardian*, June 11. https://www.theguardian.com/society/2018/jun/11/labour-mp-jess-phillips-calls-for-end-to-online-anonymity-after-600-threats

Rawls, John. 1971. *A Theory of Justice*. Cambridge: Harvard University Press.

Real, Mary Jane N. 2005. *International Consultation on Women Human Rights Defenders: Evaluation Report*. Chiang Mai: International Campaign on Women Human Rights Defenders.

Real, Mary Jane N. 2009. *Women Human Rights Defenders International Coalition Report*. Chiang Mai: WHRDIC.

Reaume, A. H. 2018. "There Is a Whisper Network in Politics. To Protect Young Women, It Has to End." *Globe & Mail*, January 25. https://www.theglobeandmail.com/opinion/there-is-a-whisper-network-in-politics-to-protect-young-women-it-has-to-end/article37734862/

Render, Jacinta. 2019. "Beto O'Rourke, Bernie Sanders, Cory Booker, and Pete Buttigieg in Miniature Coming to a Website near You." *ABC News*, March 21. https://abcnews.go.com/Politics/beto-rourke-bernie-sanders-cory-booker-pete-buttigieg/story?id=61843386

Renkl, Margaret. 2017. "The Raw Power of #MeToo." *New York Times*, October 19. https://www.nytimes.com/2017/10/19/opinion/the-raw-power-of-metoo.html

Rérolle, Raphaëlle. 2019. "L'Académie Française Se Résout à la Féminisation des Noms de Métiers." *Le Monde*, February 28. https://www.lemonde.fr/societe/article/2019/02/28/l-academie-francaise-se-resout-a-la-feminisation-des-noms-de-metiers_5429632_3224.html

Research and Advocacy Unit. 2011. *Politically Motivated Violence against Women in Zimbabwe 2000–2010: A Review of the Public Domain Literature*. Harare: RAU.

Restrepo Sanín, Juliana. 2016. *Mujeres y Participación Política: El Fenómeno de la Violencia contra las Mujeres en Política*. Bogotá: Netherlands Institute for Multiparty Democracy.

Restrepo Sanín, Juliana. 2018a. "The Law and Violence against Women in Politics." Politics & Gender 14(4): 676–680.

Restrepo Sanín, Juliana. 2018b. *Violence against Women in Politics in Latin America*. Ph.D. Diss., Rutgers University.

Restrepo Sanín, Juliana. 2020. "Violence against Women in Politics: Latin America in an Era of Backlash." Signs 45(2): 302–310.

Rheault, Ludovic, Erica Rayment, and Andreea Musulan. 2019. "Politicians in the Line of Fire: Incivility and the Treatment of Women on Social Media." *Research & Politics* 6(1): 1–7.

Rhodes, Mandy. 2016. "Nicola Sturgeon: 'If the Miscarriage Hadn't Happened, Would I Be First Minister Now? I'd Like to Think Yes.'" *Sunday Times*, September 4. https://www.thetimes.co.uk/article/nicola-sturgeon-if-the-miscarriage-hadnt-happened-would-i-be-first-minister-now-id-like-to-think-yes-07m3btgck

Richards, Joanna. 2016. *Let Her Finish: Gender and Deliberative Participation in Australian Senate Estimates Hearings*. B.Phil. Thesis, University of Canberra.

Ricchiardi, Sherry. 2018. "TrollBusters: Online Pest Control for Women Journalists." *International Journalists Network*, February 20. https://ijnet.org/en/story/trollbusters-online-pest-control-women-journalists

Riley-Smith, Ben, and Martin Evans. 2016. "Brick Thrown through Angela Eagle's Office Window after She Announces Labour Leadership Bid." *Telegraph*, July 12. https://www.telegraph.co.uk/news/2016/07/12/brick-thrown-through-angela-eagles-office-window-after-she-annou/

Ritchie, Jessica. 2013. "Creating a Monster: Online Media Constructions of Hillary Clinton during the Democratic Primary Campaign, 2007–8." *Feminist Media Studies* 13(1):102–119.

Ritzen, Yarno. 2018. "MeTooEP: Addressing sexual harassment in the European Parliament." *Al Jazeera*, October 15. https://www.aljazeera.com/news/2018/10/metooep-addressing-sexual-harassment-european-parliament-181014121756159.html

Rohde, David. 2008. "Many Women Stay Away from the Polls in an Uneasy Pakistani City." *New York Times*, February 19. https://www.nytimes.com/2008/02/19/world/asia/19peshawar.html

Rojas Valverde, María Eugenia. 2010. "Gender-Based Political Harassment and Violence: Effects on the Political Work and Public Roles of Women." *New Solutions* 230(4): 527–535.

Rojas Valverde, María Eugenia. 2012. *Acoso y Violencia Política en Contra de Mujeres Autoridades Públicas Electas en los Gobiernos Locales-Municipales en Bolivia*. La Paz: ONU Mujeres, ACOBOL, and AECID.

Rojas Valverde, María Eugenia. 2014. *Derechos Políticos de las Mujeres: Entre la Seguridad y la Violencia Política de Alto Riesgo*. La Paz: Tribunal Supremo Electoral.

Rosen, Andrew. 1974. *Rise Up, Women! The Militant Campaign of the Women's Social and Political Union 1903–1914*. New York: Routledge.

Ross, Andrea, and Kyle Muzyka. 2016. "Albertans Chant 'Lock Her Up' about Rachel Notley at Rally against Carbon Tax." *CBC News*, December 4. https://www.cbc.ca/news/canada/edmonton/chris-alexander-lock-her-up-chant-anti-carbon-tax-1.3880911

Ross, Karen. 2002. "Women's Place in 'Male' Space: Gender and Effect in Parliamentary Contexts." *Parliamentary Affairs* 55(1): 189–201.

Rothschild, Cynthia. 2005. *Written Out: How Sexuality Is Used to Attack Women's Organizing*. New York/New Brunswick: IGLHRC and CWGL.

Rouse, Wendy L. 2017. *Her Own Hero: The Origins of the Women's Self-Defense Movement*. New York: New York University Press.

Rousseau, Sandrine. 2017. *Parler*. Paris: Flammarion.

Rousseff, Dilma. 2016. "Impeachment: El Discurso Completo de Dilma Rousseff Ante el Senado." *La Tinta*, August 30. https://latinta.com.ar/2016/08/impeachment-el-discurso-completo-de-dilma-rousseff-ante-el-senado/

Rubim, Linda, and Fernanda Argolo, eds. 2018. *O Golpe na Perspectiva de Gênero*. Salvador: Edufba.

Rudman, Laurie A., and Kimberly Fairchild. 2004. "Reactions to Counterstereotypic Behavior: The Role of Backlash in Cultural Stereotype Maintenance." *Journal of Personality & Social Psychology* 87(2): 157–176.

Rudman, Laurie A., Corinne A. Moss-Racusin, Julie E. Phelan, and Sanne Nauts. 2012. "Status Incongruity and Backlash Effects: Defending the Gender Hierarchy Motivates Prejudice against Female Leaders." *Journal of Experimental Social Psychology* 48(1): 165–179.

Ruiz-Grossman, Sarah. 2017. "Senator Used to 'Avoid Elevators' as Congressional Intern for Fear of Sexual Harassment." *Huffington Post*, November 14. https://www.huff-post.com/entry/mccaskill-sexual-harassment-congress_n_5a0b8018e4b0b17ffce11e6f

Ruz, Camila, and Justin Parkinson. 2015. "'Suffrajitsu': How the Suffragettes Fought Back Using Martial Arts." *BBC News*, October 5. https://www.bbc.com/news/magazine-34425615

Saferworld. 2013. *"It's Dangerous to Be the First": Security Barriers to Women's Public Participation in Egypt, Libya, and Yemen*. London: Saferworld.

Saltzman, Linda E. 2004. "Issues Related to Defining and Measuring Violence against Women." *Journal of Interpersonal Violence* 19(11): 1235–1243.

Samara Centre. 2018. "Elephant on the Hill." https://www.samaracanada.com/research/parliament-system/elephant-on-the-hill

Sanbonmatsu, Kira. 2008. "Gender Backlash in American Politics?" *Politics & Gender* 4(4): 634–642.

SAP International. 2003. *Reviving Democracy*. Colombo: SAP International.

SAP International. 2006. *Cries of Women in Politics*. Kathmandu: SAP International.

SAP International. 2007. *Invisible Faces of Violence on Women in Politics: Breaking the Silence*. Kathmandu: SAP International.

SAP International. 2009. *Proceeding Reporting of the 2nd South Asian Regional Conference on Violence against Women in Politics on "Combating Violence against Women in Politics: Revisiting Policies, Politics, and Participation."* Lalitpur: SAP International.

SAP International. 2010. *Violence against Women in Politics: Defining Terminologies and Concepts*. Lalitpur: SAP International.

SAP International. 2011. *Incidents that Changed the Course of Women Politicians*. Lalitpur: SAP International.

"Sarah Hanson-Young: Australia Senator Wins Defamation Case." 2019. *BBC News*, November 25. https://www.bbc.com/news/world-australia-50541277

Saussure, Ferdinand. 2011 [1959]. *Course in General Linguistics*. Trans. Wade Baskin. New York: Columbia University Press.

Sawer, Marian. 2013. "Misogyny and Misrepresentation: Women in Australian Parliaments." *Political Science* 65(1): 105–117.

Scalora, Mario J., Jerome V. Baumgartner, William Zimmerman, David Callaway, MA Hatch Maillette, Christmas N. Covell, Russell E. Palarea, Jason A. Krebs, and David O. Washington. 2002. "An Epidemiological Assessment of Problematic Contacts to Members of Congress." *Journal of Forensic Science* 47(6): 1360–1364.

Schneider, Monica C., and Angela L. Bos. 2014. "Measuring Stereotypes of Female Politicians." *Political Psychology* 35(2):245–266.

Schoeneman-Morris, Katherine A., Mario J. Scalora, Grace H. Chang, William J. Zimmerman, and Yancey Garner. 2007. "A Comparison of Email versus Letter Threat Contacts toward Members of the United States Congress." *Journal of Forensic Sciences* 52(5): 1142–1147.

Schor, Elana, and Rachael Bade. 2018. "Critics Blast Senate Harassment Bill as Soft on Lawmakers." *Politico*, May 23. https://www.politico.com/story/2018/05/23/capitol-hill-harassment-policy-senate-congress-604122

Schultz, Vicki. 1998. "Reconceptualizing Sexual Harassment." *Yale Law Journal* 107(6): 1683–1805.

Schwartz, Jason. 2017. "Trump's 'Fake News' Mantra a Hit with Despots." *Politico*, December 8. https://www.politico.com/story/2017/12/08/trump-fake-news-despots-287129

Schwarzmantel, John. 2010. "Democracy and Violence: A Theoretical Overview." *Democratization* 17(2): 217–234.

Segrave, Kerry. 2014. *Beware the Masher: Sexual Harassment in American Public Places, 1880–1930*. Jefferson, NC: McFarland & Co.

Sekaggya, Margaret. 2010. *HRC/16/44: Report of the Special Rapporteur on the Situation of Human Rights Defenders*. New York: United Nations.

Semakafu, Ave Maria. 2016. *Violence against Women in Elections: VAWE Evidence for 2015 Tanzania General Elections*. Dar es Salaam: Tanzania Women Cross-Party Platform and UN Women.

Settle, Michael. 2018. "Mhairi Black Believed to Be First MP to Use the C-word in Commons Debate as She Reveals Torrent of Online Abuse." *Herald*, March 7. https://www.heraldscotland.com/news/16070295.mhairi-black-believed-to-be-first-mp-to-use-the-c-word-in-commons-debate-as-she-reveals-torrent-of-online-abuse/

"Sex Harassment, Stalking Greet 25% of First-Time Assemblywomen." 2019. *Asahi Shimbun*, March 26. http://www.asahi.com/ajw/articles/AJ201903260061.html

Shabi, Rachel. 2009. "Israeli Papers Brush Women Out of Cabinet." *Guardian*, April 3. https://www.theguardian.com/world/2009/apr/04/livnat-landver-photos-israel

Shafy, Samiha. 2011. "Egyptian Woman Tells of 'Virginity Tests.'" *Spiegel Online*, October 6. https://www.spiegel.de/international/world/horribly-humiliating-egyptian-woman-tells-of-virginity-tests-a-767365.html

Shea, Daniel M., and Alex Sproveri. 2012. "The Rise and Fall of Nasty Politics in America." PS: Political Science & Politics 45(3): 416–421.

Shearing, Hazel. 2018. "This Is the Abuse the Suffragettes Received For Trying To Win the Right to Vote." *BuzzFeed News*, February 6. https://www.buzzfeed.com/hazelshearing/heres-the-abuse-the-suffragettes-received-for-trying-to-win

Sheeler, Kristina Horn, and Karrin Vasby Anderson. 2013. *Woman President: Confronting Postfeminist Political Culture*. College Station: Texas A & M University Press.

Sheffield, Carole J. 1989. "The Invisible Intruder: Women's Experiences of Obscene Phone Calls." *Gender & Society* 3(4): 483–488.

Shelton, J. Nicole, and Rebecca E. Stewart. 2004. "Confronting Perpetrators of Prejudice: The Inhibitory Effects of Social Costs." *Psychology of Women Quarterly* 28(3): 215–223.

Sherwell, Philip. 2016. "How Duterte is Using Rumors of a Sex Tape to Slut-Shame a Senator." *Newsweek*, October 10. https://www.newsweek.com/2016/10/21/how-duterte-using-rumors-sex-tape-slut-shame-senator-508254.html

Šimonović, Dubravka. 2018a. *HRC/38/47: Report of the Special Rapporteur on Violence against Women, Its Causes and Consequences on Online Violence against Women and Girls from a Human Rights Perspective.* New York: UN.

Šimonović, Dubravka. 2018b. *A/73/301: Report of the Special Rapporteur on Violence against Women, Its Causes and Consequences on Violence against Women in Politics.* New York: UN.

Smith, Joanna. 2018. "Female MPs Share Stories of Sexual Harassment On and Off Parliament Hill in Survey." *Toronto Star*, January 2. https://www.thestar.com/news/canada/2018/01/02/female-mps-share-stories-of-sexual-harassment-on-and-off-parliament-hill-in-survey.html

Smith, Paige Hall, Jason B. Smith, and Jo Anne L. Earp. 1999. "Beyond the Measurement Trap: A Reconstructed Conceptualization and Measurement of Woman Battering." *Psychology of Women Quarterly* 23(1): 177–193.

Sobieraj, Sarah. 2018. "Bitch, Slut, Skank, Cunt: Patterned Resistance to Women's Visibility in Digital Publics." *Information, Communication, & Society* 21(11): 1700–1714.

Söderberg Kovacs, Mimmi. 2018. "Introduction: The Everyday Politics of Electoral Violence in Africa." In *Violence in African Elections*, ed. Mimmi Söderberg Kovacs and Jesper Bjarnesen. New York: Zed, 1–26.

Solnit, Rebecca. 2014. *Men Explain Things to Me*. Chicago: Haymarket Books.

Solnit, Rebecca. 2018. "How Many Husbands Control the Votes of Their Wives? We'll Never Know." *Guardian*, November 19. https://www.theguardian.com/commentisfree/2018/nov/19/voter-intimidation-republicans-democrats-midterm-elections

Sones, Boni. 2005. *Women in Parliament: The New Suffragettes.* London: Politico's.

Sonnad, Nikhil. 2018. "Spain's Controversial Battle over Whether to Make its Constitution Gender-Neutral." *Quartz*, July 18. https://qz.com/1329801/spain-is-battling-over-whether-to-make-its-constitution-gender-neutral/

Soohoo, Cynthia, and Diana Hortsch. 2011. "Who Is a Human Rights Defender? An Essay on Sexual and Reproductive Rights Defenders." *University of Miami Law Review* 56(3): 981–998.

Spender, Dale. 1980. *Man Made Language*. New York: Pandora.

Spender, Dale. 1982. *Women of Ideas and What Men Have Done to Them.* London: Pandora.

Spring, Mariana, and Lucy Webster. 2019. "A Web of Abuse: How the Far Right Disproportionately Targets Female Politicians." *BBC Newsnight*, July 15. https://www.bbc.com/news/blogs-trending-48871400

Sreberny-Mohammadi, Annabelle, and Karen Ross. 1996. "Women MPs and the Media." *Parliamentary Affairs* 49(1):103–116.

Staniland, Paul. 2014. "Violence and Democracy." *Comparative Politics* 47(1): 99–118.

Stanko, Elizabeth. 1985. *Intimate Intrusions: Women's Experience of Male Violence.* London: Routledge and Kegan Paul.

Stanko, Elizabeth. 1990. *Everyday Violence: How Men and Women Experience Sexual and Physical Danger*. London: Pandora.

Stark, Cynthia. 2019. "Gaslighting, Misogyny, and Psychological Oppression." *Monist* 102(2): 221–235.

Stark, Evan. 2007. *Coercive Control*. New York: Oxford University Press.

Stark, Evan. 2009. "Rethinking *Coercive Control*." *Violence against Women* 15(12): 1509–1525.

Stevenson, Mark. 2008. "Mexican Woman Fights for Voting Rights." *Christian Science Monitor*, February 12. https://www.csmonitor.com/World/Americas/2008/0212/p04s01-woam.html

Storm, Hannah, and Helena Williams, eds. 2012. *No Woman's Land: On the Frontlines with Female Reporters*. London: INSI.

Stout, Jane G., and Nilanjana Dasgupta. 2011. "When *He* Doesn't Mean *You*: Gender-Exclusive Language as Ostracism." *Personality & Social Psychology Bulletin* 36(6): 757–769.

Straus, Scott, and Charlie Taylor, 2012. "Democratization and Electoral Violence in Sub-Saharan Africa, 1990–2008." In *Voting in Fear: Electoral Violence in Sub-Saharan Africa*, ed. Dorina Bekoe. Washington, DC: United States Institute for Peace Press, 15–38.

Sue, Derald Wing. 2010. *Microaggressions in Everyday Life*. Hoboken, NJ: John Wiley & Sons.

Suler, John. 2004. "The Online Disinhibition Effect." *CyberPsychology & Behavior* 7(3): 321–326.

Summers, Anne. 2013. *The Misogyny Factor*. Sydney: NewSouth.

Swim, Janet K., Kristen M. Eyssell, Erin Quinlivan Murdoch, and Melissa J. Ferguson. 2010. "Self-Silencing to Sexism." *Journal of Social Issues* 66(3): 493–507.

Swim, Janet K., and Lauri L. Hyers. 1999. "Excuse Me—What Did You Just Say?!: Women's Public and Private Responses to Sexist Remarks." *Journal of Experimental Social Psychology* 35(1): 68–88.

Swim, Janet K., and Charles Stangor, eds. 1998. *Prejudice: The Target's Perspective*. New York: Academic Press.

Swinson, Jo. 2018. *Equal Power*. London: Atlantic.

Sylvester, Rachel, and Alice Thomson. 2019. "Jess Phillips Interview: Anyone Could Kill Me. But I Don't Live My Life Frightened." *The Times*, May 10. https://www.thetimes.co.uk/article/jess-phillips-interview-anyone-could-kill-me-but-i-dont-live-my-life-frightened-xkwx859dw

Tadros, Mariz. 2015. "Contentious and Prefigurative Politics: Vigilante Groups' Struggle against Sexual Violence in Egypt (2011–2013)." *Development & Change* 46(6): 1345–1368.

Tadros, Mariz. 2016. "Understanding Politically Motivated Sexual Assault in Protest Spaces: Evidence from Egypt (March 2011 to June 2013)." *Social & Legal Studies* 25(1): 93–110.

Tajali, Mona, and Sarah Farhan. 2018. "Women's Candidacy and Violence against Women in the Politics of Iraq." *Jadaliyya*, July 19. https://www.jadaliyya.com/Details/37780

Tandoc, Edson C., Zheng Wei Lim, and Richard Ling. 2018. "Defining 'Fake News.'" *Digital Journalism* 6(2): 137–153.

Terah, Flora Igoki. 2008. *They Never Killed My Spirit . . . but They Murdered My Only Child*. Meru: Olive Marketing and Publishing.

Terkel, Amanda. 2017. "Minnesota Legislator Who Called Out White Male Colleagues Won't Apologize." *Huffington Post*, April 5. https://www.huffpost.com/entry/melissa-hortman-white-males_n_58e5401fe4b0fe4ce087b9d5

Thomas, Melanee, and Amanda Bittner, eds. 2017. *Mothers and Others*. Vancouver: University of British Columbia Press.

Torres García, Isabel. 2010. *Derechos Políticos de las Mujeres y Acoso Político Como Práctica de Discriminación*. San José: ONU-Habitat Costa Rica.

Tougas, Francine, Rupert Brown, Ann M. Beaton, and Stéphane Joly. 1995. "Neosexism: Plus Ça Change, Plus C'est Pareil." *Personality & Social Psychology Bulletin* 21(8): 842–849.

Traister, Rebecca. 2018. *Good and Mad: The Revolutionary Power of Women's Anger*. New York: Simon & Schuster.

Trionfi, Barbara, and Javier Luque. 2019. *Newsroom Best Practices for Addressing Online Violence against Journalists*. Vienna: International Press Institute.

Tuchman, Gaye. 1978. "The Symbolic Annihilation of Women by the Mass Media." In Gaye Tuchman, Arlene Kaplan Daniels, and James Benet, eds. *Hearth and Home*. New York: Oxford University Press, 3–38.

Tumber, Howard, and Frank Webster. 2006. *Journalists under Fire: Information War and Journalistic Practices*. Thousand Oaks, CA: Sage.

UN. 1948. *Universal Declaration of Human Rights*. New York: UN.

UN. 1979. *Convention on the Elimination of All Forms of Discrimination against Women*. New York: UN.

UN. 1993a. *Resolution 48/104: Declaration on the Elimination of Violence against Women*. New York: UN.

UN. 1993b. *Vienna Declaration and Programme of Action*. New York: UN.

UN. 2007. *DPKO/DFS–DPA Joint Guidelines on Enhancing the Role of Women in Post-Conflict Electoral Processes*. New York: UN.

UN Commission of Inquiry. 2010. *Report into the Facts and Circumstances of the Assassination of Former Pakistani Prime Minister Mohtarma Benazir Bhutto*. New York: UN.

UN Department of Economic and Social Affairs. 2014. *Guidelines for Producing Statistics on Violence against Women*. New York: UN.

UN General Assembly. 1998. *Resolution 53/144: Declaration on the Right and Responsibility of Individuals, Groups and Organs of Society to Promote and Protect Universally Recognized Human Rights and Fundamental Freedoms*. New York: UN.

UN General Assembly. 2011. *Resolution 66/130: Women and Political Participation*. New York: UN.

UN General Assembly. 2013a. *Resolution 68/163: The Safety of Journalists and the Issue of Impunity*. New York: UN.

UN General Assembly. 2013b. *Resolution 68/181: Protecting Women Human Rights Defenders*. New York: UN.

UN General Assembly. 2015. *Resolution 70/162: The Safety of Journalists and the Issue of Impunity*. New York: UN.

UN General Assembly. 2018. *Resolution 73/148: Intensification of Efforts to Prevent and Eliminate All Forms of Violence against Women and Girls: Sexual Harassment*. New York: UN.

UN Human Rights Council. 2008. *Resolution 7/8: Mandate of the Special Rapporteur on the Situation of Human Rights Defenders*. Geneva: HRC.

UN Human Rights Council. 2013. *HRC/23/50: Report of the Working Group on the Issue of Discrimination against Women in Law and in Practice*. New York: UN.

UN Secretary-General. 2003. *Report 58/380: Human Rights Defenders*. New York: UN.

UN Secretary-General. 2010. *Report 65/354: Women's Participation in Peacebuilding*. New York: UN.

UN Secretary-General. 2013a. *Report 68/184: Measures Taken and Progress Achieved in the Promotion of Women and Political Participation*. New York: UN.

UN Secretary-General. 2013b. *Report 525: Women and Peace and Security*. New York: UN Security Council.

UN Secretary General. 2015. *Report 716: Women and Peace and Security*. New York: UN Security Council.

UN Secretary General. 2017. *Report 72/290: The Safety of Journalists and the Issue of Impunity*. New York: UN.

UN Security Council. 2006. *Resolution 1738: Protection of Civilians in Armed Conflict*. New York: UN.

UN Security Council. 2015. *Resolution 2222: Protection of Civilians in Armed Conflict*. New York: UN.

UNDP and UN Women. 2015. *Inclusive Electoral Processes*. New York: UNDP and UN Women.

UNDP and UN Women. 2017. *Preventing Violence against Women in Elections: A Programming Guide*. New York: UNDP and UN Women.

UNESCO. 1997. *Resolution 29: Condemnation of Violence against Journalists*. Paris: UNESCO.

UNESCO. 2007. *Press Freedom: Safety of Journalists and Impunity*. Paris: UNESCO.

UNESCO. 2012. *UN Plan of Action on the Safety of Journalists and the Issue of Impunity*. Paris: UNESCO.

UNESCO. 2017. *Resolution 39: Strengthening UNESCO Leadership in the Implementation of the United Nations Plan of Action on the Safety of Journalists and the Issue of Impunity*. Paris: UNESCO.

UN Women. 2011. *Addressing Violence within the Framework of Women's Political Participation: A Toolkit for Managing and Preventing Political Violence against Women*. New York: UN Women.

UN Women, Office of the High Commissioner on Human Rights, and UN Special Rapporteur on Violence against Women. 2018. *Violence against Women in Politics: Expert Group Meeting Report and Recommendations*. New York: UN Women and Office of the High Commissioner on Human Rights.

U.S. Senate. 1913. *Suffrage Parade Hearing, March 6–17*. Washington, DC: U.S. Senate.

Valentino, Nicholas A., Ted Brader, Eric W. Groenendyk, Krysha Gregorowicz, and Vincent L. Hutchings. 2011. "Election Night's Alright for Fighting: The Role of Emotions in Political Participation." *Journal of Politics* 73(1): 156–170.

Valentino, Nicholas A., Carly Wayne, and Marzia Oceno. 2018. "Mobilizing Sexism: The Interaction of Emotion and Gender Attitudes in the 2016 U.S. Presidential Election." *Public Opinion Quarterly* 82(S1): 213–235.

Vandello, Joseph A., Jennifer K. Bosson, Dov Cohen, Rochelle M. Burnaford, and Jonathan R. Weaver. 2008. "Precarious Manhood." *Journal of Personality & Social Psychology* 95(6): 1325–1339.

Van der Vet, Freek, and Laura Lyytikäinen 2015. "Violence and Human Rights in Russia: How Human Rights Defenders Develop their Tactics in the Face of Danger, 2005–2013." *International Journal of Human Rights* 19(7): 979–998.

Van Zoonen, Liesbet. 1998. "'Finally, I Have My Mother Back': Politicians and Their Families in Popular Culture." *Harvard International Journal of Press/Politics* 3(1):48–64.

Vera-Gray, F. 2017. *Men's Intrusion, Women's Embodiment.* New York: Routledge.

Vera-Gray, F. 2018. *The Right Amount of Panic: How Women Trade Freedom for Safety.* Bristol, UK: Policy Press.

Vial, Andrea C., Jaime L. Napier, and Victoria L. Brescoll. 2016. "A Bed of Thorns: Female Leaders and the Self-Reinforcing Cycle of Illegitimacy." *Leadership Quarterly* 27(3): 400–414.

Vick, Karl. 2018. "Time Person of the Year 2018: The Guardians and the War on Truth." *Time*, December 24. https://time.com/person-of-the-year-2018-the-guardians/

Vickery, Jacqueline Ryan, and Tracy Everbach, eds. 2018. *Mediating Misogyny.* New York: Palgrave.

Vigo, Julian. 2015. "The Man Who Has It All." *Huffington Post*, November 17. https://www.huffingtonpost.co.uk/julian-vigo/the-man-who-has-it-all-twitter_b_8547634.html

Vock, Daniel C. 2017. "As Outcry Over Sexual Harassment Grows, Focus Shifts to State Legislatures." *Governing*, October 18. https://www.governing.com/topics/politics/gov-sexual-harassment-state-legislatures.html

Walker, Peter. 2019. "UKIP MEP Candidate Blamed Feminists for Rise in Misogyny." *Guardian*, April 22. https://www.theguardian.com/politics/2019/apr/22/ukip-mep-candidate-carl-benjamin-blamed-feminists-for-rise-in-male-violence

Walsh, Clare. 2001. *Gender and Discourse.* New York: Routledge.

Walters, Mark Austin, and Jessica Tumath. 2014. "Gender 'Hostility,' Rape, and the Hate Crime Paradigm." *Modern Law Review* 77(4): 563–596.

Wang, Amy B. 2017. "Senators Say #MeToo: McCaskill, Others Share Their Stories of Sexual Harassment." *Washington Post*, October 21.

Ward, L. Monique. 2016. "Media and Sexualization." *Journal of Sex Research* 53(4–5):560–577.

Warner, Mary R. 1977. *The Dilemma of Black Politics: A Report on Harassment of Black Elected Officials.* Sacramento: National Association of Human Rights Workers.

Watters, Haydn. 2015. "MPs' Sexual Harassment Code of Conduct Outlined in House Report." *CBC*, June 8. https://www.cbc.ca/news/politics/mps-sexual-harassment-code-of-conduct-outlined-in-house-report-1.3105023

Watts, Charlotte, and Cathy Zimmerman. 2002. "Violence against Women: Global Scope and Magnitude." *Lancet* 359(9313): 1232–1237.

Weisburd, Steven Bennett, and Brian Levin. 1994. "On the Basis of Sex: Recognizing Gender-Based Bias Crimes." *Stanford Law & Policy Review* 5(2): 21–47.

Weldon, S. Laurel. 2006. "The Structure of Intersectionality: A Comparative Politics of Gender." *Politics & Gender* 2(2): 235–248.

West, Robin L. 2000. "The Difference in Women's Hedonic Lives: A Phenomenological Critique of Feminist Legal Theory." *Wisconsin Women's Law Journal* 15: 149–215.

Wexler, Lesley, Jennifer K. Robbennolt, and Colleen Murphy. 2019. "#MeToo, Time's Up, and Theories of Justice." *University of Illinois Law Review* 1: 45–111.

White, Rebecca Hanner. 2018. "Title VII and the #MeToo Movement." *Emory Law Journal Online* 68: 1014–1033.

WHRDIC. 2015. *Gendering Documentation: A Manual For and About Women Human Rights Defenders*. http://www.defendingwomen-defendingrights.org/wp-content/uploads/2016/09/GENDERING-DOCUMENTATION-FINAL-3-min.pdf

Wille, Petter, and Janika Spannagel. 2019. "The History of the UN Declaration on Human Rights Defenders." Universal Rights Group [blog], March 11. https://www.universal-rights.org/blog/the-un-declaration-on-human-rights-defenders-its-history-and-drafting-process/

Williams, Jamillah Bowman. 2018. *#MeToo and Public Officials: A Post-Election Snapshot of Allegations and Consequences*. Washington, DC: Georgetown University Law Center.

Williams, Rachel. 2012. "Edith Garrud: A Public Vote for the Suffragette Who Taught Martial Arts." *Guardian*, June 25. https://www.theguardian.com/lifeandstyle/2012/jun/25/edith-garrud-suffragette-martial-arts

Wills, Kate. 2016. "Man Who Has It All: Parody Gender Equality Twitter Account Has Hit a Nerve." *Independent*, February 24. https://www.independent.co.uk/life-style/gadgets-and-tech/despite-his-sarky-tweets-on-gender-equality-women-just-love-themanwhohasitall-a6893921.html

Wingrove, Josh, Bill Curry, and Chris Hannay. 2017. "Trudeau Suspends Two MPs over 'Personal Misconduct' Allegations." *Globe and Mail*, November 5. https://www.theglobeandmail.com/news/politics/liberals-suspend-two-mps-over-personal-misconduct-allegations/article21453310/

Wolfe, Lauren. 2011. *The Silencing Crime: Sexual Violence and Journalists*. New York: Committee to Protect Journalists.

Workman, Alice. 2016. "Surprise! Female Politicians More Likely To Be Negatively Interrupted Than Their Male Colleagues." *BuzzFeed*, November 24. https://www.buzzfeed.com/aliceworkman/negatively-interrupted-way-m

Workman, Alice. 2017. "An Australian Politician Is Being Trolled After a Year-Old 'Mansplaining' Video Was Posted By A Conservative American Commentator." *BuzzFeed News*, May 28. https://www.buzzfeed.com/aliceworkman/trolled-for-mansplaining

World Bank. 2016. *Women, Business, and the Law 2016*. Washington, DC: World Bank Group.

Wright, Katharine A.M., and Jack Holland. 2014. "Leadership and the Media: Gendered Framings of Julia Gillard's 'Sexism and Misogyny' Speech." *Australian Journal of Political Science* 49(3):455–468.

Yaksic, Mónica, and María Eugenia Rojas. 2010. *Paquete de Servicios: Construyendo Municipios Libres de Violencia Política*. La Paz: UNFPA and ACOBOL.

Yoder, Janice D. 1991. "Rethinking Tokenism: Looking Beyond Numbers." *Gender & Society* 5(2): 178–192.

Yousafzai, Malala, with Christina Lamb. 2013. *I Am Malala*. New York: Little, Brown and Company.

"Yvette Roudy: 'Le Ciel des Machos M'est Tombé sur la Tête." 2019. *France Culture*, March 15. https://www.franceculture.fr/politique/yvette-roudy-le-ciel-des-machos-mest-tombe-sur-la-tete

Zaki, Hind Ahmed. 2017. *In the Shadow of the State: Gender Contestation and Legal Mobilization in the Context of the Arab Spring in Egypt and Tunisia*. Ph.D. Diss., University of Washington.

Zeng, Jinyan. 2015. "China's Feminist Five: 'This Is the Worst Crackdown on Lawyers, Activists, and Scholars in Decades.'" *Guardian*, April 17. https://www.theguardian.com/lifeandstyle/2015/apr/17/chinas-feminist-five-this-is-the-worst-crackdown-on-lawyers-activists-and-scholars-in-decades

Zimmerman, Dan, and Candace West. 1975. "Sex Roles, Interruptions, and Sciences in Conversations." In *Language and Sex*, ed. Barrie Thomas and Nancy Henley, 105–129. Rowley: Newbury House.

# INDEX

*For the benefit of digital users, indexed terms that span two pages (e.g., 52–53) may, on occasion, appear on only one of those pages.*